PELICAN B[

A729

ENGELS: SELECTED WRITINGS

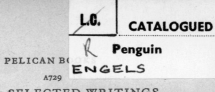

W. O. Henderson, Reader in International Economic
History at the University of Manchester, was born in
London in 1904. He was educated at Nottingham
High School; Downing College, Cambridge; the
University of Hamburg; and the London School of
Economics. He has held university posts at Cam-
bridge, Liverpool, Hull and Manchester. During the
war he was a lecturer to H.M. Forces in England and
the Middle East.

Amongst Dr Henderson's publications are: *The
Lancashire Cotton Famine* (1934), *Britain and Industrial Europe* 1750–1870 (1954 and 1965), *The
Genesis of the Common Market* (1962) and *J. C.
Fischer and his Diary of Industrial England* 1814–51
(1966). His previous work on Engels includes an
English translation and introduction to the latter's
book, *The Condition of the Working Class in England*,
and *Engels as a Military Critic* (with W. H. Chaloner).

Engels

Selected Writings

EDITED AND INTRODUCED
BY W.O. HENDERSON

PENGUIN BOOKS

Penguin Books Ltd, Harmondsworth, Middlesex, England
Penguin Books Inc., 3300 Clipper Mill Road, Baltimore, Md. 21211, U.S.A.
Penguin Books Australia Ltd, Ringwood, Victoria, Australia

—

First published 1967

—

This selection © W. O. Henderson, 1967

—

Made and printed in Great Britain by
C. Nicholls & Company Ltd
Set in Monotype Plantin

Contents

5

CONTENTS

Acknowledgements

THE editor thanks his colleague Dr W. H. Chalenor for looking through the proofs of this book and for allowing him to reprint extracts from Engels's *The Condition of the Working Class in England* (translated by W. O. Henderson and W. H. Chalenor, 1958) and *Engels as Military Critic* (edited by W. O. Henderson and W. H. Chalenor, 1959). For these extracts my thanks are also due to Manchester University Press for *Engels as Military Critic* and to Basil Blackwell Ltd for *The Condition of the Working Class in England.*

Acknowledgements

General Introduction

FRIEDRICH ENGELS was the first and the greatest of Karl Marx's disciples. Lenin wrote of their forty years' collaboration: 'In ancient history there are many moving stories of friendship. The European proletariat may say that its science was created by two scholars and fighters whose relations to each other surpassed the most moving stories of human friendship among the ancients.' Marx and Engels were both men of outstanding ability and force of character, but from the first it was Marx who led and Engels who followed. Engels declared that 'Marx stood higher, saw further and took a wider and quicker view than all the rest of us. Marx was a genius: the rest of us were talented at best.' The precise relationship between the two men may defy analysis but together they formed a powerful intellectual partnership which has profoundly influenced world affairs. Their writings were the powerhouse which generated the explosive doctrines which rocked the world. Marx and Engels were largely responsible for the rise of a new Socialism which they called Communism to differentiate it from the old Socialism of Robert Owen, Saint–Simon, Fourier and Weitling. Their political activities stimulated the growth of national Socialist parties and of the international Socialist movement.

Marx and Engels collaborated closely in their literary work. They were jointly responsible for writing *The Holy Family* and *The German Ideology* in the 1840s. Various articles appearing under Marx's name in the *New York Daily Tribune* in the 1850s were written by Engels or by Marx and Engels together. In Engels's *Anti-Dühring* there was a chapter contributed by Marx. But it was in the production of *Zur Kritik der politischen Ökonomie* – Marx's first major work – and of the first volume of *Das Kapital* that their cooperation was closest. Marx was living in London and Engels was in Manchester when these books were written. The numerous letters in the Marx-Engels correspondence concerning *Das Kapital* show how much Marx relied upon Engels's advice and judgement at every stage of the work. Engels was always ready to comment upon Marx's economic theories – on surplus value, on rent, on commercial crises, on the bullion controversy and so forth – and to place at his friend's disposal his detailed knowledge of the cotton trade. In March 1858, for example, Marx asked Engels for information concerning the life of cotton machines in the factory of Ermen and Engels in Manchester. That Marx – the scholar who worked long hours in the library of the British Museum – should have shown such a remarkable grasp of the practical affairs of the world of business was doubtless due largely to the information that he secured from his friend in Manchester. When the first volume of *Das Kapital* appeared in 1867 Engels endeavoured to bring it to the attention of the public by trying to place articles about it in leading English and German periodicals. He also arranged for his friend Samuel Moore of Manchester to translate the book into English but it took Moore (later in association with E. A. Aveling) twenty years to complete the task.

Engels helped Marx in another way. For Marx – as his daughter Eleanor later recalled – the 1850s and 1860s were 'years of horrible poverty'. Marx did not earn enough as a free-lance journalist to support his family and – although in dire financial straits – he made no serious efforts to secure full-time employment. He declared: 'I must follow my goal through thick and thin and I shall not allow bourgeois society to turn me into a money-making machine.' So Engels accepted a post as a clerk with the Manchester cotton firm of Ermen and Engels (his father being one of the partners) in order to earn enough money not only to keep himself but to send remittances to Marx. It was these funds which enabled Marx to carry on with his researches in the British Museum library. Engels heartily disliked working in an office and he did not relish living in Manchester but he felt that he must sacrifice his own literary ambitions to enable Marx to write *Das Kapital*. In the Marx-Engels correspondence there are dozens of letters in which Marx appealed to Engels for money to pay the rent and the tradesmen's bills. On £200 per annum Engels was at first not in a position to help Marx as much as he would have wished though he did supplement his gifts by writing articles for the *New York Daily Tribune* for which Marx was paid. By 1860, however, Engels was earning over £1,000 a year and in 1864 he became a partner in the business. Now at last he was able to help Marx on a more generous scale. But Marx was still unable to make ends meet. In a single month in 1868 Engels sent Marx £10 to save his property from being distrained for debt, £15 to pay a gas bill, and £40 for expenses connected with the wedding of one of his daughters. When Engels retired from business in 1870 he made his friend an allowance of £350 a year. Marx fully appreciated what Engels had done for him. When the first volume of *Das Kapital* was finished he wrote to his friend: ' So this volume is ready. Its completion is due to you and to you alone! Without your sacrifice on my behalf I could never have got through the immense amount of work that has been put into the three volumes. I embrace you full of thanks.'

The second and third volumes of *Das Kapital* were not published in Marx's lifetime. They were written in the 1860s and 1870s but Marx never completed the final revision that would be necessary before the volumes could be sent to the printer. When Marx died Engels again gave up his own literary projects to devote much of his time to the herculean task of putting Marx's manuscripts in order and preparing them for publication. Engels had been so closely associated with Marx for forty years that he was obviously in a better position than anyone else to decide on the final form that the second and third volumes should take. He was, moreover, one of the few people who had mastered Marx's handwriting, which was very difficult to read. The second volume of *Das Kapital* appeared in 1885 and the third volume (in two parts) in 1894. So it was only a few months before his own death that Engels completed the task of making the whole of Marx's masterpiece available to the public.

Marx and Engels not only collaborated in writing books and articles which analysed various problems of economics, history, philosophy and politics from the standpoint of dialectical materialism. They collaborated as revolutionary agitators to put their ideas into practice. Engels stood shoulder to shoulder with Marx in his numerous political activities. In 1846 he went to

Paris as the agent of the Brussels Communist Correspondence Committee which was Marx's first organ for the propagation of his views. In a letter of 23 October 1846 Engels reported to the Correspondence Committee that he had succeeded in persuading a small group of German socialist exiles to transfer their allegiance from Proudhon to Marx and to accept his own definition of Communism. This was as follows:

(1) To achieve the interests of the proletariat in opposition to those of the bourgeoisie;

(2) to do this through the abolition of private property and its replacement by community of goods;

(3) to recognize no means of carrying out these objectives other than a democratic revolution by force.

In later years Lenin expressed the view that the meeting at which Engels's principles were accepted could be regarded as the genesis of the German Socialist Party.

Engels also explained Marx's ideological views to a conference of the League of the Just which was held in London in the summer of 1847. Marx was absent as he could not raise the fare from Brussels. At this conference the League of the Just, which had been a secret revolutionary society, was reorganized as a public association called the Communist League. Engels was satisfied with his work at the conference since his definition of its aims had been accepted. It was agreed that the League should work for the abolition of capitalism and the establishment of a classless society. A second conference was held later in the year. This time both Marx and Engels attended. Engels acted as secretary. The conference approved a new constitution, accepted the Marxist ideology, and authorized Marx and Engels to prepare the final version of the statement of the League's policy.

Even before the conference met Engels had prepared an early draft of *The Communist Manifesto*. He had written to Marx from Paris:

Think over the Confession of Faith a bit. Let's call it 'the Communist Manifesto' and drop the idea of putting it in the form of a catechism. As we shall have to include some history – more or less – in it I think that the present form of the document is quite unsuitable. I shall bring with me a draft that I have prepared. It is in simple narrative form but miserably worded and written in fearful haste. I begin: 'What is Communism?' And then I deal at once with the proletariat – the history of its origins and the difference between the modern proletariat and workers in former times. Next I discuss the antithesis between the proletariat and the bourgeoisie. At the end I deal with commercial crises and I shall provide a summing-up. In between all this I deal with all sorts of secondary matters and I end by discussing the policy of the Communist Party in so far as this should be made public.

It is clear that Engels had an important share in the production of *The Communist Manifesto* at every stage of the drafting.

In the following year revolution broke out in Germany. Engels went to Cologne, the centre of political agitation in the Rhineland, where Marx had founded the *Neue Rheinische Zeitung*. Engels became one of the editors of this paper and wrote a number of leading articles as well as contributions on foreign and military affairs. He later claimed that 'no paper has been able to electrify the workers as this one did'. When the reaction triumphed in 1849 Engels moved to London, after a brief interlude of campaigning in the insurrection in Baden. Here he joined Marx and other exiles from the Continent. But he soon took a post in Manchester to earn money for himself and for Marx. To some extent he lost touch with the revolutionaries of 1848 and he was not involved to any great extent in the internal squabbles of the Communist League which led to its dissolution. For twenty years he took little part – except for an occasional pamphlet – in revolutionary political agitation. He was not concerned with the founding of the Working Men's International Association in 1864. It was not until he had retired from business and moved to London in 1870 that he served on the Council of the First International. When this organization disintegrated Engels took little active part in politics but he kept in close touch with Socialist leaders in many countries. Between the end of the First International and the establishment of the Second International Marx and Engels – and Engels alone after Marx's death – formed a vital link between Socialist parties all over the world. Engels's gift for languages was a great asset in the maintenance of this voluminous correspondence.

Engels collaborated with Marx not only in political agitation designed to overthrow the capitalist system but also in numerous controversies with reformers who supported policies different from those of the pioneers of the Marxist movement. Together in the 1840s they attacked the Young Hegelians in *The Holy Family* and the Utopian Socialists in *The German Ideology* and *The Communist Manifesto*. In the 1860s they both viewed Lassalle's agitation among the German workers with deep suspicion. Their fears were justified since the socialists in Germany were, for a time, split between the Lassalleans and the Marxists. When the socialists came together again in 1875 both Marx and Engels vigorously criticized the concessions that had been made to the Lassalleans. Meanwhile Marx and Engels had been involved in a bitter controversy with the anarchist Bakunin – a quarrel which contributed to the collapse of the First International. Next came controversies with German socialist heretics who presumed to deviate from strict Marxist orthodoxy. Engels dealt with Dr Mülberger in a series of articles on the housing question in 1872–3. A few years later he attacked Dr Dühring for imagining that he could revise Marx's ideology. And when the Anti-Socialist Law was in force in Germany Engels joined Marx in criticizing faint-hearted comrades who were prepared to submit to Bismarck and accept the dissolution of their party without offering any resistance. When the German Socialists summoned up enough courage to defy Bismarck they were strongly supported by Engels who became a regular contributor to their journal *Der Sozialdemokrat*. In his later years – particularly after Marx's death – Engels was ever vigilant to rebuke any socialist leaders who showed signs of departing from the path of Marxian orthodoxy.

It would, however, be a mistake to regard Engels simply as Marx's *alter ego*. Although the two men cooperated closely for many years in working out Marxian doctrines of politics, economics, history and philosophy and although they never ceased to foster the development of national and international organizations dedicated to the overthrow of capitalism and the establishment of Socialism, nevertheless Engels had a life of his own and made his individual contribution to the Socialist cause. Engels's achievements as a young man – before the long period of collaboration with Marx – should not be ignored. In an outstanding article published in the *Deutsch-Französische Jahrbücher* in 1844 Engels sharply criticized current liberal economic doctrines and advocated the abolition of private property which he believed lay at the root of the social evils which afflicted capitalist society. Fifteen years later Marx still regarded the article as 'a brilliant outline' of the subject. Just as some of the principles of Marxian economics had already been discussed in this early essay so the doctrines of historical materialism and the class struggle were to be found in Engels's book on *The Condition of the Working Class in England* which was published in 1845. Marx gave the book high praise and Engels's reputation as a scholar was now established in a small circle of revolutionary socialists. It was, however, many years before the work was widely known and recognized as a classic – if not unbiased – analysis of the effects of the industrial revolution upon the factory workers.

The Condition of the Working Class in England was a hard-hitting political tract. The forceful language with which social evils were denounced eventually gave the book a place in German political literature comparable with Thomas Carlyle's pamphlet on Chartism in England. Engels denounced the social evils of industrial society in the middle of the nineteenth century more effectively than they had ever been attacked before by a German writer. Moreover Engels went to the heart of various economic and social problems which were still being treated somewhat superficially by many of his contemporaries. While orthodox economists were discussing problems of rent, prices and the rational use of scarce resources, Engels drew attention to the fundamental problem of economic growth. He was one of the first economists to discuss the trade cycle and to offer an explanation for this phenomenon. He saw the significance of the growth of big business at the expense of small undertakings. These topics were later discussed more thoroughly by Marx but to deal with them at all in 1845 was no mean achievement. And

Engels's chapter on the great towns examined problems of town planning in a way which was far ahead of his time. It was because Engels appreciated the real significance of the factors which were changing the industrial society of his day that his book is still being read while the writings of so many of his contemporaries have fallen into oblivion.

Engels's experiences in the revolution of 1848-9, particularly his participation in the brief campaign in Baden, aroused his interest in military affairs. He wrote an account of the Baden insurrection which his biographer Gustav Mayer has called 'a masterpiece of German descriptive prose'. In Manchester in the 1850s he began a serious study of the art of war. He saw that professional armies had rarely had any difficulty in suppressing popular risings in 1848-9 and that any future revolt of the proletariat would have to be conducted in a different way. Before long Engels was contributing articles to the *New York Daily Tribune* and other journals on military affairs and he became a recognized authority on the subject. In one of his articles he discussed the technique of revolution in a passage that later had a strong influence on Lenin's thinking on these matters. Engels wrote:

Insurrection is an art quite as much as war or any other, and subject to certain rules of proceeding which, when neglected, will produce the ruin of the party neglecting them. Those rules, logical deductions from the nature of the parties and the circumstances one has to deal with in such a case, are so plain and simple that the short experience of 1848 had made the Germans pretty well acquainted with them. First, never play with insurrection unless you are fully prepared to face the consequences of your play. Insurrection is a calculus with very indefinite magnitudes, the value of which may change every day; the forces opposed to you have all the advantages of organization, discipline, and habitual authority; unless you bring strong odds against them you are defeated and ruined. Secondly, the insurrectionary career once entered upon, act with the greatest determination, and on the offensive. The defensive is the death of every armed rising: it is lost before it measures itself with its enemies. Surprise your antagonists while their forces are scattering, prepare new successes, however small, but daily; keep up the moral ascendancy which the first successful rising has given you; rally those vacillating elements to your side which always follow the strongest impulse, and which always look out for the safe side; force your enemies to a retreat before they can collect their strength against you; in the words of Danton, the greatest master of revolutionary policy yet known, *de l'audace, encore de l'audace, et toujours de l'audace.*

In the 1870s Engels's greatest achievement was his trenchant answer to Dr Dühring's newfangled socialist notions. Engels's *Anti-Dühring* was written at Marx's request. Engels complained to Marx: 'You can lie warm in bed and study ground rent in general and Russian agrarian conditions in particular with nothing to disturb you – but I am to sit on a hard bench, swill cold wine, suddenly interrupt everything again and get after the scalp of the boring Dühring.' The book began as an attack on Dühring's 'bumptious pseudo-science' but ended as a brilliant outline of Marx's philosophical and economic theories. Marx's *Das Kapital* was a volume for scholars. The workers were not likely to read it and their knowledge of Marxism came to them second-hand. *Anti-Dühring* for the first time gave the public in ringing phrases that everyone could follow, the gist of the doctrines that Marx and Engels had painfully hammered out over the years. Three chapters were published as a pamphlet and 10,000 copies were quickly sold in Germany. Translations appeared in many languages. A generation of young socialists obtained their first grounding in Marxian ideology from Engels's pamphlet.

Today only the most dedicated Marxist scholars would have the patience to plough through the whole of Engels's collected works. Some of his writings were ephemeral in character – articles hastily written to earn a few guineas for Marx. Others were of a polemic nature and dealt with long forgotten squabbles among the singularly quarrelsome early socialists. On the other hand some of Engels's essays on military topics – such as his vivid account of the insurrection in Baden in 1849 – will always be of interest to historians. And his historical works, such as the essay on the Peasant War in Germany, have a special interest as early examples of the Marxist approach to the study of history. Two of Engels's books have stood the test of time. More than a century after it was written his early work on *The Condition of the Working Class in England* still has an assured place among the socialist classics. And his *Anti-Dühring* remains one of the clearest expositions of Marxian philosophy and economics.

Career of Friedrich Engels

1820   (28 November) Friedrich Engels born at Barmen.

1837   Left grammar school.

1837–8   In his father's office at Barmen.

1838–41   In Heinrich Leupold's office in Bremen. Wrote articles for Hamburg *Telegraph für Deutschland* (edited by Karl Gutzkow) and *Morgenblätter für gebildete Leser*.

1841–2   Served for one year in the Guards Artillery of the Prussian army. Associated with the Berlin 'Young Hegelians' known as 'The Free'. Contributed to the Cologne *Rheinische Zeitung* (edited by Karl Marx).

1842   First meeting with Marx at Cologne.

1842–4   In the office of Ermen and Engels in Manchester. Collected material for his book on the English workers.

1844   (August) Second meeting of Marx and Engels in Paris.

1844–5   In Barmen. Wrote *Condition of the Working Class in England* (1845). Actively supported Hess's Communist agitation in Elberfeld and Barmen.

1845   Joined Marx in Brussels. Visited Manchester with Marx (summer, 1845).

1845–8   Collaborated with Marx in writing *The Holy Family* (1845), *The German Ideology* (1845–6) and in establishing the *Communist League* (1847). Visited Paris (autumn 1846) and London (1847) on behalf of the Brussels Correspondence Committee.

1848   *The Communist Manifesto* (by Marx and Engels) published. Revolution in Germany. Engels joined Marx in Cologne and became one of the editors of the *Neue Rheinische Zeitung*.

1849   Took part in the abortive Baden rising as Willich's adjutant.

1850–70 In Manchester for twenty years with the firm of Ermen and Engels.

1850   Contributed to the second *Neue Rheinische Zeitung* (edited by Marx).

1851–2   Wrote articles on 'Revolution and Counter Revolution in

Germany' which appeared under Marx's name in the *New York Daily Tribune*.

1856   Visit to Ireland.

1857   Contributed articles on military topics to the *New American Cyclopaedia*. Work interrupted by Engels's illness.

1859   Wrote the pamphlet *Po und Rhein*.

1860   Wrote articles on military matters for the *Volunteer Journal for Lancashire and Cheshire*.
Death of Engels's father.

1863   Death of Mary Burns with whom Engels had lived for nearly twenty years.

1864   Became a partner in the firm of Ermen and Engels. Establishment of First International in London.

1867   Publication of Volume I of Karl Marx, *Das Kapital*.

1869   (July) Engels retired from business.
(September) Visit to Ireland with Lizzie Burns and Eleanor Marx.

1870–95   Resided in London.

1870–1   Contributed articles to the *Pall Mall Gazette* on the Franco-Prussian War.

1878   Publication of *Anti-Dühring*.

1878–90   Bismarck's Anti-Socialist Law in Germany.

1880   Meeting of Engels and the German Socialist leader Bebel in London.

1882   Death of Karl Marx.

1885   Volume II of *Das Kapital* (edited by Engels) published.

1887   Edited English translation of Volume I of *Das Kapital*.

1888   Bernstein and other members of the exiled staff of the *Sozialdemokrat* moved from Zürich to London where they were in close contact with Engels.
Engels visited the United States with Professor Schorlemmer and Edward and Eleanor Aveling.

1891   Erfurt Programme of the German Socialist Party.

1893   Honorary President of International Socialist Congress held at Zürich.
Visited Vienna and Berlin.

1894   Volume III of *Das Kapital* (edited by Engels) published in two parts.

1895   (5 August) Death of Engels in London.

I. ENGELS AND THE ENGLISH WORKERS

Introduction

ENGELS settled permanently in England at the age of thirty and always took a lively interest in the fortunes of the working-class movements of his adopted country. On his first visit to Manchester in 1842–44 he devoted his free time 'almost exclusively to the intercourse with plain working men'. He quickly found ample evidence of working-class discontent as the excitement caused by the Plug Plot riots, when cotton-factory boilers had been brought to a halt by workers removing the plugs, had barely subsided. His visits to factories and slums in the manufacturing districts of the north provided Engels with much of the material for his book on *The Condition of the Working Class in England* which eventually came to be regarded by Socialists as a classic exposure of the fate of the workers in an industrial society. His chapter on the great towns is one of the most vivid in the book while his discussion of English working-class movements showed a wide knowledge of Owenite Socialism, trade unionism, and Chartism as well as the agitations in favour of the Ten Hours Bill and against the new Poor Law. For five years – between 1845 and 1850 – Engels was engaged in propagating Communism on the Continent and he played an active part in the German revolution of 1848–9 but he found time to finish *The Condition of the Working Class in England* and to write on various aspects of the working-class movement such as the Manchester builders' strike of 1845 and the Ten Hours Bill.

Engels wrote comparatively little on English working-class movements during the twenty years that he lived in Manchester but there are references in his correspondence with Marx which show that he had by no means forgotten the men and women in the factories and mines. Marx and Engels were puzzled and disappointed at the failure of the English industrial proletariat to fulfil its role of leading the workers of the world in a grand assault upon their capitalist oppressors. According to Marxist theory England – as the country which had first experienced an Industrial Revolution – should have been the first to witness the collapse of the capitalist system. But English capitalism survived the commercial crises of 1847 and 1857 as well as the social distress brought about by the Cotton Famine. Marx and Engels tried to encourage Julian Harney and Ernest Jones in their efforts to revive Chartism but without success. No workers' party arose in the 1850s or the 1860s to challenge the Tories and the Whigs. As far as England was concerned the establishment of the International Working Men's Association in London in 1864 had little immediate effect on the apathy of the industrial workers regarding any concerted action – other than trade union activity – to remedy their grievances. Engels's comment on the results of the general election of 1868, which brought Gladstone to power, was a measure of his anger at the persistent failure of all his confident prophecies that the days of the established order in England were numbered. Meanwhile his visits to Ireland gave Engels a new insight into the degraded condition of an impoverished peasantry.

At the time of Engels's first visit to England in the 1840s the centre of both trade union activity and of the Chartist movement had been in the northern industrial districts. But when he retired from business and settled in London in 1870 the focus of the working-class movement had moved to the capital. The organization of the unskilled workers into new unions and the founding of the Social Democratic Federation, the Fabians, and the Independent Labour Party were signs of a fresh advance by the workers on both the industrial and the political fronts. Despite many other calls on his time Engels contributed to English left-wing journals, and his letters to Socialist correspondents abroad show his continued interest in the fortunes of the English workers. He attributed the slow progress of the working-class movement in England partly to divisions between different groups of workers and partly to the fact that some crumbs from the vast profits of colonial exploitation fell to the workers and blinded them to the evils of the capitalist system. One of Engels's last letters on English working-class politics – written to Schlüter in the year of his death – ended on a pessimistic note, for he could still see few signs of the establishment of a genuine working-class party that could successfully challenge both the Conservatives and the Liberals.

1. The Condition of the Working Class in England in 1844[1]

(i) Manchester in 1844

MANCHESTER lies at the foot of the southern slopes of a chain of hills which stretches from Oldham between the valleys of the Irwell and the Medlock to its last spur on Kersal Moor, which is both the race-course and the *Mons Sacer*[2] of Manchester. Manchester proper lies on the left bank of the Irwell, between this river and two smaller streams, the Irk and the Medlock, which flow into the Irwell at this point. Salford lies on the right bank of the Irwell in a sharp bend of the river, while Pendleton lies further to the west. Higher Broughton and Lower Broughton are situated to the north of the River Irwell, while Cheetham Hill is situated to the north of the Irk. Hulme lies south of the River Medlock and Chorlton-on-Medlock lies further to the east. Beyond Chorlton-on-Medlock, in the east of Manchester, lies Ardwick. The whole of this built-up area is commonly called Manchester, and contains about 400,000 people. This is probably an underestimate rather than an exaggeration.[3] Owing to the curious lay-out of the town it is quite possible for someone to

1. [Extract from the chapter on 'The Great Towns' in F. Engels, *The Condition of the Working Class in England* translated and edited by W. O. Henderson and W. H. Chaloner (1958). The first German edition appeared in 1845. The standard German edition is in *Marx-Engels Gesamtausgabe*, Part I, Vol. 4, pp. 5–282. (Words and phrases in brackets in the text and footnotes in square brackets have been added by the editor.)]

2. [The *Mons Sacer* was a hill near Rome to which, according to legend, the *plebs* seceded. Kersal Moor was the scene of numerous Radical and Chartist political meetings in the early nineteenth century.]

3. [The municipal borough of Manchester had been established in 1838. Its nucleus was the ancient *township* of Manchester to which had been added the townships of Hulme, Chorlton-upon-Medlock, Ardwick and Cheetham and also the district of Beswick. (The ancient *ecclesiastical parish* of Manchester, of course, covered a very much wider area, which included 30 townships). In 1844 the Manchester Borough Council stated that the population of the borough amounted to 235,139. See A. Redford and I. S. Russell, *History of Local Government in Manchester*, Vol. 2 (1940), p. 67 and map, facing p. 26. Engels's estimate of 400,000 presumably refers to a built-up area including not only the borough of Manchester but also the borough of Salford and other adjacent townships.]

live for years in Manchester and to travel daily to and from his work without ever seeing a working-class quarter or coming into contact with an artisan. He who visits Manchester simply on business or for pleasure need never see the slums, mainly because the working-class districts and the middle-class districts are quite distinct. This division is due partly to deliberate policy and partly to instinctive and tacit agreement between the two social groups. In those areas where the two social groups happen to come into contact with each other the middle classes sanctimoniously ignore the existence of their less fortunate neighbours. In the centre of Manchester there is a fairly large commercial district, which is about half a mile long and half a mile broad. This district is almost entirely given over to offices and warehouses. Nearly the whole of this district has no permanent residents and is deserted at night, when only policemen patrol its dark, narrow thoroughfares with their bull's eye lanterns. This district is intersected by certain main streets which carry an enormous volume of traffic. The lower floors of the buildings are occupied by shops of dazzling splendour. A few of the upper storeys on these premises are used as dwellings and the streets present a relatively busy appearance until late in the evening. Around this commercial quarter there is a belt of built up areas on the average one and a half miles in width, which is occupied entirely by working-class dwellings. This area of workers' houses includes all Manchester proper, except the centre, all Salford and Hulme, an important part of Pendleton and Chorlton, two thirds of Ardwick and certain small areas of Cheetham Hill and Broughton. Beyond this belt of working-class houses or dwellings lie the districts inhabited by the middle classes and the upper classes. The former are to be found in regularly laid out streets near the working-class districts – in Chorlton and in the remoter parts of Cheetham Hill. The villas of the upper classes are surrounded by gardens and lie in the higher and remoter parts of Chorlton and Ardwick or on the breezy heights of Cheetham Hill, Broughton and Pendleton.[1] The upper classes enjoy healthy country air and

1. [L. M. Hayes wrote: 'In Manchester, about the year 1840 and onwards, the middle classes began to realize that town life was not very desirable, and families began migrating and settling in the various suburbs': *Reminiscences of Manchester and some of its local surroundings from the year* 1840 (1905), p. 51.]

live in luxurious and comfortable dwellings which are linked to the centre of Manchester by omnibuses which run every fifteen or thirty minutes. To such an extent has the convenience of the rich been considered in the planning of Manchester that these plutocrats can travel from their houses to their places of business in the centre of the town by the shortest routes, which run entirely through working-class districts, without even realizing how close they are to the misery and filth which lie on both sides of the road. This is because the main streets which run from the Exchange in all directions out of the town are occupied almost uninterruptedly on both sides by shops, which are kept by members of the lower middle classes. In their own interests these shopkeepers should keep the outsides of their shops in a clean and respectable condition, and in fact they do so. These shops have naturally been greatly influenced by the character of the population in the area which lies behind them. Those shops which are situated in the vicinity of commercial or middle-class residential districts are more elegant than those which serve as a façade for the workers' grimy cottages. Nevertheless, even the less pretentious shops adequately serve their purpose of hiding from the eyes of wealthy ladies and gentlemen with strong stomachs and weak nerves the misery and squalor which are part and parcel of their own riches and luxury. Deansgate, for example, changes in character as one goes due south from the Old Church. At first there are warehouses and factories. Next come shops of a somewhat inferior character. But on leaving the commercial quarter for the south, the traveller passes shops of an ever inferior character and the street becomes dirtier, while taverns and gin palaces become increasingly frequent. When he reaches the end of the street the appearance of the shops can leave no doubt in his mind that no one but the workers would dream of patronizing them. Market Street which runs in a south-easterly direction from the Exchange possesses the same characteristics. At first it is lined with really high-class shops, in the upper storeys of which there are offices and warehouses. Market Street runs into Piccadilly, with its huge hotels and warehouses, but the further continuation of Piccadilly, London Road, which lies near the River Medlock, has a very different appearance. Here are to

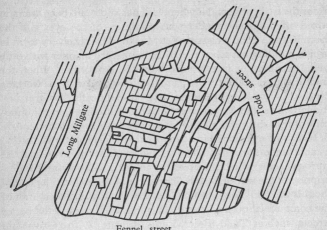

Fennel street

be found factories, public houses and shops which cater for the needs of the lower middle classes and the workers. By the time Ardwick Green is reached, the street has changed its character yet again and is flanked with residences occupied by the upper and middle classes. Beyond Ardwick Green lie the big gardens and the country villas of the wealthier factory owners and merchants. It is therefore possible for anyone who knows Manchester to judge the social character of any district merely by observing the appearance of the buildings fronting the road through which he is passing. On the other hand it is impossible to get a *true* picture from the main thoroughfare of the conditions of the working-class districts which lie immediately behind the façade of the principal streets.

I am quite aware of the fact that this hypocritical town-planning device is more or less common to all big cities. I realize, too, that owing to the nature of their business, shopkeepers inevitably seek premises in main thoroughfares. I know that in such streets there are more good houses than bad ones, and that the value of land is higher on or near a main thoroughfare than in the back streets. But in my opinion Manchester is unique in the systematic way in which the working classes have been barred from the main streets. Nowhere else has such care been taken to avoid offending the tender susceptibilities of the eyes and the nerves of the middle classes. Yet Manchester is the very town in which building has taken place in a haphazard manner with little or no planning or interference from the authorities. When the middle classes zealously proclaim that all is well with the working classes, I cannot help feeling that the politically 'progressive' industrialists, the Manchester 'bigwigs',[1] are not quite so innocent of this shameful piece of town planning as they pretend.

It may be mentioned incidentally that nearly all the industrial establishments are situated on the banks of the three rivers or the various canals which intersect the town. I will now give a description of the working-class districts of Manchester. The first of them is the Old Town, which lies between the northern limit of the commercial quarter and the River Irk. Here even the better streets, such as Todd Street, Long Millgate, Withy Grove and Shudehill are narrow and tortuous. The houses are dirty, old and tumble-down. The side streets have been built in a disgraceful fashion. If one enters the district near the 'Old Church' and goes down Long Millgate, one sees immediately on the right-hand side a row of antiquated houses where not a single front wall is standing upright. This is a remnant of the old Manchester of the days before the town became industrialized. The original inhabitants and their children have left for better houses in other districts, while the houses in Long Millgate, which no longer satisfied them, were left to a tribe of workers containing a strong Irish element. Here one is really and truly in a district which is quite obviously given over entirely to the working classes, because even the shopkeepers and the publicans of Long Millgate make no effort to give their establishments a semblance of cleanliness. The condition of this street may be deplorable, but it is by no means as bad as the alleys and courts which lie behind it, and which can be approached only by covered passages so narrow that two people cannot pass. Anyone who has never visited these courts and alleys can have no idea of the fantastic way in which the houses have been packed together in disorderly confusion in

1. [Engels, in the first German edition of 1845, wrote 'big Whigs' in English. Either phrase would make sense in this context.]

impudent defiance of all reasonable principles of town planning. And the fault lies not merely in the survival of old property from earlier periods in Manchester's history. Only in quite modern times has the policy of cramming as many houses as possible on to such space as was not utilized in earlier periods reached its climax. The result is that today not an inch of space remains between the houses and any further building is now physically impossible. To prove my point I reproduce (p. 33) a small section of a plan of Manchester. It is by no means the worst slum in Manchester and it does not cover one-tenth of the area of Manchester.

This sketch will be sufficient to illustrate the crazy lay-out of the whole district lying near the River Irk. There is a very sharp drop of some 15 to 30 feet down to the south bank of the Irk at this point. As many as three rows of houses have generally been squeezed on to this precipitous slope. The lowest row of houses stands directly on the bank of the river while the front walls of the highest row stand on the crest of the ridge in Long Millgate. Moreover, factory buildings are also to be found on the banks of the river. In short the layout of the upper part of Long Millgate at the top of the rise is just as disorderly and congested as the lower part of the street. To the right and left a number of covered passages from Long Millgate give access to several courts. On reaching them one meets with a degree of dirt and revolting filth, the like of which is not to be found elsewhere. The worst courts are those leading down to the Irk, which contain unquestionably the most dreadful dwellings I have ever seen. In one of these courts, just at the entrance where the covered passage ends, there is a privy without a door. This privy is so dirty that the inhabitants of the court can only enter or leave the court if they are prepared to wade through puddles of stale urine and excrement. Anyone who wishes to confirm this description should go to the first court on the bank of the Irk above Ducie Bridge. Several tanneries are situated on the bank of the river and they fill the neighbourhood with the stench of animal putrefaction. The only way of getting to the courts below Ducie Bridge is by going down flights of narrow dirty steps and one can only reach the houses by treading over heaps of dirt and filth. The first court below Ducie Bridge is called Allen's Court. At the time of the cholera (1832) this court was in such a disgraceful state that the sanitary inspectors (of the local Board of Health) evacuated the inhabitants. The court was then swept and fumigated with chlorine. In his pamphlet Dr Kay gives a horrifying description of conditions in this court at that time.[1] Since Kay wrote this pamphlet, this court appears to have been at any rate partly demolished and rebuilt. If one looks down the river from Ducie Bridge one does at least see several ruined walls and high piles of rubble, side by side with some recently-built houses. The view from this bridge, which is mercifully concealed by a high parapet from all but the tallest mortals, is quite characteristic of the whole district. At the bottom the Irk flows, or rather, stagnates. It is a narrow, coal-black, stinking river full of filth and rubbish which it deposits on the more low-lying right bank. In dry weather this bank presents the spectacle of a series of the most revolting blackish-green puddles of slime from the depths of which bubbles of miasmatic gases constantly rise and create a stench which is unbearable even to those standing on the bridge forty or fifty feet above the level of the water. Moreover, the flow of the river is continually interrupted by numerous high weirs, behind which large quantities of slime and refuse collect and putrefy. Above Ducie Bridge there are some tall tannery buildings, and further up there are dye-works, bone mills and gasworks. All the filth, both liquid and solid, discharged by these works finds its way into the River Irk, which also receives the contents of the adjacent sewers and privies. The nature of the filth deposited by this river may well be imagined.[2] If one looks

1. Dr J. P. Kay, *The Moral and Physical Condition of the Working Classes employed in the Cotton Manufacture in Manchester* (2nd enlarged edn., 1832). [Engels added the comment: 'This is an excellent book although the author confuses the factory workers with the working classes in general.' The description of Allen's Court appears on pages 38 to 40 of the second edition of Kay's pamphlet. There was no reference to Allen's Court in the first edition. In the following year (1833) another Manchester physician, Henry Gaulter, published an equally revolting description of Allen's Court in *The Origin and Progress of the Malignant Cholera in Manchester* (1833), pp. 50–51. See also pages 44–49, 114 and plan facing page 206.]

2. [Engels's vivid descriptions of the Medlock and the confluence of the Rivers Irwell and Irk have obscured the fact that the Manchester rivers were not uniformly filthy. Sir John and Lady Clapham wrote: 'From the foulest corner of the greatest of them [i.e. the new towns], that corner in Manchester-Salford at the junction of the Irwell and the Irk where Engels, in 1844, saw "the

Plan of Manchester and its suburbs

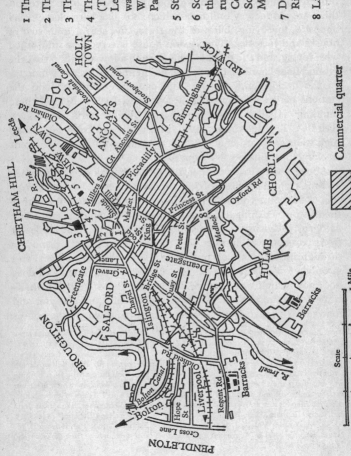

1 The Exchange

2 The Collegiate Church

3 The Workhouse

4 The Paupers' Cemetery (The station of the Leeds-Liverpool Railway runs between the Workhouse and the Paupers' Cemetery)

5 St Michael's Church

6 Scotland Bridge over the River Irk (The street running from the Collegiate Church to Scotland Bridge is Long Millgate)

7 Ducie Bridge over the River Irk

8 Little Ireland

Commercial quarter

Scale

0   ¼   ½   ¾   1 Mile

at the heaps of garbage below Ducie Bridge one can gauge the extent to which accumulated dirt, filth and decay permeates the courts on the steep left bank of the river. The houses are packed very closely together and since the bank of the river is very steep it is possible to see a part of every house. All of them have been blackened by soot, all of them are crumbling with age and all have broken window panes and window frames. In the background there are old factory buildings which look like barracks. On the opposite, low-lying, bank of the river, one sees a long row of houses and factories. The second house is a roofless ruin, filled with refuse, and the third is built in such a low situation that the ground floor is uninhabitable and has neither doors nor windows. In the background one sees the paupers' cemetery, and the stations of the railways to Liverpool and Leeds. Behind these buildings is situated the workhouse, Manchester's 'Poor Law Bastille'. The workhouse is built on a hill and from behind its high walls and battlements seems to threaten the whole adjacent working-class quarter like a fortress.

Above Ducie Bridge the left bank of the Irk becomes flatter and the right bank of the Irk becomes steeper and so the condition of the houses on both sides of the river becomes worse rather than better. Turning left from the main street which is still Long Millgate, the visitor can easily lose his way. He wanders aimlessly from one court to another. He turns one corner after another through innumerable narrow dirty alleyways and passages, and in only a few minutes he has lost all sense of direction and does not know which way to turn. The area is full of ruined or half-ruined buildings. Some of them are actually uninhabited and that means a great deal in this quarter of the town. In the houses

most horrible dwellings which he had ever yet beheld", two and a half miles up a gentle hill brought you to the sand and heather of Kersal Moor, where there was horse-racing at Whitsuntide until 1846, and Chartist mass meetings later. (Next year the race-course was moved nearer in.) Not more than a mile and a half upstream from the foul corner, the little bourgeois of the forties thought that the river bathing was excellent; they knew "a stretch of clean, nice, yellow sand, in which after our dip we could roll and dry ourselves in the hot summer sun". There or thereabouts, the first Manchester and Salford regatta was rowed in September, 1842': Sir John and Lady Clapham, 'Life in the New Towns' (*Early Victorian England 1830-1865*, ed. G. M. Young, Vol. 1, (1934), p. 228). The Claphams' quotation is from L. M. Hayes, *Reminiscences of Manchester and some of its local surroundings from the year 1840* (1905), pp. 61-2.]

one seldom sees a wooden or a stone floor, while the doors and windows are nearly always broken and badly fitting. And as for the dirt! Everywhere one sees heaps of refuse, garbage and filth. There are stagnant pools instead of gutters and the stench alone is so overpowering that no human being, even partially civilized, would find it bearable to live in such a district. The recently constructed extension of the Leeds railway which crosses the Irk at this point has swept away some of these courts and alleys, but it has thrown open to public gaze some of the others. So it comes about that there is to be found immediately under the railway bridge a court which is even filthier and more revolting than all the others. This is simply because it was formerly so hidden and secluded that it could only be reached with considerable difficulty (but is now exposed to the human eye). I thought I knew this district well, but even I would never have found it had not the railway viaduct made a breach in the slums at this point. One walks along a very rough path on the river bank, in between clothes-posts and washing lines to reach a chaotic group of little, one-storeyed, one-roomed cabins. Most of them have earth floors, and working, living and sleeping all take place in the one room. In such a hole, barely six feet long and five feet wide, I saw two beds – and what beds and bedding! – which filled the room, except for the fireplace and the doorstep. Several of these huts, as far as I could see, were completely empty, although the door was open and the inhabitants were leaning against the door posts. In front of the doors filth and garbage abounded. I could not see the pavement, but from time to time, I felt it was there because my feet scraped it. This whole collection of cattle sheds for human beings was surrounded on two sides by houses and a factory and on a third side by the river. (It was possible to get to this slum by only two routes.) One was the narrow path along the river bank, while the other was a narrow gateway which led to another human rabbit warren which was nearly as badly built and was nearly in such a bad condition as the one I have just described.

Enough of this! All along the Irk slums of this type abound. There is an unplanned and chaotic conglomeration of houses, most of which are more or less uninhabitable. The dirtiness of the interiors of these premises is fully in keeping with the filth that surrounds them. How can people dwelling in such places keep clean! There are not even adequate facilities for satisfying the most natural daily needs. There are so few privies that they are either filled up every day or are too far away for those who need to use them. How can these people wash when all that is available is the dirty water of the Irk? Pumps and piped water are to be found only in the better-class districts of the town. Indeed no one can blame these helots of modern civilization if their homes are no cleaner than the occasional pigsties which are a feature of these slums. There are actually some property owners who are not ashamed to let dwellings such as those which are to be found below Scotland Bridge. Here on the quayside a mere six feet from the water's edge is to be found a row of six or seven cellars, the bottoms of which are at least two feet beneath the low-water level of the Irk. What can one say of the owner of the corner house – situated on the opposite bank of the river above Scotland Bridge – who actually lets the upper floor although the premises downstairs are quite uninhabitable, and no attempt has been made to board up the gaps left by the disappearance of doors and windows? This sort of thing is by no means uncommon in this part of Manchester, where, owing to the lack of conveniences, such deserted ground floors are often used by the whole neighbourhood as privies.

We shall now leave the Irk in order to investigate the workers' houses on the other side of Long Millgate. This is a rather more recently built area which runs from St Michael's Church to Withy Grove and Shudehill. Here at any rate there is more evidence of a planned building. In place of the chaotic layout (just described) we find that at least both the long through alleys and the cul-de-sacs are straight. The courts, built according to a plan, are usually square. On the other side of Long Millgate not a single house was erected in accordance with any sort of plan. Now we are in an area where although individual houses form part of a pattern the alleys and courts have been laid out in an irregular and unsystematic fashion without regard. The alleys may be straight but they change direction sharply, so that the unsuspecting stranger is continually finding himself in a blind alley or in a street which is leading him to the spot he left a few moments before. Only those who are reasonably acquainted with this maze can find their way through it. The ventilation of these streets and courts – if such a word could be used of this area – is just as inadequate as in the district along the Irk. Although this district is in some respects better than the slums in the valley of the Irk – at any rate the houses are rather newer and the streets do sometimes have gutters – nevertheless it must be pointed out that here there is nearly always a cellar dwelling underneath each house. In the valley of the Irk, on the other hand, it is rare to find cellar dwellings because of the greater age of the buildings and the more slovenly method of construction. Filth, heaps of refuse and ashes and dirty pools in the streets are common to both districts. However, in the area with which we are now concerned there are additional circumstances most deleterious to public cleanliness. There are large numbers of pigs, some of which are allowed to roam freely in the narrow streets, snuffling among the garbage heaps, while others are kept in little sties in the courts. In this area, as in most of the working-class districts of Manchester, pig breeders rent the courts and build the sties there. In nearly every court there are one or more little nooks in which pigs are kept. The inhabitants of the court throw all their garbage into these sties. This fattens the pigs, but also has the highly undesirable effect of impregnating the air – already stale because it is confined between four walls – with the disagreeable odour of decaying animal and vegetable matter. A wide and reasonably decent thoroughfare, Miller's Street, has been driven through this area and by this means the worst of the slums have been more or less hidden from the public gaze. If, however, any-one has sufficient curiosity to leave his road and go along one of the many alleys which lead to the courts, he will come across pigs and filth every twenty paces.[1]

This, then, is the Old Town of Manchester. On re-reading my description of the Old Town I must admit that, far from having exaggerated anything, I have not written vividly enough to im-press the reader with the filth and dilapidation of a district which

---

1. [It is impossible to translate Engels's play on words involved in the use of the word 'Schweinerei' in this last sentence.]

is quite unfit for human habitation. The shameful lay-out of the Old Town has made it impossible for the wretched inhabitants to enjoy cleanliness, fresh air and good health. And such a district of at least twenty to thirty thousand inhabitants lies in the very centre of the second city in England, the most important factory town in the world. It is here that one can see how little space human beings need to move about in, how little air – and what air! – they need to breathe in order to exist, and how few of the decencies of civilization are really necessary in order to survive. It is true that this is the *Old Town* and Manchester people stress this when their attention is drawn to the revolting character of this hell upon earth. But that is no defence. Everything in this district that arouses our disgust and just indignation is of relatively recent origin and belongs to the industrial age. The two or three hundred houses which survive from the earlier period of Manchester's history have long ago been deserted by their original inhabitants. It is only industry which has crammed them full of the hordes of workers who now live there. It is only the modern industrial age which has built over every scrap of ground between these old houses to provide accommodation for the masses who have migrated from the country districts and from Ireland. It is only the industrial age that has made it possible for the owners of these shacks, fit only for the accommodation of cattle, to let them at high rents for human habitations. It is only modern industry which permits these owners to take advantage of the poverty of the workers, to undermine the health of thousands to enrich themselves. Only industry has made it possible for workers who have barely emerged from a state of serfdom to be again treated as chattels and not as human beings. The workers have been caged in dwellings which are so wretched that no one else will live in them, and they actually pay good money for the privilege of seeing these dilapidated hovels fall to pieces about their ears. Industry alone has been responsible for all this and yet this same industry could not flourish except by degrading and exploiting the workers. It is true that this quarter of the town was originally built on a poor site, which offered few prospects for satisfactory development. But have either the landowners or the authorities done anything to improve matters when new buildings were erected? Far from adopting any such policy those responsible for recent developments have built houses in every conceivable nook and cranny. Even small passages which were not absolutely necessary have been built over and stopped up. The value of the land rose with the expansion of industry. The more the land rose in value the more furious became the search for new building sites. The health and comfort of the inhabitants were totally ignored, as a result of the determination of landlords to pocket the maximum profit. No hovel is so wretched but it will find a worker to rent it because he is too poor to pay for better accommodation. But the middle classes salve their consciences by arguing that this state of affairs obtains only in the Old Town. Let us therefore see what the New Town has to offer.

The New Town, also known as Irish Town, on the other side of the Old Town, is situated on the clayey soil of the rising ground between the River Irk and St George's Road. This district does not give one the impression that it is part of a big city. The New Town is composed of single rows of houses and groups of streets which might be small villages, lying on bare clayey soil which does not produce even a blade of grass. The houses – or rather the cottages – are in a disgraceful state because they are never repaired. They are filthy and beneath them are to be found damp, dirty cellar dwellings; the unpaved alleys lack any form of drainage. The district is infested with small herds of pigs; some of them are penned up in little courts and sties, while others wander freely on the neighbouring hillside. The lanes in this district are so filthy that it is only in very dry weather that one can reach it without sinking ankle-deep at every step. Near St George's Road these isolated groups of houses are built closer together and one reaches a maze of lanes, blind alleys and back passages and courts. The nearer one gets to the centre of the town, the more closely packed are the houses and the more irregular is the lay-out of the streets. On the other hand, the streets here are often paved or at least have adequate pavements and gutters; but the filth, and the disgusting conditions of the houses, particularly the cellars, remain unchanged.

It is pertinent at this stage to make some general observations on the normal lay-out of working-class quarters and the normal plan of constructing artisans' dwellings in Manchester. We have seen how, in the Old Town, there has been no systematic planning and that the siting of the houses has been purely fortuitous. Builders who erected new houses put them up without regard to the situation of older neighbouring property. The tiny gaps which exist between the houses are called 'courts' for want of a more appropriate name. There is more evidence of planning in the rather newer parts of the Old Town, as well as in other working-class districts which date from the first stages of the Industrial Revolution. Here the spaces between the blocks of dwellings consist of regular – generally square – courts, from which there is access to the streets by a covered passage. (This may be seen from the accompanying diagram.) From the point

street

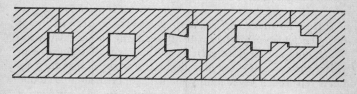

street

of view of the health of the workers cooped up in these dwellings, this type of regular lay-out with wholly inadequate ventilation is even worse than the unplanned streets of the Old Town. The air simply cannot escape and it is only up the chimneys of the houses – when fires happen to be burning – that any draught is provided to help the foul air from the courts to escape.[1] More-

1. And yet, one of the wise English Liberals asserts in the *Report* of the Children's Employment Commission that courts such as these are masterpieces of town planning because they act in the same way as a number of little open spaces which facilitate ventilation and the circulation of the air. Or course the air would circulate if every court had two or four wide uncovered entrances opposite each other. In fact these courts never have even one. Nearly all have only narrow, covered entries. [This is a reference to a statement made by R. D. Grainger on the 'Manufactures of Birming-

over the houses surrounding such courts are usually built back
to back, with a common rear wall,[1] and this alone is sufficient to
hinder any adequate circulation of the air, and since the police
do not concern themselves with the state of these courts[2]
everything thrown into the courts is allowed to lie there un-
disturbed, so that it is not surprising that dirt and heaps of ashes
and filth are to be found there. I have had occasion to visit some
of the courts lying in Miller's Street where the level of the
ground was actually six inches lower than the level of the main
street and yet no drains are available to carry away the water
which accumulates in wet weather.

Subsequently another method of constructing workers' houses
was introduced, but this has never become universal. Workers'
cottages are now hardly ever built singly, but always in larger
numbers – a dozen or even sixty at a time. A single contractor
will build one or two whole streets at a time. The way in which
these houses are built is illustrated by the accompanying diagram:

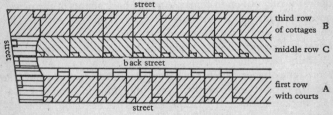

The cottages which face the street (at the bottom of the

ham' in the *Appendix to the 2nd Report* of the Children's Employment Commission
Part 1, p. F 23, para. 212. Grainger wrote: 'The great number of courts [in Birming-
ham], amounting five years ago to 2,030, must also promote the general health, being
in fact so many small squares scattered over the town.']

1. [It will be seen that this fact is not illustrated in the diagram printed by Engels.]

2. [The Manchester Corporation's *police* force would not concern itself about
these matters as it was not its function to do so. The courts were at this period
regarded as private property. Professor Redford states: 'There were no powers in
the local Acts for compelling the removal of middens from courts, passages and
vacant lands ... the only way in which redress could be obtained was by cumbrous
and costly legal proceedings': A. Redford and I. S. Russell, *History of Local Government in Manchester*, Vol. 2, p. 148. In 1844, however, the Manchester Police Act was
passed and this gave the local inspectors of nuisances rather wider powers.]

diagram) are of a somewhat superior character (Class A) and are fortunate enough to have a back door and a little backyard. The highest rents are charged for these cottages. Behind the back wall of these yards there is a narrow alley called a back street, which is enclosed at both ends. Access to this back street is either through a little entry or a covered passage. The cottages which have their front doors looking out on to the back street (Class C) pay the lowest rent and are indeed the most neglected. They have a party wall in common with the third row of cottages which face the street (at the top of the diagram). This third row of cottages (Class B) pay a lower rent than the first class of cottages (A) but a higher rent than the middle row (C). This method of construction ensures that the first row of cottages (A) is well ventilated. The ventilation of the cottages in the third row (B) is at any rate no worse than that to be found in the houses built on the older plan (which have a street frontage as distinct from a court frontage). On the other hand the middle row of cottages (C) is just as badly ventilated as the older houses with front doors looking out on to courts. And the back streets of the newer houses are just as disgustingly filthy as the newer courts. The contractors prefer the newer lay-out, not only because it economizes space, but because it gives them an opportunity of successfully exploiting the better paid workers who can pay higher rents for cottages which have front doors facing the street (A and B), (as distinct from the back alley). This method of building workers' cottages in three rows is to be found throughout Manchester and indeed all over Lancashire and Yorkshire. Sometimes the old and the new method of construction are found side by side, but generally they are located in different parts of towns so that it is possible to distinguish without difficulty the older working-class districts from the newer.

There is also a third system of building working-class houses, which may be called the back-alley type of construction. This system predominates to an overwhelming degree in the working-class quarter (of Ancoats) to the east of St George's Road, on both sides of the Oldham Road and Great Ancoats Street. It is also the commonest method of construction throughout the working-class districts of Manchester and its suburbs.

In the larger district we have just mentioned, which goes under the name of Ancoats, are to be found the majority, and the largest, of Manchester's factories. They are situated on canals and are colossal, six- or seven-storey buildings, towering, with their slender chimney-stacks, over the tiny cottages of the workers. The inhabitants of this district are for the most part factory workers, although hand-loom weavers are to be found in the worst streets. The streets lying closest to the centre of the town are the oldest and therefore the worst, though they are paved and have drains. I include in my description some streets parallel to Oldham Road and Great Ancoats Street (which lie outside Ancoats). Further to the north-east there are several newly-built streets. Here the cottages have a clean and tidy appearance, for the doors and window frames have been newly painted and the rooms whitewashed. More fresh air gets into the streets themselves, while the empty spaces between the houses are larger and more frequent (than in the older districts). But these remarks apply only to a relatively small number of the dwellings, because nearly every cottage has its inhabited cellar and many of the streets are unpaved and undrained. Above all, the present pleasing appearance of these cottages is only a pretence, because after ten years it will have vanished.[1] It is not only the lay-out of the streets, but the construction of the cottages themselves which is to be condemned. When newly built these cottages have a pleasant appearance and give the impression of being well-built. Their massive brick walls may well deceive the observer. Anyone looking at a newly-built row of workers' dwellings without examining either the back alleys or the construction of the houses might well be inclined to accept the assertions of the 'progressive'[2] manufacturers who claim that nowhere are the workers so well housed as in England. A closer inspection, however, soon reveals the fact that the walls of these cottages are as thin as it is possible to make them. The outer cellar walls which carry the weight of the ground floor and the

1. [Engels apparently assumes that no repainting would be carried out.]
2. [Engels used the phrase 'liberale Fabrikanten'.]

roof, are only one brick thick. Generally the bricks are laid so that the long sides are together and the appearance of the wall from the outside may be represented as follows:

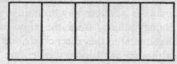

Yet I have seen several cottages of the same height – some actually still being built – where the thickness of the walls is equal to that of only half a brick. This is because the bricks are laid end to end, so that the outside wall has the following appearance:

This method of construction is adopted partly in order to save materials and partly because the builder is never the owner of the land on which the cottages are put up. The English practice is to lease building land for twenty, thirty, forty, fifty or ninety-nine years. When the lease falls in, possession of the land and the buildings on it reverts to the ground landlord, who does not have to pay any compensation for unexhausted improvements. The builder, therefore, constructs the cottages of a type unlikely to survive beyond the period of the lease. Since some leases are as short as twenty or thirty years it is easy to understand that builders are not likely to sink much capital into cottages built on such land. Moreover, the owners of the houses who are either bricklayers, joiners and carpenters or factory owners, are generally not prepared to spend very much money on repairing and maintaining their property. This is partly because they are not prepared to sacrifice any part of their profits, and partly owing to the system of short leases to which we have referred. When unemployment is rife during periods of bad trade whole rows of cottages often stand empty and in such circumstances they soon become virtually uninhabitable. It is generally estimated that on the average a worker's house is habitable for only forty years. This is indeed surprising when one looks at what appear to be the massive well-built walls of new cottages. Anyone would think they were intended to last for several centuries. False economy in the original construction, failure to maintain the property in good repair, frequent periods when they are unoccupied, are among the reasons which account for the fact that after forty years working-class property is generally in a ruinous condition. Moreover, it must be remembered that the house is particularly neglected during the last ten years or so of its life. The tenants during this period, who are generally Irish, actually use up all available woodwork for firing. The district of Ancoats has developed since the first expansion of manufactures and much of the property was built during the early years of the present (i.e. nineteenth) century. Nevertheless there are already many old and dilapidated houses in Ancoats, many of which will shortly be quite uninhabitable. What a mistake it has been to waste so much capital in this way! If only a little more money had been spent on these houses when they were first built and if only a small amount of repair work had been carried out regularly these houses might have been maintained in a clean, respectable and inhabitable condition for years. In fact the property is as I have described it, and I cannot think of any more scandalous and demoralizing system of housing the workers than this. The worker is forced to live in such dilapidated dwellings because he cannot afford to rent better accommodation, or because no better cottages are available close to the factory in which he is working. It may even be that the cottage is owned by his employer and the worker is offered a job on condition that he rents the house. Of course working-class dwellings are not allowed to fall into decay quite so rapidly in a more central area where ground rents are high. In such parts of the town there is every prospect of finding a new tenant immediately an old one leaves the premises, and it is in the interests of the owners to maintain property in a habitable condition for a rather longer period. Even here, however, only the minimum amount of maintenance is carried out and some of these dwellings which have been repaired are among the worst in the country. Sometimes the threat of an epidemic arouses the normally very sluggish conscience of the health authorities and then there are signs of unwonted activity all over some working-class district. Complete rows of cellars and cottages may be closed and there are several such alleys near Oldham Road. The effects of such action soon wear off. The condemned dwellings rapidly find new tenants and the owners are placed in an advantageous position when searching for new tenants, for it is well known that the health authorities will not trouble themselves again with this property for quite a time.

These eastern and north-eastern districts of Manchester are the only ones in which the middle classes have not built any houses for themselves. This is because for ten or eleven months in the year the winds blowing from the west and south-west always carry the smoke from the factories – and there is plenty of it – over this part of the town. The workers alone can breathe this polluted atmosphere.

A large working-class quarter is growing up south of Great Ancoats Street, on a hilly, bare stretch of land. Here a few irregularly built rows and square courts of houses have been erected between which lie broken muddy tracts where no grass grows. In wet weather it is almost impossible to cross these open spaces. The cottages are all old and dirty. They are often built at the bottom of the natural depressions in the soil and forcibly remind one of the workers' dwellings in the New Town. The area crossed by the railway to Birmingham has the most houses and is therefore the worst part of the district. Here the river Medlock flows with endless twists and turns through a valley which may be compared with that of the Irk. From its entry into Manchester to its confluence with the Irwell, this coal-black, stagnant, stinking river is lined on both sides by a broad belt of factories and workers' dwellings. The cottages are all in a sorry state. The banks of the Medlock like those of the Irk are generally steep and the buildings run down to the very edge of the river. The lay-out of the streets and houses is just as bad on the Manchester side of the river as it is on the opposite side where lie the districts of Ardwick, Chorlton and Hulme. This book would never be finished if I were to describe in detail every part of this district, but I might mention that the most disgusting spot of all is one which lies on the Manchester side of the river. It is situated to the south-west of Oxford Road and is called

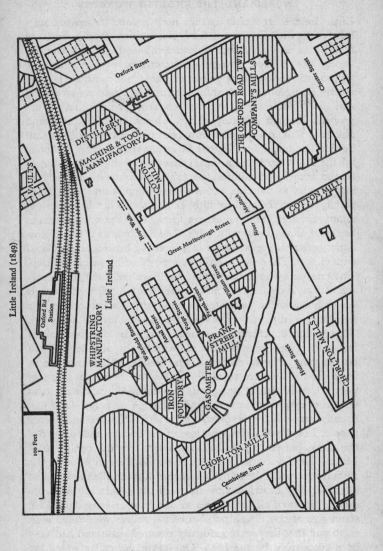

Little Ireland (1849)

Little Ireland. It lies in a fairly deep natural depression on a bend of the river and is completely surrounded by tall factories or high banks and embankments covered with buildings. Here lie two groups of about two hundred cottages, most of which are built on the back-to-back principle. Some four thousand people mostly Irish, inhabit this slum. The cottages are very small, old and dirty, while the streets are uneven, partly unpaved, not properly drained and full of ruts. Heaps of refuse, offal and sickening filth are everywhere interspersed with pools of stagnant liquid. The atmosphere is polluted by the stench and is darkened by the thick smoke of a dozen factory chimneys. A horde of ragged women and children swarm about the streets and they are just as dirty as the pigs which wallow happily on the heaps of garbage and in the pools of filth. In short, this horrid little slum affords as hateful and repulsive a spectacle as the worst courts to be found on the banks of the Irk. The inhabitants live in dilapidated cottages, the windows of which are broken and patched with oilskin. The doors and the door posts are broken and rotten. The creatures who inhabit these dwellings and even their dark, wet cellars, and who live confined amidst all this filth and foul air – which cannot be dissipated because of the surrounding lofty buildings – must surely have sunk to the lowest level of humanity. That is the conclusion that must surely be drawn even by any visitor who examines the slum from the outside, without entering any of the dwellings. But his feelings of horror would be intensified if he were to discover that on the average twenty people live in each of these little houses, which at the moment consist of two rooms, an attic and a cellar. One privy – and that usually inaccessible – is shared by about one hundred and twenty people. In spite of all the warnings of the doctors and in spite of the alarm caused to the health authorities by the condition of Little Ireland during the cholera epidemic, the condition of this slum is practically the same in this year of grace 1844 as it was in 1831. Dr Kay describes how not only the cellars but even the ground floors of all the houses in this quarter were damp. He states that at one time a number of the cellars were filled with earth and that they were gradually emptied again and had now been reoccupied by the Irish. One particular cellar which lay below the level of the river was continually flooded with water which gushed in through a hole which had been stuffed full of clay. The handloom weaver who lived there had to clean out his cellar every morning and empty the water into the street.[1]

The district of Hulme lies farther downstream on the left bank of the Medlock and this is really one big working-class quarter. Conditions in Hulme are practically identical with those already described in Ancoats. In those parts of Hulme in which the houses are built most tightly together the cottages are generally in a miserable and dilapidated state. In the less densely populated parts of the district the houses are of more modern construction and more open to the fresh air, but most of them are surrounded by filth. In general the cottages are damp and the type of lay-out, with back alleys and cellar dwellings, is similar to that of Ancoats.

On the opposite side of the Medlock, in Manchester itself, is situated a second large working-class district which lies on either side of Deansgate and stretches as far as the commercial quarter of the city. Parts of this are are just as bad as the Old Town. This is true of the area between Quay Street, Bridge Street, Princess Street and Peter Street, which lies near the commercial centre of Manchester. Here the way in which buildings have been erected close to each other is even worse than in the narrowest courts of the Old Town. Here is a maze of long narrow lanes, linking the tiny courts and passages. The exits and entrances to the courts and passages are so irregularly placed that a visitor to this labyrinth is in danger of losing his way and finding himself in a blind alley or in a passage which leads in entirely the wrong direction. Only those who know every passage and every court can find their way about. Dr Kay states that in these dilapidated and dirty houses along the narrow lanes there dwell the most demoralized classes in Manchester. There were the dens of thieves and prostitutes and as far as one can see Dr Kay's description still holds true. When the sanitary authorities made an attempt to clean up this quarter in 1831 they found that it was just as dirty

---

1. [Dr J. P. Kay, *The Moral and Physical Condition of the Working Classes . . .*, etc., pp. 35–6. The story of the weaver who had to mop out his cellar every morning was not told by Kay himself but was quoted by Kay from a report made to the Manchester magistrates by a sub-committee of the local Board of Health on 19 December 1831.]

as Little Ireland and the districts round the Irk. They found that in Parliament Street there was only one privy for three hundred and eighty people and in Parliament Passage there was only one privy for thirty houses packed with human beings.[1] I can testify that things have not improved much since Kay wrote.

If we cross the Irwell to Salford we enter a town which is built on a tongue of land enclosed by a great bend of the river. The population numbers 80,000. Salford is really all one large working-class quarter through which runs a single broad main street. At one time Salford was more important than Manchester, being the principal town for the surrounding district, which is still called Salford Hundred. This explains why here, too, there is a fairly old and therefore now very unhealthy, dirty and dilapidated district which is situated opposite the 'Old Church' of Manchester. This district is in just as bad a condition as the Old Town on the Manchester side of the Irwell. At some distance from the river there lies a more recently built-up area, but this, too, is over forty years old and therefore beginning to decay. The whole of Salford consists of courts and of lanes which are so narrow that they reminded me of the narrowest alleys I have ever seen, which are those in Genoa. From this point of view the lay-out of Salford is in general even worse than that of Manchester. Moreover, Salford is dirtier than Manchester. In Manchester the authorities do at least once in a way – say every six or ten years – inspect the working-class districts and close the very worst dwellings. They try to clean out the filthiest corners of these Augean stables. Nothing of this sort ever seems to happen in Salford. I am sure that the narrow side streets and courts of Chapel Street, Greengate and Gravel Lane have never once been cleaned since they were built. Now the railway to Liverpool crosses the district and the construction of this line has led to the removal of some of the dirtiest parts of these slums. But what good does that do? The traveller crossing this viaduct can still look down on plenty of dirt and poverty. If he takes the trouble to go through these alleyways and to peer through the open doors and windows into the houses and cellars he can satisfy himself time and time again that the Salford workers inhabit dwellings

1. [Kay, op. cit., pp. 36–7.]

in which it is impossible to live in either cleanliness or comfort. Exactly the same conditions are to be found in the outlying districts of Salford – in Islington, along Regent Road, and behind the railway to Bolton. The working-class quarter situated between Oldfield and Cross Lane – it is divided by Hope Street – is one of the innumerable courts and lanes which are in a very bad condition. This district is just as dirty and overcrowded as the Old Town of Manchester. It was here that I found a man, who seemed to be about sixty years of age, living in a cow-shed. He had constructed a sort of chimney for his square-shaped hovel, which had no floor-boards, no plaster on the walls and no windows. He had installed a bedstead and here he lived although the rain came through the decaying roof. The man was too old for regular work, but he earned a living by removing manure and garbage with his handcart. Pools of filth lay close to his shed.

Such are the various working-class districts of Manchester which I myself was able to see during my twenty months' stay in that town. I may sum up the impressions of my visits to these districts by stating that 350,000 workers in Manchester and the surrounding districts nearly all live in inferior, damp, dirty cottages; that the streets are generally in a disgraceful state of filth and disrepair, and that the lay-out of the dwellings reflects the greed of the builder for profits from the way in which ventilation is lacking. In a word, the workers' dwellings of Manchester are dirty, miserable and wholly lacking in comforts. In such houses only inhuman, degraded and unhealthy creatures would feel at home. And I am not the only one who takes this point of view. I have shown that Dr Kay's recorded impressions of these districts tallied exactly with my own. I will add only a passage from a book by Nassau Senior, who is a Liberal and a fanatical opponent of all independent trade unions. His views are highly esteemed and recognized as authoritative by the great manufacturers. Nassau Senior writes:

But when I went through their (i.e. the Manchester operatives') habitations in Irish Town, and Ancoats, and Little Ireland my only wonder was that tolerable health could be maintained by the inmates of such houses. These towns, for such they are in extent and population, have been erected by small speculators with an utter disregard to everything except immediate profit. A carpenter and a bricklayer club to buy a patch of ground,[1] and cover it with what they call houses. In one place we saw a whole street following the course of a ditch, in order to have deeper cellars (cellars for people, not for lumber) without the expense of excavations. *Not a house in this street escaped cholera*.[2] And generally speaking throughout these suburbs the streets are unpaved, with a dunghill or a pond in the middle; the houses built back to back, without ventilation or drainage; and whole families occupy each a corner of a cellar or of a garret.[3]

I have already mentioned the unusual activity of the health authorities at the time of the cholera (in 1831–2). When this epidemic threatened, the middle classes in Manchester were panic-stricken. They suddenly remembered the existence of the unhealthy dwellings of the poor; and they were greatly alarmed lest every one of these slums should become a centre from which this pestilence should spread death and destruction in all directions, and so reach the dwellings of the wealthier classes. A Board of Health was immediately appointed to inspect these slums and to make a detailed report to the municipal authorities.[4]

The investigations of this body covered all the police districts of Manchester with the exception of the 11th. Dr Kay, who was a member of the Board, gives some extracts from the report.[5] Altogether 6,915 houses were inspected. These, of course, were all in Manchester proper (i.e. the township) and not in Salford or other adjacent districts. Of these 6,915 houses, 2,565 needed immediate whitewashing of the interior, 960 'were out of repair',[6]

1. That is to say, to lease for a number of years [inserted in the text by Engels].

2. [Engels's italics.]

3. Nassau W. Senior, *Letters on the Factory Act, as it affects the cotton manufacture, addressed to the Right Honourable, the President of the Board of Trade* (1837), pp. 24–5.

4. [The Board of Health for the township of Manchester was set up in November 1831. It reported to the local magistrates and corresponded extensively with the Committees of the Manchester Police Commissioners.]

5. [See Kay, *The Moral and Physical Condition of the Working Classes* . . ., etc.]

6. [Engels quotes these four words in English. The table prepared by the Manchester Board of Health showing the classification of houses inspected in the town is reproduced both by Kay (op. cit., p. 31) and Gaskell (*The Manufacturing Population of England* . . . (1833), p. 134). In Kay's pamphlet column 3 of this table is headed 'No. of houses reported as requiring repair', but in Gaskell's book the phrase used is 'Houses out of repair'. This suggests that Engels had Gaskell's book in front of him when writing this passage.]

939 were without adequate drainage, 1,435 were damp, 452 were badly ventilated while 2,221 lacked privies. Of the 687 streets inspected 248 were unpaved, 53 were only partially paved, 112 were badly ventilated and 352 contained 'heaps of refuse, stagnant pools, ordure, etc.'[1] It was, of course, quite out of the question to clean an Augean stable of this sort before the onset of the cholera. All that could be done was to clean some of the filthiest streets and houses. Otherwise everything remained as before. It goes without saying that the places reverted in a few months to their previous filthy condition. Little Ireland was an example of this. This same Board of Health reported also on the condition of the interiors of these slum dwellings, and this investigation revealed conditions similar to those which we have already described in London, Edinburgh and elsewhere. Dr Kay wrote:

A whole (Irish) family is often accommodated on a single bed, and sometimes a heap of filthy straw and a covering of old sacking hide them in one undistinguished heap, debased alike by penury, want of economy and dissolute habits. Frequently the inspectors found two or more families crowded into one small house, containing only two apartments, one in which they slept, and another in which they ate; and often more than one family lived in a damp cellar, containing only one room, in whose pestilential atmosphere from twelve to sixteen persons were crowded. To these fertile sources of disease were sometimes added the keeping of pigs and other animals in the house, with other nuisances of the most revolting character.[2]

It may be added that many families which have only one room take in boarders and lodgers, and it is not uncommon for both men and women lodgers to sleep in the same bed as their married hosts. The *Report . . . on . . . the Sanitary Condition of the Labouring Population* mentions half a dozen cases in Manchester in which a man sleeps not only with his wife but also with his adult sister-in-law.[3]

1. [Kay, op. cit., p. 30, quoted also by R. A. Slaney, *State of the Poorer Classes in Great Towns* (1840), p. 18.]

2. [Kay, op. cit., p. 32. Engels's translation of this passage into German contains a number of small errors and changes.]

3. [Evidence of James Riddall Wood (pp. 124–5): 'I have met with instances of a man, his wife, and his wife's sister, sleeping in the same bed together. I have known at least a half-a-dozen cases in Manchester in which that has been regularly practised, the unmarried sister being an adult.']

Common lodging houses, too, are very numerous in Manchester. Dr Kay stated that in 1831 there were 267 of them in the township of Manchester,[1] and since that date their numbers have no doubt considerably increased. As each lodging house accommodates between twenty and thirty persons, the total number of people sleeping in them on any one night must be between five and seven thousand. The character of these houses and their clients is the same as in other towns. In every room five or seven beds are made up on the floor and human beings of both sexes are packed into them indiscriminately. There is no need for me to discuss the physical and moral state of these dens of vice. Every one of these houses is a breeding-ground of crime and also the scene of much conduct of an unnatural and revolting character. Many of these offences might never have been committed at all had those who perpetrated them not visited lodging houses, which are hot-beds of unnatural vice.

Gaskell estimates that twenty thousand people live in cellars in Manchester proper.[2] This statement is confirmed by an estimate in the *Weekly Dispatch* 'from official sources' that 12 per cent of the workers live in cellars. The number of workers may be taken as 175,000 and 12 per cent of this number is 21,000.[3] As there are just as many cellars in the suburbs as in Manchester itself the

1. [Kay, op. cit., Table of 'pauper lodging houses', p. 33.]

2. P. Gaskell, *The Manufacturing Population of England* ... (1833). This book is mainly a description of the Lancashire workers. The author is a Liberal but he was writing at a time before it was regarded as a tenet of Liberalism to praise the 'good fortune' of the workers. Consequently Gaskell is an objective observer and does not ignore the evils of the modern factory system. He was, however, writing before the results of the inquiries of the Royal Commission on the Labour of Children in Factories [1833]. In the circumstances he makes use of some unreliable material and commits himself to assertions subsequently contradicted by the Royal Commission. Gaskell's book should, as far as its details are concerned, be used with some caution, not only for this reason, but also because the author, like Kay, confuses the factory hands with the working classes in general. With these reservations Gaskell's book can be recommended. I have used Gaskell's book extensively when writing the introduction to the present work. [On p. 138 of this work Gaskell stated that 'upwards of 20,000 individuals live in cellars in Manchester alone'.]

3. [*Weekly Dispatch* no. 2219, 5 May 1844 – article on 'Wild Beasts *v.* rational beings'. In this article the total population of Manchester is given as 200,000. The same figure had been given in *Report of a Committee of the Manchester Statistical Society on the Condition of the Working Classes in an extensive manufacturing district in 1834, 1835 and 1836* (1838). See also Slaney, *State of the Poorer Classes in Great Towns* (1840), p. 19.]

total number of workers living in cellars in Greater Manchester must be between forty and fifty thousand. So much for the dwellings of the workers in the large towns.

(ii) Working-Class Movements in England, 1844[1]

Even if I had not given so many examples as I have done to illustrate the condition of the working classes in England, it would still be self-evident that the proletariat can hardly feel happy at the present situation. It will surely be granted that the state of affairs I have described is not one in which either an individual or a social class can think, feel and live in a civilized manner. The workers must strive to escape from this position, which degrades them to the level of animals. They must try to achieve for themselves a better and more human status. They can do this only by attacking the interests of the middle classes who live by exploiting the workers. But the bourgeoisie defends its interests in the most vigorous fashion. It has at its disposal not only the power of property, but also the resources of the authority of the State. Every attempt the worker makes to free himself from his present bondage meets with the open hostility of the bourgeoisie.

Moreover, the worker is made perpetually aware of the fact that the middle classes treat him as if he were an inanimate object and a piece of property rather than a human being, and for this reason alone he is the declared enemy of the bourgeoisie. I have already given a hundred examples, and I could have given another hundred, to illustrate the fact that under present circumstances the worker can only retain his self-respect by rising in anger against the middle classes. There can be no doubt that the worker is well able to protest with all the fury at his command against the tyranny of the capitalist, if only because of the way in which he has been brought up – or rather his lack of proper upbringing. In addition, the fact that there is now a large hot-blooded Irish element in the English proletariat also stimulates the workers' animosity against their oppressors. The English worker today is no longer an Englishman (of the old school). He no longer

1. [Chapter 9 of *The Condition of the Working Class in England*.]

resembles his capitalist neighbour in being a mere machine for making money. His capacity for feeling has developed. He has thrown off his native Nordic reserve. He has cast aside his inhibitions. Given free rein, his passions have therefore been able to develop so that they now readily stimulate him to action. Among the middle classes the emphasis laid on the cultivation of the reasoning faculty has greatly increased the tendency towards selfishness and, indeed, has promoted greed to the position of a guiding principle in the conduct of affairs. For the bourgeoisie, love of money has become the ruling passion of life. All this is lacking in the worker, who is therefore able to give full play to passions as strong and unbridled as those of the foreigner. All feelings of patriotism have been crushed in the heart of the worker.

We have seen the only way in which the worker can retain his self-respect is by fighting against the way of life imposed upon him. It is natural, therefore, that it is when he is taking action against his oppressors that the English worker is seen at his best. It is then that he appears to the fullest advantage – manly, noble and attractive. We shall see that all the vigour and activity of the worker is concentrated upon this struggle. We shall see that even his efforts to cultivate his mind have a direct connexion with his fight against the bourgeoisie. It is true that we shall have to report isolated cases of violence and even brutality. It must be remembered, however, that in England the social war has been openly declared. There are occasions on which it is in the interest of the middle classes to wage this war with the weapons of hypocrisy, and to try and cover up their deeds under the disguise of peace and even of philanthropy. When this happens the worker can reply only by tearing off this mask of hypocrisy, so as to reveal the true state of affairs. Acts of violence committed by the working classes against the bourgeoisie and their henchmen are merely frank and undisguised retaliation for the thefts and treacheries perpetrated by the middle classes against the workers.

Since its beginning in the early days of the Industrial Revolution the revolt of the workers against the middle classes has passed through several phases. I do not propose to examine here the historical significance of these phases in the history of the English people. This must be reserved for a later study. For the time

being I propose to confine myself to a bri[ef] [o]f the principal facts concerning the hostility of the [...] the middle
classes in order to show what effect thi[s] upon the development of the English proletariat. [...] st and the least

Criminal activities were the first, t[he] worker lived in
successful manifestation of this hosti[...] re better off than
poverty and want, and saw that other [...] gent to appreciate
he was. The worker was not sufficien[t] fer – for after all he
why he, of all people, should be the o[...] , and sheer necessity
contributed more to society than the [...] l respect for private
drove him to steal in spite of his t[...] w crime has increased
property. We have already pointed [...] wn that there has been
as industry has expanded. It has b[een] [...] ber of arrests and the
a constant relationship between [...]
annual consumption of bales of co[...] l that crime did not for-

The workers, however, soon [...] heir thefts, could protest
ward their cause. The criminal [...] ly as individuals. All the
against the existing social or[der] against the individual law-
mighty forces of society were [...] ir overwhelming power. In
breaker and crushed him wit[h] most stupid form of protest
addition theft was the blinde[st] ne the universal expression of
and consequently this never [...] zation, although many workers
the workers' reaction to indu[...] with those who broke the law.
doubtless sympathized priv[...] f the workers, as a class, to the
The first organized resistan[ce] associated with the movements
bourgeoisie, was the viole[nt] machinery. This occurred in the
against the introduction [of] rial Revolution. Even the earlier
earliest stage of the Ind[ustrial] uch as Arkwright, were attacked in
inventors of new machin[...] destroyed. Subsequently there were
this way and their machi[...] breaking. These generally followed
many instances of mach[ine] nters' riots in Bohemia in 1844, when
the same course as the [...] ines were destroyed.
both workshops and m[...]

This type of protest [...] is also far from universal. It was limited
to certain localities an[d] was confined to resistance to one aspect of
industrial change. If t[he] immediate object of the machine breaker
was attained, then th[e] defenceless law breakers had to face the
full fury of the esta[b]lished order. The criminals were severely

punished and the rebellion unchecked. It was... on of the new machinery went on... new method of expr... cessary for the workers to find a ... ir discontent.

This was facilitat... w passed by the old unreformed oligarchical Tory p... This Act repealed the Combination Laws, and it... y which would certainly not have been carried through... e of Commons after the Reform Act of 1832, because... rm of the franchise gave legal recognition to the con... ween the bourgeoisie and the proletariat and raised th... of the bourgeoisie to that of the ruling class. The repeal... ombination Laws in 1824 annulled all the legislation w... d formerly forbidden workers to unite for the protection ... interests. In this way the workers secured the right of ... ociation, which had hitherto been confined to members ... bourgeoisie and aristocracy.[1] There have, of course, alwa... n secret societies among the workers, but there are no subs... achievements to their credit. Symons reports the existence ... h societies in Scotland, and mentions that as early as 1812 a... t combination of weavers in Glasgow called a general strike... imilar strike took place in 1822. On this occasion two wo... who refused to join the union, and were regarded by th... ellow-workers as traitors to their class, were blinded by sul... acid.[3] In 1818 a union of coal miners was strong enough to b... about a general stoppage of work throughout Scotland.[4] The... nions bound their members by an oath of fidelity and secre... nd kept accurate mem-

1. [Engels's account of the repeal of the Com[bination] Laws is not in accordance with the facts. See Mrs M. D. George's two article[s]... *Economic History* (supplement to the *Economic Journal*), Vol. 1, no. 2, May 1927, 214–28, and *Economic History Review*, Vol. 6, no. 2, April 1936, pp. 172–8.]

2. [All that Symons says is: 'In 1812, a seriou... rike took place at Glasgow among the weavers, and they were tried under the[n] combination laws': J. C. Symons, *Arts and Artisans at Home and Abroad* (1839), 143.]

3. See Symons, op. cit., pp. 139–43. [Symons quo... from material supplied to him by the Sheriff's Clerk of Glasgow. From this acco... it appears that three men were attacked in this way on different occasions – Wilki... Armstrong and M'Callum. It seems that only M'Callum was actually blinded.]

4. [One of the documents submitted to Symons by t... Glasgow Sheriff's Clerk stated: 'In January 1818, I was called (says the Procurator... fiscal) to aid in protecting Mr Dixon of the Calder Iron Works, against an alarming ... mbination of the colliers throughout Scotland...' (See Symons, op. cit., p. 137).]

bership lists, possessed funds and rendered regular financial accounts. Local branches were established, but the secrecy in which affairs of these unions had to be conducted crippled their development. As soon as the workers were granted the right of free association in 1824 trade unions sprang up all over England and they became powerful. Unions were set up by workers in all branches of industry, their declared object being to protect the individual artisan against the tyranny and indifference of the middle classes. They aimed at fixing wages by collective bargaining with their employers. They wished to regulate wages according to the profits of the employers. They desired to raise wages whenever a favourable opportunity presented itself. Their policy was to maintain uniform rates of wages in different occupations throughout the country. Consequently the trade unions negotiated with the capitalists to secure the establishment of wage-scales which would be universally applied, and they threatened to strike against any individual employer who refused to pay wages at this level. Trade unionists tried to restrict the number of apprentices in each trade. By setting limits on the expansion of the labour force in this way they hoped to maintain competition between employers for the available skilled workers, and so to keep wages high. Unionists also strenuously opposed attempts to reduce wages by such underhand methods as the introduction of new machinery and tools. Finally unemployed workers received financial assistance from their unions. This was done either by a direct grant from the union funds or by supplying the unemployed worker with a card, which certified that he was a union member, and therefore entitled to receive subsistence and information about vacant jobs, from other branches when he was seeking work in other parts of the country. These arrangements are called 'the tramping system' and those who use them to find work are called 'tramps'.[1] In order to carry out their policy the trade unions appoint two salaried officials known as the president and the secretary. It is necessary to pay these officials, because no employers can be expected to give them work. The affairs of the trade union are controlled by a

1. [For this system, see E. J. Hobsbawm, 'The Tramping Artisan' (*Economic History Review* 2nd series, Vol. 3, no. 3, 1951, pp. 299–320).]

committee which is responsible for collecting the weekly subscriptions of the members and for seeing that the funds are used for carrying out the objects of the association. Should some real advantage appear to be gained from doing so, the skilled workers in one district try, if possible, to combine with similar unions in other districts to form a federation which holds regular meetings of delegates. There have been isolated attempts to hold national conferences representing unionists in particular trades. On several occasions, the first being in 1830, efforts have been made to establish a universal trade union for the whole country, delegates from all types of trade unions being summoned. Attempts to form nation-wide associations, however, have generally proved abortive, and even when initially successful, have never lasted for very long. Only if circumstances brought about a quite exceptional wave of enthusiasm would a union of this kind be both possible and successful.[1]

The following steps are taken by trade unions to gain their ends: if one or more masters refuse to pay the wages demanded by the union, a deputation waits upon the employer. Alternatively a petition is handed in, and this procedure shows clearly that the workers appreciate the absolute power wielded by the manufacturer in his little kingdom. If nothing is achieved by these methods, the union orders its members to down tools and all the workers go home. This is called a 'turn-out' or strike. If all the employers are involved then the strike is a general one. If only some of the manufacturers refuse to pay the wages suggested by the union, then only a partial strike is called. Provided that proper notice of the strike has been given – and this is not always done – this course of action is legal. No further pressure on the employers is possible within the existing law. These legal methods of resistance are, however, too weak to be effective, so long as there are workers who are either not members of the union or who can be bribed by the bourgeoisie to desert their union. When there is only a partial stoppage it is easy for the employer to secure workers from amongst these blacklegs, who are called 'knobsticks', and so break the resistance of the workers

1. [See G. D. H. Cole, *Attempts at General Union: a study in British Trade Union History, 1818–1834* (1953).]

who are loyal to the union. Usually these blacklegs are threatened by the loyal union members. They are molested and beaten up. Everything is done to intimidate them. As soon as one of the blacklegs who has been assaulted brings a charge, the power of the trade union is nearly always broken on the very first occasion on which one of its members is guilty of a breach of the peace. The law-abiding bourgeoisie controls the administration of justice and in this way ensures the defeat of the union.

The history of trade unionism is the story of many defeats of the workers and of only a few isolated victories. It is obvious that all these efforts on the part of trade unionists cannot change the economic law by which wages are fixed according to supply and demand in the labour market. Consequently the trade unions are helpless in the face of the major factors influencing the economy. Thus, if there is a trade depression, the unions themselves have to acquiesce in a reduction of wages or go out of existence. Similarly if there is a striking increase in the demand for labour the trade unions are not in a position to secure for their members higher wages than those which they would in any case obtain as a result of free competition between the capitalists for skilled men. On the other hand, the trade unions are in a position to exercise considerable influence over minor and less important factors in the economy. If the manufacturers did not have to face mass organized opposition from the workers they would always increase their own profits by continually reducing wages. Competition between the manufacturers themselves would force the individual capitalist to depress the wages of his workers to the minimum. Unless exceptional circumstances prevail, it is true to say that the united opposition of the workers can limit the evil consequences of unrestrained competition between manufacturers. It is one thing for a manufacturer to reduce wages when all other manufacturers are doing the same thing because the general state of the economy makes this necessary. It is another matter for one employer to attempt to cut wages on his own account at a time when there is no economic justification for doing so. The manufacturer who does this knows that he will have to meet a strike, which will injure him because his capital will lie idle and his machinery will go rusty. He knows that he cannot be sure of imposing a reduction in wages, while he can be certain that, if successful, his example will be followed by his rivals. This will lead to a fall in the price of the goods he is making and will soon deprive him of any advantage gained by the original reduction in wages. Again the trade unions are often able to bring about a more rapid increase in wages after a trade crisis than would occur if the workers were entirely unorganized. It is not in the interest of the individual manufacturer to raise wages until he is forced to do so by the competition of rival manufacturers. In fact, the workers themselves demand more wages as soon as business improves and they are often able to force the manufacturer to pay higher wages by threatening a strike. If the manufacturer is short of workers he is not able to resist such a demand. But as we have pointed out, the trade unions are unable to make any headway against the more important factors influencing the state of the labour market. In such circumstances hunger gradually forces the operatives to go back to work on whatever terms the employer dictates. Even if only a few of the strikers return to work, the power of the union is broken, since the labour of the blacklegs and the fact that there are still supplies of goods in the market enable the middle classes to overcome the worst consequences of the disturbance caused to business by the stoppage. Union funds are soon exhausted if large sums have to be disbursed in strike-pay. Small shopkeepers are prepared to sell goods on credit, at a high rate of interest, but only for a short time. Consequently necessity forces the worker back under the yoke of the middle classes. The workers have discovered that most strikes are unsuccessful. In their own interests the manufacturers do not wish to cut wages unless a reduction is unavoidable. Indeed it is the organized opposition of the workers that has forced the employers to adopt this policy. If a reduction in wages has to take place because the state of business makes this imperative the workers' standard of life naturally falls. It may well be asked why the workers go on strike when it is clear that the stoppage cannot prevent a reduction in wages which cannot be avoided owing to slack trade. The answer is, simply, that the workers must protest both against a reduction in wages and also against the circumstances which make that reduction necessary. They must assert that since they are human beings they do not propose to submit to the pressure of inexorable economic forces. On the contrary they demand that economic forces should be adapted to suit *their* convenience. If trade unionists failed to register their protest by striking, their silence would be regarded as an admission that they acquiesced in the pre-eminence of economic forces over human welfare. Such acquiescence would be a recognition of the right of the middle classes to exploit the workers when business was flourishing and to let the workers go hungry when business was slack. The workers must protest against this state of affairs so long as they have not lost all human feeling. Their protest takes the form of strikes because Englishmen are practical people, who believe in the efficacy of deeds rather than words. They are not German theorists, who cheerfully go to sleep as soon as their protest has been officially received and left to slumber in a pigeon-hole for ever. The practical manner in which Englishmen protest has helped to set certain limits to the greed of the middle classes. It has kept alive the opposition of the workers to the overweening political and social power of the capitalist class. But the workers are also learning from practical experience that trade unions and strikes are not of themselves sufficient to break the might of the middle classes. The real importance, however, of trade unions and strikes is that they constitute the first attempt of the workers to put an end to competition amongst themselves. They are based on a recognition of the fact that the power of the middle classes over the workers is due entirely to the existence of competition between workers themselves – that is to say, their lack of solidarity and their internecine rivalries. Trade unions have proved to be so dangerous to the existing social order simply because they have – if only to a limited degree – firmly opposed that competition of workers among themselves, which is the very cornerstone of modern society. The workers could not have chosen a more vulnerable chink in the armour of the middle classes and of the present social structure than by organizing trade unions and strikes. The sovereign power of property must come to an end if competition among workers is impaired and if all the operatives are determined not to allow themselves to be exploited by the middle classes. Wages have come to depend upon the law of supply and demand and upon the state of the labour market at any particular moment, simply because the workers have hitherto allowed themselves to be treated as chattels which can be bought and sold. The whole modern system of political economy, with its law of wages, will collapse as soon as the workers make up their minds that they are not going to allow themselves to be passively bought and sold any longer. Its doom is sealed as soon as they act like human beings who can think as well as toil, and show their determination to secure a just share of the fruits of their labour. It is true that the law of wages would eventually come into force again if the workers went no further than to secure the removal of competition amongst themselves. But such a limitation of their aims would bring the present trade union movement to an end, and would actually cause a revival of competition among the workers. Such a policy is out of the question. Necessity will force the trade unions to bring to an end not merely *one* aspect of competition, but all competition. And this result will be achieved. Every day it becomes clearer to workers how they are affected by competition. They appreciate even more clearly than the middle classes that it is competition among the capitalists that leads to those commercial crises which cause such dire suffering among the workers. Trade unionists realize that commercial crises must be abolished, and they will soon discover *how* to do it.

It is obvious that the activities of the trade unions contribute substantially towards inflaming the bitterness and hatred of the workers against the capitalist class. This explains why, in times of exceptional unrest, individual trade unionists, acting with or without the knowledge of their leaders, are guilty of deeds which can be explained only by the existence of hatred nourished in the depths of despair, and by ungovernable passions which cannot be restrained. I have already illustrated this when I mentioned cases of vitriol throwing, and I will now select a few more examples. In 1831, at a time of serious labour unrest, young Mr (Thomas) Ashton, (the son of) a manufacturer of Hyde, near

Manchester, was shot dead one evening while walking across some fields. No trace of the murderer was ever discovered.[1] There is no doubt that this deed was committed by the workers and inspired by vengeance. There have been many cases of arson and of attempts to wreck workshops by using explosives. On Friday, 29 September 1843, an explosion caused serious damage to Mr Padgin's saw-making factory in Howard Street, Sheffield. The device used was a piece of piping filled with powder and sealed at both ends.[2] On the next day, 30 September, a similar attempt at sabotage occurred at Mr Ibbetson's factory for making cutlery and files at Shales Moor, near Sheffield. Mr Ibbetson had made himself obnoxious to the workers because he had played a leading part in various middle-class movements. Moreover he paid low wages, he refused to employ trade unionists and used the machinery of the Poor Law for his own ends. At the time of the trade depression of 1842, he forced his workers to accept a reduction in wages by reporting to the Guardians the names of those men who rejected his terms. They were therefore declared ineligible for relief because they had refused to accept work when it was offered to them. Much damage was done to Mr Ibbetson's works by this explosion. The only regret expressed by workers who came to see the damage was 'that the whole concern was not blown over the church'.[3] On Friday, 6 October 1843, there was

1. [See *Annual Register*, 1831, Chronicle, pp. 7–8. Engels's statement that the murderers were never apprehended is incorrect. Three years after the crime had been committed, two brothers, Joseph and William Mosley, and William Garside, were tried at Chester Assizes for the murder. William Mosley turned King's evidence (there were rewards at stake amounting to £2,000) and the other two were convicted and eventually hanged in London (*Annual Register*, 1834, Chronicle, pp. 290–6). Engels's blunder may be due to reliance on the account of the affair given by P. Gaskell in *The Manufacturing Population of England* (1833), pp. 299–300, at a time when the murderers had not been caught].

2. [*Northern Star*, no. 308, 7 October 1843, p. 3, col. 2.]

3. [*Northern Star*, no. 308, 7 October, 1843, p. 3, col. 1. Engels appears to have based his account of Ibbetson on the *Northern Star*'s remarks:

'The cause of the attempt seems to be a mystery, although rumour attributes it to the odium that attaches to Mr Ibbetson as an employer. He is a leading man among the Methodists, and the great gun of the 'free-booters' [i.e. Free Traders]: his works is a refuge for all *outlaws*, or men who will not join the Union and who are working considerably under the general prices of the town. It is said too that he took advantage of the late depression and went to the Board of Guardians, and caused men who were receiving parish relief to be compelled to work for his prices or perish for want. . . .']

an attempt at arson at Ainsworth and Crompton's mill at Bolton. No damage was done. This was the third or fourth attempt to burn down this factory within a very short space of time.[1] At a meeting held on Wednesday, 10 January 1844, the police surveyor showed the Sheffield Borough Council a bomb made of cast iron. It had been discovered in Mr Kitchen's works in Earl Street, Sheffield. It contained four pounds of powder and was equipped with a fuse. It was clear that the fuse had been lit, but the flame had gone out before reaching the powder.[2] On Sunday, 21 January 1844, an explosion occurred in a saw-mill owned by Messrs Bentley and White of Bury in Lancashire. This was caused by a quantity of gunpowder, thrown into the workshop with disastrous results.[3] The Soho (Grinding) Wheel works in Sheffield were set on fire on Thursday, 1 February 1844, and completely gutted.[4] These six cases have all occurred within four months, and are due solely to the hatred of the workers for their employers. I need hardly stress the fact that this is evidence of a deplorable state of industrial relations. These incidents prove that the social war has broken out in England and rages unchecked even during a period of commercial prosperity such as existed in the latter part of 1843. And yet the English middle classes are blind to what is happening. The most striking case, however, is that of the Glasgow thugs,[5] which came before the local assizes from 3 to 11 January 1838.[6] It is clear from these proceedings that a trade union of cotton spinners had existed in Glasgow since (at least) 1816,[7] and that they were exceptionally well-organized and powerful. Members were bound by oath to

1. [*Manchester Guardian*, 11 October 1843, p. 6, col. 5.]

2. [*Northern Star*, no. 323, 20 January 1844, p. 5, col. 2, quoting *The Times*, 13 January 1844.]

3. [*Manchester Guardian*, Wednesday, 24 January 1844, p. 7, col. 2. Engels gave the date wrongly as 20 January.]

4. [*Sheffield and Rotherham Independent*, Saturday, 3 February 1844.]

5. These workers were called thugs after the well-known tribe in India whose sole occupation is the murder of all strangers who fall into their hands.

6. [Accounts of the trial may be found in Archibald Swinton (ed.) *Report of the Trial of Thomas Hunter, Peter Hacket, Richard M'Neil, James Gibb and William M'Lean, operative cotton-spinners in Glasgow* ... (Edinburgh, 1838) and *Annual Register* for 1838 (Chronicle), pp. 6–12.]

7. [*Annual Register* for 1838, p. 7 (evidence of James Moat) and p. 8 (evidence of James Murdoch).]

accept the decision of the majority. All strikes were controlled by a secret committee, the composition of which was unknown to most members of the union. This committee had unrestricted control over the finances of the union. The Committee put a price on the heads of all blacklegs[1] and obnoxious factory owners, and deliberately organized arson in factories. One factory to be set on fire had women blacklegs on the premises who had taken the place of men at the spinning machines. A certain Mrs Mac-Pherson, the mother of one of these girls, was murdered and those responsible were shipped off to America at the expense of the union.[2] As early as 1820 a blackleg named M'Quarry had been shot at and injured. The perpetrator of this deed had been awarded £15 by the union.[3] Subsequently a man named Graham had been shot at and the person who shot him received £20. He was, however, caught and sentenced to transportation for life.[4] Finally, in May 1837, there were disturbances in Glasgow owing to strikes at the Oakbank and Mile-end (cotton) factories during which a dozen blacklegs were roughly handled. In July of the same year there was fresh unrest and a blackleg named (John) Smith was so badly mishandled[5] that he died. The members of the secret committee were now arrested, and were brought to trial. The president and principal members of the committee were found guilty of forming an illegal association, intimidating and injuring blacklegs and burning down the factory[6] of James and Francis Wood. They were sentenced to seven years' transportation.[7] What do our good Germans say to all this?[8]

1. [Engels uses the word 'knobstick' which was current when he wrote in 1845.]

2. [*Annual Register* for 1838, p. 9 (evidence of James Murdoch). From the account of James Murdoch's evidence given in the *Annual Register* it is not clear exactly when Mrs MacPherson was murdered but it was certainly not in 1837.]

3. [*Annual Register* for 1838, p. 9 (evidence of James Murdoch).]

4. [*Annual Register* for 1838, p. 9 (evidence of James Murdoch).]

5. [Although Engels uses the word 'mishandled', Smith was in fact shot in the back: *Annual Register* for 1838, pp. 10–11.]

6. [The indictment says 'house' not 'factory': *Annual Register* for 1838, p. 6.]

7. [A verdict of 'not proven' was returned on eight of the twelve counts in the indictment: *Annual Register* for 1838, pp. 6, 12.]

8. 'What kind of "wild-justice" must it be in the hearts of these men that prompts them, with cold deliberation, in conclave assembled, to doom their brother workman, as the deserter of his order and his order's cause, to die as a traitor and deserter; and have him executed, since not by any public judge and hangman, then by a private one; – like your old Chivalry *Femgericht* (sic), and Secret-Tribunal, suddenly

The capitalist, and particularly the factory owners, who come into direct contact with the working classes, are strongly opposed to trade unions. They are continually trying to persuade the workers that such associations are useless. In so far as the capitalists appeal to the science of economics in support of their case, they are using arguments which might be regarded as valid. But simply because their case rests on economic grounds it is only a half-truth, and can have no application whatsoever to the workers' actual conditions. The very fact that the middle classes press these arguments with such zeal is proof enough that the advice they are giving to the workers is by no means unbiased. On the one hand it is obvious that a strike will harm the middle classes. On the other hand it is equally clear that anything the factory owners put in their pockets must necessarily be filched from those of the workers. The workers are well aware of the fact that trade unions are able, to some extent, to curb the insatiable propensity of the employers to indulge in competitive wage-cutting. Even if the workers did not fully appreciate this they would nevertheless contrive to strike simply in the hope of injuring their natural enemies, the factory owners. In a war any injury to one side is of advantage to the other, and since a state of war does in fact exist between the workers and the employers, it is natural that the working classes should adopt the same policy as is adopted by the Great Powers when hostilities break out between them. Of all members of the middle classes our old friend, Dr Ure, is the most rabid opponent of all trade union activity. He positively foams at the mouth in his fury at the 'secret tribunals' of the cotton spinners, who are the most powerful section of organized labour. (Ure wrote:)

They boasted of possessing a dark tribunal, by the mandates of which they could paralyse every mill whose master did not comply

---

in this strange guise become new; suddenly rising once more on the astonished eye, dressed now not in mail-shirts, but in fustian jackets, meeting not in Westphalian forests but in the paved Gallowgate of Glasgow! Not loyal loving obedience to those placed over them, but a far other temper, must animate these men! It is frightful enough. Such temper must be widespread, virulent among the many, when even in its worst acme, it can take such a form in a few.' T. Carlyle, *Chartism* (1839), p. 40.

with their wishes, and so bring ruin on the man who had given them profitable employment for many a year.[1]

He speaks of a time 'when the inventive head and the sustaining heart of trade were held in bondage by the unruly lower members . . .'[2] What a pity that the good doctor cannot palm his fairy stories off on to the English workers as easily as Menenius Agrippa pulled the wool over the eyes of the plebs in the days of ancient Rome! Finally Dr Ure tells the following story: on one occasion the mule spinners producing coarse yarn 'abused their powers beyond endurance'. They received high wages, but this did not awaken any sense of gratitude towards their employers. Nor did it induce them to improve their minds in any way. When Dr Ure refers to 'improvement of mind' he really means that the workers should occupy themselves with innocuous studies which might actually benefit their employers. In many cases increased wages led to sinful pride. The money was actually used to support strikes by refractory workmen. One group of mill-owners[3] after another have suffered from this arbitrary abuse of power. On one occasion when these unhappy industrial disputes affected Hyde, Dukinfield and neighbouring districts, the mill-owners, fearing lest French, Belgian and American competitors would drive them out of the market, asked the firm of Sharp, Roberts and Company whether Mr (Richard) Roberts[4] could not invent an automatic mule 'in order to emancipate the trade from galling slavery and impending ruin'.[5] '. . . he produced in the course of a few months, a machine apparently instinct with the thought, feeling, and tact of the experienced workman . . . Thus, the *Iron Man*, as the operatives fitly call it, sprang out of the hands of our modern Prometheus at the bidding of Minerva – a creation destined to restore order among the industrious classes, and to confirm to Great Britain the empire of art. The news of this

1. [Dr Andrew Ure, *The Philosophy of Manufactures* (1835), p. 282.]
2. [ibid., page 282.]
3. [Engels wrote 'Fabrikanten' (i.e. factory owners) but Dr Ure had written 'millowners' (op. cit., p. 366).]
4. [Engels gives the name Sharp instead of the correct one, Roberts (Ure, op. cit., p. 366). For Richard Roberts, see H. W. Dickinson 'Richard Roberts. his life and inventions' (*Trans: Newcomen Society*, Vol. 25, 1945–7, pp. 123–27).]
5. [Ure, op. cit., p. 367.]

Herculean prodigy spread dismay through the Union, and even long before it left its cradle, so to speak, it strangled the Hydra of misrule.'[1] Dr Ure goes on to state that the invention of the four-colour and five-colour printing machines in the textile industry was brought about by unrest among the (journeymen) calico-printers.[2] Ure gives several other examples to illustrate his point, including the installation of a new sizing machine for dressing warp when the yarn dressers showed signs of insubordination.[3] And this is the same author who only a little earlier in the same book had devoted several pages to explaining how beneficial machinery was to the workers! Dr Ure, of course, is by no means the only critic of trade unions. In evidence before the Factories Enquiry Commission, several manufacturers, including the well-known industrialist, Mr (Henry) Ashworth, lost no opportunity of venting their wrath on combinations of workers.[4] These clever representatives of the middle classes – like certain (reactionary) governments – denounce all movements that they do not understand as inspired by the machinations of wicked agitators, evilly-disposed persons, demagogues, tub-thumpers and irresponsible youths. They claim that the paid agents of the trade unions foment this unrest, because it is a bread and butter question as far as they are concerned. In fact, of course, it is the middle classes themselves who make it necessary for the trade unions to support these agents, because the bourgeoisie refuses to allow them to earn a livelihood in industry.

The incredible frequency of strikes affords the best proof of the extent to which the social war now rages in England. Not a week passes – indeed hardly a day passes – without a strike occurring somewhere. There are numerous causes for these stoppages – reductions in wages, refusals to raise wages, the employment of non-union labour, the continued existence of abuses or bad conditions of work, the introduction of new machinery and a hundred other causes. Nevertheless, these strikes are often nothing more than skirmishes in the social war, though sometimes they develop into more serious clashes. They may be only

1. [Ure, op. cit., p. 367.] 2. [Ure, op. cit., p. 369.] 3. [Ure, op. cit., p. 370.]
4. [*First Report* of the Central Board of the Factories Enquiry Commission (1833) p. 50 and evidence, E4–7. See last paragraph of evidence.]

minor engagements but they prove conclusively that the decisive battle between the proletariat and the bourgeoisie is approaching. These stoppages of work are a training ground for the industrial proletariat and a preparation for the great campaign which draws inevitably nearer. Strikes are the manifestoes by which particular groups of trade unionists pledge their adherence to the cause of the working classes. The *Northern Star* is the only newspaper which contains reports of all aspects of the workers' movement. Anyone who examines all the issues which have appeared in a year will realize that both urban and rural industrial workers are united in trade unions and are accustomed from time to time to demonstrate openly against the tyranny of the middle classes. Trade unionism is an ideal preparation for social war. It is in these organizations that the characteristic courage of the English-man finds its best expression. Continental observers argue that Englishmen – particularly English workers – lack the courage to succeed as revolutionaries because English workmen seem to accept middle-class rule without complaint: it is said that, unlike the French, they are not always prepared to man the barricades at a moment's notice.[1] This opinion is entirely erroneous. The English workers are as courageous as those of any other country. They are just as discontented as the French, but their methods of fighting are different. The French workers have politics in their blood, and so they fight social evils with political weapons.

1. [Compare the opening paragraphs of chapter III ('Manchester Insurrection') of Thomas Carlyle's *Past and Present* (1843), pp. 14–15 (Everyman edition, 1912):

'Blusterowski, Colacorde, and other Editorial prophets of the Continental-Democratic Movement, have in their leading-articles shown themselves disposed to vilipend the late Manchester Insurrection, as evincing in the rioters an extreme backwardness to battle; nay as betokening, in the English People, itself perhaps a want of the proper animal courage indispensable in these ages. A million hungry operative men started up, in utmost paroxysm of desperate protest against their lot; and, ask Colacorde and company, How many shots were fired? Very few in comparison! Certain hundreds of drilled soldiers sufficed to suppress this million-headed hydra, and tread it down, without the smallest appeasement or hope of such, into its subterranean settlements again, there to reconsider itself. Compared with our revolts in Lyons, in Warsaw and elsewhere, to say nothing of incomparable Paris City past or present, what a lamblike Insurrection!

'The present Editor is not here, with his readers, to vindicate the character of Insurrections; nor does it matter to us whether Blusterowski and the rest may think the English a courageous people or not courageous. In passing, however, let us mention that, to our view, this was not an unsuccessful Insurrection; that as Insurrections go, we have not heard lately of any that succeeded so well.']

The English workers hold aloof from politics, which they look upon as a game played solely in the interest of middle-class groups. Therefore, instead of fighting against the government, the English workers strike directly at their middle-class enemies and, for the time being, this struggle can be waged only by peaceful means and not by violence. In France commercial depression and the resulting social distress led in 1834 to the armed rising of the Lyons workers in favour of the Republic. In England, somewhat similar conditions in 1842 led to a general strike in Manchester in support of the People's Charter and higher wages. Courage is needed not only by armed rebels but also by strikers. Indeed, it is obvious that a striker needs greater courage and a keener and steadier determination than the man at the barricades. It is no mere trifle for a worker with first-hand experience of poverty to face hunger and distress with wife and child for months on end and still remain steadfast in the cause. Death or the galleys face the French worker who takes part in an armed rising. But what is such a fate compared with that of the English striker who daily sees his family in the grip of slow starvation, and who knows that in the long run he cannot escape the vengeance of the middle classes, who are determined to crush him under the capitalist yoke? We propose later to give an example of the obstinate, unconquerable spirit of the English workers, which only surrenders to superior strength when all further resistance is obviously hopeless. The character of the English worker indeed deserves our respect when we see how in such circumstances he bears his sufferings with patient fortitude and determination. The striker's steadfastness is tested a hundred times a day and still he stands firm. Men who are prepared to suffer so much to break the will of a single obstinate factory owner will one day be able to smash the power of the whole bourgeoisie.

(It might be argued that failure of the Plug Plots riots in Lancashire in 1842 showed that English workers lacked the courage of their convictions.) But it is easy to account for the failure of this strike movement. The conflict was badly timed, for the workers allowed themselves to be provoked by the middle classes into taking premature action. The men were far from clear in their own minds as to why they were on strike. Above all the workers were not united.

But, apart from failures of this kind, ample evidence exists of the courage of the English workers – particularly when they have clearly defined social objectives in view. The Welsh rising of 1839 is a case in point.[1] I propose to discuss at greater length a strike which culminated in violence in Manchester when I was there in May 1843. Messrs Pauling and Henfrey decided to increase the size of the bricks made at their works. They naturally proposed to charge more for the new bricks than for the smaller ones but they failed to raise the wages of the men who made them. A wage-claim was rejected by the employers, the men went on strike and the men's trade union supported them by blacklisting the firm. Messrs Pauling and Henfrey succeeded, though not without great difficulty, in securing blackleg labour from Manchester and district. The strikers threatened with violence those who persisted in working for the firm and then Messrs Pauling and Henfrey engaged twelve men, all ex-soldiers or former policemen, and armed them with flintlocks for the defence of the brick yard. Having failed to intimidate the blacklegs, the strikers proceeded to sterner measures. At ten o'clock one night a disciplined force of strikers – the front rank armed with blunderbusses – marched on the brickworks, which were only four hundred yards away from an infantry barracks.[2] The strikers pressed on. As soon as they saw the guards, they fired on them, trampled on the wet bricks spread out to dry, scattered the stacks of finished bricks and destroyed everything in their path. Then they broke into the house of the manager, beat up his wife, and destroyed the furniture. Meanwhile the guards were able to fire on the strikers from a safe vantage point which they had taken up behind a hedge. The rioters were now standing around a kiln in which bricks were being fired; they were clearly silhouetted against the fire. Consequently every bullet fired by the guards found its mark, while the return fire of the strikers was wholly ineffective. The firing went on for

1. [For the Newport rising, see David Williams, *John Frost: a study in Chartism* (1959).]

2. [The brickworks were] at the junction of Cross Lane and Regent Road – see plan of Manchester, p. 33.

over half-an-hour until supplies of ammunition ran out. By this time, however, the object of the attack – the demolition of what could be destroyed in the brickyard – had been accomplished. When the military appeared the brickmakers retreated to Eccles, which is three miles from Manchester. Shortly before reaching Eccles, a roll-call was held and each man had to answer to his number. The men thereupon dispersed, but it is not surprising that they immediately fell into the hands of the police who were closing in upon them from all sides. The number of wounded must have been very considerable, but only some of them were arrested. One of them had been hit three times, in the thigh, the calf and the shoulder, and yet had managed to walk for over four miles. Surely it cannot be denied that these strikers showed all the courage needed by revolutionaries and did not flinch from a hail of bullets.[1] The circumstances of the demonstrations of 1842 were quite different. Then unarmed crowds, who had no clear common objective in view, were easily held in check by a handful of dragoons and police in enclosed market places. The forces of law and order had only to block a few roads leading to the markets. These demonstrators were not lacking in courage, for they would have behaved in the same way even had the minions of the bourgeoisie not put in an appearance. When the workers have a clear objective, they show no lack of courage. A example of this was at Birley's mill which eventually had to be protected by the mounting of artillery.[2]

Incidentally it may be worth while saying a word or two here concerning the sanctity of law in England. The middle classes certainly are all in favour of the sanctity of the law. That is not surprising. They have made the law; they approve of it; they are protected by it and they gain advantages from it. The bourgeoisie appreciate that, even although some particular enactment may injure their interests, the whole body of laws protects their interests. The middle classes know full well how firmly their position in the social order is buttressed by this principle of the sanctity of law – a principle established by an act of will on the

1. [For the attack on the brickworks, see *Northern Star*, no. 289, 27 May 1843 p. 5, col. 5: 'Atrocious and Alarming Outrage'.]

2. [For the riot at Birley's mill, see *Northern Star*, no. 248, 13 August 1842, p. 5, col. 1.]

part of one section of society and passively accepted by the other section. The middle classes hold fast to the sanctity of law because they believe that the law has been made, like their God, in their own image. That is why the policeman's truncheon, which is really their own weapon, is such a reassuring symbol of authority. But the worker naturally regards the law in quite a different way. He knows from long and bitter experience that the law is a rod which the bourgeoisie has in readiness for him. The worker has no confidence in the law and, if at all possible, he avoids it. It is ridiculous to assert that the English workers are afraid of the police. In Manchester policemen are beaten up every week by the workers, and last year the workers even attempted to storm a police station which was protected by iron doors and shutters. I have already pointed out that the victory of the police in the disturbances caused by the strikes of 1842 was due solely to the vacillation of the workers.

Since the workers do not respect the law, but merely submit to it when they are not strong enough to change it, it is natural that they should put proposals for new laws. It is natural that they should aim at replacing the law of the middle classes by the law of the working classes. This proposed law of the proletariat is the People's Charter, which is purely political in outward form and calls for a fully democratic House of Commons. Chartism is the expression of a common policy which unites the workers solidly against the middle classes. When workers make common cause in trade unions or when they combine to go on strike to fight the middle classes their opposition is of only a local or piecemeal character. When there were signs that the economic struggle against the bourgeoisie was being fought on a wide front, this could hardly be ascribed to the deliberate intentions of the workers. It was a purely political movement – Chartism – which was mainly responsible for uniting the workers against their oppressors. The whole working class is behind the great Chartist assault on the middle classes – above all against the political and legal fortress which the bourgeoisie has erected to guard its interests. The origins of Chartism are to be found in the 1780s, when a democratic party developed simultaneously with the growth of the proletariat. The French Revolution fostered this democratic movement, particularly in London. After the end of the Napoleonic Wars in 1815 the movement – now known as the 'Radical' party – was strongest in Birmingham and Manchester. The Radicals allied themselves with the Liberal middle classes to break the power of the oligarchy which dominated the un-reformed House of Commons and to secure the passing of the Reform Bill. Since then the organization of the Radicals has steadily improved and they have moved to the left to become a working-class party opposed to the middle classes.

In (1838) the London Working Men's Association, under the leadership of William Lovett, drew up the People's Charter.[1] It had six points: (i) Every male adult over the age age of 21, being of sound understanding and not convicted of any criminal offence, was to be entitled to a vote. (ii) Parliament was to be elected annually. (iii) Members of Parliament to be paid, so that membership of the House of Commons should be open to the poorest. (iv) Voting for members of Parliament to be by ballot, to prevent bribery and intimidation of the voters by the middle classes. (v) Equal electoral districts, so that each member of Parliament should represent the same number of voters. (vi) Abolition of the – admittedly ineffective – property qualification for candidates for election, who are supposed to possess landed property to the (annual) value of £300.[2] This provision would have qualified every voter to be a candidate.

These six points are all concerned with the constitution of the House of Commons. They may look innocent enough, but if they were granted they would undermine the whole English Consti-tution, including the position of the Queen and the House of Lords. The so-called monarchical and aristocratic elements of the Constitution can survive only because it is in the interests of the middle classes to maintain the façade of a sham monarchy and aristocracy, neither of which enjoys more than the outward semblance of authority. But as soon as public opinion is solidly behind the House of Commons – as soon as the Commons

1. [The People's Charter was first published on 8 May 1838, not in 1835 as stated by Engels.]
2. [According to the Act of 1710 the property qualification of candidates for borough seats was the possession of land bringing in an income of £300 a year and in the case of county seats, £600 a year.]

represent the will of the whole people and not merely of the middle classes – that body will become all-powerful and Queen and Lords will lose even the last trappings of outward authority. The English worker has no respect whatever either for the Queen or the nobility. The middle classes place Queen and peerage on a pinnacle and accord them every honour, but in fact leave them with little effective power. An English Chartist is a republican, though he seldom, if ever, uses the term. He prefers to describe himself as a democrat, although he gives his sympathy to republican parties all over the world. Indeed, he is more than a republican, because the democracy that he supports is not only political (but social and economic as well).

Nevertheless it may be observed that, although from its beginnings in 1835[1] Chartism was a working-class movement, it was not sharply differentiated from the Radical movement supported by the lower middle classes. Working-class Radicalism went hand in hand with bourgeois Radicalism. The two groups mingled in their annual National Conventions and both accepted the points of the Charter as their objective. At one time they appeared to form a united party. At that time the lower middle classes were bitterly disappointed over the results of the Reform Bill and they were badly hit by the commercial depression of 1837–9. Consequently they were in a highly bellicose and blustering mood and threw themselves heart and soul into the Chartist movement. Here in Germany no one appreciates the full-blooded vigour of this agitation. The Chartists incited the people to take up arms and rise in revolt. The days of the French Revolution were recalled when the making of pikes became a popular hobby. In 1838 a certain Methodist minister called Stephens, advocated violence at a mass meeting of workers in Manchester:

There is no need for you to fear the power of Government. Do not be afraid of the soldiers, bayonets and cannon, with which your oppressors threaten you. You have something which is mightier than them all. You possess a weapon against which bayonets and cannon are powerless, and a ten-year-old child can wield this weapon. All you

1. [The origin of Chartism is usually dated in the following year, 1836, which saw the foundation of the London Working Men's Association.]

need to do is to take a bundle of straw dipped in pitch and a few matches, and we shall see what Government and its hundreds of thousands of soldiers will be able to do when this weapon is boldly used.[1]

At the same time the characteristic social aspect of the working-class side of the Chartist movement was clearly demonstrated. Thus this same Stephens told a demonstration of 200,000 people at Kersal Moor, the *Mons Sacer* of Manchester[2]:

This question of Universal Suffrage was a knife and fork question after all; this question was a bread and cheese question, notwithstanding all that had been said against it, and if any man asked him what he meant by Universal Suffrage, he would answer that every working man in the land had a right to have a good coat to his back, a comfortable abode in which to shelter himself and his family, a good dinner upon his table and no more work than was necessary for keeping him in health, and as much wages for that work as would keep him in plenty, and afford him the enjoyment of all the blessings of life which a reasonable man could desire (*Tremendous cheers*).[3]

Two other popular agitations, which were very closely associated with Chartism, were those against the new Poor Law and in favour of the Ten Hours Bill. The Tory, Oastler, was very active at public demonstrations at this time. The national petition in favour of the People's Charter was adopted at Birmingham, but there were also hundreds of other petitions demanding various social reforms for the benefit of the workers. The agitations were as active in 1839 as they had been in the previous year. Towards the end of 1839, however, the enthusiasm of the

1. We have seen how the workers are taking this advice to heart. [This footnote was omitted in Mrs F. K. Wischnewetzky's translation of 1887. This speech of Stephens's has been retranslated from the German. For the Rev. Joseph Rayner Stephens, see the *Dictionary of National Biography*. Examples of speeches in which he incited the workers to violence may be found in G. J. Holyoake, *Life of Joseph Rayner Stephens, preacher and political orator* (1881), chap. VII, pp. 112–131 and *Wigan Gazette*, 16 November 1838. For the technique of torchlight processions at this time see R. G. Gammage, *The History of the Chartist Movement . . .*, Part I (1854), pp. 103–8.]

2. [Two references to Kersal Moor as the 'Mons Sacer' of Manchester had already been made in Croker's article on the Anti-Corn Law agitation in the *Quarterly Review* of December 1842, Vol. 71, no. clxi, pp. 268, 275.]

3. [*Northern Star*, no. 46, 29 September, 1838, p. 6 – meeting at Kersal Moor, on Monday, 24 September. Engels gives only a very abbreviated version of this well-known passage in the speech. For the significance of the meeting at which this speech was made, see M. Hovell, *The Chartist Movement* (1918), pp. 118–19.]

workers appeared to be waning. Thereupon Bussey, Taylor and Frost[1] planned simultaneous risings in the North of England, in Yorkshire and in Wales. Frost's plans were betrayed, his rising broke out prematurely, and it was easily suppressed. The Northern plotters heard the news of Frost's failure in time to cancel their plans. Two months later, in January 1840, several so-called 'spy-outbreaks' took place in Sheffield, Bradford and elsewhere in Yorkshire,[2] and after that the unrest gradually subsided.[3]

Meanwhile the attention of the middle classes was diverted to a more practical and more advantageous plan. This was the repeal of the Corn Laws. The Anti-Corn Law League was founded in Manchester and this resulted in a loosening of the bonds which linked the Radical elements in the bourgeoisie with the proletariat. The workers soon realized that they would gain little from the repeal of the Corn Laws, which would, however, be very beneficial to the middle classes. In the circumstances the working classes were not prepared to support the agitation for Corn Law repeal. In 1842, when there was much economic distress and social unrest, the agitation in favour of Corn Law repeal revived and was as vigorous as it had been in 1839. On this occasion it was the wealthy members of the middle classes engaged in industry who supported the movement, because they had been particularly hard hit by the commercial crisis.[4] The

1. [For Peter Bussey, Dr John Taylor and the events of 1839 see Mark Hovell, *The Chartist Movement* (1918), chap. XI: 'Sedition, Privy Conspiracy and Rebellion (1839–1840)'; for John Frost, see above p. 73.]

2. [For these minor outbreaks see Hovell, op. cit., pp. 186–7. By using the English words 'spy-outbreaks' Engels appears to imply that they were fomented by *agents provocateurs*.]

3. [Engels's account of the origins and course of the Plug Plot riots of 1842 is undoubtedly based upon that given in an article on the Anti-Corn Law agitation in the *Quarterly Review* of December 1842 (Vol. 71, no. cxli, pp. 244–314). It was written by a rabid Tory, J. W. Croker, and made a vicious and unscrupulous attack upon the League. For Croker's authorship of this article, see *The Correspondence and Diaries of the late Rt. Hon. John Wilson Croker* ... (ed. L. J. Jennings), Vol. 2 (1884), pp. 388–93 and M. F. Brightfield, *John Wilson Croker* (1940), pp. 433, 453, 458. Engels was not, as Halévy stated, 'an eye witness' of the riots (E. Halévy, *The Age of Peel and Cobden: a History of the English People*, 1841–1852 (1947), p. 22, fn. 1). Croker was supplied with material for the article by the Home Secretary, Sir James Graham, and the Prime Minister, Sir Robert Peel, himself read the proofs.]

4. [*Quarterly Review*, December 1842, p. 270.]

Anti-Corn Law League – a federation of societies which had developed from the original association founded by the Manchester manufacturers[1] – now adopted a decidedly Radical and bellicose attitude. The journals and agitators of the League became frankly revolutionary in tone. This change in the attitude of the leaders of the League may be attributed to the fact that (Peel's) Conservative Government had been in power since 1841.[2] The League incited the workers to revolt in much the same way as the Chartists had done a few years before. Meanwhile the workers themselves were by no means inactive, for after all they had suffered most from the depression of 1842. This is shown by the fact that in 1842 the Chartists drew up a national petition which secured three and a half million signatures. Although the working-class and bourgeois wings of the Radical party had become somewhat estranged, circumstances nevertheless brought them together again in 1842. On 14 February[3] of that year a meeting of Liberals and Chartists was held in Manchester and agreement was reached on the terms of a petition which demanded not only the repeal of the Corn Laws but also the adoption of the Charter. On the following day both parties endorsed this decision and approved the petition. In the spring and summer of 1842 there was much unrest and distress. The middle classes were determined to push through Corn Law repeal while conditions remained favourable – business depression, social misery and widespread unrest. Since the Tories were now in office, the middle classes on this occasion actually deviated for a time from their normal respect for the sanctity of the law. They wanted to gain their ends by revolutionary means and they wanted the support of the working classes for their policy. The workers were to pull the chestnuts out of the fire and burn their fingers for the benefit of the middle classes. Already in many quarters there was a revival of the plan already put forward by

1. [The Anti-Corn Law League had been founded as far back as 1839.]
2. [*Quarterly Review*, December 1842, pp. 254–8.]
3. [Engels wrote 15 February, but see *Northern Star*, No. 223, 19 February 1842, p. 3, col. 2, on 'The Chartists and the League'. The writer of the *Quarterly Review* article also gave 15 February as the date of this meeting (December 1842 p. 270).]

the Chartists in 1839. This project was called a 'Sacred Month' and there was to be a general strike during that period. But in 1842 it was not the workers who wanted to go on strike. It was the manufacturers who wanted to close their factories and lock out their workers, in the hope that unemployed men would leave the towns and swarm into the countryside over the estates of the landed aristocracy.[1] In this way the factory owners hoped to force the Government and the Tory Parliament to repeal the Corn Laws. If this plan had been put into operation it would, of course, have culminated in a workers' rising. But the middle classes kept themselves safely in the background and could await the success of their schemes. If the worst came to the worst, the middle classes would not themselves be compromised. In July (1842) business began to improve. It was now or never (for the middle-class plot). Although *trade was actually getting better*,[2] three Stalybridge firms proposed to reduce their employees' wages. I would not care to say whether they did this on their own initiative, or whether they had an understanding with other manufacturers, particularly the members of the Anti-Corn Law League. Two of the Stalybridge firms soon gave up the idea of cutting wages, but William Bayley and Brothers stood fast by their decision. When their workers complained to them they replied that if they were not satisfied with the firm's offer, 'You had, perhaps, better go and play for a few days.'[3] The remark was no more than a piece of sarcasm, but the men took their employers at their word. The men left the factory cheering loudly and marched through Stalybridge, calling upon workers in other mills to join them. In a few hours every mill in the town stood idle and the workers had marched off in procession to Mottram Moor for a meeting. This was on 5 August. Five thousand of the men marched from Stalybridge to Ashton and Hyde on 8 August. This led to the closure of all the factories and collieries in the

1. [*Quarterly Review*, December 1842, pp. 258, 271.]

2. See the trade reports from Manchester and Leeds from the end of July to the beginning of August [1842]. [*Quarterly Review*, December 1842 (pp. 185–6), published reports from the *Manchester Guardian* and *Leeds Mercury* of July and August 1842 to the effect that trade was reviving in the Northern textile districts.]

3. [*Quarterly Review*, December 1842, pp. 291–2.]

immediate neighbourhood.[1] At their meetings the men did not demand the repeal of the Corn Laws, as the middle classes had hoped. They demanded 'a fair day's wages for a fair day's work'.[2] On 9 August they marched to Manchester. Here, the municipal authorities, who were all Liberals, allowed the demonstrators to enter the town, and on their arrival all the factories closed down. The first occasion upon which the demonstrators were resisted was on 11 August, when they had reached Stockport, and this was because they attacked the workhouse, the favourite child of the English middle classes.[3] On the same day there was a general strike in Bolton, coupled with much unrest, but here again the authorities refrained from checking these demonstrations[4]; soon the rising had spread to all the industrial districts, and everybody was on strike with the exception of those who were getting the harvest in or engaged in handling foodstuffs. The angry strikers showed very great self-control. They had been manoeuvred into this situation against their better judgement. With one exception – (Hugh Hornby) Birley, the Manchester Tory – the employers had offered no resistance to the strike, and this was absolutely contrary to their normal practice.[5] When the whole business started the workers had no definite objective in mind,[6] but they were at least united on one point. They were all determined not to be shot down to oblige their Anti-Corn Law League employers.[7] Some of them hoped to gain the People's Charter, others thought that it was premature to hope for the Charter and would have been satisfied with a return to the wage-rates of 1840.[8] This was why the rising collapsed completely: had it been a deliberate and carefully thought-out workers' insurrection from the beginning it would probably have succeeded. In fact, masses of workers were turned

1. [*Quarterly Review*, December 1842, p. 293.]

2. [ibid., December 1842, p. 293. The Rev. J. R. Stephens had used this phrase in a speech at Norwich as early as November 1838: *Northern Star*, 10 November 1838.]

3. [*Quarterly Review*, December 1842, pp. 301–3.]

4. [ibid., December 1842, p. 300.]

5. [*Quarterly Review*, December 1842, p. 295. For a recent account of this incident see G. Kitson Clark, 'Hunger and Politics in 1842': *Journal of Modern History*, Vol. 25, no. 4, December 1953, pp. 362–3.]

6. [*Quarterly Review*, December 1842, pp. 293–4.]

7. [ibid., December 1842, pp. 297–8.]

8. [ibid., December 1842, p. 294.]

loose on the streets by their employers whether they liked it or not. They had no definite objective in view, and so could achieve nothing. Meanwhile the middle classes had not moved a finger to implement the alliance of 14 February 1842.[1] The bourgeoisie soon realized that it was not possible to use the workers as cats-paws; the middle classes realized that they themselves had endangered their own position by departing from their normal role as guardians of law and order. So they promptly became once more staunch upholders of the principle of the sanctity of the law. They now allied themselves with the Government against the workers, whom they had first stirred up and then let loose upon the streets. They themselves, together with their trusty henchmen, were sworn in as special constables. Even the German merchants of Manchester wasted their time by parading through the town as special constables, smoking cigars and carrying staves. In Preston the special constables fired on the crowd. Suddenly the aimless insurgents found themselves opposed not only by Government troops but also by all the resources that the capitalists could summon to their aid. The workers, who in any case had no common objective in view, gradually dispersed, and the insurrection petered out without serious consequences. Afterwards the middle classes disgraced themselves by committing one shameful act after another; they tried to whitewash their own conduct by pretending to be horri-fied by this most recent example of popular violence. Such an attitude was hardly consistent with their own inflammatory lan-guage of the previous spring. Now the middle classes blamed the rising on Chartist 'agitators', although actually they themselves were far more to blame for the outbreak than the Chartists. Once more the middle classes came forward as champions of the sanctity of the law. The brazen effrontery of this attitude was surely unique. We have seen that the Chartists had played a very minor part in the outbreak, for they did no more than to make the most of the opportunities afforded by the situation. The middle classes themselves would have been only too glad to do the same thing. But it was the Chartists who were brought to trial and punished, while the middle classes came to no harm

1. [See above, p. 80 and footnote 3.]

and actually took advantage of the stoppage of work to dispose of their stocks at a good profit.[1]

The failure of this rising led to a complete split between the working classes and the bourgeoisie. Hitherto the Chartists had made little attempt to hide the fact that they were prepared to try all means, not excluding revolutionary methods, to gain their ends. The middle classes had by now realized the danger to their own position of any violent upheaval, and so were opposed to the use of 'physical force'. They were prepared to secure their ends only by the use of moral force – as if this were anything else but a threat eventually to resort to physical force in one form or another. (At this time two fundamental issues divided the Chartists from the middle classes.) One concerned the respective merits of physical force and moral force. But this difference of opinion was subsequently resolved when the Chartists asserted that they also were firmly opposed to the use of physical force – and the Chartists are quite as worthy of credence as the Liberal middle classes. The second – and more important – point at issue between the Chartists and the middle classes was the question of the repeal of the Corn Laws, and here the shining integrity of the Chartist movement was fully in evidence. The Radical middle classes had a direct interest in Corn Law repeal, but the working classes had not. So the Chartists split into two groups. Although on paper their political programmes might appear to be identical, these rival sections of the movement in fact pursued different and irreconcilable objectives.

When a National Convention was held at Birmingham in (December 1842 and) January 1843, Sturge, the representative of the Radical middle classes, suggested that the word 'Charter' be dropped from the rules of the Association. The reason he advanced for making this proposal was that owing to the popular rising in the previous year the word 'Charter' had now acquired a sinister and revolutionary significance. We might add that the name 'Charter' had, in fact, had such a significance for some years without Mr Sturge having found it necessary to say anything about it. The workers refused to drop the name 'Chartist' and Sturge was outvoted. The worthy Quaker thereupon sud-

1. [*Quarterly Review*, December 1842, pp. 304–5.]

denly rediscovered his long-lost loyalty and led a minority of the Radical middle classes from the hall to found a Complete Suffrage Union.[1] The middle classes, who had so recently been tainted with Jacobinism, were now so anxious to forget their former policy that they actually dropped the use of the familiar phrase 'Universal Suffrage' in favour of the ridiculous term 'Complete Suffrage'. The workers hooted with derision and quietly went their own way.

From this moment Chartism became a purely working-class movement, and was free from all the trammels of bourgeois influence. The periodicals which supported (Complete Suffrage) Union – the *Weekly Dispatch*, the *Weekly Chronicle*, the *Examiner*, etc. – gradually lapsed into that somnolence which is typical of all the other Liberal newspapers. They had less and less to say about Radicalism; they espoused Free Trade, attacked the Ten Hours Bill and all other reforms which would have benefited the working classes. The Radical bourgeoisie made common cause with the Liberals in attacking the Chartists. The main plank in their platform was now Corn Law repeal, which for Englishmen is the issue of free competition. And so the Radical section of the middle class fell under the domination of the Liberals, and now plays a very miserable role indeed on the political scene.

On the other hand, the Chartist workers resumed the fight of the lower classes against the middle class in all its aspects. They detested free competition which had brought so much misery to the proletariat, and the Chartists were therefore the declared enemies of the bourgeoisie, who stood for this abominable principle. Should no limit whatever be set to the freedom of competition, the position of the workers would be worse than ever. The reforms hitherto demanded by the workers had included the Ten Hours Bill, protection of workers against capitalists, a fair wage, security of employment, and the repeal of the new Poor Law. All these proposals are in direct opposition to free competition and free trade, and they are all just as much a part of Chartism as the 'Six Points'. It is therefore not surprising that the workers have no use for free competition, Free Trade or

1. [See Mark Hovell, *The Chartist Movement* (1918), pp. 264–5.]

Corn Law repeal. They are completely indifferent to the fate of the Corn Laws, but detest wholeheartedly the supporters of Repeal. The middle classes, to a man, are quite incapable of appreciating the workers' attitude to these questions. The Corn Law issue is fundamental. It divides the proletariat from the bourgeoisie and the Chartists from the Radicals. The middle class world cannot grasp the significance of this, because the middle classes are incapable of understanding the working classes.

Herein lies the difference between Chartist democracy and all former brands of bourgeois political democracy. *Chartism is essentially a social movement.*[1] The middle-class Radicals had regarded the 'Six Points' of the Charter as the be-all and end-all of the movement, but the working classes consider that the 'Six Points' and any further constitutional reforms to which they might give rise, are only a means to an end. Nowadays the rallying cry of the Chartists is: 'Political power brings social happiness.' The 'knife and fork question' to which the Reverend (J. R.) Stephens referred in 1838 was in those days accepted by only a section of the Chartists as the aim of their movement. By 1845 it had become the slogan of the entire movement. Not one of the Chartists today is content to agitate solely for the political objectives of the 'Six Points'. It is true that the form of Socialism professed by the Chartists is not a very highly developed one. It is true that the main Chartist remedy for distress is the introduction of smallholdings[2] – an anachronism since smallholdings disappeared with the rise of modern industry. It is true that most of the Chartists' practical proposals, such as the demand for 'the protection of the worker',[3] might at first sight appear to be an attempt to return to the conditions of an age which has

1. [At this point Mrs F. K. Wischnewetzky added the words 'a class movement' for which there is no authority in the original German edition of 1845. But Engels approved the English translation of 1887.]

2. [Engels uses the words 'allotment system' in English in the first German edition of 1845. It is now generally called the system of smallholdings. For O'Connor's land scheme, to which this is a reference, see Mark Hovell, *The Chartist Movement* (1918), pp. 267–84.]

3. [The meaning of this vague phrase is not clear. It might refer to the protection of craftsmen such as the handloom weavers who were waging a losing battle against machines.]

passed away. Nevertheless, these proposals of the Chartists are not so impractical as they might appear on the surface. They do at least clarify the issue which faces the English working classes. The proletariat must either give up the fight against the power of competition and fall back into its former servitude or the workers must themselves utterly destroy the competition system. Again, it will be appreciated that at the moment Chartism is in a state of flux. Chartism has shaken off those supporters who regarded it as a purely political movement. The result is that today the significant feature of Chartism lies in its social aims. And it is this aspect of Chartism which must inevitably develop in the future. It cannot be long before Chartism moves towards Socialism. This is particularly likely to happen during the next commercial crisis in England. In view of the present prosperity of manufacturers and commerce the latest date at which this crisis may be expected is the year 1847.[1] Indeed it will probably strike the economy next year (1846). The magnitude and fury of this crisis will be far greater than that of any former business depression. When it comes the workers will suffer so severely that they are certain to demand radical social remedies rather than purely political measures and it is a foregone conclusion that the workers will then get their Charter.[2] But at the moment the workers are by no means clear in their own minds as to what they can achieve once the Charter has been accepted, and it will be absolutely necessary for them to devote a great deal of thought to this matter, so that they will know to what use to put political power when they achieve it. Meanwhile the Socialist agitation is making progress. In this connexion we are concerned with English Socialism only in so far as it influences the workers. The English Socialists demand the gradual introduction of 'home colonies of united interests'[3] of between 2,000 and 3,000 people. These communities will be engaged in both industry and

1. [In the German edition of 1892 Engels added the triumphant footnote: 'Arrived punctually.']

2. [Engels made no comment on the non-fulfilment of this prophecy in later editions of his book.]

3. [See, for example, the use of this phrase in the original rules of the Rochdale Pioneers Society of 1844, printed by Bland, Brown and Tawney, *English Economic History: Select Documents* (1914), p. 643.]

agriculture. The members enjoy equal rights and (their children are to receive) the same education. Other objects of the Socialists include easier divorce, and the introduction of an enlightened system of government, with complete freedom of opinion. Punishments are to be abolished and are to be replaced by more intelligent treatment of criminals. These are the practical proposals of the Socialists. We are not concerned for the moment with the theoretical principles of English Socialism. Robert Owen was the founder of Socialism.[1] He was a mill-owner himself and, although his theories developed from an appreciation of the antagonism between the middle classes and the workers, nevertheless his practical proposals unduly favoured the bourgeoisie and were often less than just to the proletariat. The Socialists are mild-mannered and entirely law-abiding. They accept existing conditions, however bad they may be, and refuse to countenance any other method of reform save that of the peaceful persuasion of public opinion. In fact, however, the public will never be convinced by the Socialist arguments, which are at present presented in far too abstract a form. At the same time the English Socialists are constantly bewailing the demoralization of the lower orders. But they fail to recognize that this dissolution of the social order is in fact a sign of progress. They cannot see that the demoralization of private interests and the hypocrisy of the capitalist classes are far worse than any failings that the workers may possess. They do not appreciate the significance of historical development. They want to realize the Communist ideal immediately and do not grasp the fact that the transition to this state of society can be achieved only by the pursuit of a definite policy culminating in the dissolution of the existing social order. It is true that they do understand why the working classes are the sworn enemies of the middle classes. Yet although this enmity is the only means by which the workers can further their aims, the modern English Socialists preach the much less effective doctrine of philanthropy and universal love. The Socialists understand only the psychological development of man and are concerned with the improvement of humanity in

1. [For Robert Owen, see F. Podmore, *The Life of Robert Owen* (2 vols., 1906) and Margaret Cole, *Robert Owen of New Lanark* (1954).]

the abstract. This abstract approach to the problem takes no account of the extent to which modern man has been moulded by the past. In fact the whole world and, indeed, all individuals in it are the product of historical circumstances. The English Socialists are consequently too intellectual and too metaphysical, with the result that their practical achievements have been negligible. They have secured some support from the working classes, but only a small minority of the proletariat is imbued with the Socialist creed. But it must be admitted that this tiny minority includes those workers with the best education and the firmest characters. In its present form Socialism in England will never be a rallying cry for the workers. The Socialists will have to come down to earth, if only for a short time, and support the Charter as a practical objective. On the other hand, genuine working-class Socialists, who have played their part in a Chartist movement purged of its middle-class elements, will before long play an important role in the political development of the English people. There are already many such working-class Socialists, some of whom entered the movement through Chartism.[1] English Socialism rests on a firmer foundation than French Socialism. On the other hand French Socialism has made greater progress than English Socialism. English Socialists will have to learn something from the example of their French comrades, so that they can ultimately make further progress themselves. Meanwhile it is not to be expected that the French Socialists will be standing still.

It may be added that the lack of religious belief among the proletariat is most clearly seen in the Socialist doctrines. This is all the more significant when we consider that although English workers reject religion in practice without much conscious thought, they nevertheless recoil from an open admission of their lack of faith. Once more it may be expected that hard necessity will force the workers to give up their religious beliefs. They will come more and more to realize that these beliefs serve only to weaken the proletariat and to keep them obedient and faithful to the capitalist vampires.

1. [Engels added a footnote to German edition of 1892: 'Socialists, of course, in the general sense of the term and not in the Owenite sense.'

We have seen that the Chartists and the Socialists are the two main groups into which the working-class movement is divided. The Chartists are genuine members of the working class, true representatives of the proletariat; but their policy is far less mature than that of the Socialists. The Socialists, on the other hand, are more far-sighted, and have put forward practical proposals to relieve working-class distress. Unfortunately, when their movement started the Socialists were not in a position to join forces with the proletariat because of their middle-class origin. The next step will be to unite Socialism and Chartism, and give an English dress to the principles of French Communism. This process has indeed already begun. Only when it is finally accomplished will the working classes really rule England. While this is happening it may be expected that the growth and evolution of the Chartist movement will be favoured by political and social changes (that can be confidently anticipated).

We have examined three aspects of the working-class movement – Trade Unionism, Chartism and Socialism. These three movements differ in character to a great extent, though there is a not inconsiderable overlap in their membership. They have, of course, frequently differed on points of policy. All three have from their own resources established schools and reading rooms to provide educational facilities for their members. Nearly all the Socialist and Chartist groups maintain such educational centres. Many local trade union branches and working men's clubs provide similar facilities. Here the children receive a genuine proletarian education, free from middle-class influences, while the reading rooms contain very few books or newspapers except those devoted to the interests of the working classes. The middle classes naturally regard these institutions with great alarm and they have succeeded in withdrawing some of them from the influence of the workers and turning them into new centres called Mechanics' Institutes. These new institutes are organs of the middle classes and their purpose is to encourage the study of those branches of 'useful knowledge' which it is to the advantage of the bourgeoisie that the workers should possess.[1] The

1. [For an instance of this, in 1843–45, see W. H. Chaloner, *The Social and Economic Development of Crewe*, 1780–1923, (1950), pp. 234–5.

Mechanics Institutes provide classes in those fields of scientific study which are thought likely to wean the workers from their opposition to the middle classes. The middle classes hope also that by fostering such studies they will stimulate the inventive powers of the workers to the eventual profit of the bourgeoisie. At the moment the workers are not interested in the natural sciences. Since they live in great cities and work for very long hours they have little opportunity of obtaining any first-hand knowledge of nature at all. Mechanics' Institutes also offer classes in that brand of political economy which takes free competition as its God. The teachers of this subject preach the doctrine that it does not lie within the power of the workers to change the existing economic order. The proletariat is told that they must resign themselves to starving without making a fuss. In the Mechanics Institutes the teaching is uninspired and flabby. The students are taught to be subservient to the existing political and social order. All that the worker hears in these schools is one long sermon on respectful and passive obedience in the station in life to which he has been called.

Of course the vast majority of the workers will have nothing to do with these institutes and patronize working-class reading rooms where they can join groups which can discuss matters which really affect their own interests. The smug middle classes thereupon intone 'Dixi et salvavi'[1] and contemptuously turn their backs upon workers who actually 'prefer the impassioned harangues of wicked demagogues to the advantages of a sound education.' There can be no doubt that the workers are interested in acquiring a sound education, provided that it is not tainted by the 'wisdom' spread by prejudiced middle-class teachers. This is proved by the popularity of lectures on economics and on scientific and aesthetic topics which are frequently held at working-class institutes, particularly those run by Socialists. I have sometimes come across workers, with their fustian jackets falling apart, who are better informed on geology, astronomy and other matters, than many an educated member of the middle classes in Germany. No better evidence of the

1. [The full phrase is: *Dixi et salvavi animam meam* – I have spoken and saved my soul.]

extent to which the English workers have succeeded in educating themselves can be brought forward than the fact that the most important modern works in philosophy, poetry and politics are in practice read only by the proletariat. The middle classes, enslaved by the influences generated by their environment, are blinded by prejudice. They are horror-stricken at the very idea of reading anything of a really progressive nature. The working classes, on the other hand, have no such stupid inhibitions and devour such works with pleasure and profit. In this connexion the Socialists have a wonderful record of achievement, for they have promoted the education of the workers by translating the works of such great French materialist philosophers as Helvétius, Holbach and Diderot. These books, as well as many standard English books, have been widely circulated among the workers in cheap editions.[1] (D. F.) Strauss's *Life of Jesus*[2] and (P.-J.) Proudhon's book on *Property*[3] are also read in England only by the workers. Again it is the workers who are most familiar with the poetry of Shelley and Byron. Shelley's prophetic genius has caught their imagination, while Byron attracts their sympathy by his sensuous fire and by the virulence of his satire against the existing social order. The middle classes, on the other hand, have on their shelves only ruthlessly expurgated 'family' editions of these writers. These editions have been prepared to suit the hypocritical moral standards of the bourgeoisie.

1. [The file of Robert Owen's periodical *The New Moral World* contains advertisements for popular editions of Shelley's *Queen Mab* and translations of Rousseau's *Social Contract* and of Holbach's *System of Nature*.]

2. [In an article entitled 'Die Lage Englands' – a review of Thomas Carlyle's *Past and Present* which originally appeared in the *Deutsch-Französische Jahrbücher* (ed. by Karl Marx and Arnold Ruge, Paris, 1844, Parts I and II, pp. 86–114 and pp. 181–182), reprinted in *Gesamtausgabe . . .*, Part I, Vol. 2 (1930), pp. 405–431 – Engels stated that when Strauss's book on Jesus appeared no 'respectable' person in England would translate it and no 'respectable' bookseller would sell it. But a 'Socialist lecturer' made a translation which was issued in parts which were sold at a penny each. And so 'it was the workers of Manchester, Birmingham and London who were Strauss's only readers in England': *Gesamtausgabe*, Part I, Vol. 2: F. Engels, *Werke und Schriften bis Anfang* 1844 *nebst Briefen und Dokumenten* (Marx-Engels–Lenin Institute, 1930), pp. 407–8. The 'Socialist lecturer' was Henry Hetherington (1792–1849) who apparently used Littré's French translation of 1839. The first authorized translation of Strauss's book – by Mary Ann Evans (George Eliot) – appeared in 1846, in three volumes.]

3. [Proudhon's well-known work *Qu'est-ce la Propriété?* (1840) was not translated into English until 1876.]

Bentham and Godwin – particularly the latter – are the two great practical philosophers of recent times, and both are virtually studied only by the workers. It is true that Bentham has a school of followers among the middle-class Radicals, but only enlightened working-class students and Socialists have been able to evolve a progressive doctrine from his writings. Such are the foundations upon which the English working classes are building up their own literature. It is to be found mainly in periodicals and pamphlets, and it is far superior in content to the whole body of middle-class literature. We shall discuss this matter again later.

Finally, it may be observed that it is the factory workers, particularly in the Lancashire cotton districts, who form the solid core of the working-class movement. Manchester is the headquarters of the most powerful trade unions, the focal point of Chartism, and the stronghold of the Socialist movement. As one branch of handicraft industry after another is transformed by the factory system, so more and more workers flock into the various working-class movements. The wider the gulf which separates workers from capitalists, the more openly class-conscious does the proletariat become. The small independent master craftsmen of Birmingham, although they suffer, in company with the workers, from recurrent trade depressions, are poised uneasily between the Chartism of the proletariat and the Radicalism of the petty shopkeepers. In general, however, all the industrial workers support one or other of the three main working-class movements, and so are ranged against the capitalists and the bourgeoisie. They are all proud to call themselves 'working men',[1] which is the usual opening form of address in the speeches at Chartist meetings. The workers are conscious of the fact that they form a separate class, and have their own interests, policies, and points of view, which are opposed to those of the capitalist property owners. Above all they are conscious of the fact that on their shoulders rests the real power of the nation and the hope of its future progress.

1. [In English in the original.]

2. Ireland in 1856[1]

ENGELS TO MARX   *23 May 1856*

Our tour in Ireland took us from Dublin to Galway on the west coast, then twenty miles north inland, then to Limerick, down the River Shannon to Tarbert, Tralee, Killarney and back to Dublin. We covered between 450 and 500 miles and we have seen about two thirds of the country. Dublin has the appearance of a small one-time capital and the buildings are entirely English in character. A comparison between Dublin and London would be the same as a comparison between Düsseldorf and Berlin. Except for Dublin the whole of Ireland – especially the towns – reminds one of France or northern Italy since there is a pleasing profusion of policemen, priests, lawyers, officials and country squires and a total absence of any industry whatever. It would be difficult to understand how all these parasites live if the distress of the peasants did not supply an answer to the problem.

'Strong measures' are to be seen in every corner of the country. The government meddles with everything and there is no trace of any so-called self-government. Ireland may be regarded as the first English colony. Because of its proximity to the mother country Ireland is still governed in the traditional way. Here one can see that the so-called liberty of English citizens is based upon the oppression of the colonies. I have never seen so many policemen in any country. The bleary look of the bibulous Prussian policeman is developed to its highest perfection among the Irish constables who carry carbines, bayonets and handcuffs.

Ruined edifices are characteristic of the Irish countryside. The oldest date from the fifth and sixth centuries, the most recent from the nineteenth century. And every intervening period is represented. The oldest ruins are those of churches. After 1100 the ruins are of castles and churches. After 1800 the ruins are those of peasants' cottages. All western Ireland – especially in the

1. [Based upon translation in Karl Marx and Friedrich Engels, *On Britain* (Foreign Languages Publishing House, Moscow, 1953), pp. 489–91.]

neighbourhood of Galway – is covered with ruined cottages. Most of them have only been deserted since 1846. I never thought that famine could have such tangible reality. Whole villages are devastated. And among the deserted villages lie the fine parks of the lesser landlords – mostly lawyers – who are almost the only people still living there. This state of affairs is due to famine, emigration and clearances. Even the fields have no cattle. The land is deserted and nobody wants it.

In County Clare, south of Galway, conditions are rather better. Here at any rate there are cattle. The hills towards Limerick are well cultivated, mostly by Scottish farmers. In that district the ruins have been cleared away and the country has a bourgeois appearance. In the south-west there are many mountains and bogs but also remarkably luxuriant forest land. Beyond that district – especially in Tipperary and towards Dublin – there are fine pastures which are gradually coming into the hands of substantial farmers.

Ireland has been utterly ruined by the English wars of conquest from 1100 to 1850 – for it is a fact that the campaigns and the state of siege have lasted as long as that. There can be no question that most of the ruins were due to destruction in time of war. The result is that for all their fanatical nationalism the Irish feel that they are no longer at home in their own country. Ireland for the English! That is now being realized. The Irish know that they cannot compete with the English who are better equipped in every way. Emigration will continue until the almost exclusively Celtic character of the people has gone to the dogs. How often have the Irish started out to achieve something and every time they have been crushed, politically and industrially. Continual oppression has artificially turned the Irish into an utterly impoverished people and now, as everyone knows, they fulfil the function of supplying England, America and Australia with prostitutes, casual labourers, pimps, thieves, swindlers, beggars and other rabble. The aristocracy is also impoverished. Everywhere else the landowners have been absorbed by the middle classes but in Ireland they have been reduced to a state of complete poverty. The country seats are set in enormous and amazingly beautiful parks but all around is waste land. And how such land can produce rents is impossible to see. These land-lords are a comical lot. You would laugh fit to burst if you could see them. Most of them are tall, strong, handsome chaps who wear enormous moustaches under colossal Roman noses. They give themselves the false military airs of retired colonels and travel around the country in search of all sorts of pleasures. But if you inquire about them you will find that they haven't a penny, that they are up to their ears in debts, and that they live in dread of the Encumbered Estates Court. If you do not come over soon I will write again and tell you about the corrupt and repressive measures that the English use in order to rule Ireland. England thought of these methods long before Bona-parte!

3. The General Election of 1868[1]

Engels to Marx   *18 November 1868*
What do you say to the elections in the factory districts? Once again the working class has discredited itself terribly. Manchester and Salford have returned three Tories to two Liberals – includ-ing moreover the milk-and-water Bayley. Bolton, Preston, Blackburn, etc. have returned practically only Tories. In Ashton it looks as if Milner Gibson has gone to the wall. Ernest Jones is nowhere despite the cheering. Everywhere the working class is the rag, tag and bobtail of the official parties, and if any party has gained strength from the new voters it is the Tories. The small towns, the half-rotten boroughs, are the salvation of bourgeois liberalism. Now the roles of the two parties will be reversed – the Tories will now be in favour of more members for the big towns and the Liberals will support unequal representation.

In Manchester the electorate has risen from 24,000 to nearly 48,000 and the Tories have increased their votes from 6,000 to between 14,000 and 15,000. The Liberals allowed much to slip by them and Mr Henry did a lot of damage. But it cannot be

1. [Based on translation in Karl Marx and Friedrich Engels, *On Britain* (Foreign Languages Publishing House, Moscow, 1953), pp. 499–500.]

denied that the increase in working-class voters has brought the Tories more than a simple percentage increase. They have improved their relative position. On the whole this is a good thing. It now looks as if Gladstone will get a *narrow* majority and so he will have to keep the ball rolling and reform the Reform Act. If he had a big majority he would, as usual, leave everything to Providence.

But it all shows up the disastrous political ineptitude of the English working class. The *parson* has shown unexpected power and so has the cringing to respectability. Not a single working-class candidate had the ghost of a chance but my Lord Tom Noddy or any *parvenu* snob could have the workers' votes with pleasure. . . .

4. The English Working-Class Movement in 1879[1]

ENGELS TO BERNSTEIN   *17 June 1879*

At the present time and for many years past the English working-class movement has confined itself within a narrow circle of strikes for higher wages and shorter hours. These strikes are an end in themselves and are not an expedient or a means of propaganda. The trade unions in their charters actually bar all political action on principle and in this way they stop the proletariat as a class from taking part in any working-class movement. Politically the workers are divided into Conservatives and Liberal Radicals. They support either a Disraeli ministry or a Gladstone ministry. In England one can speak of a genuine labour movement only in so far as strikes take place. But, whether they are won or lost, the strikes do not get the movement on a single step further. In the trade depressions of the last few years the capitalists have purposely fomented strikes so as to have a pretext for closing down their factories and mills. Some poeple, like those behind the London *Freiheit*, try to inflate these strikes – which do not enable the working-class movement to make any headway – into

1. [Based on translation in Karl Marx and Friedrich Engels, *On Britain* (Foreign Languages Publishing House, Moscow, 1953), p. 510.]

struggles of world importance. This can only do harm to our movement. No attempt should be made to conceal the fact that at the moment England has no labour movement in the Continental sense. In the circumstances I do not think that you will lose much if you do not receive any reports concerning the activities of the English trade unions.

5. Articles from *The Labour Standard*, 1881

(i) A Fair Day's Wages for a Fair Day's Work[1]

This has now been the motto of the English working-class movement for the last fifty years. It did good service in the time of the rising Trades Unions after the repeal of the infamous Combination Laws in 1824; it did still better service in the time of the glorious Chartist movement, when the English workmen marched at the head of the European working class. But times are moving on, and a good many things which were desirable and necessary fifty, and even thirty years ago, are now antiquated and would be completely out of place. Does the old, time-honoured watchword too belong to them?

A fair day's wages for a fair day's work? But what is a fair day's wages, and what is a fair day's work? How are they determined by the laws under which modern society exists and develops itself? For an answer to this we must not apply to the science of morals or of law and equity, nor to any sentimental feeling of humanity, justice, or even charity. What is morally fair, what is even fair in law, may be far from being socially fair. Social fairness or unfairness is decided by one science alone – the science which deals with the material facts of production and exchange, the science of political economy.

Now what does political economy call a fair day's wages and a fair day's work? Simply the rate of wages and the length and intensity of a day's work which are determined by competition of employer and employed in the open market. And what are they, when thus determined?

1. [*The Labour Standard*, 7 May 1881.]

A fair day's wages, under normal conditions, is the sum required to procure to the labourer the means of existence necessary, according to the standard of life of his station and country, to keep himself in working order and to propagate his race. The actual rate of wages, with the fluctuations of trade, may be sometimes above, sometimes below this rate; but, under fair conditions, that rate ought to be the average of all oscillations.

A fair day's work is that length of working day and that intensity of actual work which expends one day's full working power of the workman without encroaching upon his capacity for the same amount of work for the next and following days.

The transaction, then, may be thus described – the workman gives to the capitalist his full day's working power; that is, so much of it as he can give without rendering impossible the continuous repetition of the transaction. In exchange he receives just as much, and no more, of the necessaries of life as is required to keep up the repetition of the same bargain every day. The workman gives as much, the capitalist gives as little, as the nature of the bargain will admit. This is a very peculiar sort of fairness.

But let us look a little deeper into the matter. As, according to political economists, wages and working days are fixed by competition, fairness seems to require that both sides should have the same fair start on equal terms. But that is not the case. The capitalist, if he cannot agree with the labourer, can afford to wait, and live upon his capital. The workman cannot. He has but wages to live upon, and must therefore take work when, where, and at what terms he can get it. The workman has no fair start. He is fearfully handicapped by hunger. Yet, according to the political economy of the capitalist class, that is the very pink of fairness.

But this is a mere trifle. The application of mechanical power and machinery to new trades, and the extension and improvements of machinery in trades already subjected to it, keep turning out of work more and more 'hands'; and they do so at a far quicker rate than that at which these superseded 'hands' can be absorbed by, and find employment in, the manufactures of the country. These superseded 'hands' form a real industrial army of reserve for the use of Capital. If trade is bad they may starve, beg, steal or go to the workhouse; if trade is good they are ready at hand to expand production; and until the very last man, woman, or child of this army of reserve shall have found work – which happens in times of frantic over-production alone – until then will its competition keep down wages, and by its existence alone strengthen the power of Capital in its struggle with Labour. In the race with Capital, Labour is not only handi-capped, it has to drag a cannon-ball riveted to its foot. Yet that is fair according to capitalist political economy.

But let us inquire out of what fund does Capital pay these very fair wages? Out of capital, of course. But capital produces no value. Labour is, besides the earth, the only source of wealth; capital itself is nothing but the stored-up produce of labour. So that the wages of Labour are paid out of labour, and the working man is paid out of his own produce. According to what we may call common fairness, the wages of the labourer ought to consist in the produce of his labour. But that would not be fair according to political economy. On the contrary, the produce of the work-man's labour goes to the capitalist, and the workman gets out of it no more than the bare necessaries of life. And thus the end of this uncommonly 'fair' race of competition is that the produce of the labour of those who do work, gets unavoidably accumu-lated in the hands of those that do not work, and becomes in their hands the most powerful means to enslave the very men who produced it.

A fair day's wages for a fair day's work! A good deal might be said about the fair day's work too, the fairness of which is per-fectly on a par with that of the wages. But that we must leave for another occasion. From what has been stated it is pretty clear that the old watchword has lived its day, and will hardly hold water nowadays. The fairness of political economy, such as it truly lays down the laws which rule actual society, that fairness is all on one side – on that of Capital. Let, then, the old motto be buried for ever and replaced by another:

POSSESSION OF THE MEANS OF WORK – RAW MATERIAL, FACTORIES, MACHINERY – BY THE WORKING PEOPLE THEMSELVES.

(ii) The Wages System[1]

In a previous article we examined the time-honoured motto, 'A fair day's wages for a fair day's work,' and came to the conclusion that the fairest day's wages under present social conditions is necessarily tantamount to the very unfairest division of the workman's produce, the greater portion of that produce going into the capitalist's pocket, and the workman having to put up with just as much as will enable him to keep himself in working order and to propagate his race.

This is a law of political economy, or, in other words, a law of the present economical organization of society, which is more powerful than all the Common and Statute Law of England put together, the Court of Chancery included. While society is divided into two opposing classes – on the one hand, the capitalists, monopolizers of the whole of the means of production, land, raw materials, machinery; on the other hand, labourers, working people deprived of all property in the means of production, owners of nothing but their own working power; while this social organization exists the law of wages will remain all-powerful, and will every day afresh rivet the chains by which the working man is made the slave of his own produce – monopolized by the capitalist.

The Trades Unions of this country have now for nearly sixty years fought against this law – with what result? Have they succeeded in freeing the working class from the bondage in which Capital – the produce of its own hands – holds it? Have they enabled a single section of the working class to rise above the situation of wages-slaves, to become owners of their own means of production, of the raw materials, tools, machinery required in their trade, and thus to become the owners of the produce of their own labour? It is well known that not only have they not done so, but that they never tried.

Far be it from us to say that Trades Unions are of no use because they have not done that. On the contrary, Trades

1. [*The Labour Standard*, 21 May 1881.]

Unions in England, as well as in every other manufacturing country, are a necessity for the working classes in their struggle against capital. The average rate of wages is equal to the sum of necessaries sufficient to keep up the race of workmen in a certain country according to the standard of life habitual in that country. That standard of life may be very different for different classes of workmen. The great merit of Trades Unions, in their struggle to keep up the rate of wages and to reduce working hours, is that they tend to keep up and to raise the standard of life. There are many trades in the East End of London whose labour is not more skilled and quite as hard as that of bricklayers and bricklayers' labourers, yet they hardly earn half the wages of these. Why? Simply because a powerful organization enables the one set to maintain a comparatively high standard of life as the rule by which their wages are measured; while the other set, disorganized and powerless, have to submit not only to unavoidable but also to arbitrary encroachments of their employers: their standard of life is gradually reduced, they learn how to live on less and less wages, and their wages naturally fall to that level which they themselves have learnt to accept as sufficient.

The law of wages, then, is not one which draws a hard and fast line. It is not inexorable within certain limits. There is at every time (great depression excepted) for every trade a certain latitude within which the rate of wages may be modified by the results of the struggle between the two contending parties. Wages in every case are fixed by a bargain, and in a bargain he who resists longest and best has the greatest chance of getting more than his due. If the isolated workman tries to drive his bargain with the capitalist he is easily beaten and has to surrender at discretion; but if a whole trade of workmen form a powerful organization, collect among themselves a fund to enable them to defy their employers if need be, and thus become enabled to treat with these employers as a power, then, and then only, have they a chance to get even that pittance which according to the economical constitution of present society, may be called a fair day's wages for a fair day's work.

The law of wages is not upset by the struggles of Trades

Unions. On the contrary, it is enforced by them. Without the means of resistance of the Trades Unions the labourer does not receive even what is his due according to the rules of the wages system. It is only with the fear of the Trade Union before his eyes that the capitalist can be made to part with the full market value of his labourer's working power. Do you want a proof? Look at the wages paid to the members of the large Trades Unions, and at the wages paid to the numberless small trades in that pool of stagnant misery the East End of London.

Thus the Trades Unions do not attack the wages system. But it is not the highness or lowness of wages which constitutes the economical degradation of the working class: this degradation is comprised in the fact that, instead of receiving for its labour the full produce of this labour, the working class has to be satisfied with a portion of its own produce called wages. The capitalist pockets the whole produce (paying the labourer out of it) because he is the owner of the means of labour. And, therefore, there is no real redemption for the working class until it becomes owner of all the means of work – land, raw material, machinery, and thereby also the owner of THE WHOLE OF THE PRODUCE OF ITS OWN LABOUR.

(iii) Trades Unions I[1]

In our last issue we considered the action of Trades Unions as far as they enforce the economical law of wages against employers. We return to this subject, as it is of the highest importance that the working classes generally should thoroughly understand it.

We suppose no English working man of the present day needs to be taught that it is the interest of the individual capitalist, as well as of the capitalist class generally, to reduce wages as much as possible. The produce of labour, after deducting all expenses, is divided, as David Ricardo has irrefutably proved, into two shares: the one forms the labourer's wages, the other the capitalist's profits. Now, this net produce of labour being, in every individual case, a given quantity, it is clear that the share

1. [*The Labour Standard*, 28 May 1881.]

called profits cannot increase without the share called wages decreasing. To deny that it is the interest of the capitalist to reduce wages, would be tantamount to saying that it is not his interest to increase his profits.

We know very well that there are other means of temporarily increasing profits, but they do not alter the general law, and therefore need not trouble us here.

Now, how can the capitalists reduce wages when the rate of wages is governed by a distinct and well-defined law of social economy? The economical law of wages is there, and is irrefutable. But, as we have seen, it is elastic, and it is so in two ways. The rate of wages can be lowered, in a particular trade, either directly, by gradually accustoming the work people of that trade to a lower standard of life, or, indirectly, by increasing the number of working hours per day (or the intensity of work during the same working hours) without increasing the pay.

And the interest of every individual capitalist to increase his profits by reducing the wages of his work-people receives a fresh stimulus from the competition of capitalists of the same trade amongst each other. Each one of them tries to undersell his competitors, and unless he is to sacrifice his profits he must try and reduce wages. Thus, the pressure upon the rate of wages brought about by the interest of every individual capitalist is increased tenfold by the competition amongst them. What was before a matter of more or less profit, now becomes a matter of necessity.

Against this constant, increasing pressure unorganized labour has no effective means of resistance. Therefore, in trades without organization of the work-people, wages tend constantly to fall and the working hours tend constantly to increase. Slowly, but surely, this process goes on. Times of prosperity may now and then interrupt it, but times of bad trade hasten it on all the more afterwards. The work-people gradually get accustomed to a lower and lower standard of life. While the length of working day more and more approaches the possible maximum, the wages come nearer and nearer to their absolute minimum – the sum below which it becomes absolutely impossible for the workman to live and to reproduce his race.

There was a temporary exception to this about the beginning of this century. The rapid extension of steam and machinery was not sufficient for the still faster increasing demand for their produce. Wages in these trades, except those of children sold from the workhouse to the manufacturer, were as a rule high; those of such skilled manual labour as could not be done without were very high; what a dyer, a mechanic, a velvet-cutter, a hand-mule spinner, used to receive now sounds fabulous. At the same time the trades superseded by machinery were slowly starved to death. But newly-invented machinery by-and-by superseded these well-paid workmen; machinery was invented which made machinery, and that at such a rate that the supply of machine-made goods not only equalled, but exceeded, the demand. When the general peace, in 1815, re-established regularity of trade, the decennial fluctuations between prosperity, over-production, and commercial panic began. Whatever advantages the work-people had preserved from old prosperous times, and perhaps even increased during the period of frantic over-production, were now taken from them during the period of bad trade and panic; and soon the manufacturing population of England submitted to the general law that the wages of unorganized labour constantly tend towards the absolute minimum.

But in the meantime the Trades Unions, legalized in 1824, had also stepped in, and high time it was. Capitalists are always organized. They need in most cases no formal union, no rules, officers, etc. Their small number, as compared with that of the workmen, the fact of their forming a separate class, their constant social and commercial intercourse stand them in lieu of that; it is only later on, when a branch of manufacturers has taken possession of a district, such as the cotton trade has of Lancashire, that a formal capitalists' Trade Union becomes necessary. On the other hand, the work-people from the very beginning cannot do without a strong organization, well-defined by rules and delegating its authority to officers and committees. The Act of 1824 rendered these organizations legal. From that day Labour became a power in England. The formerly helpless mass, divided against itself, was no longer so. To the strength given by union and common action soon was added the force of a well-filled exchequer – 'resistance money,' as our French brethren expressively call it. The entire position of things now changed. For the capitalist it became a risky thing to indulge in a reduction of wages or an increase of working hours.

Hence the violent outbursts of the capitalist class of those times against Trades Unions. That class had always considered its long-established practice of grinding down the working class as a vested right and lawful privilege. That was now to be put a stop to. No wonder they cried out lustily and held themselves at least as much injured in their rights and property as Irish landlords do nowadays.

Sixty years' experience of struggle have brought them round to some extent. Trades Unions have now become acknowledged institutions, and their action as one of the regulators of wages is recognized quite as much as the action of the Factories and Workshops Acts as regulators of the hours of work. Nay, the cotton masters in Lancashire have lately even taken a leaf out of the work-people's book, and now know how to organize a strike, when it suits them, as well or better than any Trade Union.

Thus it is through the action of Trades Unions that the law of wages is enforced as against the employers, and that the work-people of any well-organized trade are enabled to obtain, at least approximately, the full value of the working power which they hire to their employer; and that, with the help of State laws, the hours of labour are made at least not to exceed too much that maximum length beyond which the working power is prematurely exhausted. This, however, is the utmost Trades Unions, as at present organized, can hope to obtain, and that by constant struggle only, by an immense waste of strength and money; and then the fluctuations of trade, once every ten years at least, break down for the moment what has been conquered, and the fight has to be fought over again. It is a vicious circle from which there is no issue. The working class remains what it was, and what our Chartist forefathers were not afraid to call it, a class of wages slaves. Is this to be the final result of all this labour, self-sacrifice, and suffering? Is this to remain for ever the highest aim of British workmen? Or is the working class of this country at last to attempt breaking through this vicious circle, and to find an issue out of it in a movement for the ABOLITION OF THE WAGES SYSTEM ALTOGETHER?

Next week we shall examine the part played by Trades Unions as organizers of the working class.

(iv) Trades Unions II[1]

So far we have considered the functions of Trades Unions as far only as they contribute to the regulation of the rate of wages and ensure to the labourer, in his struggle against capital, at least some means of resistance. But that aspect does not exhaust our subject.

The struggle of the labourer against capital, we said. That struggle does exist, whatever the apologists of capital may say to the contrary. It will exist so long as a reduction of wages remains the safest and readiest means of raising profits; nay, so long as the wages system itself shall exist. The very existence of Trades Unions is proof sufficient of the fact; if they are not made to fight against the encroachments of capital what are they made for? There is no use in mincing matters. No milksop words can hide the ugly fact that present society is mainly divided into two great antagonistic classes – into capitalists, the owners of all the means for the employment of labour, on one side; and working men, the owners of nothing but their own working power, on the other. The produce of the labour of the latter class has to be divided between both classes, and it is this division about which the struggle is constantly going on. Each class tries to get as large a share as possible; and it is the most curious aspect of this struggle that the working class, while fighting to obtain a share only of its own produce, is often enough accused of actually robbing the capitalist!

But a struggle between two great classes of society necessarily becomes a political struggle. So did the long battle between the middle or capitalist class and the landed aristocracy; so also does the fight between the working class and these same capitalists. In every struggle of class against class, the next end fought for is political power; the ruling class defends its political supremacy,

1. [*The Labour Standard*, 4 June 1881.]

that is to say its safe majority in the Legislature; the inferior class fights for, first a share, then the whole of that power, in order to become enabled to change existing laws in conformity with their own interests and requirements. Thus the working class of Great Britain for years fought ardently and even violently for the People's Charter, which was to give it that political power; it was defeated, but the struggle had made such an impression upon the victorious middle class that this class, since then, was only too glad to buy a prolonged armistice at the price of ever-repeated concessions to the working people.

Now, in a political struggle of class against class, organization is the most important weapon. And in the same measure as the merely political or Chartist Organization fell to pieces, in the same measure the Trades Unions Organization grew stronger and stronger, until at present it has reached a degree of strength unequalled by any working-class organization abroad. A few large Trades Unions, comprising between one and two millions of working men, and backed by the smaller or local Unions, represent a power which has to be taken into account by any Government of the ruling class, be it Whig or Tory.

According to the traditions of their origin and development in this country, these powerful organizations have hitherto limited themselves almost strictly to their function of sharing in the regulation of wages and working hours, and of enforcing the repeal of laws openly hostile to the workmen. As stated before, they have done so with quite as much effect as they had a right to expect. But they have attained more than that – the ruling class, which knows their strength better than they themselves do, has volunteered to them concessions beyond that. Disraeli's Household Suffrage gave the vote to at least the greater portion of the organized working class. Would he have proposed it unless he supposed that these new voters would show a will of their own – would cease to be led by middle-class Liberal politicians? Would he have been able to carry it if the working people, in the management of their colossal Trade Societies, had not proved themselves fit for administrative and political work?

That very measure opened out a new prospect to the working class. It gave them the majority in London and in all manufacturing towns, and thus enabled them to enter into the struggle against capital with new weapons, by sending men of their own class to Parliament. And here, we are sorry to say, the Trades Unions forgot their duty as the advanced guard of the working class. The new weapon has been in their hands for more than ten years, but they scarcely ever unsheathed it. They ought not to forget that they cannot continue to hold the position they now occupy unless they really march in the van of the working class. It is not in the nature of things that the working class of England should possess the power of sending forty or fifty working men to Parliament and yet be satisfied for ever to be represented by capitalists or their clerks, such as lawyers, editors, etc.

More than this, there are plenty of symptoms that the working class of this country is awakening to the consciousness that it has for some time been moving in the wrong groove; that the present movements for higher wages and shorter hours exclusively, keep it in a vicious circle out of which there is no issue; that it is not the lowness of wages which forms the fundamental evil, but the wages system itself. This knowledge once generally spread amongst the working class, the position of Trades Unions must change considerably. They will no longer enjoy the privilege of being the only organizations of the working class. At the side of, or above, the Unions of special trades there must spring up a general Union, a political organization of the working class as a whole.

Thus there are two points which the organized Trades would do well to consider, firstly, that the time is rapidly approaching when the working class of this country will claim, with a voice not to be mistaken, its full share of representation in Parliament. Secondly, that the time also is rapidly approaching when the working class will have understood that the struggle for high wages and short hours, and the whole action of Trades Unions as now carried on, is not an end in itself, but a means, a very necessary and effective means, but only one of several means towards a higher end: the abolition of the wages system altogether.

For the full representation of labour in Parliament as well as for the preparation of the abolition of the wages system, organizations will become necessary, not of separate Trades, but of the working class as a body. And the sooner this is done the better. There is no power in the world which could for a day resist the British working class organized as a body.

(v) A Working Men's Party[1]

How often have we not been warned by friends and sympathizers, 'Keep aloof from party politics!' And they were perfectly right, as far as present English party politics are concerned. A labour organ must be neither Whig nor Tory, neither Conservative nor Liberal, or even Radical, in the actual party sense of that word. Conservatives, Liberals, Radicals, all of them represent but the interests of the ruling classes, and various shades of opinion predominating amongst landlords, capitalists, and retail tradesmen. If they do represent the working class, they most decidedly misrepresent it. The working class has interests of its own, political as well as social. How it has stood up for what it considers its social interests, the history of the Trades Unions and the Short Time movement shows. But its political interests it leaves almost entirely in the hands of Tories, Whigs, and Radicals, men of the upper class, and for nearly a quarter of a century the working class of England has contented itself with forming, as it were, the tail of the 'Great Liberal Party'.

This is a political position unworthy of the best organized working class of Europe. In other countries the working men have been far more active. Germany has had for more than ten years a Working Men's party (the Social Democrats), which owns ten seats in Parliament, and whose growth has frightened Bismarck into those infamous measures of repression of which we give an account in another column.[2] Yet in spite of Bismarck, the Working Men's party progresses steadily; only last week it carried sixteen elections for the Mannheim Town Council and one for the Saxon Parliament. In Belgium, Holland, and Italy the example of the Germans has been imitated; in every one of these countries a Working Men's party exists, though the voter's

1. [*The Labour Standard*, 23 July 1881.]
2. [A reference to the Anti-Socialist Exceptional Law adopted by the German Reichstag in 1878.]

qualification there is too high to give them a chance of sending members to the Legislature at present. In France the Working Men's Party is just now in full process of organization; it has obtained the majority in several Municipal Councils at the last elections, and will undoubtedly carry several seats at the general election for the Chamber next October. Even in America where the passage of the working class to that of farmer, trader, or capitalist, is still comparatively easy, the working men find it necessary to organize themselves as an independent party. Everywhere the labourer struggles for political power, for direct representation of his class in the Legislature – everywhere but in Great Britain.

And yet there never was a more widespread feeling in England than now, that the old parties are doomed, that the old shibboleths have become meaningless, that the old watchwords are exploded, that the old panaceas will not act any longer. Thinking men of all classes begin to see that a new line must be struck out, and that this line can only be in the direction of democracy. But in England, where the industrial and agricultural working class forms the immense majority of the people, democracy means the dominion of the working class, neither more nor less. Let, then, that working class prepare itself for the task in store for it – the ruling of this great empire; let them understand the responsibilities which inevitably will fall to their share. And the best way to do this is to use the power already in their hands, the actual majority they possess in every large town in the kingdom, to send to Parliament men of their own order. With the present household suffrage, forty or fifty working men might easily be sent to St Stephen's, where such an infusion of entirely new blood is very much wanted indeed. With only that number of working men in Parliament, it would be impossible to let the Irish Land Bill become, as is the case at present, more and more an Irish Land Bull, namely, an Irish Landlords' Compensation Act; it would be impossible to resist the demand for a redistribution of seats, for making bribery really punishable, for throwing election expenses, as is the case everywhere but in England, on the public purse, etc.

Moreover, in England a real democratic party is impossible

unless it be a working men's party. Enlightened men of other classes (where they are not so plentiful as people would make us believe) might join that party and even represent it in Parliament after having given pledges of their sincerity. Such is the case everywhere. In Germany, for instance, the working-men representatives are not in every case actual working men. But no democratic party in England, as well as elsewhere, will be effectively successful unless it has a distinct working-class character. Abandon that, and you have nothing but sects and shams.

And this is even truer in England than abroad. Of Radical shams there have been unfortunately enough since the break-up of the first working men's party which the world ever produced – the Chartist party. Yes, but the Chartists were broken up and attained nothing. Did they, indeed? Of the six points of the People's Charter, two, vote by ballot and no property qualification, are now the law of the land. A third, universal suffrage, is at least approximately carried in the shape of household suffrage; a fourth, equal electoral districts, is distinctly in sight, a promised reform of the present Government. So that the break-down of the Chartist movement has resulted in the realization of fully one half of the Chartist programme. And if the mere recollection of a past political organization of the working class could effect these political reforms, and a series of social reforms besides, what will the actual presence of a working men's political party do, backed by forty or fifty representatives in Parliament?

We live in a world where everybody is bound to take care of himself. Yet the English working class allows the landlord, capitalist, and retail trading classes, with their tail of lawyers, newspaper writers, etc., to take care of its interests. No wonder reforms in the interest of the workman come so slow and in such miserable dribbles. The work-people of England have but to will it, and they are the masters to carry every reform, social and political, which their situation requires. Then why not make that effort?

(vi) Social Classes – necessary and superfluous[1]

The question has often been asked, in what degree are the different classes of society useful or even necessary? And the answer was naturally a different one for every different epoch of history considered. There was undoubtedly a time when a territorial aristocracy was an unavoidable and necessary element of society. That, however, is very, very long ago. Then there was a time when a capitalist middle class, a *bourgeoisie* as the French call it, arose with equally unavoidable necessity, struggled against the territorial aristocracy, broke its political power, and in its turn became economically and politically predominant. But, since classes arose, there never was a time when society could do without a working class. The name, the social status of that class has changed; the serf took the place of the slave, to be in his turn relieved by the free working man – free from servitude but also free from any earthly possessions save his own labour force. But it is plain: whatever changes took place in the upper, non-producing ranks of society, society could not live without a class of producers. This class, then, is necessary under all circumstances – though the time must come, when it will no longer be a class, when it will comprise all society.

Now, what necessity is there at present for the existence of each of these three classes?

The landed aristocracy is, to say the least, economically useless in England, while in Ireland and Scotland it has become a positive nuisance by its depopulating tendencies. To send the people across the ocean or into starvation, and to replace them by sheep or deer – that is all the merit that the Irish and Scotch landlords can lay claim to. Let the competition of American vegetable and and animal food develop a little further, and the English landed aristocracy will do the same, at least those that can afford it, having large town estates to fall back upon. Of the rest, American food competition will soon free us. And good riddance – for their political action, both in the Lords and Commons, is a perfect national nuisance.

But how about the capitalist middle class, that enlightened

1. [*The Labour Standard*, 6 August 1881.]

and liberal class which founded the British colonial empire and which established British liberty? The class that reformed Parliament in 1832, repealed the Corn Laws, and reduced tax after tax? The class that created and still directs the giant manufactures, and the immense merchant navy, the ever spreading railway system of England? Surely that class must be at least as necessary as the working class which it directs and leads on from progress to progress.

Now the economical function of the capitalist middle class has been, indeed, to create the modern system of steam manufactures and steam communications, and to crush every economical and political obstacle which delayed or hindered the development of that system. No doubt, as long as the capitalist middle class performed this function it was, under the circumstances, a necessary class. But is it still so? Does it continue to fulfil its essential function as the manager and expander of social production for the benefit of society at large? Let us see.

To begin with the means of communication, we find the telegraphs in the hands of the Government. The railways and a large part of the sea-going steamships are owned, not by individual capitalists who manage their own business, but by joint-stock companies whose business is managed for them by *paid employees*, by servants whose position is to all intents and purposes that of superior, better paid work-people. As to the directors and shareholders, they both know that the less the former interfere with the management, and the latter with the supervision, the better for the concern. A lax and mostly perfunctory supervision is, indeed, the only function left to the owners of the business. Thus we see that in reality the capitalist owners of these immense establishments have no other action left with regard to them, but to cash the half-yearly dividend warrants. The social function of the capitalist here has been transferred to servants paid by wages; but he continues to pocket, in his dividends, the pay for those functions though he has ceased to perform them.

But another function is still left to the capitalist, whom the extent of the large undertakings in question has compelled to 'retire' from their management. And this function is to speculate with his shares on the Stock Exchange. For want of something better to do, our 'retired' or in reality superseded capitalists, gamble to their hearts' content in this temple of mammon. They go there with the deliberate intention to pocket money which they were pretending to earn; though they say, the origin of all property is labour and saving – the origin perhaps, but certainly not the end. What hypocrisy to forcibly close petty gambling houses, when our capitalist society cannot do without an immense gambling house, where millions after millions are lost and won, for its very centre! Here, indeed, the existence of the 'retired' shareholding capitalist becomes not only superfluous, but a perfect nuisance.

What is true for railways and steam shipping is becoming more and more true every day for all large manufacturing and trading establishments. 'Floating' – transforming large private concerns into limited companies – has been the order of the day for the last ten years and more. From the large Manchester warehouses of the City to the ironworks and coalpits of Wales and the North and the factories of Lancashire, everything has been, or is being, floated. In all Oldham there is scarcely a cotton mill left in private hands; nay, even the retail tradesman is more and more superseded by 'co-operative stores', the great majority of which are co-operative in name only – but of that another time. Thus we see that by the very development of the system of capitalist's production the capitalist is superseded quite as much as the handloom-weaver. With this difference, though, that the handloom-weaver is doomed to slow starvation, and the superseded capitalist to slow death from overfeeding. In this they generally are both alike, that neither knows what to do with himself.

This, then, is the result: the economical development of our actual society tends more and more to concentrate, to socialize production into immense establishments which cannot any longer be managed by single capitalists. All the trash of 'the eye of the master', and the wonders it does, turns into sheer nonsense as soon as an undertaking reaches a certain size. Imagine 'the eye of the master' of the London and North Western Railway! But what the master cannot do the workman, the wages-paid servants of the Company, *can* do, and do it successfully.

Thus the capitalist can no longer lay claim to his profits as 'wages of supervision,' as he supervises nothing. Let us remember that when the defenders of Capital drum that hollow phrase into our ears.

But we have attempted to show, in our last week's issue, that the capitalist class had also become unable to manage the immense productive system of this country; that they on the one hand expanded production so as to periodically flood all the markets with produce, and on the other became more and more incapable of holding their own against foreign competition. Thus we find that, not only can we manage very well without the interference of the capitalist class in the great industries of the country, but that their interference is becoming more and more a nuisance.

Again we say to them, 'Stand back! Give the working class the chance of a turn.'

6. The English Workers in 1895

ENGELS TO H. SCHLÜTER[1]   1 *January* 1895

Things here (in England) are much the same as in your country.[2] The socialist instinct is getting stronger and stronger among the *masses*, but as soon as it is a question of translating the instinctive impulses into clear demands and ideas people at once begin to disagree. Some go to the Social-Democratic Labour Federation, others to the Independent Labour Party, still others go no further than the trade union organization, etc., etc. In brief, nothing but sects and no party. The leaders are almost all pretty unreliable fellows. The candidates for the top leadership are very numerous but by no means conspicuously fitted for the posts, while the two big bourgeois parties stand there, purse in hand, on the look-out for someone they can buy.

Besides, so-called 'democracy' here is very much restricted by

1. [From Karl Marx and Frederich Engels, *On Britain* (Foreign Languages Publishing House, Moscow, 1953), pp. 537.]
2. [United States of America.]

indirect barriers. A periodical costs a terrible amount of money, a parliamentary candidature ditto, living the life of an M.P. ditto, if only on account of the enormous correspondence entailed. A checking-up of the miserably kept electoral register likewise costs a lot and so far only the two official parties can afford the expense. Anyone, therefore, who does not sign up with either of these parties has little chance of getting on the election list of candidates. In all these respects people here are a long way behind the Continent, and are beginning to notice this. Furthermore we have no second ballots here and a relative majority or – as you Americans say – plurality suffices. At the same time everything is arranged for *only two* parties. A third party can at most turn the scales in favour of one of the other two until it equals them in strength . . . Yet here, as in your country, once the workers know what they want, the state, the land, industry and everything else will be theirs.

II. ENGELS AND THE GERMAN WORKERS

Introduction

ENGELS was the son of a Barmen cotton manufacturer and even as a schoolboy he appreciated the sufferings both of the craftsmen and the factory workers in his home town. In one of his earliest articles, written at the age of nineteen, he sharply criticized the factory owners of the Wupper valley. In 1845 he horrified his family by actively supporting Moses Hess's campaign of Communist propaganda in Elberfeld and Barmen. Soon afterwards he was engaged in Communist activities in Brussels and Paris, but when revolutions broke out in Germany in 1848 he joined Marx in Cologne as one of the editors of the *Neue Rheinische Zeitung*. In the following year he returned to Elberfeld to share the fortunes of the workers who had risen in revolt. The local Committee of Public Safety placed him in charge of maintaining the defences of the town but he was asked to leave within a few days since the middle classes feared that he was planning to set up a 'red republic'. Soon afterwards Engels took part in an abortive rising in Baden. When the revolutionary movement collapsed Engels went into exile in Manchester. Even during the period of reaction in the 1850s there were workers in Elberfeld and Solingen who still regarded Engels as their leader and they looked forward to his eventual return to Germany.

In the 1860s there was a revival of the working-class movement in Germany which was inspired by the speeches and pamphlets of Ferdinand Lassalle. But many of the old revolutionaries of 1848 distrusted the new Socialist leader. Marx and Engels regarded Lassalle as a shallow thinker and a flashy adventurer who was using the workers for his own political advancement. They could not deny that by founding the General German Workers Union Lassalle had awakened the workers from their long political slumber. But Lassalle's discussions with Bismarck seemed to confirm their worst suspicions. Lassalle's career was cut short in 1864 when he was killed in a duel. The German Socialists were now divided. Some were Marxists who accepted the programme of the Communist Manifesto and joined the First International. Others supported Lassalle's programme which included a demand for the establishment of state-aided industrial cooperative societies. Marx and Engels pressed the new Socialist leaders in Germany – Wilhelm Liebknecht and August Bebel – to accept unification with the Lassalleans only on the basis of Marxist doctrines. Marx and Engels were bitterly disappointed that substantial concessions were made to Lassalle's followers when the rival parties were united in 1875 under the banner of the Gotha Programme.

In 1878 these disputes were forgotten when the Anti-Socialist Law outlawed the German Socialist Party. At first it seemed as if Bismarck had succeeded in crushing the Socialists since several of their leaders were prepared to obey the law and to further their cause only by legal means. But after a conference held at Wyden in Switzerland the German Socialist Party decided to fight Bismarck 'with all the means at its disposal'. In defiance of the law thousands of copies of the *Sozialdemokrat* (a new socialist periodical published first in Zürich and then in London) were smuggled into Germany every week. Engels contributed to this paper and gave the German socialists every encouragement in their struggle against the Anti-Socialist Law. In 1890, after the fall of Bismarck, the law was allowed to lapse. And in the following year the new Erfurt Programme of the German Socialist Party was firmly based on Marx's doctrines. 'We have the satisfaction of seeing the Marxian critique win all along the line,' he wrote to Sorge on 24 October 1891. 'Even the last trace of Lassalleanism has been removed.'

1. The Workers of Wuppertal, 1839[1]

. . . In Elberfeld there are no signs of that bright and energetic love of life that is to be found almost everywhere else in Germany. It is true that first impressions do not bear this out since on any evening cheerful apprentices can be seen singing their songs as they march down the streets. But their songs are low vulgar ditties that come from throats inflamed by brandy and not the popular German folk songs of which we can be proud. All the public houses are full, particularly on Sundays. Closing time is at 11 o'clock and then the drunken fellows leave the inns and sleep off the effects of intoxication in the gutter. The most wretched of all are the carriers. They are a completely demoralized crew who have no steady jobs or permanent lodgings. At daybreak they creep out of the holes where they have spent the night – haylofts and barns or even front doorsteps and dunghills. The authorities are dealing with the problem to some extent by restricting the number of carriers.

Factory work is obviously one of the main reasons for this state of affairs. Confinement in a small space and inhaling more dust and charcoal fumes than oxygen – often from the age of six – inevitably robs the workers of all health and strength. The weavers who work at home are bent over their looms from morning until night and their backs are injured by the heat from their stoves. Those who do not fall into the hands of the Pietists[2] fall under the influence of alcohol. Since Pietism flourishes here in a peculiarly impudent and revolting form it naturally calls forth an opposite extreme. And so there is a gulf between the 'respectable people' – or Pietists – and the vulgar mob. Such a division – quite apart from the character of the two groups –

1. [Extract from Engels's newspaper articles on 'Briefe aus dem Wuppertal', reprinted in *Gesamtausgabe*, Part I, Vol. 2 (1930), and E. Engelberg, *Die Klassiker des wissenschaftlichen Kommunismus zur deutschen Arbeiterbewegung* (1955,) pp. 7–9.]

2. [Pietism, a German form of Puritanism, flourished in Elberfeld and Barmen in the early nineteenth century.]

would in itself be enough to prevent the development of a healthy society, and the disappearance of one group would not solve the problem since both of them are riddled with consumption. The few healthy people to be seen in Elberfeld are joiners or other craftsmen who have migrated from other parts of the country. There are some healthy local tanners but after three years they are physically and mentally exhausted. Three out of five people die from consumption which has been caused by drinking spirits.

Factors which explain the hold that consumption has gained upon the people include the reckless manner in which the factory owners exploit their workers and the existence of a peculiar form of Pietism which actually threatens to extend its influence still further. There is terrible distress among the lower classes, particularly among the factory operatives in the valley of the River Wupper. Syphilis and chest complaints exist to an extent that is difficult to credit. In Elberfeld alone, 1,200 out of 2,500 children of school age grow up in the mills simply because the greedy factory owners would rather pay half wages to a child than full pay to an adult. The rich factory owners have highly elastic consciences and no Pietist will go to Hell for ruining one child more or less – especially if he goes to church twice on a Sunday. There can be no doubt that it is the Pietest factory owners who are the worst employers. They resort to any excuse to cut wages on the plea that the less money a worker has in his pocket the less he can spend on drink. Yet when it comes to an election for a new pastor the Pietist factory owners take the lead in bribing the voters!

2. Communism in Elberfeld in 1845[1]

ENGELS TO MARX   22 *February–7 March* 1845
... Elberfeld has seen an age of miracles. Yesterday we held our third Communist meeting in the largest room of the best hotel in the town. Forty people came to the first meeting, 130 to the

1. [Translated from *Gesamtausgabe*, Part III, Vol. I, pp. 14–15.]

second, and at least 200 to the third. All Elberfeld and Barmen
was represented from the aristocracy of wealth to the ordinary
shopkeepers. Only the workers failed to turn up. Hess[1] made a
speech and poems by Müller, Püttmann and Shelley were
recited. An article in the *Bürgerbuch*[2] on Communist settlements
was read. Afterwards the discussion continued until one in the
morning.

Our propaganda is making extraordinary progress. People can
talk of nothing but Communism and we are getting new recruits
every day. Communism in the valley of the Wupper is a fact –
virtually already a power in the land. You cannot imagine how
favourable the situation is here. The most stupid, the most idle
and the most philistine people, who once had no interest whatever in what was going on, now begin almost to revel in Communism. How long it will last I do not know. The police are in
real difficulties and do not know what action to take. The
Landrat, who is the dirtiest dog of the lot, is in Berlin at the
moment. But if we are banned we will find a way round the ban
and if that fails we shall have stirred people up so much that in
future anything that we write will be read with avidity.

3. The Elberfeld Rising of 1849[3]

THE *Neue Rheinische Zeitung* did not fail to be represented on
the barricades of Elberfeld. Since various false rumours are
circulating about our part in the affair we shall give our readers
a brief report on what actually happened.

Friedrich Engels, an editor of the *Neue Rheinische Zeitung*, went
from Cologne to Elberfeld on 10 May. On the way he stopped at
Solingen and collected two boxes of ammunition which the local
workers had seized when they stormed the arsenal at Gräfrath.

1. [Moses Hess was one of the leading Communist agitators in Elberfeld and
Barmen at this time. His headquarters were in the Stadt London hotel in Barmen.]
2. [*Deütsches Bürgerbuch für 1845*, edited by Püttman and published in Darmstadt
(1845).]
3. [Article in the *Neue Rheinische Zeitung*, 17 May 1849; reprinted in: Karl Marx
und Friedrich Engels, *Die Revolution von 1848. Auswahl aus der 'Neuen Rheinischen
Zeitung'* (1955), pp. 306–9.]

When he got to Elberfeld Engels gave the local Committee of Public Safety a report on the state of affairs in Cologne. He placed himself at the disposal of the Committee. The Military Commission of the Committee of Public Safety at once issued the following order which authorized Engels to supervise the defence works of the town:

The Military Commission of the Committee of Public Safety hereby authorizes Herr Friedrich Engels to inspect all the town's barricades and to complete the defence works. All pickets on the barricades are requested to give Herr Engels any assistance that he may require. Elberfeld, 11 May, 1849 (signed) Hühnerbein, Troost.

On the following day the artillery was also placed at Engels's disposal by the following order:

Citizen F. Engels is hereby empowered to set up cannon where he thinks best. He is authorized to requisition the services of the labourers that he requires. The expenses will be borne by the Committee of Public Safety.
Elberfeld, 12 May, 1849.
On behalf of the Committee of Public Safety
(signed) Pothmann, Hühnerbein, Troost.

On the very day that he arrived in Elberfeld Engels organized a company of pioneers and strengthened the barricades at various exits from the town. He attended all the meetings of the Military Commission. His suggestion that Herr Mirbach should be appointed Commander-in-Chief was unanimously accepted by the Commission. He continued his activities on the following day. He changed several of the barricades and pickets and strengthened the pioneer companies. As soon as Mirbach arrived Engels placed himself at the disposal of the Commander-in-Chief and took part in all the war councils. During the whole of his stay in Elberfeld Engels enjoyed the complete confidence of the free corps and of the armed workers of Berg and the Mark.

As soon as Engels arrived, Herr Riotte, a member of the Committee of Public Safety, asked him why he had come to Elberfeld. Engels replied that he had come because he had been sent from Cologne and because he believed that he could perhaps make himself useful in a military capacity. Moreover as he had been born in Berg, Engels considered that it was a matter of honour to stand shoulder to shoulder with the people of Berg on the first occasion that they had taken up arms. Engels declared that he wanted to devote himself entirely to his military duties and to hold himself completely aloof from the political side of the movement. It was obvious that only a black-red-gold movement[1] was possible in Elberfeld at the moment and that any opposition to the German Constitution was to be avoided. Herr Riotte declared that he was entirely satisfied with Engels's statement.

When Engels accompanied Mirbach, the Commander-in-Chief, on a general inspection on the Engelnberg on the morning of 14 May, he was approached by Herr Höchster (another member of the Committee of Public Safety). Höchster declared that – although he himself had no criticism whatever to make of Engels's conduct – the middle classes in Elberfeld were greatly alarmed at Engels's presence in the town. They feared that Engels might proclaim the red republic at any time and they all hoped that Engels would leave Elberfeld.

Engels declared that he would not stay where he was not wanted but that he was not prepared to desert his post in a cowardly fashion. He demanded that the request that he should leave Elberfeld should be made by the Committee of Public Safety in writing and should be signed by all the members. Herr Höchster brought the matter before the Committee of Public Safety on the same day. The Committee passed the following resolution:

Citizen Friedrich Engels of Barmen, recently resident in Cologne, is thanked for his services in this town. But as his continued presence in Elberfeld might give rise to misunderstandings concerning the character of the movement Engels is asked to leave the town today.

Before the passing of this resolution Engels had declared that he would accept the decision of the Committee of Public Safety only if he received a direct order from Mirbach to leave Elberfeld. He had suggested Mirbach's appointment as Commander-in-Chief and he would not leave until Mirbach relieved him of his duties.

1. [i.e. a movement in support of the draft German constitution drawn up by the Frankfurt National Assembly.]

On the morning of 15 May, Mirbach was persuaded by the Committee of Public Safety to sign its resolution concerning Engels and copies of the resolution were posted in the town. The free corps and the armed workers were highly incensed at the decision of the Committee of Public Safety. They demanded that Engels should stay in Elberfeld and they declared that they were prepared to sacrifice their lives to protect him. Engels went to the insurgents and calmed them down. He referred them to Mirbach and declared that since he had proposed Mirbach's appointment as Commander-in-Chief and had complete confidence in Mirbach he could not be the first to disobey him.

After making a final reconnaissance of the district Engels handed over his command to his adjutant and left Elberfeld. The workers of Berg and the Mark, who have given such wonderful loyalty and support to our editor, may rest assured that the present movement is merely a curtain-raiser to a new and different movement. That new movement will be a thousand times more serious than the present movement because it will concern the real interests of the workers themselves. The new revolutionary insurrection will be a direct consequence of the present movement and the workers may be certain that as soon as it breaks out Engels – and all the other editors of the *Neue Rheinische Zeitung* – will be at their side. No power on earth will drive them from their posts.

4. The Insurrection in Baden in 1849[1]

ENGELS TO MRS MARX   *Vevey, 25 July 1849*
YOU and Marx will be wondering why I have been silent for such a long time. I will explain. On the very day that I wrote to Marx from Kaiserslautern the news came that Homburg had been occupied by the Prussians and that communications with Paris had been cut. So I was unable to post my letter. I went to Willich. In Kaiserslautern I had held aloof from the so-called

1. [Translated from *Gesamtausgabe*, Part III, Vol. I, pp. 109–10.]

revolution but when the Prussians came I could not resist the temptation to take part in the campaign. Willich was the only officer who had any ability so I went to him and became his adjutant. I took part in four engagements and two of them (particularly the one at Rastatt) were of some significance. I discovered that the much vaunted courage to attack recklessly is a most ordinary accomplishment. The whistling of bullets is a trifling matter. I saw plenty of cowardice during the campaign but there were less than a dozen cases of cowardice *in the face of the enemy*. I did see plenty of courage that bordered on folly.

I have come through all right and now that it is all over I am glad that a representative of the *Neue Rheinische Zeitung* took part in the campaign because the lousy democrats of Baden and the Palatinate are now boasting of all sorts of deeds of heroism that they never performed. (If nobody from the *Neue Rheinische Zeitung* had been there) it would have been the same old story – the gentlemen of the *Neue Rheinische Zeitung* are afraid to fight. Not a single one of the gentlemanly democrats took up arms. But Kinkel and I did. Kinkel joined our corps as a musketeer and distinguished himself. In his first engagement he received a wound in the head and was taken prisoner. After our corps had covered the retreat of the Baden army we crossed over into Switzerland 24 hours later after everybody else. Yesterday we arrived at Vevey . . .

5. Ferdinand Lassalle[1]

ENGELS TO MARX   *7 March 1856*

. . . Lassalle.[2] One might feel sorry for the fellow because of his great talents but the whole affair is really too aggravating. We have always had to keep a devilish sharp eye on him. He is a real Jew from the Slav frontier and he has always been ready to

1. [Translated from *Gesamtausgabe*, Part III, Vol. 2, p. 122.]

2. [Marx had written to Engels on 5 March 1856 that he had received a complaint from the Düsseldorf workers concerning Lassalle's conduct. Lassalle was accused of having turned against the workers and of using the workers' party for his own ends (*Gesamtausgabe*, Part III, Vol. 2, p. 118).]

exploit party affairs for his private ends. Moreover it is disgusting to see how he is always trying to push his way into the world of the upper classes. He is a greasy Jew disguised under brilliantine and flashy jewels. All this simply meant that we had to watch him very carefully. But if he starts doing things that directly affect the party no one can blame the Düsseldorf workers for hating him. I'll see Lupus[1] this evening and I will discuss the affair with him. None of us has ever trusted Lassalle though we have of course defended him against H. Bürger's follies. I agree with the advice that you have given to the workers of Düsseldorf. If he does anything openly against the party – then we shall have him. At the moment he has not overstepped the mark and we do not want a scandal just now ...

ENGELS TO MARX[2]   20 May 1863

... Lassalle's agitation and the rumpus that it has caused in Germany is after all beginning to be awkward for us. It is high time that you finished your book if only in order to secure new disciples (of a different character than Lassalle) in the fight against the middle classes. From one point of view it is a good thing that we have now again secured a foothold in Germany for our propaganda against the middle classes but it is most unfortunate that Itzig[3] should have provided us with this foothold ...

ENGELS TO MARX[4]   Manchester, 4 September 1864

I HAD been occupied with all kinds of business affairs and so I had not opened your letter when your wire arrived. You can imagine how surprised I was at the news. Whatever Lassalle may have been as a person, a writer, and a scholar there can be no doubt that as a politician he was one of the most important chaps in Germany. Just now he was being a very uncertain friend and in the future he would almost certainly have been our enemy. But it comes as a shock when one realizes how Germany ruins

1. [Nickname of Wilhelm Wolff.]
2. [Translated from *Gesamtausgabe*, Part III, Vol. 3, pp. 140–41]
3. [Nickname for Lassalle.]
4. [Translated from *Gesamtausgabe*, Part III Vol. 3, p. 188.]

all her political extremists who have some sort of ability. What rejoicings there will be in the ranks of the factory owners and those dirty dogs of the Progressive Party. Lassalle was the only fellow in Germany they really feared.

And what an extraordinary way to die. This would-be Don Juan really falls in love with the daughter of a Bavarian ambassador and wants to marry her. Then he comes up against a rejected suitor of the lady – who incidentally is a swindler from Rumania – and gets himself shot dead by his rival. That could only happen to Lassalle with his unique character – part Jew, part cavalier, part clown, part sentimentalist. How can a politician of his calibre let himself be shot dead by a Rumanian adventurer?

ENGELS TO MARX[1]   *Manchester, 27 January 1865*

... It is gradually becoming clear that the worthy Lassalle was no more than a common rascal. We have always judged people by their deeds and not by their words and I see no reason why we should make an exception in favour of the late lamented Itzig. He may have been able to justify his actions to himself in a plausible fashion because he was so vain, but viewed impartially his behaviour was plain roguery and a betrayal of the whole working class movement to the Prussians. And what is worse the silly chump failed to get a quid pro quo from Bismarck. He did not get any definite promise and certainly no firm guarantee from Bismarck. He seems to have persuaded himself that he *had* to get the better of Bismarck just as he *had* to kill Rakowitz.[2]

ENGELS TO MARX[3]   *13 February 1865*

... It is clear that Itzig has given the Socialist movement a Tory-Chartist twist which will be hard to destroy. He has deflected the workers' movement in Germany on to quite new lines. Everywhere there are signs of a disgusting kow-towing to reaction. We shall have some trouble with that. Mark my words! The miserable wretches will say: 'What is Engels up to? What

1. [Translated from *Gesamtausgabe*, Part III, Vol. 3, p. 218.]
2. [Rakowitz killed Lassalle in a duel.]
3. [Translated from *Gesamtausgabe*, Part III Vol. 3, pp. 234-5.]

has he been doing all this time? How can he speak in our name and tell us what to do? All he does is to sit in Manchester and exploit the workers!' I don't care a tinker's cuss but it will come all the same and we shall have Baron Itzig to thank for it.

ENGELS TO KAUTSKY[1]   23 February 1891

... You say that Bebel has written to you to say that Marx's treatment of Lassalle has caused bad blood among the old followers of Lassalle. That may be so. These people do not know the real story and nothing seems to have happened to enlighten them about it. It is not my fault if they do not know that Lassalle's reputation was due to the fact that for years Marx allowed Lassalle to parade the results of Marx's researches as his own. Moreover owing to his inadequate knowledge of economics Lassalle distorted Marx's views into the bargain. But I am Marx's literary executor and consequently I have a duty to perform in this matter.

Lassalle has belonged to history for twenty-six years. When the Anti-Socialist Law was in force historical criticism of Lassalle fell into abeyance but the time has at last come when such criticism must be made. Lassalle's position in relation to Marx must be made clear. The legend which glorifies Lassalle and conceals the truth about him can surely not be allowed to become an article of faith in the Socialist Party. However highly Lassalle's services to socialism may be rated his historical role in the movement remains an equivocal one. Lassalle the socialist is dogged at every step by Lassalle the demagogue. The Lassalle of the Hatzfeldt case[2] shows through Lassalle the agitator and Lassalle the political organizer. Whatever he did Lassalle was completely cynical in his choice of weapons to get what he wanted and he preferred to surround himself with dubious and corrupt creatures who could be used as mere tools and then discarded. Until 1862 Lassalle was definitely a vulgar Prussian democrat with strong Bonapartist leanings and that is shown by his letters to Marx which I have just been reading. Then for purely personal

1. [Translation based on that in Karl Marx and Friedrich Engels, *Selected Correspondence* (Foreign Languages Publishing House, Moscow), pp. 509–10.]
2. [Between 1845 and 1854 Lassalle devoted much of his time to the affairs of the Countess Hatzfeldt who was endeavouring to secure a divorce from her husband.]

reasons Lassalle changed course and began his political agitation. Within two years he was advising the workers to support the monarchy against the middle classes. Lassalle intrigued with Bismarck. In character and outlook the two men had much in common. Lassalle's intrigues could certainly have led to the betrayal of the socialist movement had he not – fortunately for himself – been shot in time.

In his political writings what is correct is what has been borrowed from Marx. But these borrowings are so mixed up with the errors that Lassalle made all by himself that it is difficult to distinguish between truth and error. Those workers who feel injured by Marx's judgement know Lassalle only through his two years of political agitation – and even those years are seen through rose coloured spectacles. But historical criticism cannot for ever stand hat in hand before such prejudices. It was my duty finally to settle accounts between Marx and Lassalle. That has been done and for the time being I am content to let the matter rest. I have other things to do just now. The ruthless judgement of Marx on Lassalle which has appeared in print will have some effect and it will give courage to others. But if my hand is forced I shall have no choice in the matter and I shall have to make a clean sweep of the Lassalle myth once and for all.

6. The Gotha Programme of 1875[1]

ENGELS TO BEBEL   *18–28 March 1875*
... You ask for the views of Marx and myself on the question of the unification of the German Socialist parties. Unfortunately we are in the same position as yourself. Neither Liebknecht nor anyone else has told us anything. We know only what is in the newspapers and they gave no information until about a week ago when the draft programme was issued. And what we saw certainly was a surprise. In the past our party has often held out the hand of reconciliation to the followers of Lassalle. If the

1. [Translated from E. Engelberg, *Die Klassiker des wissenschaftlichen Kommunismus zur deutschen Arbeiterbewegung* (1955), pp. 161–5.]

amalgamation of the parties were impossible we offered a coalition. And every time the Hasenclevers, the Hasselmanns and the Tölckes scornfully rejected our overtures. Now a babe in arms can see that these gentlemen must be in a devilish fix if they come to us of their own accord with an offer of reconciliation. In view of the well-known character of these chaps it is our duty to take advantage of their difficulties and to insist that they should give us every possible guarantee. This is the only way to make certain that these fellows are never again in a position to repair their broken image in the eyes of the German workers. They ought to have been received with extreme coolness and caution. It should have been made clear to them that if they wanted unification they must drop their sectarian slogans and their demands for state aid for industrial cooperative enterprises. They must be prepared to accept either the Eisenach programme of 1869 or a revised version of this programme adapted to modern conditions. Our Party has *absolutely nothing to learn* from Lassalle's followers as far as theoretical principles are concerned and that is what matters in drawing up a party programme. The Lassalleans, on the other hand, have much to learn from us in this respect. The first condition of unification should be that the Lassalleans should cease to be sectarian Lassalleans. They should agree either to give up altogether their notion that state aid for industrial cooperative associations is a magic cure for all the ills of the world or at least they should acknowledge that such state aid is no more than a subordinate temporary measure – one of many possible measures which might be proposed. The Gotha programme shows that we are a hundred times superior to the Lassalleans as far as theoretical arguments are concerned. But we are much inferior to them in political cunning. Once again 'honest folk' have been thoroughly cheated by dishonest characters.

First, the Gotha programme repeats the pompous – but historically erroneous – assertion of Lassalle that 'society is divided into two groups – the working class and all other classes which are only a mass of reactionaries'. This statement is correct only in a few isolated cases. It was true, for example, in France at the time of the Paris Commune when there was a working-class revolution. It would be true in a country where the bourgeoisie has moulded the state and society entirely in its own image and where the lower middle-class democrats have carried out this process to its logical conclusion. If the lower middle-class democrats in Germany were really a part of 'a reactionary mass' how could the Social Democratic Workers' Party cooperate for years with the *Volkspartei* (Popular Party)? How can the *Volkstaat*[1] follow the political line of the lower middle class democratic *Frankfurter Zeitung*? And how can one insert in the Gotha programme seven demands which are taken word for word from the programme of the Popular Party? . . .

Secondly, for practical purposes the Gotha programme completely denies the principle that the working-class movement is an international movement. And that denial has been accepted by the very people who upheld the principle in the most honourable manner for five years under the most difficult conditions. German workers today stand in the forefront of the European movement and that is almost entirely due to the fact that they adopted a genuinely international policy during the Franco-Prussian war. No other working class would have behaved so well. And now the German workers are to deny the principle that their movement is international in character at the very moment when foreign workers are firmly resisting all the attempts of their rulers to suppress the international aspect of the movement. What is left of the international working-class movement in the Gotha programme? Is it the prospect however faint of the future collaboration of the European workers to secure their freedom? Not at all. We are promised merely a future 'international brotherhood' – a 'United States of Europe' which is the policy of the bourgeois League of Peace.

Thirdly, our people have been forced to swallow Lassalle's 'iron law of wages'. This 'law' is derived from a completely out-of-date economic theory – namely the theory that the worker receives on the average only a *minimum* wage because (according to Malthus's theory of population) there is always a surplus of labour. But Marx has proved conclusively in *Das Kapital* that the laws governing wages are very complicated and that the level

---

1. [The *Volkstaat*, edited by Wilhelm Liebknecht, was the organ of the German Social Democratic Workers' Party between 1869 and 1876.]

of wages is influenced by various factors in various circumstances. Marx has shown that the laws of wages far from being 'iron laws' are highly elastic and that Lassalle was quite wrong in imagining that his catchphrase was the solution to a complex problem . . .

Fourthly, the sole social demand contained in the Gotha programme is Lassalle's proposal for state aid for industrial co-operative enterprises in its most naked form – exactly as Lassalle stole it from Buchez. And that has been done in spite of the fact that Bracke has exposed the utter futility of this plan.[1] The scheme has been put forward once more although all – or virtually all – our party speakers have denounced it when attacking the followers of Lassalle. Our party cannot sink lower than that . . .

Fifthly, nothing is said in the Gotha programme about the organization of the workers in trade unions. And this is a very important matter since the trade unions are the real class organs of the proletariat. It is trade unions which enable the workers to fight their daily battles with the capitalists. It is trade unions which are the training ground for the workers. And trade unions are so firmly entrenched that they simply cannot be destroyed even by the most powerful reaction – such as the reaction in Paris just now. In view of the strength of the trade union movement in Germany the unions should undoubtedly be mentioned in the Gotha programme and a place should be left free for them in the organization of the Socialist Party.

All this has been done by our people to oblige the Lassalleans. And what have they given us in return? A lot of pretty muddled *democratic* demands have found their way into the Gotha programme. Some are fashionable at the moment – popular law-making for example which exists as the referendum in Switzerland where it does more harm than good. Popular *administration* would be better. And nothing is said of the basic requisite of all freedoms – that all bureaucrats should be responsible to the normal courts (under common law) for their official actions towards ordinary citizens. I will not comment any more on the fact that the Gotha programme includes demands for academic freedom and freedom of conscience. These are the stock in trade

1. [W. Bracke, *Der Lassallesche Vorschlag* (1873).]

of every middle-class liberal programme and look somewhat out of place in our programme. The 'free people's state' has been turned into the 'free state'. A 'free state', from a grammatical point of view, is a state which is free in relation to its own citizens – i.e. a state with a despotic government. All the talk about the state should be dropped, particularly since we have now had the experience of the Paris Commune which was not really a state in the accepted sense of the word. The anarchists have thrown the term 'peoples state' into our faces until we are sick of it. Yet Marx's pamphlet against Proudhon and then the Communist Manifesto both clearly stated that a state automatically dissolves itself and vanishes when a socialist society is established. The state is merely a temporary phenomenon which Socialists can use in the revolutionary struggle. So it is complete nonsense to speak of the 'free people's state'. For a time the proletariat may still *need* the state as a means of holding down its enemies but as soon as genuine freedom is established the state as such ceases to exist. We suggest that the word 'state' should be replaced in the Gotha programme by the word 'community' (*Gemeinwesen*) which is a good old German word and may be regarded as the equivalent of the French word 'commune'.

'The removal of all social and political inequalities' is a very dubious phrase with which to replace 'the removal of all class distinctions'. There will always be *certain* inequalities in the standard of life in different countries, provinces and places. They can be reduced to a minimum but they can never be entirely removed. The inhabitants of mountain districts will always live in a different sort of way from the townsman. The notion that a socialist society is a society of *equals* is a biased French idea inherited from the old revolutionary slogan: 'Liberty, equality, fraternity'. This idea could be justified as a necessary *phase of development* in its own place and time. But – like all the biased views of the earlier schools of Socialism – the idea of equality should now be regarded as out of date since it only leads to confusion and hampers a precise examination of the problem.

I will stop now although almost every word in this weak and flabby programme is open to criticism. If this programme is adopted neither Marx nor I could *ever* recognize the *new* party which would be erected on this programme. And we should have to consider very seriously what attitude we should adopt in private and in public towards the new party. You must realize that outside Germany *we* are made responsible for every single pronouncement and action of the German Social Democratic Workers' Party. In his *Politics and Anarchy* Bakunin made us responsible for every careless word that Liebknecht had said or written since the establishment of the *Demokratisches Wochenblatt*. People imagine that Marx and I control everything from London. You know as well as I do that Marx and I have never interfered in any way with the internal affairs of the German Party. And if we have intervened we have done so only in order to try to put right blunders – and then *only* blunders concerning the theory of Socialism – which we felt needed correction. You must see for yourself that the Gotha programme may precipitate a crisis. Marx and I could easily be forced to decline to accept any responsibility whatsoever for the actions of the Party. The official programme of a party is usually less important than its actions. But a *new* programme is always a flag that is publicly raised and foreigners pass judgements upon its contents. The new Gotha programme should never be a retreat from the old Eisenach programme. The probable attitude of foreign workers to the new programme should also be considered. What will they think of the way in which the German Socialist proletariat is bowing down before the shade of Lassalle?

7. The German Anti-Socialist Law, 1879–90[1]

ENGELS TO J. P. BECKER   1 *July 1879*
... It is quite understandable that Liebknecht's untimely meekness in the Reichstag[2] should have created a very bad impression

---

1. [Based on translation in Karl Marx and Friedrich Engels, *Selected Correspondence* (Foreign Languages Publishing House, Moscow), p. 387.]

2. [When a minor state of siege was proclaimed in Berlin, Wilhelm Liebknecht declared in a speech to the Reichstag on 17 March 1879 that the German Socialist Party was not a revolutionary organization and that it would obey the Anti-Socialist Law.]

in Latin Europe as well as among Germans wherever they may be. We said so at once in our letter. The good old days of leisurely political agitation in Germany – interrupted occasionally by six weeks or six months in prison – have gone for ever. No matter what may be the outcome of the present conflict the new Socialist movement will start on a more or less revolutionary basis. This new agitation must inevitably be much more resolute in character than the first phase of our movement which has now come to an end. The slogan about the 'peaceful attainment' of our aims will no longer be necessary and in any case it will not be taken seriously any more. By making this slogan impossible and by thrusting the Socialist movement in a revolutionary direction Bismarck has rendered us a great service. This far outweighs any harm that he may have done to our cause by interfering with our propaganda . . .

ENGELS TO BERNSTEIN[1]   *30 November 1881*

If any piece of news could have helped to put Marx to some extent on his feet again it was the result of the Reichstag elections. Never has any proletariat done so well. In England after the great failure of 1848 the working classes became apathetic and allowed themselves to be exploited by the middle classes although the trade unions did fight for higher wages. In France, the proletariat vanished from the scene after the coup d'état of 2 December. But in Germany the proletariat has suffered three years of grim repression and continual pressure. No organization of the workers has been able to function openly. Yet our lads are standing four square in all their old self-confidence and strength. Indeed, in one respect they are more powerful than they were before because the centre of gravity of the socialist movement has moved from the semi-rural districts of Saxony to the great industrial towns. Most of our supporters in Saxony were handloom weavers whose livelihood has been threatened by the power loom. They have survived by supplementing their starvation wages with additional earnings from gardening or carving toys. These people are in a backward stage of economic development

1. [Translated from E. Engelberg, *Die Klassiker des wissenschaftlichen Kommunismus zur deutschen Arbeiterbewegung* (1955), pp. 170–1.]

and their technique of industrial production is one which is on the decline. They cannot be regarded as the natural representatives of revolutionary Socialism. But the workers in the great industrial plants in the towns are the natural representatives of revolutionary socialism. Unlike the last of the English handloom weavers who became the core of the 'Conservative Working Men' the Saxon weavers are by no means reactionaries by nature but in the long run they are unreliable supporters of Socialism. Since they are scattered over the countryside and since they suffer from the most grinding poverty they are more easily subject to political pressure than the workers in the great towns. And one must admire the heroism – and the facts are to be found in the pages of the *Sozialdemokrat* – shown by so many of these poor devils in resisting their oppressors.

All the same they cannot be regarded as a sound nucleus for a great national movement. At certain times – between 1865 and 1870 for example – their distress made them more ready to support socialism than the workers in the great towns. But their poor standard of living also makes them unreliable supporters of our cause. A drowning man clutches at any straw and cannot wait for the boat from the shore that will save him. The piece of straw is the tariff and State Socialism while the boat is the socialist revolution. It is significant that in traditionally Socialist constituencies it is virtually only the conservatives who have any chance against us . . .

Now things have changed. Berlin, Hamburg, Breslau, Leipzig, Dresden, Mainz, Offenbach, Barmen, Elberfeld, Solingen, Nürnberg, Frankfurt am Main, Hanau as well as Chemnitz and the Erzgebirg district – that gives us quite a different basis. The class which naturally supports a revolution because of its economic position has become the nucleus of our movement. Moreover the movement has spread its influence uniformly over all the industrial regions of Germany. Formerly support for socialism was confined to a few local centres but now it has become a truly national movement. And that is what scares the middle classes most of all.

As for the Socialist deputies in the Reichstag one must just hope for the best although I have grave doubts about some of them. It would be a misfortune if Bebel were not elected. He alone has the skill to keep in order the many newcomers who will certainly have all sorts of plans up their sleeves. Bebel alone can stop them from making fools of themselves. . . .

ENGELS TO BERNSTEIN[1]   *18 January 1883*

. . . We are delighted by the way in which Grillenberger and the *Sozialdemokrat* have answered Puttkamer's hypocrisy.[2] That is the way to do it. Do not twist and turn when your opponent strikes you. Do not whine and moan and stammer excuses and say that you do not mean any harm. So many Socialists still do this. What you have to do is to hit back and give your opponent two or three blows for every one that he can deliver. We have always followed an aggressive policy and so far I think that we have nearly always beaten our enemies. In an order to his generals old Fritz[3] once declared: 'The genius of our troops lies in attack and that is a very good thing.' But if Kayser[4] withdraws during the Reichstag debate on the Anti-Socialist law . . . and wails that we are revolutionaries only in a Pickwickian sense – what then? This is what should have been said: 'The Reichstag and the Bundesrat exist only because of a revolution. Old William[5] was a revolutionary when he swallowed three crowns and one free city. All legality – the so called "basis of law" – is nothing more than the product of countless revolutions against the will of the people and directed against the people'. . .

ARTICLE IN THE 'SOZIALDEMOKRAT'   *27 September 1890*[6]

. . . I have twice had the honour and the good fortune to write regularly for a journal under very favourable conditions, for I

1. [Based on translation in Karl Marx and Friedrich Engels, *Selected Correspondence* (Foreign Languages Publishing House, Moscow), p. 431.]
2. [This refers to attacks on Puttkamer, the Prussian Minister of the Interior, at the time of the renewal of the Anti-Socialist Law.]
3. [Frederick the Great.]
4. [Kayser was a right wing Socialist deputy in the Reichstag.]
5. [Wilhelm I, the first Emperor of the united Reich of 1871.]
6. [This was the last number of the *Sozialdemokrat*, the organ of the German Socialist Party during the period of the Anti-Socialist Law. The paper was published first in Zürich and then in London and was smuggled into Germany. The extracts from Engels's article have been translated from E. Engelberg, *Die Klassiker des wissenschaftlichen Kommunismus zur deutschen Arbeiterbewegung* (1955).]

have enjoyed the two greatest blessings that any contributor could desire – complete freedom of the press and the knowledge that my articles were being read by the very people I wished to influence.

The first time was in 1848–9 when I was associated with the *Neue Rheinische Zeitung*. A revolution was taking place in those days and for that reason alone I was delighted to work for a daily newspaper. I could see the effect of every word that I wrote. And our articles were influencing public opinion like the explosion of a bomb.

The second time was when I wrote for the *Sozialdemokrat*. And that too was in a period of revolution because at the Wyden conference the German Socialist Party found its soul again and decided to take up the struggle once more 'with all the means at its disposal' – legal and illegal. The *Sozialdemokrat* was the very embodiment of illegality. For the *Sozialdemokrat* there was no German constitution, no German penal code and no Prussian common law. In defiance of all the laws of the Reich and the Federal States the *Sozialdemokrat* forced its way across the frontiers of the Holy German Empire. Policemen, spies, agents provocateurs and customs officials doubled and trebled the watch on the frontiers. But their efforts were in vain. Subscribers regularly received the paper when it was due almost with the certainty of a bill of exchange. No Stephan[1] could stop the German Post Office from handling the paper. And there were over 10,000 subscribers in Germany. Moreover in 1848 the middle-class subscribers to the banned newspapers rarely paid their bills but the workers have paid for their *Sozialdemokrat* for twelve years with exemplary punctuality. As an old hand at revolutionary activities I have often rejoiced at the quiet efficiency of the cooperation between the editors, the distributors, and the subscribers. I was delighted at the businesslike way in which the revolutionary job was done week after week and year after year.

All the trouble and risks that had to be taken to distribute the paper were fully justified. The high standard attained by the *Sozialdemokrat* was not merely due to the fact that it was the only Socialist paper which enjoyed the advantage of complete freedom

1. [Heinrich von Stephan was the German Postmaster General.]

of the press. The principles of the party were stated with unusual clarity and precision and there was no deviation from them. And while the German bourgeois press is incredibly dull the *Sozial-demokrat* reflected the cheerful humour with which our workers are accustomed to fight the chicaneries of the police.

Moreover the *Sozialdemokrat* was much more than a mere mouthpiece of the Socialist deputies in the Reichstag. When the majority of the parliamentary party supported the Steamship Subsidy Bill in 1885 the *Sozialdemokrat* took the opposite point of view. The majority of the deputies passed a resolution denouncing the *Sozialdemokrat*. Today it must seem incomprehensible to the deputies themselves that they should have done such a thing. The struggle lasted for exactly three weeks. It was on 2 April 1885 that the deputies passed their resolution. On 30 April a joint statement of the editors and the deputies appeared in the *Sozialdemokrat* which made it clear that the deputies had given up their claim to dictate the policy of the paper....

The *Sozialdemokrat* was the flag of the German Socialist Party. Now the Party has emerged victorious from a struggle that has lasted for twelve years. The Anti-Socialist Law is no more. Bismarck has fallen from power. The mighty German Reich set all its forces in motion against us. The Party defied the Reich and now the Reich has had to admit defeat. In future the government of the Reich will again deal with us in accordance with the established laws of the land. And we will now return to the paths of legality. But let it be remembered that our victory was won by striking hard with illegal weapons....

III. THE ECONOMIST

Introduction

MARX and Engels collaborated so closely in their writings on economics that it is sometimes difficult to assess what each of them contributed to the final result. Many letters passed between Marx and Engels concerning the first volume of *Das Kapital*. Since Engels was working in the offices of the cotton firm of Ermen and Engels in Manchester he was able to supply Marx with accurate and detailed information concerning business practices in England. The Marx-Engels correspondence also includes letters in which Engels commented on Marx's economic theories. The second and third volumes of *Das Kapital* were prepared for publication by Engels after Marx's death. Engels made two important contributions of his own to Marxian economics. The first was an early essay which Engels wrote in 1844 before his close association with Marx began. In this article, which appeared in the *Deutsch-Französische Jahrbücher*, he vigorously attacked the theories of the English liberal economics of that time. Many years later – in 1878 – Engels wrote a criticism of Dr Dühring's version of Socialist economic theory. This included a clear statement, in a popular and simplified form, of the main theories of Marxian economics contained in the first volume of *Das Kapital*. Three chapters of this book subsequently appeared as a pamphlet entitled *Socialism, Utopian and Scientific* and this had a wide sale. Engels not only worked closely with Marx in the preparation of the first volume of *Das Kapital* and other economic works but he also did much to popularize Marx's theories and to make them known among workers who would be unlikely to master Marx's learned works.

1. Outlines of a Critique of Political Economy, 1844[1]

Economics

POLITICAL economy came into being as a natural result of the expansion of trade. With the appearance of the science of economics unscientific swindling was replaced by a more highly developed system of licensed fraud – a complete get-rich economy.

Political economy – the science of how to make money – was born of the mutual envy and greed of the merchants. It bears on its brow the mark of the most loathsome selfishness. At one time people still held the naïve belief that gold and silver were wealth and they thought that the universal prohibition of the export of the 'precious' metals was a matter of the greatest urgency. Nations faced each other like misers. Each clasped his precious money bags to his bosom. Each eyed his neighbours with distrust and envy. Every conceivable means was employed to lure from nations with whom one had commercial relations as much ready cash as possible. Everyone wished to retain snugly within his own frontiers all the cash that had been happily accumulated.

A rigorously consistent pursuit of this principle would have killed commerce. So a step forward from this first stage was taken. People came to realize that capital locked up in a chest was dead capital, while capital in circulation multiplied itself continuously. So they became more philanthropic. They sent off their ducats as call-birds to bring others back with them. They recognized that there is no harm in paying A too much for his goods so long as the goods can be sold to B at a still higher price.

The *mercantile system* was built on these foundations. The avaricious character of commerce was already, to some extent, beginning to be hidden. Nations drew a little closer together.

1. [First published in the *Deutsch-Französische Jahrbücher*, 1844. Translation based on Karl Marx, *Economic and Philosophic Manuscripts of 1844* (Foreign Languages Publishing House, Moscow, 1961). Appendix, pp. 175–209. The subheadings have been inserted by the editor.]

They concluded commercial agreements: they did business with one another: and – to make larger profits – they treated one another with all possible love and kindness. Fundamentally, however, the old lust for money survived. So did the selfishness which from time to time erupted in wars. And in those days wars were all due to commercial rivalries. It also became evident in those days that commerce – like robbery – is based on the law of the strong hand. No scruples were felt about exacting by cunning and violence such treaties as were held to be the most advantageous.

The cardinal point of the whole mercantile system was the theory of the balance of trade. Since people still believed that gold and silver were real wealth they considered that the only profitable transactions were those which brought hard cash into the country. To find out if cash was coming into the country exports were compared with imports. When exports were greater than imports it was believed that the difference had come into the country in hard cash and that the country was richer by the difference between exports and imports. It was therefore the task of the economists to ensure that at the end of each year exports should show a favourable balance over imports. And for the sake of this ridiculous illusion thousands of men have been slaughtered! Commerce, too, has had its crusades and its inquisitions.

The eighteenth century was the age of revolution. Economics too were revolutionized. But all the revolutions of the eighteenth century lacked balance and were bogged down in antitheses. Abstract materialism was opposed to abstract spiritualism: the republic was opposed to the monarchy: the social contract was opposed to divine right. In the same way the revolution in economics did not get beyond antitheses. Existing fundamental ideas were not challenged. Materialism did not question the Christian contempt for – and humiliation of – Man but merely postulated Nature instead of the Christian God as the Absolute facing Man. In politics no one dreamt of examining the premises of the State as such. Similarly the economists never thought of questioning *the validity of private property*. Consequently the new economics represented only a partial step forward. The economists had to betray and disavow their own premises. They had to resort to sophistry and hypocrisy to cover up the contradictions in which they became involved. All this they had to do so as to reach conclusions to which they were driven not by the premises from which they started but by the humane spirit of the eighteenth century. Economists assumed a philanthropic character. Their favours were withdrawn from the producers and bestowed upon the consumers. They solemnly threw up their hands in horror at the bloody terror of the mercantile system and proclaimed commerce to be a bond of friendship and union among nations as among individuals. All this was pure splendour and magnificence. Yet the old premises reasserted themselves soon enough and the new sham philanthropy was overshadowed by Malthus's theory of population. This was the crudest and most barbarous theory that ever existed. It was a system of despair which struck down all the beautiful phrases about loving one's neighbour and world citizenship. The old premises begot and reared the factory system and modern slavery which is just as cruel and inhuman as the slavery of the ancient world. Modern economics – the system of Free Trade based upon Adam Smith's *Wealth of Nations* – is revealed as the same old hypocrisy, inconsistency and immorality which now everywhere confronts free humanity.

In spite of this can Adam Smith's system be regarded as an advance on previous systems? Of course it can. It was an advance and a necessary advance into the bargain. It was necessary to overthrow the mercantile system with its monopolies and hindrances to trade so that the true consequences of private property could be brought to light. It was necessary to push all petty, local, and national considerations into the background so that the struggle of our time could become a universal human struggle. It was necessary for the theory of private property to leave the purely empirical path of merely objective inquiry. This theory had to acquire a more scientific character. And those who supported the theory had to accept responsibility for its consequences. The whole problem had to be elevated to a universally human sphere. It was necessary to carry the immorality of the old economics to its logical conclusion. This could only be done by denying it and by veiling it in hypocrisy.

We gladly concede that only the establishment and development of Free Trade now makes it possible for us to take the economics of private property a stage further. But we must at the same time have the right to show the complete invalidity of Free Trade both from a theoretical and a practical point of view.

Our criticism of the economists must become more severe the closer we come to our own day. Adam Smith and Malthus could see only scattered fragments of the modern capitalist system. But the economists of today can examine the fully-grown capitalist system. The consequences of the system and all its contradictions are there for everybody to see. Yet modern economists still attempt to justify the entire system without ever examining the premises upon which it is based. The more modern the economist the more dishonest does he become. With every day that passes the sophistry of the economist increases so as to prevent his science from lagging behind the times. This is why Ricardo is more guilty than Adam Smith. This is why MacCulloch and Mill are more guilty than Ricardo.

Modern economists cannot even judge the mercantile system correctly. Their own system of economics is one-sided and they are still fenced in by the premises of the old mercantile system. We need a new economic theory which rises above the opposition of the two systems (mercantilism and Free Trade), which criticizes the premises common to both of them, and which starts from purely human and universal premises. Only such a theory can place the two older theories in proper perspective.

The supporters of Free Trade are more inveterate monopolists than the old mercantilists. The sham humanity of the modern economists hides a barbarism unknown to their predecessors. The confusion of ideas of which the mercantilists were guilty was simple and consistent compared with the double tongued logic of their critics. Neither the mercantilists nor the Free Traders can reproach the other with anything which would not recoil upon themselves.

This explains why the liberal economists of today cannot understand Friedrich List's attempt to restore the mercantilist system. For us this presents no difficulty. It is obvious that the inconsistencies of liberal economics must necessarily dissolve again into their basic components. Just as theology must either return to blind faith or progress towards free philosophy so Free Trade must either lead to the restoration of monopolies or progress to the abolition of private property.

The only *positive* advances which liberal economics has made is the unfolding of the laws of private property. These laws are contained in modern liberal economic theory although they are not yet fully revealed or clearly expressed. It follows that on all matters where it is a question of deciding which is the shortest road to wealth – i.e. in all strictly economic controversies – the protagonists of Free Trade have right on their side. They are right when they are attacking monopolists. But of course they are not right when they criticize the opponents of private property. Indeed the English Socialists have proved long ago – both from a theoretical and a practical point of view – that they are in a position to solve economic problems more correctly than the liberal economists.

In our criticisms of modern theories of economics we shall examine fundamental ideas first of all and we shall then expose the contradictions introduced by the system of Free Trade. Finally we shall follow to their logical conclusions both sides of the contradictory arguments.

The use of the term 'national wealth' has arisen only because the liberal economists have a passion for generalizations. While private property exists this term is meaningless. The 'national wealth' of England is very great and yet the English people are the poorest in the world. One should either dismiss the term 'national wealth' completely or we should accept such premises as would give it some meaning. The same criticism may be made of terms like 'national economy' and 'political or public economy'. As things are at present the science of economics should be called '*private* economy' since its public connexions exist only for the sake of private property.

Commerce

If private property exists then trade inevitably follows. Commerce, like everything else in a society dominated by private property, must become a direct source of gain for the trader.

This means that everyone must try to sell as dear as possible and to buy as cheaply as possible. So whenever buying and selling occurs two men with diametrically opposed interests confront each other. The confrontation is decidedly antagonistic since each knows the intentions of the other. Each knows that the interests of the other fellow are opposed to his own interests. Hence there is mutual distrust. And this mistrust is justified. It is the application of immoral means to attain an immoral end. The first maxim of trade is the concealment of everything that might reduce the value of the article in question. In commerce one is allowed to take the utmost advantage of the ignorance and the trust of the opposing party. One may bestow fictitious qualities on a commodity that one wishes to sell. In other words trade is legalized fraud. Actual trading practices conform with this theory and any truthful merchant will bear this out.

The mercantile system had a certain artless Catholic candour and did not in the least try to hide the immoral nature of trade. It openly paraded its mean avarice. The mutually-hostile attitude of the nations in the eighteenth century, loathsome envy and commercial jealousy were all the logical consequences of trade as such. Public opinion had not yet become humanized. So no attempt was made to hide things which resulted from the inhuman hostile nature of trade itself.

But when Adam Smith – the *economic Luther* – criticized established economic theories, things had changed considerably. The century had been humanized: reason had asserted itself: morality began to claim its eternal rights. Progressive ideas could not be squared with extorted commercial treaties, with trade wars or with the surly isolation of the nations of the world. Protestant hypocrisy replaced Catholic candour. Adam Smith proved that humanity, too, was rooted in the very nature of commerce. He showed that trade – instead of being 'the most fertile source of discord and animosity' – must become a 'bond of union and friendship among nations as among individuals'. He argued that by and large it lay in the nature of things for trade to be profitable to *all* parties concerned.

Adam Smith was right to eulogize trade as humane. There is nothing absolutely immoral in the world. Trade, too, has an aspect wherein it pays homage to morality and humanity. But what homage! The law of force and the open highway robbery of the Middle Ages became humanized when they passed over into trade. Commerce became humanized when mercantilism replaced the phase when the export of money was forbidden. Then the mercantile system itself was humanized. Naturally it is in the interest of the trader to be on good terms with the one from whom he buys cheap as well as with the other to whom he sells dear. A nation therefore acts very imprudently if it fosters feelings of animosity in nations with which it is engaged in commerce. Friendly trade means more profitable trade. And that is the humanity of commerce. This hypocritical way of misusing morality for immoral purposes is the pride of the Free Trade system.

'Have we not overthrown the barbarism of the monopolies?' exclaim the hypocrites. 'Have we not carried civilization to distant parts of the world?' 'Have we not brought about the fraternization of the peoples and reduced the number of wars?' Of course you have done all this. But *how* have you done it? You have destroyed small monopolies so that property – the *one* great basic monopoly – may function more freely. You have brought civilization to the ends of the earth so as to subject new lands to your vile avarice. You have accomplished the fraternization of the peoples – but it is the fraternization of thieves. You have reduced the number of wars so as to earn bigger profits in peacetime and so as to intensify to the utmost the enmity between individuals – the ignominious war of competition! When have you done anything from purely humanitarian motives? When have you ever acted in conformity with the principle that there is no clash between the interests of the individual and the interests of society as a whole? When have you acted morally except when such action coincides with your own interests? When have you acted morally without harbouring at the back of your mind immoral and egotistical motives? Liberal economics has done its best to make enmity universal. By dissolving nationalities it has transformed mankind into a horde of ravenous beasts – for what else are competitors? And these beasts devour one another just *because* each has interests which are identical with all the others. After this preparatory work there remained but one step to take before the goal was finally reached. This was the dissolution of the family.

To accomplish this, modern political economy has been able to make use of its own beautiful invention – the factory system. The last vestige of common interests, the community of possessions held by the family, is being undermined by the factory system and – at least here in England – is already in the process of dissolution. It is a common practice for children as soon as they are able to work – i.e. as soon as they reach the age of nine – to spend their wages themselves and to look upon their parental home as a mere boarding house. How can it be otherwise? What else can result from the separation of interests that is the basis of the Free Trade system? Once a principle is set in motion it works by its own impetus through all its consequences whether the economists like it or not.

The economist, however, does not know himself what cause he serves. He does not realize that despite all his egotistical reasoning he nevertheless is a link in the chain of the universal progress of mankind. He does not know that by dissolving all sectional interests he merely paves the way for the great transformation to which the century is moving – the reconciliation of mankind with nature and with itself.

Value

The next category established by trade is *value*. There is no quarrel between the modern economists and their mercantilist predecessors over value – just as there is none over all the other categories – because the monopolists are so obsessed with getting rich that they have no time to bother about categories. All arguments concerning these matters stem from the modern economists.

The economist who lives by antitheses of course has a *double* value – abstract (i.e. 'real') value and exchange value. There was a long dispute concerning the nature of real value between the English economists (who defined real value as the costs of production) and the French economist Say (who measured real value by the utility of a commodity). The dispute was not settled in the early part of the century and eventually it became dormant without a decision having been reached. In fact the economists cannot decide anything.

The English economists – particularly MacCulloch and Ricardo – argue that the abstract value of any commodity is determined by the costs of production. They say that the 'exchangeable value'[1] of a commodity – i.e. its value in trade – is something quite different. Why are the costs of production the measure of value? Because no one would normally sell a product for less than it cost him to make – leaving on one side any question of competition. But how does 'selling' come into the picture? It is 'abstract value' that we are discussing, not *trade* value. So trade turns up again and we were specifically supposed to leave it aside! And what trade! A trade in which competition is to be ignored. Yet competition is a cardinal factor in commerce. So we have first an 'abstract value' and then an 'abstract trade' – i.e. a trade without competition. We might as well have a man without a body or a thought without a brain. And does the economist never stop to think that as soon as competition is left out of account there is no guarantee at all that the producer will sell his commodity just at the cost of production. What a muddle!

Let us suppose for a moment that the economist is right. Imagine someone making an utterly useless article with great exertion and at great expense. And suppose that no one wants this article. Do production costs represent the 'value' of such a commodity? 'Of course not', says the economist. 'Who will want to buy it?' So we suddenly have both Say's despised utility but (with the idea of buying) competition as well. It cannot be done. The economist cannot for one moment stick to his own abstractions. Theoretical 'value' and its determination by costs of production is simply an abstraction and nothing more.

Once more let us imagine for a moment that the economist is right. If so how will he determine the costs of production without taking competition into account? When we come to examine the

1. ['Exchangeable value' in English in the original.]

costs of production we shall see that these costs, too, are based on competition so that it is again clear that the economist cannot substantiate his claims.

If we turn to Say we find the same abstraction. The utility of a commodity is something purely subjective which cannot be decided with absolute certainty. And anyhow 'utility' cannot be decided so long as the economist still deals with antitheses. According to Say's theory, necessities ought to be more valuable than luxuries. So long as private property exists the only possible way of arriving at a more or less objective (and apparently general) decision on the utility of a commodity is by taking competition into account. Yet competition is precisely the thing which is not taken into account. Once the existence of competition is accepted production costs must also be considered since no one will sell an article for less than it has cost him to produce. Here too the one side of the argument passes over involuntarily into the other.

Let us try to clear up the confusion. The value of an article includes both the factors which the contending economists have so rudely and so unsuccessfully attempted to separate. Value is the relation of production costs to utility. The first conception of 'value' is used when a person decides whether he should make an article or not. He considers whether the utility of the article will balance the cost of making it. Only then can we apply the notion of 'value' to 'exchange'. If two articles cost exactly the same to produce, it is utility that finally decides which is the more valuable.

Utility is the only just basis of exchange, but who is to decide the utility of an article? If it is decided by the mere opinion of the buyer and seller then *one* of them will be cheated. Or is utility to be regarded as some quality inherent in the article and not apparent to the buyer or the seller? If so then the exchange involves coercion and both the buyer and the seller consider that they have been cheated. Only by getting rid of private property can we get rid of the opposition between the real inherent utility of an article and the determination of that utility. Only in that way can one overcome the opposition between the determination of utility and the freedom of the buyer and the seller. Once we have got rid of private property there can no longer be any question of buying and selling as they exist today.

How do matters stand at present? We have seen how the idea of value has been violently torn asunder and how the two parts are each substituted for the whole. Production costs – distorted from the outset by competition – are supposed to be 'value' itself. Similarly mere subjective 'utility' – and no other kind of utility can exist at this stage – is supposed to be 'value'. To strengthen these lame definitions we must, in both cases, resort to the idea of competition. The best of it is that English economists consider that competition represents utility (not production costs) while Say holds exactly the opposite view. What kind of utility and what kind of production costs are they talking about? Their 'utility' depends on chance or fashion or the whim of the rich, while, their 'production costs' fluctuate with the fortuitous relationship of supply and demand.

The difference between 'real value' and 'exchange value' is based on the fact that the value of an article is different from the so-called 'equivalent' given for it in commerce. And that means that the 'equivalent' is not an equivalent at all. What is called the 'equivalent' is really the 'price' of an article and if economists were honest they would refer to 'exchange value' as 'price'. The economists, however, have to keep up some sort of pretence that 'price' is somehow bound up with 'value'. If they did anything else the immorality of commerce would become too obvious. It is quite correct – and it is a fundamental law of private property – that *price* is determined by the reciprocal action of production costs and competition. This purely empirical law was the first to be discovered by the economists. From this law the economists then abstracted 'real value'. And 'real value' was the price of an article when competition was in a state of equilibrium. It was the price when demand and supply covered each other. What is left are the costs of production. And economists proceed to call these costs 'real value'. In fact the costs of production are merely the factor which determines the price of an article. So everything in economics is turned upside down. Value is made *dependent* upon the price whereas it is really the *origin* of price. As Feuerbach has observed, this inversion is the essence of abstraction.

Factors of Production

Economists state that there are three elements in the cost of producing an article. They are (i) the rent of the piece of land required to produce the raw material, (ii) the capital with its profit, and (iii) the wages of the labour required for production and manufacture. It is obvious two of these elements – capital and labour – are identical since the economists themselves confess that capital is 'stored up labour'. So we are left with only two elements – land (provided by nature) and human labour (which includes capital). But there is a third element that economists ignore. That is the mental element of thought and invention which is different from the physical element of sheer labour. Why should the economists bother about the spirit of invention? Have not all inventions come flying to the economists without any effort on their part? Has *one single* invention ever cost the economists a penny? So why should the economists bother about inventions in their calculation of the costs of producing an article? Economists regard land, capital and labour as the conditions of wealth and that is all. Science is no concern of the economists. What does it matter to the economists that they have received the gifts of science through the work of men like Berthollet, Davy, Liebig, Watt and Cartwright? And have not the advances in science and the inventions of these men greatly increased production? The economists do not know how to calculate such things. Scientific progress goes beyond the statistics of the economists. But if society were organized in a rational manner and if we could overcome the antagonism between the different interests discussed by economists the mental factor would certainly be accepted as an element in the costs of production. In this connexion it is certainly gratifying to know that the promotion of science brings its natural reward. We know that a single achievement of science such as James Watt's steam engine has brought more wealth to the world in the first fifty years of its existence than the world has spent on the promotion of science since the beginning of time.

We have shown that there are two factors which influence production – nature and man. And man's contribution is both mental and physical, so we can now return to the economists and heir costs of production.

Rent

Economists argue that anything which cannot be manufactured has no value. This proposition will be examined more closely later on. If 'price' is substituted for 'value' the statement is valid in a society based upon private property. If land were as easily available as air no one would pay rent. In fact land is limited in extent so that a rent has to be paid for a piece of monopolized land. Alternatively a piece of land can be bought outright. After we have been enlightened in this way about the origin of ground rent it is very strange to be told by economists that the rent of land is the difference between the yield from the rented land and the yield from the worst land worth cultivating at all. It is well known that this definition of rent was first fully developed by Ricardo. This definition is doubtless correct in practice if one assumes that a fall in demand has an *immediate* effect upon rent and at once puts a corresponding amount of the worst land out of cultivation. Since this does not happen Ricardo's definition is inadequate. Moreover Ricardo's definition does not explain the cause of rent and must be dismissed for that reason alone. In opposition to this definition Colonel T. P. Thompson, the champion of the Anti-Corn Law League, revived Adam Smith's definition of rent and amplified it. According to Thompson rent is the relation between the competition of those striving for the use of the land and the limited quantity of available land. Here at least is a return to the origin of rent. But this explanation fails to take into account the varying fertility of the soil, just as Ricardo's explanation leaves out competition.

So again we have two biased – and consequently imperfect – definitions. As with 'value' so with 'rent' we shall have to bring the two definitions together so as to find the correct definition. And our definition will come from an examination of the development of rent itself. Rent is the relation between nature and man. Nature contributes the productivity of the soil (and this consists of *natural* fertility and *human* improvements) while man contributes competition. Economists may shake their heads over this definition but they will disavow to their horror that it embraces everything relevant to this problem.

The *landowner* is the merchant. The landowner is a robber when he exploits for his own benefit the growth of population which intensifies competition and increases the value of his estate. The landowner is a thief because he turns to his personal advance something that he has not done himself. He practises robbery both when he *leases his land* and when he later seizes for himself the improvements made by his tenant. This is the secret of the ever increasing wealth of the great landowners.

We are not responsible for enunciating the principles which brand as robbery the landowner's method of making money. These principles are that everybody has a right to the product of his labour and that no one shall reap what he has not sown. And the principles are imperfect since the first excludes the duty of feeding children while the second deprives each generation of the right to live since each generation starts with what it inherits from the last generation. These principles are implications of private property. One must either carry out the principles or abandon private property.

Indeed the original act of appropriating the land is justified by the assertion of the still earlier *common* right to land. So wherever we turn private property leads us into contradictions.

The earth is the first condition of our existence. To make it an object of trade was the last step towards making human beings an object of trade. To buy and sell land is an immorality surpassed only by the immorality of selling oneself into slavery. The original appropriation of land meant that a few people monopolized the earth and excluded other people from using it. But the original act of appropriation yields nothing in immorality to the subsequent trade in land.

If we abandon private property we can discover the rational idea which lies at the root of rent. The 'value' of the land – now divorced from it as 'rent' – would then revert to the land itself. This 'value' (measured by the productivity of equal areas of land subjected to equal applications of labour) should be included as part of the cost of production when determining the value of products. Like rent it is the relation of productivity to competition. And we shall discuss the nature of *real* competition later.

Our analysis of the writings of economists has shown that capital and labour were originally identical; that in the process of production capital (itself the result of labour) is immediately transformed into the material used by labour; and that the temporary separation of capital from labour immediately gives way to the unity of capital and labour. Nevertheless economists persist in separating capital from labour and fail to recognize their unity except by defining capital as 'stored up labour'. This separation of capital from labour is due to the existence of private property. It is simply the inner dichotomy of labour which represents this separation and arises out of it. Once this separation has been accomplished capital is again divided into (i) the original capital, and (ii) profit or the increment which capital receives in the process of production. In practice, however, the two types of capital are immediately lumped together again and are once more set to work together. Indeed even profit is divided into (i) interest, and (ii) profit proper. The absurdity of these subdivisions is carried to extreme limits in the case of interest. It is quite obvious that loans at interest are immoral. To receive money by simply lending money and without doing any work is immoral but it is inherent in private property. The immorality of this practice has long ago been recognized by the ordinary unsophisticated man in the street and in such matters he is usually right. All these minute subdivisions stem from the original separation of capital and labour. They stem also from the culmination of this separation which is the division of mankind into capitalists and workers. Every day this division becomes more acute. And we shall show later that the division between capitalists and workers *must* become even greater in the future. In the final analysis this division between capital and labour – like the separation of labour from capital – is an impossibility. No one can determine precisely the exact share that land, capital and labour have in the production of any particular article. The three factors of production cannot be measured and compared. The land creates the raw material – but only with the help of both capital and labour. Capital presupposes land and labour. Labour, in turn, presupposes *at least* land and usually capital as well. The functions of these three factors of production are quite different and cannot be measured by inventing a fourth factor as a common denominator. So, under existing conditions, there is no common measure by which we can allocate the proceeds of land, capital and labour. The decision concerning the allocation is actually made by competition which is an entirely alien and fortuitous measure. Competition represents the cunning power which the strong can exercise over the weak. Rent implies competition. Profit on capital is determined entirely by competition. And the way in which wages are fixed will be discussed later.

If private property is abandoned all these unnatural divisions disappear. The difference between interest and profit vanishes. So does the difference between capital and labour. The significance of profit is reduced to the extent to which capital determines the costs of production. Profit thus remains inherent in capital just as capital itself reverts to its original unity with labour.

Labour

Labour is the main factor in production. Economists call it the 'source of wealth' yet it comes off badly in their theories. Just as capital was previously separated from labour so now labour is divided again. The product of labour is separated from labour as wages. And wages are determined by competition. As we have seen there is no objective standard by which labour's share in producing an article can be determined. If private property is abolished we get rid of this unnatural division. Labour then becomes its own reward. The true significance of wages comes to light. We are in a position to appreciate the significance of labour in determining the cost of making an article.

Private Property and Competition

So long as private property exists everything is regulated by competition. Economists worship competition. It is their dearest daughter whom they ceaselessly caress – and beware of her Medusa's head!

When private property was established the production of

commodities was divided into the 'natural' aspect and the 'human aspect'. It was divided into land (which is sterile unless fertilized by man) and human activity (which cannot exist without land to work on). We have seen how human activity itself was divided into capital and labour which confronted each other as enemies. So the three elements of production are antagonistic to each other instead of giving each other material support. To make matters worse the existence of private property has led to the sub-division of all the factors of production. One landed estate confronts another: one piece of capital confronts another: one unit of the labour force confronts another. And this happens simply because private property isolates everyone in the crudest fashion in spite of the fact that everyone really has the same interests as his neighbour. The immorality of the conditions in which men now find themselves is consummated in this clash of interests which should be identical. This consummation is competition.

Monopoly is the opposite of *competition*. Monopoly was the war cry of the mercantilists while competition is the battle cry of the liberal economists. Once more we have an antithesis which is quite unreal. Every competitor – worker, capitalist or landowner – *must* wish to be in the position to enjoy the fruits of monopoly. Each group of competitors, however small, wants to have a monopoly to the exclusion of all other competitors. Self-interest, the root of all competition, itself breeds the desire for monopoly. Competition therefore develops into monopoly. On the other hand, monopoly cannot hold back the tide of competition. Monopoly actually breeds competition. A prohibition of imports or a high tariff positively breed competition in the shape of smuggling. The contradiction inherent in competition is just the same as the contradiction inherent in private property. It is in the interest of each individual to possess everything but it is in the interest of society that everybody should possess an equal amount. The interests of society and the interests of the individual are in complete opposition. The contradiction inherent in competition is that each individual must desire to have the monopoly whilst society as a whole is bound to lose by monopoly and must therefore desire to remove it. Competition actually presupposes the existence of one monopoly. This is the monopoly of land. And here the hypocrisy of the liberals is once more evident. So long as there is a monopoly of property the possession of other monopolies is equally justified. After all, once a monopoly is established it too is invested with the rights of property. It is indeed a half-hearted measure to attack the little monopolies and to leave untouched the basic monopoly of private property! We have already referred to the principle enunciated by economists that everything which has a value is capable of being monopolized. This means that anything capable of monopoly can be subject to competition. This completely justifies our assertion that competition presupposes monopoly.

The law of competition is that supply and demand always try to balance each other – and therefore never do so. Supply and demand are torn apart and transformed into complete opposites. Supply always follows close on the heels of demand but supply never quite covers demand. Supply is always either a little too big or a little too small. It never corresponds exactly to demand. In the present unconscious condition of mankind no one knows precisely the nature of either supply or demand. If demand exceeds supply then the price of the commodity rises with the result that supply is stimulated to some extent. As soon as additional supplies reach the market there is a fall in prices. Should supply exceed demand then a significant fall in prices will take place, and this will once more stimulate demand. This process continues indefinitely and it is a permanently unhealthy state of affairs. It is a state of continual fluctuation which never achieves equilibrium. Economists think that this is a marvellous law – this constant balancing where what is gained on the swings is lost on the roundabouts. Economists regard this law as their chief glory. They cannot see enough of it and they study it in all its possible and impossible applications.

It is obvious that this is a purely natural law and not a law of the mind. It is a law which produces revolution. Economists come along with this wonderful law of supply and demand and prove that 'one can never produce too much'. Practice replies with trade crises which reappear as regularly as the comets. We now have a slump every five to seven years. For the last eight years these trade crises have come just as regularly as the great plagues did in the past. And they have brought in their train more misery and immorality than the plagues.[1] Of course these commercial crises amply confirm the law of supply and demand. But the confirmation is different from what the economists would have us believe. What are we to think of a law that can assert itself only through periodic slumps? It is just a natural law based upon the unconsciousness of those affected by it. The fluctuations of competition and the tendency to periodic slumps would disappear if the producers knew how much the consumers wanted and were then able to organize output and share the products among themselves. If we were to act like rational beings and produce commodities accordingly – instead of behaving like dispersed atoms unconscious of our neighbours – all the artificial and untenable antitheses of the economists would disappear. But commercial crises will remain so long as commodities are produced as at present in a way which leaves so much to the mercy of chance. Every new crisis must be more serious and more universal than the last. Every fresh slump must ruin more small capitalists and increase the workers who live only by their labour. This will increase the number of the unemployed and this is the main problem that worries economists. In the end commercial crises will lead to a social revolution far beyond the comprehension of the economists with their scholastic wisdom.

The perpetual fluctuation of prices created by competition completely deprives trade of its last vestige of morality. *Value* is no longer even mentioned. Economists appear to attach great importance to value. They honour the abstraction of 'value' in money form by giving it an independent existence of its own. Yet the same economic system destroys the inherent value of everything by competition. The relative value of different commodities is changed every day and even every hour by competition. Can there be any possibility of an exchange based on a moral foundation in this whirlpool? When prices are continually fluctuating everybody *must* try to hit upon the most favourable

1. John Wade, *History of the Middle and Working Classes* (third edition, London 1835), p. 211.

moment to buy and sell. Everybody must become a speculator who reaps what he has not sown. Everybody must try to enrich himself at the expense of others or else rely upon chance to win for him. The speculator always gambles on disasters – particularly on bad harvests. He tries to extract a profit from every disaster – such as the New York fire. The climax of this sort of immorality is the speculation that takes place on the stock exchange where mankind is debased to gratify the avarice of the calculating and gambling speculator. 'Honest' and 'respectable' merchants have no cause to adopt a pharisaical attitude towards gambling on the stock exchange and to exclaim 'I thank thee, O Lord . . .', etc. They are as bad as those who speculate in stocks and shares. The 'honest' merchants speculate just as much as the stock exchange gamblers. Competition compels them to do so whether they like it or not. Their trading activities are just as immoral as speculating on the stock exchange.

True competition may be defined as the relationship between the power of consumption to the power of production. In a world worthy of mankind *this* would be the only kind of competition. The community will have to calculate what it can produce with the means at its disposal. Then, in the light of the relationship of this productive power to the mass of the consumers, it will determine how far it has to raise or to lower production. It will have to decide how far luxury can be allowed and to what extent luxury must be curtailed. My readers should consult the works of the English Socialists and some of the writings of Fourier so that they can learn how to pass a correct judgement on the relationship between supply and demand and on the increase in productive power that can be anticipated from regulating the economic affairs of society in a rational manner. Under such conditions subjective competition – the contest of capital against capital and of labour against labour – will be reduced to the spirit of emulation which is part of human nature. So far only Fourier has tried to develop this idea. When subjective competition is introduced the rivalry of opposing interests will be conducted in a proper and a rational manner.

The struggle of capital against capital, labour against labour, and land against land drives production to a fever pitch at which production turns all natural and rational relations upside down. No capital can survive competition unless it is brought to the highest pitch of activity. No landed estate can be profitably cultivated if it does not continuously increase its productive power. No worker can hold his own against his competitors if he does not devote all his powers to his work. Once a person has become involved in the struggle of competition he can stand the strain only if he exerts his powers to the utmost and gives up every truly human purpose. Over-exertion inevitably leads to collapse. A time comes when the fluctuation of competition is small and a state of equilibrium is reached between supply and demand and between production and consumption. At this stage there is so much superfluous productive power available that the great mass of people has nothing to live on. People starve from sheer abundance. England has been in this crazy position for some considerable time. As an inevitable consequence of this living absurdity production is subject to still greater fluctuations than before. This is followed by the alternation of boom and crisis – over production and slump. Economists have never been able to explain this crazy situation. In an effort to offer some explanation economists have invented the theory of population. But this is just as senseless. Indeed the theory of population is even more stupid than the contradiction of wealth and poverty existing side by side. Economists *cannot afford* to accept the truth. They cannot afford to admit that the contradiction of wealth and poverty is simply the consequence of competition. Any such admission would result in the total collapse of their theories.

We can easily explain the matter. Mankind's productive powers are enormous. The productivity of the land can be increased *ad infinitum* by the application of capital, labour and scientific knowledge. According to the oldest economists and statisticians[1] Great Britain could in ten years produce enough wheat to feed a population six times as great as it is at present. Capital increases every day. The productive power of the labour force expands with the growth of population. Every day new scientific knowledge increasingly subjects the power of nature to mankind's needs. This immense productive capacity – if handled

1. A. Alison, *The Principles of Population . . .* (2 vols, 1840).

rationally in everybody's interests – would soon reduce to a minimum the work which mankind has to perform. The same thing happens when competition is rampant. But it takes place within a context of antitheses. One antithesis is that while some land is very well cultivated other land lies barren. In Great Britain and Ireland twenty million acres of good land lie uncultivated. Some capital circulates with fantastic rapidity while other capital does not circulate at all. Some men work between fourteen and sixteen hours a day while others starve for want of a job. These are contrasts which occur at the same moment in time. But there are other contrasts in events which take place one after the other. Today trade may flourish. There is a considerable demand for goods. Capital circulates with miraculous speed. Farming, too, is flourishing. The workers not merely enjoy full employment but work till they drop. Tomorrow a slump occurs. It is no longer worth while to farm the land. Acres of land are no longer cultivated. The flow of capital comes to an abrupt end. A great many workers are unemployed. The whole country suffers from surplus wealth and surplus population.

Economists cannot accept that our analysis is correct. To do so they would have to give up their theories concerning competition. They would have to recognize the inadequacy of their contrasts between production and consumption and between surplus population and surplus wealth. But there are facts which even economists cannot ignore. And to try to relate theory and fact the theory of population was invented.

The Theory of Population

It was Malthus who first put forward the theory of population. According to this theory population always presses upon the means of subsistence. Population increases in proportion to the growth of output. The inherent tendency of population to expand in excess of the available food is the root of all misery and vice. When there are too many people their numbers must somehow be reduced. They must either be killed or allowed to starve. But when this has happened the population again expands and the old misery begins all over again. Moreover this is a universal experience. It happens in both civilized and primitive societies.

In Australia, with a population density of only one per square mile, savages suffer just as much from over-population as the more civilized inhabitants of England. To take the argument to its logical conclusion one would have to say that the world was already over-populated when only one man lived on it. Malthus's theory implied that since it is the poor who are the surplus population nothing should be done for them except to make their starvation as easy as possible. The poor must be told that this cannot be helped and that their only hope is to reduce the size of their families to the absolute minimum. If this fails the best course is to establish a state institution for the painless killing of the children of the poor, such as 'Marcus' suggests.[1] Each working class family would be allowed to have two and a half children and any excess beyond this limit would be painlessly killed. Charity to the poor would be a crime since this would encourage the growth of the surplus population. Indeed it would be a good idea to declare poverty to be a crime and to turn workhouses into prisons. Indeed this has already happened in England as a result of the new 'liberal' Poor Law. It is true that Malthus's theory hardly conforms with the biblical doctrine of the perfection of God and of his creation but 'it is a poor refutation to enlist the Bible against facts'.

Should I continue to elaborate this vile and infamous theory, this blasphemy against nature and mankind? Should I pursue its consequences any further? This is surely the climax of the immorality of the economists. How insignificant are all the wars and horrors of the system of monopoly compared with this theory! Yet Malthus's theory is the keystone of the liberal system of Free Trade. The collapse of the theory of population would lead to the collapse of the entire edifice of liberal economics. This theory proves that competition is the root cause of misery, poverty and crime. Who now will dare to support it?

In his book on *The Principles of Population* Alison has shaken Malthus's theory. Alison has drawn attention to the productive powers of the soil. He has contradicted Malthus's doctrine by

1. [*An Essay on Populousness* by 'Marcus' was printed by the author in 1838 for private circulation. It obtained wider circulation when it was reprinted under the title *The Book of Murder* (1839). It is not possible to say whether 'Marcus' was a crank who expected to be taken seriously or a satirist.]

showing that each adult can produce more than he himself needs. This is self-evident for if this were not true then there could be no increase in population at all. Mankind would cease to exist, for those who were still growing up would get nothing to eat. But Alison does not go to the root of the matter and eventually he comes to the same conclusion as Malthus. Although Alison proves that Malthus's principle is wrong he cannot deny the facts that have led Malthus to propound his theory.

Malthus examined the problem in so biased a way that he failed to see the connexion between surplus population (or a surplus labour force) and surplus wealth, surplus capital and surplus landed property. The population is too large only when the productive power of the country as a whole is too large. The condition of every over-populated country – particularly England – since the time when Malthus wrote makes this abundantly clear. These were the facts which Malthus should have considered. Had he done so he must have reached the correct conclusion. In fact Malthus simply selected one isolated fact and ignored the other facts and this was why he arrived at such a crazy conclusion. Malthus's second mistake was to confuse means of subsistence with means of employment. Malthus can be praised for correctly establishing certain principles. He saw that population always presses on the means of employment. He realized that the size of the population varies with the number of people who can be employed. He saw that the size of the labour force has been regulated by the law of competition and is therefore exposed to periodic fluctuations and crises. But the means of employment are not the means of subsistence. The means of employment *eventually* expand owing to the increase of machine power and capital. But the means of subsistence increase *at once* as soon as there is an increase – however slight – in the power of production. And here a new contradiction in economics comes to light. The 'demand' that economists talk about is not a real demand and the 'consumption' that they talk about is an artificial consumption. The economists limit demand to the demands made by consumers who have an equivalent to offer for what they receive. But if it is true that every adult produces more than he can consume and that children are like trees which give an abundant return for what has been invested in them, then it follows that every worker should be able to produce far more than he needs. Consequently the community should be delighted to provide the worker with everything that he requires. And the community should look upon a large family as a welcome gift. But economists, with their sordid outlook, can think only of an equivalent that they can receive in hard cash. The economists are so involved in their antitheses that they ignore the most obvious facts as well as the soundest scientific principles.

We destroy the contradiction simply by transcending it. If the interests now opposed to each other are reconciled, the opposition between surplus population and surplus wealth disappears. The miraculous fact – more miraculous than all the miracles of all the religions put together – that a nation has to starve from sheer wealth and plenty disappears. And the crazy assertion that the earth lacks the power to feed mankind also disappears. What we have asserted is the pinnacle of Christianity. We could prove that our economic theories are essentially Christian and I shall do so in due course. Malthus's theory may be regarded as the economic aspect of the religious dogma concerning the contradiction of spiritual values and nature – and the consequent corruption of both. As far as religion is concerned the contradiction has been resolved long ago. I hope that I have shown that in the sphere of economics the contradiction is just as erroneous. I shall not be satisfied with any defence of Malthus's theory that does not from the outset explain to me – on the basis of its own principles – how a people can starve from sheer plenty. And such an assertion must be brought into harmony with reason and with the facts.

At the same time Malthus's theory has taken us a step further forward. Thanks to this theory – thanks to modern economics as a whole – our attention has been called to the productive power of the earth and of mankind. Once this economic despair has been overcome we have been secured for ever against the fear of over-population. From this theory we derive the most powerful economic arguments for a social transformation. Even if Malthus were completely right this transformation would have to be undertaken. Only this transformation – and the education of the masses which it alone can provide – will make possible that 'moral restraint' which Malthus presents as the most effective and the easiest remedy for over-population. Through Malthus's theory we have come to know that man's dependence upon competition is indeed his deepest degradation. The theory has shown us how in the last instance private property has turned man into a commodity. And the production and destruction of that commodity depends solely on demand. The theory has shown how competition has slaughtered – and every day continues to slaughter – millions of men. All this drives us to the conclusion that we must get rid of this degradation of mankind by abolishing private property, competition and opposing economic interests.

We revert to the relation of productive power to population in the hope of finally removing the universal fear of over-population. According to Malthus population increases in geometrical progression while the productive power of the land increases only in an arithmetical progress. Is this terrifying difference correct? Who has proved that the productivity of land increases in an arithmetical progression? The amount of land is limited. That is agreed. The labour force which can be used on this land increases as the population grows. Let us even assume that the increase in the yield of crops brought about by the expansion of the labour force does not always rise in proportion to the increased labour force. Even so there is another factor to be considered. This is the advance of scientific knowledge. And this of course is ignored by the economists. The progress of scientific knowledge is as unceasing and at least as rapid as the growth of population. Consider the progress made in agriculture in this century by the work of only two men – Sir Humphry Davy and Justus Liebig! Scientific knowledge is extended at least as much as any growth in population. Population grows in proportion to the size of the last generation. Scientific knowledge advances in proportion to the knowledge bequeathed to it by the previous generation. And this progress, under the most ordinary conditions, is also in geometrical progression. What is impossible to science? It is absurd to talk about over-population when 'there is enough waste land in the valley of the Mississippi for the whole population of Europe to be transplanted there'.[1] It is absurd to talk of over-population so long as only one third of the earth can be considered cultivated and so long as the production of that third itself can be raised six-fold and more by the application of improvements which are already known.

Conclusion

We have seen that competition sets capital against capital, labour against labour, landed property against landed property. And it also sets each of them against the other two. In such a struggle it is the stronger who wins. To predict the outcome of the struggle the strength of the contestants must be investigated. At first land and capital are more powerful than labour since the worker has to work in order to live while the landowner can live on his rents, and the capitalist can live on his interest. If necessary the capitalist can live on his capital or on capitalized property in land. Consequently labour secures only the very barest necessities – the mere means of subsistence – while the lion's share of what is produced falls to capital and landed property. Moreover the stronger worker drives the weaker worker out of the market just as larger capital drives out smaller capital and the larger landed properties drive out the smaller landed properties. This theoretical conclusion is confirmed by what actually happens. It is well known that large manufacturers and merchants enjoy great advantages over their smaller rivals and that big landowners enjoy great advantages over smallholders who are cultivating only a single acre. The result is that, under normal conditions, large capital and large landed property swallow small capital and small landed property. This leads to the concentration of property. When there are depressions in industry and agriculture this process of concentration is greatly accelerated. Large properties increase much more rapidly than small properties because the expenses of running large properties are proportionately smaller than the cost of running small properties. . . . The middle classes must increasingly disappear until the world is divided into millionaires and paupers and into large landowners and poor farm labourers. This process cannot be stopped by any

1. A. Alison, op. cit., p. 548.

laws or by any attempts to split up landed or industrial properties. The process must continue unless social conditions are completely changed by fusing opposing interests and by abolishing private property.

Free competition – the key to modern economic theory – is an impossibility. Monopoly at least tried to protect the consumer against shoddy goods even if in fact it could not do so. The abolition of monopoly, however, throws the door wide open to shoddy products. It has been argued that competition has its own remedy since no one will buy shoddy goods. But that implies that every consumer has an expert knowledge about everything put up for sale. This is clearly impossible. Monopoly is therefore essential and in fact many articles are produced under conditions of monopoly. Apothecaries, for example, *must* have a monopoly. Money, the most important commodity, needs a monopoly most of all. Whenever money has ceased to be a state monopoly there has been a commercial crisis. English economists – Dr Wade among them – agree that the issuing of money must be a state monopoly. But even a state monopoly is no protection against counterfeit money. One can argue in favour of monopoly or free competition without coming to a satisfactory conclusion. Monopoly produces competition while competition in its turn leads to monopoly. So monopoly and competition must be abolished by introducing a new principle which will embrace both of them.

Competition has penetrated into all human relationships and it has completed human bondage in all its aspects. Competition is the great mainspring which repeatedly jerks our dying social order – or rather disorder. But with each new effort competition also saps a part of the waning strength of our social system. Anyone who has any knowledge of the statistics of crime must have been struck by the peculiar regularity with which crime advances year after year. Moreover certain causes regularly produce certain crimes. The extension of the factory system is always followed by an increase in crime. Year by year it is possible to predict absolutely accurately for any large town or district the number of arrests, the number of criminal cases, and the number of murders, robberies and petty thefts. Such predictions have been made frequently in England. This regularity proves that even crime is subject to competition. It shows that society creates a *demand* for crime which is met by a corresponding *supply*. It shows that the gap created by the arrest, transportation or execution of a certain number of criminals is promptly filled by other criminals – just as every gap in population is at once filled by new arrivals. Uniformity in statistics of crime proves that crime presses on the means of punishment just as the people press upon the means of employment. I leave my readers to decide whether it is just to punish criminals under these circumstances.... I am merely concerned to demonstrate the extension of competition into the moral sphere and to show to what deep degradation man has been brought by the institution of private property.

In the struggle of capital and land against labour the first two factors enjoy yet another advantage over labour. This is the assistance of science. Under present conditions technical knowledge is directed against labour. Nearly all mechanical inventions, for example, have been stimulated by a shortage of labour. This is certainly true of the cotton spinning machines invented by Hargreaves, Crompton and Arkwright. Every period of intense demand for labour has led to an invention which has considerably increased the productivity of labour. In this way the demand for human labour has been reduced. The history of England from 1770 onwards proves this conclusively. The self-acting mule – the last invention in cotton spinning – was stimulated simply by the demand for labour and high wages. The self-actor halved the amount of hand-labour that was required. It crushed a projected combination of the workers against the factory owners. It destroyed the last vestige of strength which had enabled the workers to hold out in their unequal struggle against the capitalists.[1] Economists argue that in the long run new machinery benefits the workers. They say that machinery reduces costs, creates large new markets, and ultimately finds new jobs for unemployed workers. This is all very well but the economists forget that the output of the labour force is regulated by competition. Consequently the labour force is always pressing on the

1. Andrew Ure, *Philosophy of Manufactures*, pp. 366 et seq.

means of employment. When the advantages which come from new machinery are due to come into operation a surplus of competitors for jobs is already waiting for the new opportunities for employment. And so the alleged advantages derived by the workers from new machines are illusory. The disadvantages are far from illusory. Owing to the introduction of new machines half the workers lose their jobs and the other half receive lower wages. Moreover the economists forget that the division of labour is very highly developed in our civilization. Today a worker can earn a living only if he can use one particular machine for one particular operation. It is almost invariably impossible for an adult to change over from one kind of machine to a newly invented machine.

In turning my attention to the effects of machinery upon the workers I am brought to a consideration of the factory system. But this is not directly relevant to the problems that I have discussed in this essay. I have neither the time nor the inclination to pursue the matter further at the moment. I hope, however, to have an early opportunity to describe the factory system in detail and to expose its despicable immorality. And I shall at the same time mercilessly expose the hypocrisy of the economists which appears in all its glitter in the factory system.[1]

2. Review of *Das Kapital*, 1868[2]

(1)

As long as capitalists and workers have existed no book has appeared which is of such importance for the workers as *Das Kapital*. The relation between capital and labour, the hinge on which our entire present system of society turns, is here treated scientifically for the first time and with a thoroughness and acuteness of which only a German is capable. Valuable as are the

1. [Engels discussed the factory system in *The Condition of the Working Class in England*, published in 1845.]

2. [This review first appeared in the *Demokratisches Wochenblatt* (Leipzig), 21 and 28 March 1868. Translation based on that in F. Engels, *On Marx's 'Capital'* (Foreign Languages Publishing House, Moscow).]

writings of Robert Owen, Saint-Simon and Fourier – valuable as they will be in the future – it has been reserved for a German first to climb to the heights from which the whole field of modern social relations can be clearly seen in full view just as the lower mountain scenery is observed by someone standing on the top-most peak.

Hitherto economics has taught us that labour is the source of all wealth and the measure of all values. Hence two goods which have cost the same labour-time to make, possess the same value and must also be exchanged for each other, since normally only goods of equal values are exchangeable. At the same time economics teaches that there exists a kind of stored-up labour which it calls capital. This capital – owing to the auxiliary services contained in it – raises the productivity of labour a hundred- and a thousand-fold and, in return, it claims a certain compensation which is termed profit or gain. We all know that this occurs in such a way that the profits of stored-up dead labour become ever more massive, that the capital of the capitalists becomes ever more colossal, while the wages of living labour constantly decrease, and the mass of workers living solely on wages grows ever more numerous and poverty-stricken.

How is this contradiction to be solved? How can there remain a profit for the capitalist if the worker gets back the full value of the labour he adds to his product? And yet this should happen since only equal values are exchanged. On the other hand, how can equal values be exchanged, how can the worker receive the full value of his product if – as is admitted by many economists – this product is divided between him and the capitalist? Econo-mists have so far been baffled by this contradiction and write or stutter embarrassed and meaningless phrases about it. Even the early socialist critics of the capitalist system were unable to do more than draw attention to the contradiction. No one has solved it. Now at last Marx has traced the process by which this profit originates right to its ultimate source and in this way he has made everything clear.

Marx traces the development of capital by starting from the simple – and notoriously obvious – fact that the capitalists turn their capital to account by exchange. They buy goods with money and then sell those goods for more money than they originally paid. For example a capitalist buys cotton for 1,000 thalers and then sells it for 1,100 thalers and so 'earns' 100 thalers. This excess of 100 thalers over the original capital Marx calls *surplus value*. The economists assume that only equal values are exchanged and in the sphere of abstract theory this is correct. In theory the purchase of cotton and its subsequent sale can no more yield surplus value than the exchange of a silver thaler for thirty silver groschen and the re-exchange of the small coins for a silver thaler – a process by which one becomes neither richer nor poorer. Again surplus value cannot arise from sellers selling goods above their value or from buyers buying goods below their value because each is in turn buyer and seller and this would cancel itself out. Surplus value cannot arise from buyers and sellers overreaching each other since this would create no new value but would merely distribute the existing capital differently between the capitalists. Although the capitalist buys the goods at their value and sells them at their value, he gets more value out than he put in. How does this happen?

Under present social conditions the capitalist finds on the *commodity* market a commodity which has the peculiar property that *its use is a source of new value, is a creation of new value*. This commodity is *labour power*.

What is the value of labour power? The value of every commodity is measured by the labour required for its production. Labour power exists in the shape of the living worker who needs a definite amount of means of subsistence for himself and for his family, which ensures the continuance of labour power even after his death. So the labour-time necessary for producing these means of subsistence represent the value of labour power. The capitalist pays him weekly and thereby purchases the use of one week's labour of the workers. So far the economists will pretty well agree with us as to the value of labour power.

The capitalist now sets his worker to work. In a certain time the worker will have delivered as much labour as was represented by his weekly wage. Supposing that the weekly wage of a worker represents three labour days. In that case the worker who starts work on a Monday has by Wednesday evening *replaced* for the capitalist *the full value of the wage paid*. But does he then stop working? Not at all. The capitalist has bought his *week's* labour and the worker must go on working during the last three days of the week. This *surplus labour* of the worker over and above the time necessary to replace his wage is the *source of the surplus value*. It is the source of profit. It is the source of the continually growing accumulation of capital.

It is no use arguing that it is an arbitrary assumption that the worker earns in three days the wages he has received and works the remaining three days for the capitalist. Whether the worker takes exactly three days to replace his wages, or two, or four, is of course quite immaterial in this connexion. The actual number of days depends upon circumstances. What matters is that the capitalist – besides the labour he pays for – extracts from the worker labour that he *does not pay for*. This is no arbitrary assumption since if the capitalist extracted from the worker over a long period only as much labour as he paid him in wages he would have to close his factory since his whole profit would come to nought.

Marx has resolved all the apparent contradictions. The origin of surplus value (of which the capitalist's profit forms an important part) is now quite clear and natural. The value of the labour power is paid for. But this payment is much less than the value extracted by the capitalist from the labour power. It is precisely this difference – the *unpaid labour* – that constitutes the share of the capitalist (or more accurately the share of the capitalist class). Even the profit that the cotton dealer made on his cotton in the the example that we have given must consist of unpaid labour, if cotton prices have not risen. The trader must have sold to a cotton manufacturer, who is able to extract from his product a profit for himself besides the original 100 thalers, and therefore shares with him the unpaid labour that he has pocketed. In general it is this unpaid labour which maintains all the non-working members of society. The state and municipal taxes (as far as they affect the capitalist class) and the rent of the land-owners are paid from unpaid labour. It is on this unpaid labour that the whole existing social system rests.

It would be absurd to assume that unpaid labour arose only

under present conditions where production is carried on by capitalists on the one hand and by wage earners on the other. On the contrary the oppressed class has at all times had to perform unpaid labour. During the whole long period when slavery was the prevailing form of the organization of labour the slaves had to perform much more labour than was returned to them in the form of means of subsistence. The same is true of the system of serfdom right up to the abolition of peasant *corvée* labour. In this case there is a clear distinction between the time during which the peasant works for his own maintenance and the time spent in surplus labour for the feudal lord. The two types of labour were carried out at different times. The form of surplus labour has changed but the substance remains; so long as (in Marx's words) 'a part of society possesses the monopoly of the means of production, the labourer – free or not free – must add to the working time necessary for his own maintenance an extra working time in order to produce the means of subsistence for the owners of the means of production'.

(2)

In the previous article we saw that every worker employed by the capitalist performs a twofold labour. During one part of his working time he replaces the wages advanced to him by the capitalist. This part of his labour Marx calls *necessary labour*. But afterwards the worker has to go on working and during that time he produces *surplus labour* for the capitalist, a significant portion of which constitutes profit. That part of the worker's labour Marx calls *surplus labour*.

Let us assume that the worker works for three days in the week to replace his wages and for three days to produce surplus value for the capitalist. This would mean that with a twelve hour working day the worker works for six hours every day for his wages and for six hours to produce surplus value. There are only six days in the week – seven at most if Sunday is included – but it is possible to extract six, eight, ten, twelve, fifteen or even more hours of labour out of every working day. The worker sells the capitalist a working day for his day's wages. But *what is a working day*? Eight hours or eighteen?

It is in the capitalist's interest to make the working day as long as possible. The longer it is the more surplus value is produced. The worker naturally feels that every hour of labour which he performs over and above the replacement of his wage is unjustly taken from him. The worker experiences in his own body what it means to work excessive hours. The capitalist fights for his profit while the worker fights for his health. The worker fights for a few hours of rest a day so that – as a human being – he can have other occupations than simply working, sleeping and eating. Incidentally it does not depend upon the good will of any individual capitalist whether he embarks upon this struggle or not. Competition compels even the most philanthropic capitalist to join with other capitalists to arrange that his working day should be the one universally adopted.

The struggle for the fixing of the working day has lasted from the first appearance of free workers to the present day. In various trades different traditional working days prevail though in fact they are seldom observed. Only if the state fixes the working day by law and supervises its observance can one really say that there exists a normal working day. Hitherto almost the only example of this has been in the factory districts in England. Here the ten hour working day (ten and a half hours on five days and seven and a half hours on Saturdays) has been legally fixed for all women and for youths of 13 to 18. Since men cannot work without women and youths they also enjoy the benefits of a ten hour working day. The English factory workers have won this law after years of endurance and after a long stubborn struggle with the factory owners. They have won the law because of the freedom of the press and the right of association and assembly. And they have adroitly made use of the divisions within the ruling class itself. The law has become the great safeguard of the English workers. It has been gradually extended to all important branches of industry and last year (1867) to almost *all trades* – at least to all those in which women and children are employed. Marx's book contains very exhaustive material on the history of this legal regulation of the working day in England. The next North German Reichstag will also be discussing factory legislation including the regulation of factory labour. We hope that none of the deputies elected by German workers will discuss this bill without previously making themselves thoroughly conversant with Marx's book. *Much can be achieved there.* The divisions within the ruling classes are more favourable to the workers than they ever were in England because *universal suffrage compels the ruling classes to court the favour of the workers.* Four or five representatives of the proletariat are *a power* under these circumstances if they know how to use their position. They are a power above all if they know what is at stake – and the middle classes do not know this. And Marx's book gives the representatives of the workers in ready form all the material that they require.

We will pass over a number of other first-rate investigations of more theoretical interest and we will deal with the final chapter of Marx's book which deals with the accumulation of capital. Marx shows for the first time that the capitalist method of production (i.e. the economy which presupposes capitalists on the one hand and wage earners on the other) not only continually reproduces the capital of the capitalist but also continually reproduces the poverty of the workers at the same time. The system ensures that there will always exist in the future on the one hand capitalists (who are the owners of all means of subsistence, raw materials and instruments of labour) and on the other the great mass of workers (who are compelled to sell their labour power to those capitalists for an amount of the means of subsistence which at best just suffices to keep them working and to bring up a new generation of proletarians). But capital is not merely reproduced. It is continually increased and multiplied. And the power of capital over the workers who own no property is also continually increased. Just as capital itself is reproduced on an ever greater scale so the modern capitalist method of production reproduces the class of workers (who own no property) on an ever increasing scale. Marx writes: 'The accumulation of capital reproduces the relationship between capital and labour at a progressively increasing rate. On the one hand there are more capitalists and larger capitalists. On the other hand there are more wage earners . . . The accumulation of capital therefore leads to an increase of the proletariat.' But owing to the progress of machinery and to improved methods of farming fewer and fewer workers are needed to produce the same quantity of goods or food and a situation arises in which more and more workers are redundant. If industrial efficiency increases more rapidly than capital itself what becomes of the ever growing army of workers? They form an industrial reserve army. In times of bad or moderate business this reserve army is paid *below* the value of its labour or it is irregularly employed or it comes under the care of the Poor Law authorities. But the reserve army of workers is indispensable to the capitalist class when business is booming. This is quite evident in England. The reserve army of workers *always* serves to break the power of resistance of the regularly employed workers and to keep their wages down. Marx writes: 'The greater the social wealth ... the greater is the industrial reserve army ... But the greater that this reserve army is in proportion to the regularly employed labour force the greater is the mass of surplus population whose misery is in inverse ratio to its torment of labour. Finally, the more extensive the Lazarus-layers of the working class and the industrial reserve army the greater is official pauperism. *This is the absolute general law of capitalist accumulation.*'

These are some of the main laws of the modern capitalist social system. They have been strictly and scientifically proved and the official economists have been careful not even to attempt to refute them. But is this all that can be said on the problem? Certainly not. Just as sharply as Marx stresses the evils of capitalist production so also does he clearly prove that this social system has been necessary so as to develop the productive forces of society to a level which will make it possible for *all* members of society to develop equally in a manner worthy of human beings. All earlier forms of society have been too poor to do this. Capitalist production for the first time creates the wealth and the productive forces necessary before this can be achieved. At the same time it also creates the social class of oppressed workers which is more and more compelled to claim the utilization of this wealth and productive forces for the whole of society. At present the wealth and the productive forces are used only for the benefit of a class of monopolists.

3. *Socialism, Utopian and Scientific,* 1892[1]

(1)

MODERN socialism is, in its essence, the direct product of the recognition, on the one hand, of the class antagonisms, existing in the society of today, between proprietors and non-proprietors, between capitalists and wage-workers; on the other hand, of the anarchy existing in production. But, in its theoretical form, modern Socialism originally appears ostensibly as a more logical extension of the principles laid down by the great French philosophers of the eighteenth century. Like every new theory, modern Socialism had, at first, to connect itself with the intellectual stock-in-trade ready to its hand, however deeply its roots lay in material economic facts.

The great men, who in France prepared men's minds for the coming revolution, were themselves extreme revolutionists. They recognized no external authority of any kind whatever. Religion, natural science, society, political institutions, everything, was subjected to the most unsparing criticism: everything must justify its existence before the judgement-seat of reason, or give up existence. Reason became the sole measure of everything. It was the time when, as Hegel says, the world stood upon its head; first, in the sense that the human head, and the principles arrived at by its thought, claimed to be the basis of all human action and association; but by and by, also, in the wider sense that the reality which was in contradiction to these principles had, in fact, to be turned upside down. Every form of society and government then existing, every old traditional notion was flung into the lumber-room as irrational; the world had hitherto allowed itself to be led solely by prejudices; everything in the past deserved only pity and contempt. Now, for the first time, appeared the light of day, the kingdom of reason, henceforth superstition, injustice, privilege, oppression, were to be superseded by eternal truth,

1. [Three chapters from *Anti-Dühring* which appeared in Edward Aveling's English translation as a pamphlet in 1892. The introduction and the notes have been omitted.]

eternal Right, equality based on Nature and the inalienable rights of man.

We know today that this kingdom of reason was nothing more than the idealized kingdom of the bourgeoisie; that this eternal Right found its realization in bourgeois justice; that this equality reduced itself to bourgeois equality before the law; that bourgeois property was proclaimed as one of the essential rights of man; and that the government of reason, the 'Contrat Social' of Rousseau, came into being, and only could come into being, as a democratic bourgeois republic. The great thinkers of the eighteenth century could, no more than their predecessors, go beyond the limits imposed upon them by their epoch.

But, side by side with the antagonism of the feudal nobility and the burghers, who claimed to represent all the rest of society, was the general antagonism of exploiters and exploited, of rich idlers and poor workers. It was this very circumstance that made it possible for the representatives of the bourgeoisie to put themselves forward as representing, not one special class, but the whole of suffering humanity. Still further. From its origin, the bourgeoisie was saddled with its antithesis: capitalists cannot exist without wage-workers, and, in the same proportion as the medieval burgher of the guild developed into the modern bourgeois, the guild journeyman and the day-labourer, outside the guilds, developed into the proletarian. And although, upon the whole, the bourgeoisie, in their struggle with the nobility, could claim to represent at the same time the interests of the different working classes of that period, yet in every great bourgeois movement there were independent outbursts of that class which was the forerunner, more or less developed, of the modern proletariat. For example, at the time of the German reformation and the peasants' war, the Anabaptists and Thomas Münzer; in the great English revolution, the Levellers; in the great French revolution, Babeuf.

There were theoretical enunciations corresponding with these revolutionary uprisings of a class not yet developed; in the sixteenth and seventeenth centuries, Utopian pictures of ideal social conditions; in the eighteenth, actual communistic theories (Morelly and Mably). The demand for equality was no longer limited to political rights, it was extended also to the social conditions of individuals. It was not simply class privileges that were to be abolished, but class distinctions themselves. A Communism, ascetic, denouncing all the pleasures of life, Spartan, was the first form of the new teaching. Then came the three great Utopians: Saint-Simon, to whom the middle-class movement, side by side with the proletarian, still had a certain significance; Fourier; and Owen, who in the country where capitalist production was most developed, and under the influence of the antagonisms begotten of this, worked out his proposals for the removal of class distinction systematically and in direct relation to French materialism.

One thing is common to all three. Not one of them appears as a representative of the interests of that proletariat which historical development had, in the meantime, produced. Like the French philosophers, they do not claim to emancipate a particular class to begin with, but all humanity at once. Like them, they wish to bring in the kingdom of reason and eternal justice, but this kingdom, as they see it, is as far as heaven from earth, from that of the French philosophers.

For, to our three social reformers, the bourgeois world, based upon the principles of these philosophers, is quite as irrational and unjust, and, therefore, finds its way to the dust-hole quite as readily as feudalism and all the earlier stages of society. If pure reason and justice have not, hitherto, ruled the world, this has been the case only because men have not rightly understood them. What was wanted was the individual man of genius, who has now arisen and who understands the truth. That he has now arisen, that the truth has now been clearly understood, is not an inevitable event, following of necessity in the chain of historical development, but a mere happy accident. He might just as well have been born five hundred years earlier, and might then have spared humanity five hundred years of error, strife and suffering.

We saw how the French philosophers of the eighteenth century, the forerunners of the Revolution, appealed to reason as the sole judge of all that is. A rational government, rational society, were to be founded; everything that ran counter to eternal reason was to be remorselessly done away with. We saw also that this eternal reason was in reality nothing but the idealized understanding of the eighteenth century citizen, just then evolving into the bourgeois. The French Revolution had realized this rational society and government.

But the new order of things, rational enough as compared with earlier conditions, turned out to be by no means absolutely rational. The State based upon reason completely collapsed. Rousseau's 'Contrat Social' had found its realization in the Reign of Terror, from which the bourgeoisie, who had lost confidence in their own political capacity, had taken refuge first in the corruption of the Directorate, and, finally, under the wing of the Napoleonic despotism. The promised eternal peace was turned into an endless war of conquest. The society based upon reason had fared no better. The antagonism between rich and poor, instead of dissolving into general prosperity, had become intensified by the removal of the guild and other privileges, which had to some extent bridged it over, and by the removal of the charitable institutions of the Church. The 'freedom of property' from feudal fetters, now veritably accomplished, turned out to be, for the small capitalists and small proprietors, the freedom to sell their small property, crushed under the overmastering competition of the large capitalists and landlords, to these great lords, and thus, so far as the small capitalists and peasant proprietors were concerned, became 'freedom *from* property'. The development of industry upon a capitalistic basis made poverty and misery of the working masses conditions of existence of society. Cash payment became more and more, in Carlyle's phrase, the sole nexus between man and man. The number of crimes increased from year to year. Formerly, the feudal vices had openly stalked about in broad daylight; though not eradicated, they were now at any rate thrust into the background. In their stead, the bourgeois vices, hitherto practised in secret, began to blossom all the more luxuriantly. Trade became to a greater and greater extent cheating. The 'fraternity' of the revolutionary motto was realized in the chicanery and rivalries of the battle of competition. Oppression by force was replaced by corruption; the sword, as the first social lever, by gold. The right of the first night was transferred from the feudal lords to the bourgeois manufacturers.

Prostitution increased to an extent never heard of. Marriage itself remained, as before, the legally recognized form, the official cloak of prostitution, and, moreover, was supplemented by rich crops of adultery.

In a word, compared with the splendid promises of the philosophers, the social and political institutions born of the 'triumph of reason' were bitterly disappointing caricatures. All that was wanting was the men to formulate this disappointment, and they came with the turn of the century. In 1802 Saint-Simon's Geneva letters appeared; in 1808 appeared Fourier's first work, although the groundwork of his theory dated from 1799; on 1 January 1800, Robert Owen undertook the direction of New Lanark.

At this time, however, the capitalist mode of production, and with it the antagonism between the bourgeoisie and the proletariat, was still very incompletely developed. Modern industry, which had just arisen in England, was still unknown in France. But modern industry develops, on the one hand, the conflicts which make absolutely necessary a revolution in the mode of production, and the doing away with its capitalistic character – conflicts not only between the classes begotten of it, but also between the very productive forces and the forms of exchange created by it. And, on the other hand, it develops, in these very gigantic productive forces, the means of ending these conflicts. If, therefore, about the year 1800, the conflicts arising from the new social order were only just beginning to take shape, this holds still more fully as to the means of ending them. The 'have-nothing' masses of Paris, during the Reign of Terror, were able for a moment to gain the mastery, and thus to lead the bourgeois revolution to victory in spite of the bourgeoisie themselves. But, in doing so, they only proved how impossible it was for their domination to last under the conditions then obtaining. The proletariat, which then for the first time evolved itself from these 'have-nothing' masses as the nucleus of a new class, as yet quite incapable of independent political action, appeared as an oppressed suffering order, to whom, in its incapacity to help itself, help could, at best, be brought in from without, or down from above.

This historical situation also dominated the founders of Socialism. To the crude conditions of capitalistic production and the crude class conditions corresponded crude theories. The solution of the social problems, which as yet lay hidden in undeveloped economic conditions, the Utopians attempted to evolve out of the human brain. Society presented nothing but wrongs, to remove these was the task of reason. It was necessary, then, to discover a new and more perfect system of social order and to impose this upon society from without by propaganda, and, wherever it was possible, by the example of model experiments. These new social systems were foredoomed as Utopian; the more completely they were worked out in detail, the more they could not avoid drifting off into pure phantasies.

These facts once established, we need not dwell a moment longer upon this side of the question, now wholly belonging to the past. We can leave it to the literary small fry to solemnly quibble over these phantasies, which today only make us smile, and to crow over the superiority of their own bald reasoning, as compared with such 'insanity'. For ourselves, we delight in the stupendously grand thoughts and germs of thought that everywhere break out through their phantastic covering, and to which these Philistines are blind.

Saint-Simon was a son of the great French Revolution, at the outbreak of which he was not yet thirty. The Revolution was the victory of the third estate, i.e. of the great masses of the nation, *working* in production and in trade, over the privileged *idle* classes, the nobles and the priests. But the victory of the third estate soon revealed itself as exclusively the victory of a small part of this 'estate', as the conquest of political power by the socially privileged section of it, i.e., the propertied bourgeoisie. And the bourgeoisie had certainly developed rapidly during the Revolution, partly by speculation in the lands of the nobility and of the Church, confiscated and afterwards put up for sale, and partly by frauds upon the nation by means of army contracts. It was the domination of these swindlers that, under the Directory, brought France to the verge of ruin, and thus gave Napoleon the pretext for his *coup-d'état*.

Hence, to Saint-Simon the antagonism between the third estate and the privileged classes took the form of an antagonism between 'workers' and 'idlers'. The idlers were not merely the old privileged classes, but also all who, without taking any part in production or distribution, lived on their incomes. And the workers were not only the wage-workers, but also the manufacturers, the merchants, the bankers. That the idlers had lost the capacity for intellectual leadership and political supremacy had been proved, and was by the Revolution finally settled. That the non-possessing classes had not this capacity seemed to Saint-Simon proved by the experiences of the Reign of Terror. Then, who was to lead and command? According to Saint-Simon, science and industry, both united by a new religious bond, destined to restore that unity of religious ideas which had been lost since the time of the Reformation – a necessarily mystic and rigidly hierarchic 'new Christianity'. But science, that was the scholars; and industry, that was, in the first place, the working bourgeois, manufacturers, merchants, bankers. These bourgeoisie were certainly intended by Saint-Simon to transform themselves into a kind of public official, or social trustees; but they were still to hold, vis-à-vis the workers, a commanding and economically privileged position. The bankers especially were to be called upon to direct the whole of social production by the regulation of credit. This conception was in exact keeping with a time in which modern industry in France and, with it, the chasm between bourgeoisie and proletariat was only just coming into existence. But what Saint-Simon especially lays stress upon is this: what interests him first, and above all other things, is the lot of the class that is the most numerous and the most poor ('*la classe la plus nombreuse et la plus pauvre*').

Already, in his Geneva letters, Saint-Simon lays down the proposition that 'all men ought to work'. In the same work he recognizes also that the Reign of Terror was the reign of the non-possessing masses. 'See,' says he to them, 'what happened in France at the time when your comrades held sway there; they brought about a famine.' But to recognize the French Revolution as a class war, and not simply one between nobility, bourgeoisie, and the non-possessors, was, in the year 1802, a most pregnant discovery. In 1816, he declares that politics is the science of production, and foretells the complete absorption of politics by economics. The knowledge that economic conditions are the basis of political institutions appears here only in embryo. Yet what is here already very plainly expressed is the idea of the future conversion of political rule over men into an administration of things and a direction of processes of production – that is to say, the 'abolition of the State', about which recently there has been so much noise.

Saint-Simon shows the same superiority over his contemporaries, when in 1814, immediately after the entry of the allies into Paris, and again in 1815, during the Hundred Days War, he proclaims the alliance of France with England, and then of both these countries with Germany, as the only guarantee for the prosperous development and peace of Europe. To preach to the French in 1815 an alliance with the victors of Waterloo required as much courage as historical foresight.

If in Saint-Simon we find a comprehensive breadth of view, by virtue of which almost all the ideas of later Socialists, that are not strictly economic, are found in him in embryo, we find in Fourier a criticism of the existing conditions of society, genuinely French and witty, but not upon that account any the less thorough. Fourier takes the bourgeoisie, their inspired prophets before the Revolution, and their interested eulogists after it, at their own word. He lays bare remorselessly the material and moral misery of the bourgeois world. He confronts it with the earlier philosophers' dazzling promises of a society in which reason alone should reign, of a civilization in which happiness should be universal, of an illimitable human perfectibility, and with the rose-coloured phraseology of the bourgeois ideologists of his time. He points out how everywhere the most pitiful reality corresponds with the most high-sounding phrases, and he overwhelms this hopeless fiasco of phrases with his mordant sarcasm.

Fourier is not only a critic; his imperturbably serene nature makes him a satirist, and assuredly one of the greatest satirists of all time. He depicts, with equal power and charm, the swindling speculations that blossomed out upon the downfall of the Revolution, and the shopkeeping spirit prevalent in, and characteristic of, French commerce at that time. Still more masterly is his criticism of the bourgeois form of the relations between the sexes, and the position of woman in bourgeois society. He was the first to declare that in any given society the degree of woman's emancipation is the natural measure of the general emancipation.

But Fourier is at his greatest in his conception of the history of society. He divides its whole course, thus far, into four stages of evolution – savagery, barbarism, the patriarchate, civilization. This last is identical with the so-called civil, or bourgeois, society of today – i.e. with the social order that came in with the sixteenth century. He proves 'that the civilized stage raises every vice practised by barbarism in a simple fashion, into a form of existence, complex, ambiguous, equivocal, hypocritical' – that civilization moves in 'a vicious circle' – in contradictions which it constantly reproduces without being able to solve them; hence it constantly arrives at the very opposite to that which it wants to attain, or pretends to want to attain, so that, e.g. 'under civilization poverty is born of superabundance itself'.

Fourier, as we see, uses the dialectic method in the same masterly way as his contemporary, Hegel. Using these same dialectics, he argues, against the talk about illimitable human perfectibility, that every historical phase has its period of ascent and also its period of descent, and he applies this observation to the future of the whole human race. As Kant introduced into natural science the idea of the ultimate destruction of the earth, Fourier introduced into historical science that of the ultimate destruction of the human race.

Whilst in France the hurricane of the Revolution swept over the land, in England a quieter, but not on that account less tremendous, revolution was going on. Steam and the new tool-making machinery were transforming manufacture into modern industry, and thus revolutionizing the whole foundation of bourgeois society. The sluggish march of development of the manufacturing period changed into a veritable storm and stress period of production. With constantly increasing swiftness the splitting-up of society into large capitalists and non-possessing proletarians went on. Between these, instead of the former stable middle class, an unstable mass of artisans and small shopkeepers, the most fluctuating portion of the population, now led a precarious existence.

The new mode of production was, as yet, only at the beginning of its ascent; as yet it was the normal, regular method of production – the only one possible under existing conditions. Nevertheless, even then it was producing crying social abuses – the herding together of a homeless population in the worst quarters of the large towns; the loosening of all traditional moral bonds, of patriarchal subordination, of family relations; overwork, especially of women and children, to a frightful extent; complete demoralization of the working-class, suddenly flung into altogether new conditions, from the country into the town, from agriculture into modern industry, from stable conditions of existence into insecure ones that changed from day to day.

At this juncture there came forward as a reformer a manufacturer twenty-nine years old – a man of almost sublime, childlike simplicity of character, and at the same time one of the few born leaders of men. Robert Owen had adopted the teaching of the materialistic philosophers: that man's character is the product, on the one hand, of heredity, on the other, of the environment of the individual during his lifetime, and especially during his period of development. In the industrial revolution most of his class saw only chaos and confusion, and the opportunity of fishing in these troubled waters and making large fortunes quickly. He saw in it the opportunity of putting into practice his favourite theory, and so of bringing order out of chaos. He had already tried it with success, as superintendent of more than five hundred men in a Manchester factory. From 1800 to 1829, he directed the great cotton mill at New Lanark, in Scotland, as managing partner, along the same lines, but with greater freedom of action and with a success that made him a European reputation. A population, originally consisting of the most diverse and, for the most part, very demoralized elements, a population that gradually grew to 2,500, he turned into a model colony, in which drunkenness, police, magistrates, lawsuits, poor laws, charity, were unknown. And all this simply by placing the people in conditions worthy of human beings, and especially by carefully bringing up the rising generation. He was the founder of infant schools, and introduced them first at New Lanark. At the age of two the children came to school, where they enjoyed themselves so much that they could scarcely be got home again. Whilst his competitors worked their people thirteen or fourteen hours a day, in New Lanark the working-day was only ten and a half hours. When a crisis in cotton stopped work for four months, his workers received their full wages all the time. And with all this the business more than doubled in value, and to the last yielded large profits to its proprietors.

In spite of all this, Owen was not content. The existence which he secured for his workers was, in his eyes, still far from being worthy of human beings. 'The people were slaves at my mercy.' The relatively favourable conditions in which he had placed them were still far from allowing a rational development of the character and of the intellect in all directions, much less of the free exercise of all their faculties. 'And yet, the working part of this population of 2,500 persons was daily producing as much real wealth for society as, less than half a century before, it would have required the working part of a population of 600,000 to create. I asked myself, what became of the difference between the wealth consumed by 2,500 persons and that which would have been consumed by 600,000?'

The answer was clear. It had been used to pay the proprietors of the establishment 5 per cent on the capital they had laid out, in addition to over £300,000 clear profit. And that which held for New Lanark held to a still greater extent for all the factories in England. 'If this new wealth had not been created by machinery, imperfectly as it has been applied, the wars of Europe, in opposition to Napoleon, and to support the aristocratic principles of society, could not have been maintained. And yet this new power was the creation of the working-classes.' To them, therefore, the fruits of this new power belonged. The newly-created gigantic productive forces, hitherto used only to enrich individuals and to enslave the masses, offered to Owen the foundations for a reconstruction of society; they were destined, as the common property of all, to be worked for the common good of all.

Owen's Communism was based upon this purely business foundation, the outcome, so to say, of commercial calculation. Throughout, it maintained this practical character. Thus, in 1823, Owen proposed the relief of the distress in Ireland by Communist colonies, and drew up complete estimates of costs of founding them, yearly expenditure, and probable revenue. And in his definite plan for the future, the technical working-out of details is managed with such practical knowledge – ground plan, front and side and bird's eye-views all included – that the Owen method of social reform once accepted, there is from the practical point of view little to be said against the actual arrangement of details.

His advance in the direction of Communism was the turning-point in Owen's life. As long as he was simply a philanthropist, he was rewarded with nothing but wealth, applause, honour and glory. He was the most popular man in Europe. Not only men of his own class, but statesmen and princes listened to him approvingly. But when he came out with his Communist theories, that was quite another thing. Three great obstacles seemed to him especially to block the path to social reform: private property, religion, the present form of marriage. He knew what confronted him if he attacked these – outlawry, excommunication from official society, the loss of his whole social position. But nothing of this prevented him from attacking them without fear of consequences, and what he had foreseen happened. Banished from official society, with a conspiracy of silence against him in the press, ruined by his unsuccessful Communist experiments in America, in which he sacrificed all his fortune, he turned directly to the working-class and continued working in their midst for thirty years. Every social movement, every real advance in England on behalf of the workers links itself on to the name of Robert Owen. He forced through in 1819, after five years' fighting, the first law limiting the hours of labour of women and children in factories. He was president of the first Congress at which all the Trade Unions of England united in a single great trade association. He introduced as transition measures to the complete communistic organization of society, on the one hand, cooperative societies for retail trade and production. These have since that time, at least, given practical proof that the merchant and the manufacturer are socially quite unnecessary. On the other hand, he introduced labour bazaars for the exchange of the products of labour through the medium of labour-notes, whose unit was a single hour of work; institutions necessarily doomed to failure, but completely anticipating Proudhon's bank of exchange of a much later period, and differing entirely from this in that it did not claim to be the panacea for all social ills, but only a first step towards a much more radical revolution of society.

The Utopians' mode of thought has for a long time governed the socialist ideas of the nineteenth century, and still governs some of them. Until very recently all French and English Socialists did homage to it. The earlier German Communism, including that of Weitling, was of the same school. To all these Socialism is the expression of absolute truth, reason and justice, and has only to be discovered to conquer all the world by virtue of its own power. And as absolute truth is independent of time, space, and of the historical development of man, it is a mere accident when and where it is discovered. With all this, absolute truth, reason and justice are different with the founder of each different school. And as each one's special kind of absolute truth, reason and justice is again conditioned by his subjective understanding, his conditions of existence, the measure of his knowledge and his intellectual training, there is no other ending possible in this conflict of absolute truths than that they shall be mutually exclusive one of the other. Hence, from this nothing could come but a kind of eclectic, average Socialism, which, as a matter of fact, has up to the present time dominated the minds of most of the socialist workers in France and England. Hence, a mish-mash allowing of the most manifold shades of opinion; a mish-mash of such critical statements, economic theories, pictures of future society by the founders of different sects, as excite a minimum of opposition; a mish-mash which is the more easily brewed the more the definite sharp edges of the individual constituents are rubbed down in the stream of debate, like rounded pebbles in a brook.

To make a science of Socialism, it had first to be placed upon a real basis.

(2)

In the meantime, along with and after the French philosophy of the eighteenth century had arisen the new German philosophy, culminating in Hegel. Its greatest merit was the taking up again of dialectics as the highest form of reasoning. The old Greek philosophers were all born natural dialecticians, and Aristotle, the most encyclopedic of them, had already analysed the most essential forms of dialectic thought. The newer philosophy, on the other hand, although in it also dialectics had brilliant exponents (e.g. Descartes and Spinoza), had, especially through English influence, become more and more rigidly fixed in the so-called metaphysical mode of reasoning, by which also the French of the eighteenth century were almost wholly dominated, at all events in their special philosophical work. Outside philosophy in the restricted sense, the French nevertheless produced masterpieces of dialectic. We need only to call to mind Diderot's *Le Neveu de Rameau*, and Rousseau's *Discours sur l'origine et les fondements de l'inégalité parmi les hommes*. We give here, in brief, the essential character of these two modes of thought.

When we consider and reflect upon nature at large, or the history of mankind, or our own intellectual activity, at first we see the picture of an endless entanglement of relations and reactions, permutations and combinations, in which nothing remains what, where, and as it was, but everything moves, changes, comes into being and passes away. We see, therefore, at first the picture as a whole, with its individual parts still more or less kept in the background; we observe the movements, transitions, connexions, rather than the things that move, combine and are connected. This primitive, naïve, but intrinsically correct conception of the world is that of ancient Greek philosophy, and was first clearly formulated by Heraclitus: everything is and is not, for everything is fluid, is constantly changing, constantly coming into being and passing away.

But this conception, correctly as it expresses the general character of the picture of appearances as a whole, does not suffice to explain the details of which this picture is made up, and so long as we do not understand these details we must detach them from their natural or historical connexion and examine each one separately, its nature, special causes, effects, etc. This is, primarily, the task of natural science and historical research; branches of science which the Greeks of classical times, on very good grounds, relegated to a subordinate position, because they had first of all to collect materials for these sciences to work upon. A certain amount of natural and historical material must be collected before there can be any critical analysis, comparison, and arrangement in classes, orders and species. The foundations of the exact natural sciences were, therefore, first worked out by the Greeks of the Alexandrian period, and later on, in the Middle Ages, by the Arabs. Real natural science dates from the second half of the fifteenth century, and thence onward it has advanced with constantly increasing rapidity. The analysis of Nature into its individual parts, the grouping of the different natural processes and objects in definite classes, the study of the internal anatomy of organized bodies in their manifold forms – these were the fundamental conditions of the gigantic strides in our knowledge of Nature that have been made during the last four hundred years. But this method of work has also left us as legacy the habit of observing natural objects and processes in isolation, apart from their connexion with the vast whole; of observing them in repose, not in motion; as constants, not as essentially variables; in their death, not in their life. And when this way of looking at things was transferred by Bacon and Locke from natural science to philosophy, it begot the narrow, metaphysical mode of thought peculiar to the last century.

To the metaphysician, things and their mental reflexes, ideas, are isolated, are to be considered one after the other and apart from each other, are objects of investigation fixed, rigid, given once for all. He thinks in absolutely irreconcilable antitheses. 'His communication is "yea, yea; nay, nay"; for whatsoever is more than these cometh of evil.' For him a thing either exists or does not exist; a thing cannot at the same time be itself and something else. Positive and negative absolutely exclude one another; cause and effect stand in a rigid antithesis one to the other.

At first sight this mode of thinking seems to us very luminous, because it is that of so-called sound commonsense. Only sound commonsense, respectable fellow that he is, in the homely realm of his own four walls, has very wonderful adventures directly he ventures out into the wide world of research. And the metaphysical mode of thought, justifiable and necessary as it is in a number of domains whose extent varies according to the nature of the particular object of investigation, sooner or later reaches a limit, beyond which it becomes one-sided, restricted, abstract, lost in insoluble contradictions. In the contemplation of individual things, it forgets the connexion between them; in the contemplation of their existence, it forgets the beginning and end of that existence; of their repose, it forgets their motion. It cannot see the wood for the trees.

For everyday purposes we know and can say, e.g., whether an animal is alive or not. But, upon closer inquiry, we find that this is, in many cases, a very complex question, as the jurists know very well. They have cudgelled their brains in vain to discover a rational limit beyond which the killing of the child in its mother's womb is murder. It is just as impossible to determine absolutely the moment of death, for physiology proves that death is not an instantaneous, momentary phenomenon, but a very protracted process.

In like manner, every organized being is every moment the same and not the same; every moment it assimilates matter supplied from without, and gets rid of other matter; every moment some cells of its body die and others build themselves anew; in a longer or shorter time the matter of its body is completely renewed, and is replaced by other molecules of matter, so that every organized being is always itself, and yet something other than itself.

Further, we find upon closer investigation that the two poles of an antithesis, positive and negative, e.g., are as inseparable as they are opposed, and that despite all their opposition, they mutually interpenetrate. And we find, in like manner, that cause and effect are conceptions which only hold good in their application to individual cases, but as soon as we consider the individual cases in their general connexion with the universe as a whole, they run into each other, and they become confounded when we contemplate that universal action and reaction in which causes and effects are eternally changing places, so that what is effect here and now will be cause there and then, and *vice versa*.

None of these processes and modes of thought enters into the framework of metaphysical reasoning. Dialectics, on the other hand, comprehends things and their representations, ideas, in their essential connexion, concatenation, motion, origin, and ending. Such processes as those mentioned above are, therefore, so many corroborations of its own method of procedure.

Nature is the proof of dialectics, and it must be said for modern science that it has furnished this proof with very rich materials increasing daily, and thus has shown that, in the last resort, Nature works dialectically and not metaphysically; that she does not move in the eternal oneness of a perpetually recurring circle, but goes through a real historical evolution. In this connexion Darwin must be named before all others. He dealt the metaphysical conception of Nature the heaviest blow by his proof that all organic beings, plants, animals, and man himself, are the products of a process of evolution going on thought millions of years. But the naturalists who have learned to think dialectically are few and far between, and this conflict of the results of discovery with preconceived modes of thinking explains the endless confusion now reigning in theoretical natural science, the despair of teachers as well as learners, of authors and readers alike.

An exact representation of the universe, of its evolution, of the development of mankind, and of the reflection of this evolution in the minds of men, can therefore only be obtained by the methods of dialectics with its constant regard to the innumerable actions and reactions of life and death, of progressive or retrogressive changes. And in this spirit the new German philosophy has worked. Kant began his career by resolving the stable solar system of Newton and its eternal duration, after the famous initial impulse had once been given, into the result of a historic process, the formation of the sun and all the planets out of a rotating nebulous mass. From this he at the same time drew the conclusion that, given this origin of the solar system, its future death followed of necessity. His theory half a century later was established mathematically by Laplace, and half a century after that the spectroscope proved the existence in space of such incandescent masses of gas in various stages of condensation.

This new German philosophy culminated in the Hegelian system. In this system – and herein is its great merit – for the first time the whole world natural, historical, intellectual, is represented as a process, i.e. as in constant motion, change, transformation, development, and the attempt is made to trace out the internal connexion that makes a continuous whole of all this movement and development. From this point of view the history of mankind no longer appeared as a wild whirl of senseless deeds of violence, all equally condemnable at the judgement seat of mature philosophic reason, and which are best forgotten as quickly as possible; but as the process of evolution of man himself. It was now the task of the intellect to follow the gradual march of this process through all its devious ways, and to trace out the inner law running through all its apparently accidental phenomena.

That the Hegelian system did not solve the problem it propounded is here immaterial. Its epoch-making merit was that it propounded the problem. This problem is one that no single individual will ever be able to solve. Although Hegel was – with Saint-Simon – the most encylopedic mind of his time, yet he was limited, first, by the necessarily limited extent of his own knowledge, and, second, by the limited extent and depth of the knowledge and conceptions of his age. To these limits a third must be added. Hegel was an idealist. To him the thoughts within his brain were not the more or less abstract pictures of actual things and processes, but, conversely, things and their evolution were only the realized pictures of the 'Idea', existing somewhere from eternity before the world was. This way of thinking turned everything upside down, and completely reversed the actual connexion of things in the world. Correctly and ingeniously as many individual groups of facts were grasped by Hegel, yet, for the reasons just given, there is much that is botched, artificial, laboured, in a word, wrong in point of detail. The Hegelian system, in itself, was a colossal miscarriage – but it was also the last of its kind. It was suffering, in fact, from an internal and incurable contradiction. Upon the one hand, its essential proposition was the conception that human history is a process of evolution, which, by its very nature, cannot find its intellectual final term in the discovery of any so-called absolute truth. But, on the other hand, it laid claim to being the very essence of this absolute truth. A system of natural and historical knowledge, embracing everything, and final for all time, is a contradiction to the fundamental law of dialectic reasoning. This law, indeed, by no means excludes, but, on the contrary, includes the idea that the systematic knowledge of the external universe can make giant strides from age to age.

The perception of the fundamental contradiction in German idealism led necessarily back to materialism, but *nota bene*, not to the simply metaphysical, exclusively mechanical materialism of the eighteenth century. Old materialism looked upon all previous history as a crude heap of irrationality and violence; modern materialism sees in it the process of evolution of humanity, and aims at discovering the laws thereof. With the French of the eighteenth century, and even with Hegel, the conception obtained of Nature as a whole, moving in narrow circles, and forever immutable, with its eternal celestial bodies, as Newton, and unalterable organic species, as Linnæus, taught. Modern materialism embraces the more recent discoveries of natural science, according to which Nature also has its history in time, the celestial bodies, like the organic species that, under favourable conditions, people them, being born and perishing. And even if Nature, as a whole, must be said to move in recurrent cycles, these cycles assume infinitely larger dimensions. In both aspects, modern materialism is essentially dialectic, and no longer requires the assistance of that sort of philosophy which, queenlike, pretended to rule the remaining mob of sciences. As soon as each special science is bound to make clear its position in the great totality of things and of our knowledge of things, a special science dealing with this totality is superfluous or unnecessary. That which still survives of all earlier philosophy is the science of thought and its laws – formal logic and dialectics. Everything else is subsumed in the positive science of Nature and history.

Whilst, however, the revolution in the conception of Nature could only be made in proportion to the corresponding positive materials furnished by research, already much earlier certain historical facts had occurred which led to a decisive change in the conception of history. In 1831, the first working-class rising took place in Lyons; between 1838 and 1842, the first national working-class movement, that of the English Chartists, reached its height. The class struggle between proletariat and bourgeoisie came to the front in the history of the most advanced countries in Europe, in proportion to the development, upon the one hand, of modern industry, upon the other, of the newly-acquired political supremacy of the bourgeoisie. Facts more and more strenuously gave the lie to the teachings of bourgeois economy as to the identity of the interests of capital and labour, as to the universal harmony and universal prosperity that would be the consequence of unbridled competition. All these things could no longer be ignored, any more than the French and English Socialism, which was their theoretical, though very imperfect, expression. But the old idealist conception of history, which was not yet dislodged, knew nothing of economic interests; production and all economic relations appeared in it only as incidental, subordinate elements in the 'history of civilization'.

The new facts made imperative a new examination of all past history. Then it was seen that *all* past history, with the exception of its primitive stages, was the history of class struggles; that these warring classes of society are always the products of the modes of production and of exchange – in a word, of the *economic* conditions of their time; that the economic structure of society always furnishes the real basis, starting from which we can alone work out the ultimate explanation of the whole superstructure of juridical and political institutions as well as of the religious, philosophical and other ideas of a given historical period. Hegel had freed history from metaphysics – he had made it dialectic; but his conception of history was essentially idealistic. But now idealism was driven from its last refuge, the philosophy of history; now a materialistic treatment of history was propounded, and a method found of explaining man's 'knowing' by his 'being', instead of, as heretofore, his 'being' by his 'knowing'.

From that time forward Socialism was no longer an accidental discovery of this or that ingenious brain, but the necessary out-come of the struggle between two historically developed classes – the proletariat and the bourgeoisie. Its task was no longer to manufacture a system of society as perfect as possible, but to examine the historico-economic succession of events from which these classes and their antagonism had of necessity sprung, and to discover in the economic conditions thus created the means of ending the conflict. But the Socialism of earlier days was as incompatible with this materialistic conception as the conception of Nature and the French materialists was with dialectics and modern natural science. The Socialism of earlier days certainly criticized the existing capitalistic mode of production and its consequences. But it could not explain them, and, therefore, could not get the mastery of them. It could only simply reject them as bad. The more strongly this earlier Socialism denounced the exploitation of the working-class, inevitable under Capitalism, the less able was it clearly to show in what this exploitation consisted and how it arose. But for this it was necessary – (1) to present the capitalistic method of production in its historical connexion and its inevitableness during a particular historical period, and therefore, also to present its inevitable downfall; and (2) to lay bare its essential character, which was still a secret. This was done by the discovery of *surplus-value*. It was shown that the appropriation of unpaid labour is the basis of the capitalist mode of production and of the exploitation of the worker that occurs under it; that even if the capitalist buys the labour-power of his labourer at its full value as a commodity on the market, he yet extracts more value from it than he paid for; and that in the ultimate analysis this surplus-value forms those sums of value from which are heaped up the constantly increasing masses of capital in the hands of the possessing classes. The genesis of capitalist production and the production of capital were both explained.

These two great discoveries, the materialistic conception of history and the revelation of the secret of capitalistic production through surplus-value, we owe to Marx. With these discoveries Socialism became a science. The next thing was to work out all its details and relations.

(3)

The materialist conception of history starts from the proposition that the production of the means to support human life and, next to production, the exchange of things produced, is the basis of all social structure; that in every society that has appeared in history, the manner in which wealth is distributed and society divided into classes or orders, is dependent upon what is produced, how it is produced, and how the products are exchanged. From this point of view the final causes of all social changes and political revolutions are to be sought, not in men's brains, not in man's better insight into eternal truth and justice, but in changes in the modes of production and exchange. They are to be sought, not in the *philosophy*, but in the *economics* of each particular epoch. The growing perception that existing social institutions are unreasonable and unjust, that reason has become unreason, and right wrong, is only proof that in the modes of production and exchange changes have silently taken place, with which the social order adapted to earlier economic conditions is no longer in keeping. From this it also follows that the means of getting rid of the incongruities that have been brought to light, must also be present, in a more or less developed condition, within the changed modes of production themselves. These means are not to be invented by deduction from fundamental principle, but are to be discovered in the stubborn facts of the existing system of production.

What is, then, the position of modern Socialism in this connexion?

The present structure of society – this is now pretty generally conceded – is the creation of the ruling class of today, of the bourgeoisie. The mode of production peculiar to the bourgeoisie, known, since Marx, as the capitalist mode of production, was incompatible with the feudal system, with the privileges it conferred upon individuals, entire social ranks and local corporations, as well as with the hereditary ties of subordination which constituted the framework of its social organization. The bourgeoisie broke up the feudal system and built upon its ruins the capitalist order of society, the kingdom of free competition, of personal liberty, of the equality, before the law, of all commodity owners, of all the rest of the capitalist blessings. Thenceforward the capitalist mode of production could develop in freedom. Since steam, machinery, and the making of machines by machinery transformed the older manufacture into modern industry, the productive forces evolved under the guidance of the bourgeoisie developed with a rapidity and in a degree unheard of before. But just as the older manufacture, in its time, and handicraft, becoming more developed under its influence, had come into collision with the feudal trammels of the guilds, so now modern industry, in its more complete development, comes into collision with bounds within which the capitalistic mode of production holds it confined. The new productive forces have already outgrown the capitalistic mode of using them. And this conflict between productive forces and modes of production is not a conflict engendered in the mind of man, like that between original sin and divine justice. It exists, in fact, objectively, outside us, independently of the will and actions even of the men that have brought it on. Modern Socialism is nothing but the reflex, in thought, of this conflict in fact; its ideal reflection in the minds, first, of the class directly suffering under it, the working-class.

Now, in what does this conflict consist?

Before capitalistic production, i.e. in the Middle Ages, the system of petty industry obtained generally, based upon the private property of the labourers in their means of production; in the country, the agriculture of the small peasant, freeman or serf; in the towns, the handicrafts organized in guilds. The instruments of labour – land, agricultural implements, the workshop, the tool – were the instruments of labour of single individuals, adapted for the use of one worker, and, therefore, of necessity, small, dwarfish, circumscribed. But, for this very reason they belonged, as a rule, to the producer himself. To concentrate these scattered, limited means of production, to enlarge them, to turn them into the powerful levers of production of the present day – this was precisely the historic role of capitalist production and of its upholder, the bourgeoisie. In the fourth section of *Capital* Marx has explained in detail how, since the fifteenth century, this has been historically worked out through the three phases of simple cooperation, manufacture and modern industry. But the bourgeoisie, as is also shown there, could not transform these puny means of production into mighty productive forces without transforming them, at the same time, from means of production of the individual into *social* means of production only workable by a collectivity of men. The spinning-wheel, the handloom, the blacksmith's hammer, were replaced by the spinning-machine, the power-loom, the steam-hammer; the individual workshop, by the factory implying the cooperation of hundreds and thousands of workmen. In like manner, production itself changed from a series of social acts, and the products from individual to social products. The yarn, the cloth, the metal articles that now came out of the factory were the joint product of many workers, through whose hands they had successively to pass before they were ready. No one person could say of them, 'I made that, this is *my* product'.

But where, in a given society, the fundamental form of production is that spontaneous division of labour which creeps in gradually and not upon any preconceived plan, there the products take on the form of *commodities*, whose mutual exchange, buying and selling, enable the individual producers to satisfy their manifold wants. And this was the case in the Middle Ages. The peasant, e.g., sold to the artisan agricultural products and bought from him the products of handicraft. Into this society of individual producers, of commodity-producers, the new mode of production thrust itself. In the midst of the old division of labour, grown up spontaneously and upon *no definite plan*, which had governed the whole of society, now arose division of labour upon *a definite plan*, as organized in the factory, side by side with *individual* production appeared *social* production. The products of both were sold in the same market, and, therefore, at prices at least approximately equal. But organization upon a definite plane was stronger than spontaneous division of labour. The factories working with the combined social forces of a collectivity of individuals produced their commodities far more cheaply than the individual small producers. Individual production succumbed in one department after another. Socialized production revolutionized all the old methods of production. But its revolutionary character was, at the same time, so little recognized, that it was, on the contrary, introduced as a means of increasing and developing the production of commodities. When it arose, it found ready-made, and made liberal use of, certain machinery for the production and exchange of commodities; merchants' capital, handicraft, wage-labour. Socialized production thus introducing itself as a new form of the production of commodities, it was a matter of course that under it the old forms of appropriation remained in full swing, and were applied to its products as well.

In the medieval stage of evolution of the production of commodities, the question as to the owner of the product of labour could not arise. The individual producer, as a rule, had, from raw material belonging to himself, and generally his own handiwork, produced it with his own tools, by the labour of his own hands or of his family. There was no need for him to appropriate the new product. It belonged wholly to him, as a matter of course. His property in the product was, therefore, based *upon his own labour*. Even where external help was used, this was, as a rule, of little importance, and very generally was compensated by something other than wages. The apprentices and journeymen of the guilds worked less for board and wages than for education, in order that they might become master craftsmen themselves.

Then came the concentration of the means of production and of the producers in large workshops and manufactories, their transformation into actual socialized means of production and socialized producers. But the socialized producers and means of production and their products were still treated, after this change, just as they had been before, i.e. as the means of production and the products of individuals. Hitherto, the owner of the instruments of labour had himself appropriated the product, because, as a rule, it was his own product and the assistance of others was the exception. Now the owner of the instruments of labour always appropriated to himself the product, although it was no longer *his* product but exclusively the product of the *labour of others*. Thus, the products now produced socially were not appropriated by those who had actually set in motion the means of production and actually produced the commodities, but by the *capitalists*. The means of production, and production itself, had become in essence socialized. But they were subjected to a form of appropriation which presupposes the private production of individuals, under which, therefore, every one owns his own product and brings it to market. The mode of production is subjected to this form of appropriation, although it abolishes the conditions upon which the latter rests.

This contradiction, which gives to the new mode of production its capitalistic character, *contains the germ of the whole of the social antagonisms of today*. The greater the mastery obtained by the new mode of production over all important fields of production and in all manufacturing countries, the more it reduced individual production to an insignificant residuum, *the more clearly was brought out the incompatibility of socialized production with capitalistic appropriation.*

The first capitalists found, as we have said, alongside of other forms of labour, wage-labour ready-made for them on the market. But it was exceptional, complementary, accessory, transitory wage-labour. The agricultural labourer, though, upon occasion, he hired himself out by the day, had a few acres of his own land on which he could at all events live at a pinch. The guilds were so organized that the journeyman of today became the master of tomorrow. But all this changed, as soon as the means of production became socialized and concentrated in the hands of capitalists. The means of production, as well as the product, of the individual producer became more and more worthless; there was nothing left for him but to turn wage-worker under the capitalist. Wage-labour, aforetime the exception and accessory, now became the rule and basis of all production; aforetime complementary, it now became the sole remaining function of the worker. The wage-worker for a time became a wage-worker for life. The number of these permanent wage-workers was further enormously increased by the breaking-up of the feudal system that occurred at the same time, by the disbanding of the retainers of the feudal lords, the eviction of the peasants from their homesteads, etc. The separation was made complete between the means of production concentrated in the hands of the capitalists on the one side, and the producers, possessing nothing but their labour-power, on the other. *The contradiction between socialized production and capitalistic appropriation manifested itself as the antagonism of proletariat and bourgeoisie.*

We have seen that the capitalistic mode of production thrust its way into a society of commodity-producers, of individual producers, whose social bond was the exchange of their products. But every society, based upon the production of commodities, has this peculiarity: that the producers have lost control over their own social interrelations. Each man produces for himself with such means of production as he may happen to have, and for such exchange as he may require to satisfy his remaining wants. No one knows how much of his particular article is coming on the market, nor how much of it will be wanted. No one knows whether his individual product will meet an actual demand, whether he will be able to make good his cost of production or even to sell his commodity at all. Anarchy reigns in socialized production.

But the production of commodities, like every other form of production, has its peculiar, inherent laws inseparable from it; and these laws work, despite anarchy, in and through anarchy. They reveal themselves in the only persistent form of social interrelations, i.e. in exchange, and here they affect the individual producers as compulsory laws of competition. They are, at first, unknown to these producers themselves, and have to be discovered by them gradually and as the result of experience. They work themselves out, therefore, independently of the producers, and in antagonism to them, as inexorable natural laws of their particular form of production. The product governs the producers.

In medieval society, especially in the earlier centuries, production was essentially directed towards satisfying the wants of the individual. It satisfied, in the main, only the wants of the producer and his family. Where relations of personal dependence existed, as in the country, it also helped to satisfy the wants of the feudal lord. In all this there was, therefore, no exchange; the products, consequently, did not assume the character of commodities. The family of the peasant produced almost everything they wanted: clothes and furniture, as well as means of subsistence. Only when it began to produce more than was sufficient to supply its own wants and the payments in kind to the feudal lord, only then did it also produce commodities. This surplus, thrown into socialized exchange and offered for sale, became commodities.

The artisans of the towns, it is true, had from the first to produce for exchange. But they, also, themselves supplied the greatest part of their own individual wants. They had gardens and plots of land. They turned their cattle out into the communal forest, which, also, yielded them timber and firing. The women spun flax, wool, and so forth. Production for the purpose of exchange, production of commodities, was only in its infancy. Hence, exchange was restricted, the market narrow, the methods of production stable; there was local exclusiveness without, local unity within; the mark in the country, in the town, the guild.

But with the extension of the production of commodities, and especially with the introduction of the capitalist mode of production, the laws of commodity-production, hitherto latent, came into action more openly and with greater force. The old bonds were loosened, the old exclusive limits broken through, the producers were more and more turned into independent, isolated producers of commodities. It became apparent that the production of society at large was ruled by absence of plan, by accident, by anarchy; and this anarchy grew to greater and greater height. But the chief means by aid of which the capitalist mode of production intensified this anarchy of socialized production, was the exact opposite of anarchy. It was the increasing organization of production, upon a social basis in every individual productive establishment. By this, the old, peaceful, stable condition of things was ended. Wherever this organization of production was introduced into a branch of industry, it brooked no other method of production by its side. The field of labour became a battleground. The great geographical discoveries, and the colonization following upon them, multiplied markets and quickened the transformation of handicraft into manufacture. The war did not simply break out between the individual producers of particular localities. The local struggles began in their turn national conflicts, the commercial wars of the seventeenth and the eighteenth centuries.

Finally, modern industry and the opening of the world-market made the struggle universal, and at the same time gave it an unheard-of virulence. Advantages in natural or artificial conditions of production now decide the existence or non-existence of individual capitalists, as well as of whole industries and countries. He that falls is remorselessly cast aside. It is the Darwinian struggle of the individual for existence transferred from Nature to society with intensified violence. The conditions of existence natural to the animal appear as the final term of human development. The contradiction between socialized production and capitalistic appropriation now presents itself as *an antagonism between the organization of production in the individual workshop and the anarchy of production in society generally*.

The capitalistic mode of production moves in these two forms of the antagonism immanent to it from its very origin. It is never able to get out of that 'vicious circle', which Fourier had already discovered. What Fourier could not, indeed, see in his time is that this circle is gradually narrowing; that the movement becomes more and more a spiral, and must come to an end, like the movement of the planets, by collision with the centre. It is the compelling force of anarchy in the production of society at large that more and more completely turns the great majority of men into proletarians; and it is the masses of the proletariat again who will finally put an end to anarchy in production. It is the compelling force of anarchy in social production that turns the limitless perfectibility of machinery under modern industry into a compulsory law by which every individual industrial capitalist must perfect his machinery more and more, under penalty of ruin.

But the perfecting of machinery is making human labour superfluous. If the introduction and increase of machinery means the displacement of millions of manual, by a few machine, workers, improvement in machinery means the displacement of more and more of the machine-workers themselves. It means, in the last instance, the production of a number of available wage-workers in excess of the average needs of capital, the formation of a complete industrial reserve army, as I called it in 1845, available at the times when industry is working at high pressure, to be cast out upon the street when the inevitable crash comes, a constant dead weight upon the limbs of the working-class in its struggle for existence with capital, a regulator for the keeping of wages down to the low level that suits the interests of capital. Thus it comes about, to quote Marx, that machinery becomes the most powerful weapon in the war of capital against the working-class; that the instruments of labour constantly tear the means of subsistence out of the hands of the labourer; that the very product of the worker is turned into an instrument for his subjugation. Thus it comes about that the economizing of the instruments of labour becomes at the same time, from the outset, the most reckless waste of labour-power, and robbery based upon the normal conditions under which labour functions; that machinery 'the most powerful instrument for shortening labour-time, becomes the most unfailing means for placing every moment of the labourer's time and that of his family at the disposal of the capitalist for the purpose of expanding the value of his capital' (*Capital*, English edition, p.406). Thus it comes about that overwork of some becomes the preliminary condition for the idleness of others, and that modern industry, which hunts after new consumers over the whole world, forces the consumption of the masses at home down to a starvation minimum, and in doing so this destroys its own home market. 'The law that always equilibrates the relative surplus population, or industrial reserve army, to the extent and energy of accumulation, this law rivets the labourer to capital more firmly than the wedges of Vulcan did Prometheus to the rock. It established an accumulation of misery, corresponding with accumulation of capital. Accumulation of wealth at one pole is, therefore, at the same time, accumulation of misery, agony of toil, slavery, ignorance, brutality, mental degradation, at the opposite pole, i.e. on the side of the class that produces *its own product in the form of capital*' (*Capital*, p.661). And to expect any other division of the products from the capitalistic mode of production is the same as expecting the electrodes of a battery not to decompose acidulated water, not to liberate oxygen at the positive, hydrogen at the negative pole, so long as they are connected with the battery.

We have seen that the ever-increasing perfectibility of modern machinery is, by the anarchy of social production, turned into a compulsory law that forces the individual industrial capitalist always to improve his machinery, always to increase its productive force. The bare possibility of extending the field of production is transformed for him into a similar compulsory law. The enormous expansive force of modern industry, compared with which that of gases is mere child's play, appears to us now as a *necessity* for expansion, both qualitative and quantitative, that laughs at all resistance. Such resistance is offered by consumption, by sales, by the markets for the products of modern industry. But the capacity for extension, extensive and intensive, of the markets is primarily governed by quite different laws, that work much less energetically. The extension of the markets cannot keep pace with the extension of production. The collision becomes inevitable, and as this cannot produce any real solution so long as it does not break in pieces the capitalist mode of production, the collisions become periodic. Capitalist production has begotten another 'vicious circle'.

As a matter of fact, since 1825, when the first general crisis broke out, the whole industrial and commercial world, production and exchange among all civilized peoples and their more or less barbaric hangers-on, are thrown out of joint about once every ten years. Commerce is at a standstill, the markets are glutted, products accumulate, as multitudinous as they are unsaleable, hard cash disappears, credit vanishes, factories are closed, the mass of the workers are in want of the means of subsistence, because they have produced too much of the means of subsistence; bankruptcy follows upon bankruptcy, execution upon execution. The stagnation lasts for years; productive forces and products are wasted and destroyed wholesale, until the accumulated mass of commodities finally filter off, more or less depreciated in value, until production and exchange gradually begin to move again. Little by little the pace quickens. It becomes a trot. The industrial trot breaks into a canter, the canter in turn grows into the headlong gallop of a perfect steeplechase of industry, commercial credit and speculation, which finally, after breakneck leaps, ends where it began – in the ditch of a crisis. And so over and over again. We have now, since the year 1825, gone through this five times, and at the present moment (1877) we are going through it for the sixth time. And the character of these crises is so clearly defined that Fourier hit all of them off, when he described the first as a '*crise pléthorique*', a crisis from plethora.

In these crises, the contradiction between socialized production and capitalist appropriation ends in a violent explosion. The circulation of commodities is, for the time being, stopped. Money, the means of circulation, becomes a hindrance to circulation. All the laws of production and circulation of commodities are turned upside down. The economic collision has reached its apogee. *The mode of production is in rebellion against the mode of exchange.*

The fact that the socialized organization of production within the factory has developed so far that it has become incompatible with the anarchy of production in society, which exists side by side with and dominates it, is brought home to the capitalists themselves by the violent concentration of capital that occurs during crises, through the ruin of many large, and a still greater number of small, capitalists. The whole mechanism of the capitalist mode of production breaks down under the pressure of the productive forces, its own creations. It is no longer able to turn all this mass of means of production into capital. They lie fallow, and for that very reason the industrial reserve army must also be fallow. Means of production, means of subsistence, available labourers, all the elements of production and of general wealth are present in abundance. But 'abundance becomes the source of distress and want' (Fourier) because it is the very thing that prevents the transformation of the means of production and subsistence into capital. For in capitalistic society the means of production can only function when they have undergone a preliminary transformation into capital, into the means of exploiting human labour-power. The necessity of this transformation into capital of the means of production and subsistence stands like a ghost between these and the workers. It alone prevents the coming together of the material and personal levers of production; it alone forbids the means of production to function, the workers to work and live. On the one hand, therefore, the capitalistic mode of production stands convicted of its own incapacity to further direct these productive forces. On the other, these productive forces themselves, with increasing energy, press forward to the removal of the existing contradiction, to the abolition of their quality as capital, to the *practical recognition of their character as social productive forces.*

This rebellion of the productive forces, as they grow more and more powerful, against their quality as capital, this stronger and stronger command that their social character shall be recognized, forces the capitalist class itself to treat them more and more as social productive forces so far as this is possible under capitalist conditions. The period of industrial high pressure, with its unbounded inflation of credit, not less than the crash itself, by the collapse of great capitalist establishments, tends to bring about that form of the socialization of great masses of means of production, which we meet with in the different kinds of joint-stock companies. Many of these means of production and of distribution are, from the outset, so colossal, that, like the railroads, they exclude all other forms of capitalistic exploitation. At a further stage of evolution this form also becomes insufficient. The producers on a large scale in a particular branch of industry in a particular country unite in a 'Trust', a union for the purpose of regulating production. They determine the total amount to be produced, parcel it out among themselves, and thus enforce the selling price fixed beforehand. But trusts of this kind, as soon as business becomes bad, are generally liable to break up, and, on this very account, compel a yet greater concentration of association. The whole of the particular industry is turned into one gigantic joint-stock company; internal competition gives place to the internal monopoly of this one company. This has happened in 1890 with the English *alkali* production, which is now, after the fusion of 48 large works, in the hands of one company, conducted upon a single plan, and with a capital of £6,000,000.

In the trusts, freedom of competition changes into its very opposite – into monopoly; and the production without any definite plan of capitalistic society capitulates to the production upon a definite plan of the invading socialistic society. Certainly this is so far still to the benefit and advantage of the capitalists. But in this case the exploitation is so palpable that it must break down. No nation will put up with production conducted by trusts, with so barefaced an exploitation of the community by a small band of dividend-mongers.

In any case, with trusts or without, the official representative of capitalist society – the State – will ultimately have to undertake the direction of production. This necessity for conversion into State property is felt first in the great institutions for intercourse and communication – the post office, the telegraphs, the railways.

If the crises demonstrate the incapacity of the bourgeoisie for managing any longer modern productive forces, the transformation of the great establishments for production and distribution into joint-stock companies, trusts and State property, show how unnecessary the bourgeoisie are for that purpose. All the social functions of the capitalist are now performed by salaried employees. The capitalist has no further social function than that of pocketing dividends, tearing off coupons, and gambling on the Stock Exchange, where the different capitalists despoil one another of their capital. At first the capitalistic mode of production forces out the workers. Now it forces out the capitalists, and reduces them, just as it reduced the workers, to the ranks of the surplus population, although not immediately into those of the industrial reserve army.

But the transformations, either into joint-stock companies and trusts, or into State ownership, does not do away with the capitalistic nature of the productive forces. In the joint-stock companies and trusts this is obvious. And the modern State, again, is only the organization that bourgeois society takes on in order to support the external conditions of the capitalist mode of production against the encroachments, as well of the workers as of individual capitalists. The modern State, no matter what its form, is essentially a capitalist machine, the state of the capitalists, the ideal personification of the total national capital. The more it proceeds to the taking over of productive forces, the more does it actually become the national capitalist, the more citizens does it exploit. The workers remain wage-workers – proletarians. The capitalist relation is not done away with. It is rather brought to a head. But, brought to a head, it topples over. State ownership of the productive forces is not the solution of the conflict, but concealed within it are the technical conditions that form the elements of that solution.

This solution can only consist in the practical recognition of the social nature of the modern forces of production, and therefore in harmonizing the modes of production, appropriation and exchange with the socialized character of the means of production. And this can only come about by society openly and directly taking possession of the productive forces which have outgrown all control except that of society as a whole. The social character of the means of production and of the products today reacts against the producers, periodically disrupts all production and exchange, acts only like a law of Nature working blindly, forcibly, destructively. But with the taking over by society of the productive forces, the social character of the means of production and of the products will be utilized by the producers with a perfect understanding of its nature, and instead of being a source of disturbance and periodical collapse, will become the most powerful lever of production itself.

Active social forces work exactly like natural forces: blindly, forcibly, destructively, so long as we do not understand, and reckon with, them. But when once we understand them, when once we grasp their action, their direction, their effects, it depends only upon ourselves to subject them more and more to our own will, and by means of them to reach our own ends. And this holds especially for the mighty productive forces of today. As long as we obstinately refuse to understand the nature and the character of these social means of action – and this understanding goes against the grain of the capitalist mode of production and its defenders – so long these forces are at work in spite of us, in opposition to us, so long they master us, as we have shown above in detail.

But when once their nature is understood, they can, in the hands of the producers working together, be transformed from master demons into willing servants. The difference is as that between the destructive force of electricity in the lightning of the storm, and electricity under command in the telegraph and the voltaic arc; the difference between a conflagration, and fire working in the service of man. With this recognition at last of the real nature of the productive forces of today, the social anarchy of production gives place to a social regulation of production upon a definite plan, according to the needs of the community and of each individual. Then the capitalist mode of appropriation, in which the product enslaves first the producer and then the appropriator, is replaced by the mode of appropriation of the products that is based upon the nature of the modern means of production; upon the one hand, direct social appropriation, as means to the maintenance and extension of production – on the other, direct individual appropriation, as means of subsistence and of enjoyment.

Whilst the capitalist mode of production more and more completely transforms the great majority of the population into proletarians, it creates the power which, under penalty of its own destruction, is forced to accomplish this revolution. Whilst it forces on more and more the transformation of the vast means of production, already socialized, into State property, it shows itself the way to accomplishing this revolution. *The proletariat seizes political power and turns the means of production into State property.*

But, in doing this, it abolishes itself as proletariat, abolishes all class distinctions and class antagonisms, abolishes also the State as State. Society thus far, based upon class antagonisms, had need of the State. That is, of an organization of the particular class which was *pro tempore* the exploiting class, an organization for the purpose of preventing any interference from without with the existing conditions of production, and therefore, especially, for the purpose of forcibly keeping the exploited classes in the condition of oppression corresponding with the given mode of production (slavery, serfdom, wage-labour). The State was the official representative of society as a whole; the gathering of it together into a visible embodiment. But it was this only in so far as it was the State of that class which itself represented, for the time being, society as a whole; in ancient times, the State of slave-owning citizens; in the middle ages, the feudal lords; in our own time, the bourgeoisie. When at last it becomes the real representative of the whole of society, it renders itself unnecessary. As soon as there is no longer any social class to be held in subjection; as soon as class rule, and the individual struggle for existence based upon our present anarchy in production, with the collisions and excesses arising from these, are removed, nothing more remains to be repressed, and a special repressive force, a State, is no longer necessary. The first act by virtue of which the State really constitutes itself the representative of the whole of society – the taking possession of the means of production in the name of society – this is, at the same time, its last independent act as a State. State interference in social relations becomes, in one domain after another, superfluous, and then dies out of itself; the government of persons is replaced by the administration of things, and by the conduct of processes of production. The State is not 'abolished'. *It dies out.* This gives the measure of the value of the phrase 'a free State', both as to its justifiable use at times by agitators, and as to its ultimate scientific insufficiency, and also of the demands of the so-called anarchists for the abolition of the State out of hand.

Since the historical appearance of the capitalist mode of production, the appropriation by society of all the means of production has often been dreamed of, more or less vaguely, by individuals, as well as by sects, as the ideal of the future. But it could become possible, could become a historical necessity, only when the actual conditions for its realization were there. Like every other social advance, it becomes practicable, not by men understanding that the existence of classes is in contradiction to justice, equality, etc., not by the mere willingness to abolish these classes, but by virtue of certain new economic conditions. The separation of society into an exploiting and an exploited class, a ruling and an oppressed class, was the necessary consequence of the deficient and restricted development of production in former times. So long as the total social labour only yields a produce which but slightly exceeds that barely necessary for the existence of all; so long, therefore, as labour engages all or almost all the time of the great majority of the members of society – so long, of necessity, this society is divided into classes. Side by side with the great majority, exclusively bond slaves to labour, arises a class freed from directly productive labour, which looks after the general affairs of society; the direction of labour, State business, law, science, art, etc. It is, therefore, the law of division of labour that lies at the basis of the division into classes. But this does not prevent this division into classes from being carried out by means of violence and robbery, trickery and fraud. It does not prevent the ruling class, once having the upper hand, from consolidating its power at the expense of the working class, from turning their social leadership into an intensified exploitation of the masses.

But if, upon this showing, division into classes has a certain historical justification, it has this only for a given period, only under given social conditions. It was based upon the insufficiency of production. It will be swept away by the complete development of modern productive forces. And, in fact, the abolition of classes in society presupposes a degree of historical evolution, at which the existence, not simply of this or that particular ruling class, but of any ruling class at all, and, therefore, the existence of class distinction itself has become an obsolete anachronism. It presupposes, therefore, the development of production carried out to a degree at which appropriation of the means of production and of the products, and, with this, of political domination, of the monopoly of culture, and of intellectual leadership by a particular class of society, has become not only superfluous, but economically, politically, intellectually a hindrance to development.

This point is now reached. Their political and intellectual bankruptcy is scarcely any longer a secret to the bourgeoisie themselves. Their economic bankruptcy recurs regularly every ten years. In every crisis, society is suffocated beneath the weight of its own productive forces and products, which it cannot use, and stands helpless, face to face with the absurd contradiction that the producers have nothing to consume, because consumers are wanting. The expansive force of the means of production bursts the bonds that the capitalist mode of production had imposed upon them. Their deliverance from these bonds is the one precondition for an unbroken, constantly-accelerated development of the productive forces, and therewith for a practically unlimited increase of production itself. Nor is this all. The socialized appropriation of the means of production does away, not only with the present artificial restrictions upon production, but also with the positive waste and devastation of productive forces and products that are at the present time the inevitable concomitants of production, and that reach their height in the crises. Further, it sets free for the community at large a mass of means of production and of products, by doing away with the senseless extravagance of the ruling classes of today, and their political representatives. The possibility of securing for every member of society, by means of socialized production, an existence not only fully sufficient materially, and becoming day by day more full, but an existence guaranteeing to all the free development and exercise of their physical and mental faculties – this possibility is now for the first time here, but *it is here*.

With the seizing of the means of production by society, production of commodities is done away with, and, simultaneously, the mastery of the product over the producer. Anarchy in social production is replaced by systematic, definite organization. The struggle for individual existence disappears. Then for the first time, man, in a certain sense, is finally marked off from the rest of the animal kingdom, and emerges from mere animal conditions of existence into really human ones. The whole sphere of the conditions of life which environ man, and which have hitherto ruled man, now comes under the dominion and control of man, who for the first time becomes the real, conscious lord of Nature, because he has now become master of his own social organization. The laws of his own social action, hitherto standing face to face with man as laws of Nature foreign to, and dominating, him, will then be used with full understanding, and so mastered by him. Man's own social organization, hitherto confronting him as a necessity imposed by Nature and history, now becomes the result of his own free action. The extraneous objective forces that have hitherto governed history, pass under the control of man himself. Only from that time will man himself, more and more consciously, make his own history – only from that time will the social causes set in movement by him have, in the main and in a constantly growing measure, the results intended by him. It is the ascent of man from the kingdom of necessity to the kingdom of freedom.

Let us briefly sum up our sketch of historical evolution.

I. *Medieval Society*. Individual production on a small scale. Means of production adapted for individual use, hence primitive, ungainly, petty, dwarfed in action. Production for immediate consumption, either of the producer himself or of his feudal lord.

Only where an excess of production over this consumption occurs is such excess offered for sale, enters into exchange. Production of commodities, therefore, only in its infancy. But already it contains within itself, in embryo, *anarchy in the production of society at large.*

2. *Capitalist Revolution.* Transformation of industry, at first by means of simple cooperation and manufacture. Concentration of the means of production, hitherto scattered, into great workshops. As a consequence, their transformation from individual to social means of production – a transformation which does not, on the whole, affect the form of exchange. The old forms of appropriation remain in force. The capitalist appears. In his capacity as owner of the means of production, he also appropriates the products and turns them into commodities. Production has become a *social* act. Exchange and appropriation continue to be *individual* acts, the acts of individuals. *The social product is appropriated by the individual capitalist.* Fundamental contradiction, whence arise all the contradictions in which our present-day society moves, and which modern industry brings to light.

A. Severance of the producer from the means of production. Condemnation of the worker to wage-labour for life. *Antagonism between the proletariat and the bourgeoisie.*

B. Growing predominance and increasing effectiveness of the laws governing the production of commodities. Unbridled competition. *Contradiction between socialized organization in the individual factory and social anarchy in production as a whole.*

C. On the one hand, perfecting of machinery, made by competition compulsory for each individual manufacturer, and complemented by a constantly growing displacement of labourers. *Industrial reserve-army.* On the other hand, unlimited extension of production, also compulsory under competition, for every manufacturer. On both sides, unheard of development of productive forces, excess of supply over demand, over-production, glutting of the markets, crises every ten years, the vicious circle – excess here, of means of production and products – excess there of labourers, without employment and without means of existence. But these two levers of production and of social well-being are unable to work together, because the capitalist form of production prevents the productive forces from working and the products from circulating, unless they are first turned into capital – which their very superabundance prevents. The contradiction has grown into an absurdity. *The mode of production rises in rebellion against the form of exchange*. The bourgeoisie are convicted of incapacity further to manage their own social productive forces.

D. Partial recognition of the social character of the productive forces forced upon the capitalists themselves. Taking over of the great institutions for production and communication, first by joint-stock companies, later on by trusts, then by the State. The bourgeoisie demonstrated to be a superfluous class. All its social functions are now performed by salaried employees.

3. *Proletarian Revolution*. Solution of the contradictions. The proletariat seizes the public power, and by means of this transforms the socialized means of production, slipping from the hands of the bourgeoisie, into public property. By this fact, the proletariat frees the means of production from the character of capital they have thus far borne, and gives their socialized character complete freedom to work itself out. Socialized production upon a pre-determined plan becomes henceforth possible. The development of production makes the existence of different classes of society thenceforth an anachronism. In proportion as anarchy in social production vanishes, the political authority of the State dies out. Man, at last the master of his own form of social organization, becomes at the same time the lord over Nature, his own master – free.

To accomplish this act of universal emancipation is the historical mission of the modern proletariat. To thoroughly comprehend the historical conditions and thus the very nature of this act, to impart to the now oppressed proletarian class a full knowledge of the conditions and of the meaning of the momentous act it is called upon to accomplish, this is the task of the theoretical expression of the proletarian movement, scientific Socialism.

IV. THE HISTORIAN

Introduction

As historians Marx and Engels owed much to Hegel. In his lectures on the philosophy of history Hegel had argued that the great men who in the past had changed the course of world events were more than remarkable individuals. They were the embodiment of new social forces and new ideas. Each new revolution in History embodied the unconscious workings of the Absolute Mind and was a step forward towards the realization of a Divine Idea. Marx and Engels took over from Hegel the notion of historical progress towards a predetermined end. But they held that purely materialistic – and not divinely inspired – factors must be examined to arrive at the truth concerning historical change and they believed that mankind was moving not towards the realization of a Divine Idea but towards the establishment of a Communist society. Moreover they held that the economic and social forces which stimulated revolutionary changes were the struggles between rival classes in society. Marx and Engels were not professional historians conducting research from original sources. They used the standard histories available to them. They claimed that they had discovered a new approach to history and that they had found a convincing explanation of what had happened in the past. Their views on the materialistic conception of history were clearly stated as early as 1846 in their joint work on *The German Ideology* (most of which, however, was not published in the lifetime of Marx and Engels). Here they wrote that 'it is quite obvious from the start that there exists a materialistic connexion of men with one another, which is determined by their needs and their mode of production, and which is as old as men themselves. This connexion is ever taking new forms, and thus presents a "history" independently of the existence of any political or religious nonsense which would hold men together on its own.'

Engels's historical writings fall into two groups. In some of his historical studies he relied for his information upon the researches of recognized scholars but offered his readers a new interpretation of the facts. On the other hand, when he discussed very recent events – often in newspapers or periodicals – Engels was an independent writer who did not rely on the researches of other people but assembled his own materials and selected his own facts for presentation to the reader. There was, however, a vital link between the two types of Engels's historical writings since both were firmly based upon a materialist conception of history. This view of history was the theory that the development of man and of society could be understood only by examining the interaction of politics and economics in the past. Marx and Engels believed that it was only by studying the continual interplay of political and economic factors over the centuries that the history of man could really be understood. They held that in the past economic conditions had generally controlled political changes but that in the Communist society of the future political factors – the policy of an all powerful State – would successfully control man's economic destiny.

Even before he had begun to collaborate with Marx, Engels had written a brief historical introduction to his book on *The Condition of the Working Class in England* (1845) which was largely based upon Peter Gaskell's *The Manufacturing Population of England*. Engels accepted Gaskell's view that English yeomen and craftsmen had led an idyllic existence in the eighteenth century before the coming of the factory system. *The Communist Manifesto* of 1848, composed jointly by Marx and Engels, opened with a striking section which sought to explain the rise of the middle and working classes in the context of the economic developments of Europe in modern times. Soon afterwards he wrote a short history of the Peasants' War which he regarded as the first violent eruption of the class struggle in Germany. Here he was heavily indebted to W. Zimmermann's account of the Peasant War which had been published in three volumes in 1841–3. Many years later – in 1884 – he wrote a book on *The Origin of the Family, Private Property and the State* which was based upon the researches of the American scholar Lewis H. Morgan. Engels considered that Morgan 'had rediscovered in America, in his own way, the materialist conception of history that had been discovered by Marx forty years ago in his comparison of barbarism and civilization and was led by this conception to the same conclusions ... as had been reached by Marx.'

Engels's earliest essays in contemporary history appeared in the early 1850s. At that time Engels had settled in Manchester and was working in the cotton trade. He devoted some of his scanty leisure to a study of the history of the recent revolution in Germany in order to discover why this had failed. He hoped that future revolutionaries would not repeat these errors. He contributed articles to the *Neue Rheinische Zeitung* on the risings in support of the German constitution drawn up by the National Assembly at Frankfurt. Engels wrote about events of which he had personal knowledge since he had been engaged in revolutionary activities in Cologne and Elberfeld in 1848 and had served in the rebel army in the Baden rising of 1849. Subsequently he wrote a more general popular account of the revolution and subsequent reaction in Germany in 1848–9 in a series of articles which appeared (under Marx's name) in the *New York Daily Tribune*. Shortly afterwards Engels turned his attention to a study of the history of warfare and he established a considerable reputation for himself as a military critic and historian. He contributed articles on military subjects to an American encyclopedia and acted as a military correspondent for a London newspaper at the time of the Franco-Prussian war. Finally in his later years Engels wrote introductions to new editions of two of Karl Marx's essays on recent French history and tried to show how successful his friend had been in explaining 'a phase of contemporary history from the given economic situation'.

1. The Formation of the State among the Germans[1]

ACCORDING to Tacitus the Germans were a very numerous people. An approximate idea of the strength of the different German peoples is given by Caesar; he puts the number of Usipetans and Tencterans, who appeared on the left bank of the Rhine, at 180,000, including women and children. Thus, about 100,000 to a single people, considerably more than, say, the Iroquois numbered in their most flourishing period, when not quite 20,000 became the terror of the whole country, from the Great Lakes to the Ohio and Potomac. If we were to attempt to group on a map the individual peoples of the Rhine country, who are better known to us from reports, we would find that such a people would occupy on the average the area of a Prussian administrative district, about 10,000 square kilometres, or 182 geographical square miles. The *Germania Magna* of the Romans, reaching to the Vistula, comprised, however, roundly 500,000 square kilometres. Counting an average of 100,000 for any single people, the total population of *Germania Magna* would have amounted to five million – a rather high figure for a barbarian group of peoples, although 10 inhabitants to the square kilometre, or 550 to the geographical square mile, is very little when compared with present conditions. But this does not include all the Germans then living. We know that German peoples of Gothic origin, Bastarnians, Peukinians and others, lived along the Carpathian Mountains all the way down to the mouth of the Danube. They were so numerous that Pliny designated them as the fifth main tribe of the Germans; in 180 B.C. they were already serving as mercenaries of the Macedonian King Perseus, and in the first years of the reign of Augustus they were still pushing their way as far as the vicinity of Adrianople. If we assume that

1. [Chapter VIII of F. Engels, *The Origin of the Family, Private Property and the State* (German edition 1884: English translation from the edition published by the Foreign Languages Publishing House, Moscow).]

they numbered only one million, then, at the beginning of the Christian era, the Germans numbered probably not less than six million.

After settling in Germany (*Germanien*) the population must have grown with increasing rapidity. The industrial progress mentioned above is sufficient to prove it. The objects found in the bogs of Schleswig, to judge by the Roman coins found with them, date from the third century. Hence at that time the metal and textile industry was already well developed on the Baltic, a lively trade was carried on with the Roman Empire, and the wealthier class enjoyed a certain luxury – all evidences of a greater density of population. At this time, however, the Germans started their general assault along the whole line of the Rhine, the Roman frontier rampart and the Danube, a line stretching from the North Sea to the Black Sea – direct proof of the ever-growing population striving outwards. During the three centuries of struggle, the whole main body of the Gothic peoples (with the exception of the Scandinavian Goths and the Burgundians) moved towards the south-east and formed the left wing of the long line of attack; the High Germans (Herminonians) pushed forward in the centre of this line, on the Upper Danube, and the Istaevonians, now called Franks, on the right wing, along the Rhine. The conquest of Britain fell to the lot of the Ingaevonians. At the end of the fifth century the Roman Empire, exhausted, bloodless and helpless, lay open to the invading Germans.

In preceding chapters we stood at the cradle of ancient Greek and Roman civilization. Now we are standing at its grave. The levelling plane of Roman world power had been passing for centuries over all the Mediterranean countries. Where the Greek language offered no resistance all national languages gave way to a corrupt Latin. There were no longer any distinctions of nationality, no more Gauls, Iberians, Ligurians, Noricans; all had become Romans. Roman administration and Roman law had everywhere dissolved the old bodies of *consanguinei* and thus crushed the last remnants of local and national self-expression. The new-fangled Romanism could not compensate for this loss; it did not express any nationality, but only lack of nationality.

The elements for the formation of new nations existed everywhere. The Latin dialects of the different provinces diverged more and more; the natural boundaries that had once made Italy, Gaul, Spain, Africa independent territories, still existed and still made themselves felt. Yet nowhere was there a force capable of combining these elements into new nations; nowhere was there the least trace of any capacity for development or any power of resistance, much less of creative power. The immense human mass of that enormous territory was held together by one bond alone – the Roman state; and this, in time, had become their worst enemy and oppressor. The provinces had ruined Rome; Rome itself had become a provincial town like all the others, privileged, but no longer ruling, no longer the centre of the world empire, no longer even the seat of the emperors and vice-emperors, who lived in Constantinople, Treves and Milan. The Roman state had become an immense complicated machine, designed exclusively for the exploitation of its subjects. Taxes, services for the state and levies of all kinds drove the mass of the people deeper and deeper into poverty. The extortionate practices of the procurators, tax collectors and soldiers caused the pressure to become intolerable. This is what the Roman state with its world domination had brought things to: it had based its right to existence on the preservation of order in the interior and protection against the barbarians outside. But its order was worse than the worst disorder, and the barbarians, against whom the state pretended to protect its citizens, were hailed by them as saviours.

Social conditions were no less desperate. During the last years of the republic, Roman rule was already based on the ruthless exploitation of the conquered provinces. The emperors had not abolished this exploitation; on the contrary, they had regularized it. The more the empire fell into decay, the higher rose the taxes and compulsory services, and the more shamelessly the officials robbed and blackmailed the people. Commerce and industry were never the business of the Romans who lorded it over entire peoples. Only in usury did they excel all others, before and after them. The commerce that existed and managed to maintain itself for a time was reduced to ruin by official extortion; what survived was carried out in the eastern, Grecian part of the empire, but this is beyond the scope of our study. Universal impoverishment; decline of commerce, handicrafts, the arts, and of the population; decay of the towns; retrogression of agriculture to a lower stage – this was the final result of Roman world supremacy.

Agriculture, the decisive branch of production throughout antiquity, now became so more than ever. In Italy, the immense aggregations of estates (*latifundia*) which had covered nearly the whole territory since the end of the republic, had been utilized in two ways: either as pastures, on which the population had been replaced by sheep and oxen, the care of which required only a few slaves; or as country estates, on which large-scale horticulture had been carried on with masses of slaves, partly to serve the luxurious needs of the owners and partly for sale in the urban markets. The great pastures had been preserved and probably even enlarged. But the country estates and their horticulture fell into ruin owing to the impoverishment of their owners and the decay of the towns. Latifundian economy based on slave labour was no longer profitable; but at that time it was the only possible form of large-scale agriculture. Small-scale farming again became the only profitable form. Estate after estate was parcelled out and leased in small lots to hereditary tenants, who paid a fixed sum, or to *partiarii*, farm managers rather than tenants, who received one-sixth or even one ninth of the year's product for their work. Mainly, however, these small plots were distributed to *coloni*, who paid a fixed amount annually, were attached to the land and could be sold together with the plots. These were not slaves, but neither were they free; they could not marry free citizens, and intermarriage among themselves was not regarded as valid marriage, but as mere concubinage (*contubernium*), as in the case of the slaves. They were the forerunners of the medieval serfs.

The slavery of antiquity became obsolete. Neither in large-scale agriculture in the country, nor in the manufactories of the towns did it any longer bring in a return worth while – the market for its products had disappeared. Small-scale agriculture and small handicrafts, to which the gigantic production of the flourishing times of the empire was now reduced, had no room for numerous slaves. Society found room only for the domestic and luxury slaves of the rich. But moribund slavery was still sufficiently virile to make all productive work appear as slave labour, unworthy of the dignity of free Romans – and everybody was now a free Roman. On this account, on the one hand, there was an increase in the number of superfluous slaves who, having become a drag, were emancipated; on the other hand, there was an increase in the number of *coloni* and of beggared freemen (similar to the poor whites in the ex-slave states of America). Christianity is perfectly innocent of this gradual dying out of ancient slavery. It had partaken of the fruits of slavery in the Roman Empire for centuries, and later did nothing to prevent the slave trade of Christians, either of the Germans in the North, or of the Venetians on the Mediterranean, or the Negro slave trade of later years. Slavery no longer paid, and so it died out; but dying slavery left behind its poisonous sting by branding as ignoble the productive work of the free. This was the blind alley in which the Roman world was caught: slavery was economically impossible, while the labour of the free was under a moral ban. The one could no longer, the other could not yet, be the basic form of social production. Only a complete revolution could be of help here.

Things were no better in the provinces. Most of the reports we have concern Gaul. By the side of the *coloni*, free small peasants still existed there. In order to protect themselves against the brutal extortions of the officials, judges and usurers, they frequently placed themselves under the protection, the patronage, of men possessed of power; and they did this not only singly, but in whole communities, so much so that the emperors of the fourth century often issued decrees prohibiting this practice. How did this help those who sought this protection? The patron imposed the condition that they transfer the title of their lands to him, and in return he ensured them the usufruct of their land for life – a trick which the Holy Church remembered and freely imitated during the ninth and tenth centuries, for the greater glory of God and the enlargement of its own landed possessions. At that time, however, about the year 475, Bishop Salvianus of Marseilles still vehemently denounced such robbery and related that the oppression of the Roman officials and great landlords became so intolerable that many 'Romans' fled to the districts already occupied by the barbarians, and the Roman citizens who had settled there feared nothing so much as falling under Roman rule again. That poor parents frequently sold their children into slavery in those days is proved by a law forbidding this practice.

In return for liberating the Romans from their own state, the German barbarians appropriated two thirds of the entire land and divided it among themselves. The division was made in accordance with the gentile system; as the conquerors were relatively small in number, large tracts remained, undivided, partly in the possession of the whole people and partly in that of the tribes or gentes. In each gens fields and pastures were distributed among the individual households in equal shares by lot. We do not know whether repeated redivisions took place at that time; at all events, this practice was soon discarded in the Roman provinces, and the individual allotment became alienable private property, allodium. Forests and pastures remained undivided for common use; this use and the mode of cultivating the divided land was regulated by ancient custom and the will of the entire community. The longer the gens existed in its village, and the more Germans and Romans merged in the course of time, the more the consanguineous character of the ties retreated before territorial ties. The gens disappeared in the mark community, in which, however, sufficient traces of the original kinship of the members were visible. Thus, the gentile constitution, at least in those countries where mark communes were preserved – in the North of France, in England, Germany and Scandinavia – was imperceptibly transformed into a territorial constitution, and thus became capable of being fitted into the state. Nevertheless, it retained the natural democratic character which distinguishes the whole gentile order, and thus preserved a piece of the gentile constitution even in its degeneration, forced upon it in later times, thereby leaving a weapon in the hands of the oppressed, ready to be wielded even in modern times.

The rapid disappearance of the blood tie in the gens was due to the fact that its organs in the tribe and the whole people had also degenerated as a result of the conquest. We know that rule over subjugated people is incompatible with the gentile order. Here we see it on a large scale. The German peoples, masters of the Roman provinces, had to organize their conquest; but one could neither absorb the mass of the Romans into the gentile bodies nor rule them with the aid of the latter. A substitute for the Roman state had to be placed at the head of the Roman local administrative bodies, which at first largely continued to function, and this substitute could only be another state. Thus, the organs of the gentile constitution had to be transformed into organs of state, and owing to the pressure of circumstances, this had to be done very quickly. The first representative of the conquering people was, however, the military commander. The internal and external safety of the conquered territory demanded that his power be increased. The moment had arrived for transforming military leadership into kingship. This was done.

Let us take the kingdom of the Franks. Here, not only the wide dominions of the Roman state, but also all the very large tracts of land and small *Gau*[1] and mark communities, especially all the large forests, fell into the hands of the victorious Salian people as their unrestricted possession. The first thing the king of the Franks, transformed from an ordinary military commander into a real monarch, did was to convert this property of the people into a royal estate, to steal it from the people and to donate or grant it in fief to his retainers. This retinue, originally composed of his personal military retainers and the rest of the subcommanders of the army, was soon augmented not only by Romans, that is, Romanized Gauls, who quickly became almost indispensable to him owing to their knowledge of writing, their education and familiarity with the Romance vernacular and literary Latin as well as with the laws of the land, but also by slaves, serfs and freedmen, who constituted his Court and from among whom he chose his favourites. All these were granted tracts of public land first mostly as gifts and later in the form of benefices – originally in most cases for the period of the life of the king – and so the basis was laid for a new nobility at the expense of the people.

But this was not all. The far-flung empire could not be

1. [Administrative region.]

governed by means of the old gentile constitution. The council of chiefs, even if it had not long become obsolete, could not have assembled and was soon replaced by the king's permanent retinue. The old popular assembly was still ostensibly preserved, but more and more as an assembly of the sub-commanders of the army and the newly-rising notables. The free land-owning peasants, the mass of the Frankish people, were exhausted and reduced to penury by continuous civil war and wars of conquest, the latter particularly under Charlemagne, just as the Roman peasants had been during the last period of the republic. These peasants, who originally had formed the whole army, and after the conquest of the Frankish lands had been its core, were so impoverished at the beginning of the ninth century that scarcely one out of five could provide the accoutrements of war. The former army of free peasants, called up directly by the king, was replaced by an army composed of the servitors of the newly-arisen magnates. Among these servitors were also villeins, the descendants of the peasants who formerly had acknowledged no master but the king, and a little earlier had acknowledged no master at all, not even a king. Under Charlemagne's successors the ruin of the Frankish peasantry was completed by internal wars, the weakness of the royal power and corresponding usurpations of the magnates, whose ranks were augmented by the *Gau* counts, established by Charlemagne and eager to make their office hereditary, and finally by the incursions of the Normans. Fifty years after the death of Charlemagne, the Frankish Empire lay as helpless at the feet of the Normans as four hundred years previously the Roman Empire had lain at the feet of the Franks.

Not only the external impotence, but the internal order, or rather disorder, of society, was almost the same. The free Frankish peasants found themselves in a position similar to that of their predecessors, the Roman *coloni*. Ruined by war and plunder, they had to seek the protection of the new magnates or the Church, for the royal power was too weak to protect them; they had to pay dear for this protection. Like the Gallic peasants before them, they had to transfer the property in their land to their patrons, and received it back from them as tenants in different and varying forms, but always on condition of performing services and paying dues. Once driven into this form of dependence, they gradually lost their personal freedom; after a few generations most of them became serfs. How rapidly the free peasants were degraded is shown by Irminon's land records of the Abbey Saint-Germain-des-Prés, then near (now in) Paris. Even during the life of Charlemagne, on the vast estates of this abbey, stretching into the surrounding country there were 2,788 households, nearly all Franks with German names; 2,080 of them were *coloni*, 35 liti, 220 slaves and only 8 freeholders! The custom by which the patron had the land of the peasants transferred to himself, giving to them only the usufruct of it for life, the custom denounced as ungodly by Salvianus, was now universally practised by the Church in its dealings with the peasants. Feudal servitude, now coming more and more into vogue, was modelled as much on the lines of the Roman *angariae*, compulsory services for the state, as on the services rendered by the members of the German mark in bridge and road building and other work for common purposes. Thus, it looked as if, after four hundred years, the mass of the population had come back to the point it had started from.

This proved only two things, however: first, that the social stratification and the distribution of property in the declining Roman Empire corresponded entirely to the then prevailing stage of production in agriculture and industry, and hence was unavoidable; secondly, that this stage of production had not sunk or risen to any material extent in the course of the following four hundred years, and, therefore, had necessarily produced the same distribution of property and the same class division of population. During the last centuries of the Roman Empire, the town lost its supremacy over the country, and did not regain it during the first centuries of German rule. This presupposes a low stage of agriculture, and of industry as well. Such a general condition necessarily gives rise to big ruling landowners and dependent small peasants. How almost impossible it was to graft either the Roman latifundian economy run with slave labour or the newer large-scale farming run with serf labour on to such a society, is proved by Charlemagne's very extensive experiments with his famous imperial estates, which passed away leaving hardly a trace. These experiments were continued only by the monasteries and were fruitful only for them; but the monasteries were abnormal social bodies founded on celibacy. They could do the exceptional, and for that very reason had to remain exceptions.

Nevertheless, progress was made during these four hundred years. Even if in the end we find almost the same main classes as in the beginning, still, the people who constituted these classes had changed. The ancient slavery had disappeared; gone were also the beggared poor freemen, who had despised work as slavish. Between the Roman *colonus* and the new serf there had been the free Frankish peasant. The 'useless reminiscences and vain strife' of doomed Romanism were dead and buried. The social classes of the ninth century had taken shape not in the bog of a declining civilization, but in the travail of a new. The new race, masters as well as servants, was a race of men compared with its Roman predecessors. The relation of powerful landlords and serving peasants, which for the latter had been the hopeless form of the decline of the world of antiquity, was now for the former the starting point of a new development. Moreover, unproductive as these four hundred years appear to have been, they, nevertheless, left *one* great product behind them: the modern nationalities, the refashioning and regrouping of West European humanity for impending history. The Germans, in fact, had infused new life into Europe; and that is why the dissolution of the states in the German period ended, not in Norse-Saracen subjugation, but in the development from the royal benefices and patronage (commendation) to feudalism, and in such a tremendous increase in the population that the drain of blood caused by the Crusades barely two centuries later could be borne without injury.

What was the mysterious charm with which the Germans infused new vitality into dying Europe? Was it the innate magic power of the German race, as our jingo historians would have it? By no means. Of course, the Germans were a highly gifted Aryan tribe, especially at that time, in full process of vigorous development. It was not their specific national qualities that rejuvenated

Europe, however, but simply – their barbarism, their gentile constitution.

Their personal efficiency and bravery, their love of liberty, and their democratic instinct, which regarded all public affairs as its own affairs, in short, all those qualities which the Romans had lost and which were alone capable of forming new states and of raising new nationalities out of the muck of the Roman world – what were they but the characteristic features of barbarians in the upper stage, fruits of their gentile constitution?

If they transformed the ancient form of monogamy, moderated male rule in the family and gave a higher status to women than the classic world had ever known, what enabled them to do so if not their barbarism, their gentile customs, their still living heritage of the time of mother right?

If they were able in at least three of the most important countries – Germany, Northern France and England – to preserve and carry over to the feudal state a piece of the genuine constitution in the form of the mark communities, and thus give to the oppressed class, the peasants, even under the hardest conditions of medieval serfdom, local cohesion and the means of resistance which neither the slaves of antiquity nor the modern proletarians found ready at hand – to what did they owe this if not to their barbarism, their exclusively barbarian mode of settling in gentes?

And lastly, if they were able to develop and universally introduce the milder form of servitude which they had been practising at home, and which more and more displaced slavery also in the Roman Empire – a form which, as Fourier first emphasized, gave to the oppressed the means of gradual emancipation as a class (*fournit aux cultivateurs des moyens d'affranchissement collectif et progressif*) and is therefore far superior to slavery, which permits only of the immediate manumission of the individual without any transitory stage (antiquity did not know any abolition of slavery by a victorious rebellion), whereas the serfs of the Middle Ages, step by step, achieved their emancipation as a class – to what was this due if not their barbarism, thanks to which they had not yet arrived at complete slavery, either in the form of the ancient labour slavery or in that of the Oriental domestic slavery?

All that was vital and life-bringing in what the Germans infused into the Roman world was barbarism. In fact, only barbarians are capable of rejuvenating a world labouring in the throes of a dying civilization. And the highest stage of barbarism, to which and in which the Germans worked their way up previous to the migration of peoples, was precisely the most favourable one for this process. This explains everything.

2. Luther and Münzer[1]

LUTHER and Münzer, each fully represented his party by his doctrine as well as by his character, and actions.

From 1517 to 1525 *Luther* underwent quite the same changes as the present-day German constitutionalists did between 1846 and 1849, and which are undergone by every bourgeois party which, placed for a while at the head of the movement, is overwhelmed by the plebeian-proletarian party standing behind it.

When in 1517 Luther first opposed the dogmas and statutes of the Catholic Church his opposition by no means possessed a definite character. While it did not overstep the demands of the earlier burgher heresy, it did not, and could not, rule out any trend which went further. At that early stage all the oppositional elements had to be united, the most aggressive revolutionary energy displayed, and the sum of the existing heresies against the Catholic orthodoxy had to find a protagonist. In much the same way our liberal bourgeoisie of 1847 was still revolutionary, called itself socialist and communist, and clamoured for the emancipation of the working class. Luther's sturdy peasant nature asserted itself in the stormiest fashion in that first period of his activities. 'If the raging madness (of the Roman churchmen) were to continue, it seems to me no better counsel and remedy could be found

1. [Engels's history of the Peasants War in Germany (from which this account of Luther and Münzer is taken) appeared as articles in the *Neue Rheinische Zeitung* in 1850 and as a book in 1870 (English translation issued by the Foreign Languages Publishing House, Moscow, 1956).]

against it than that kings and princes apply force, arm themselves, attack those evil people who have poisoned the entire world, and put an end to this game once and for all, *with arms, not with words*. Since we punish thieves with the halter, murderers with the sword, and heretics with fire, why do we not turn on all those evil teachers of perdition, those popes, cardinals and bishops, and the entire swarm of the Roman Sodom *with arms in hand, and wash our hands in their blood*?'

But this revolutionary ardour was short-lived. Luther's lightning struck home. The entire German people was set in motion. On the one hand, peasants and plebeians saw the signal to revolt in his appeals against the clergy, and in his sermon of Christian freedom; and on the other, he was joined by the moderate burghers and a large section of the lesser nobility, and even princes were drawn into the maelstrom. The former believed the day had come to wreak vengeance upon all their oppressors, the latter only wished to break the power of the clergy, the dependence upon Rome, the Catholic hierarchy, and to enrich themselves on the confiscation of church property. The parties stood aloof of each other, and each found its spokesmen. Luther had to choose between them. He, the protégé of the Elector of Saxony, the revered professor of Wittenberg who had become powerful and famous overnight, the great man with his coterie of servile creatures and flatterers, did not hesitate a single moment. He dropped the popular elements of the movement, and took the side of the burghers, the nobility and the princes. His appeals for a war of extermination against Rome were heard no more. Luther now preached *peaceful progress* and *passive resistance*. Invited by Hutten to visit him and Sickingen in the castle of Ebern, the seat of the nobility's conspiracy against clergy and princes, Luther replied: ' I do not wish the Gospel *defended by force and bloodshed*. The world was conquered by the Word, the Church is maintained by the Word, the Word will also put the Church back into its own, and Antichrist, who gained his own without violence, will fall without violence.'

From this tendency, or, to be more exact, from this more definite delineation of Luther's policy, sprang that bartering and haggling over institutions and dogmas to be retained or reformed, that disgusting diplomatizing, conciliating, intriguing and compromising, which resulted in the Augsburg Confession,[1] the finally importuned articles of a reformed burgher church. It was quite the same kind of petty bargaining that was recently repeated in political form *ad nauseam* at the German national assemblies, conciliatory gatherings, chambers of revision, and Erfurt parliaments.[2] The Philistine nature of the official Reformation was most markedly evident at these negotiations.

There were good reasons for Luther, henceforth the recognized representative of the burgher reform, to preach lawful progress. The bulk of the towns espoused the cause of moderate reform, the petty nobility became more and more devoted to it, and a section of the princes struck in, while another vacillated. Success was as good as won, at least in a large part of Germany. The remaining regions could not in the long run withstand the pressure of moderate opposition in the event of continued peaceful development. Any violent upheaval, meanwhile, was bound to bring the moderate Party into conflict with the extremist plebeian and peasant party, to alienate the princes, the nobility, and certain towns from the movement, leaving the alternative of either the burgher party being overshadowed by the peasants and plebeians, or the entire movement being crushed by Catholic restoration. And there have been examples enough lately of how bourgeois parties seek to steer their way by means of lawful progress between the Scylla of revolution and the Charybdis of restoration, after gaining the slightest victory.

Under the general social and political conditions prevailing in that day the results of every change were necessarily advantageous to the princes, and inevitably increased their power. Thus it came about that the more completely the burgher reform fell under the control of the reformed princes, the more sharply it broke away from the plebeian and peasant elements. Luther himself became more and more their vassal, and the people well knew what they were doing when they accused him of having

1. [A statement of the Lutheran doctrine, read to Emperor Charles V at the Imperial Diet in Augsburg in 1530.]

2. [Allusion is made to the parliament of representatives of German states that comprised the 'German Union' created by Prussia, which sat at Erfurt from 20 March to 29 April 1850.]

become, as the others, a flunkey of the princes, and when they stoned him in Orlamünde.

When the Peasant War broke out Luther strove to adopt a mediatory attitude in regions where the nobility and the princes were mostly Catholic. He resolutely attacked the governments. He said they were to blame for the rebellion in view of their oppression; it was not the peasants, but God himself, who rose against them. Yet, on the other hand, he said, the revolt was ungodly, and contrary to the Gospel. In conclusion he called upon both parties to yield and reach a peaceful understanding.

But in spite of these well-meaning mediatory offers, the revolt spread swiftly, and even involved Protestant regions dominated by Lutheran princes, lords and towns, rapidly outgrowing the 'circumspect' burgher reform. The most determined faction of the insurgents under Münzer made its headquarters in Luther's immediate proximity at Thuringia. A few more successes, and the whole of Germany would be in flames, Luther surrounded and perhaps piked as a traitor, and the burgher reform swept away by the tide of a peasant-plebeian revolution. There was no more time for circumspection. All the old animosities were forgotten in the face of the revolution. Compared with the hordes of peasants, the servants of the Roman Sodom were innocent lambs, sweet-tempered children of God. Burgher and prince, noble and clergyman, Luther and the Pope, all joined hands 'against the murderous and plundering peasant hordes'.[1] 'They must be *knocked to pieces*, *strangled* and *stabbed*, *covertly* and *overtly*, by everyone who can, just as one must kill a *mad dog*!' Luther cried. 'Therefore, dear sirs, help here, save there, stab, knock, strangle them everyone who can, and should you lose your life, bless you, no better death canst thou ever attain.' There should only be no false mercy for the peasant. Whoever hath pity on those whom God pities not, whom He wishes punished and destroyed, belongs among the rebels himself. Later the peasants would themselves learn to thank God when they would have to give up one cow in order to enjoy the other in peace, and

1. [The title of a pamphlet against the peasant movement published by Luther in May 1525, at the height of the Peasant War.]

the princes would learn through the revolution the spirit of the mob that must be ruled by force only. 'The wise man says: *cibum, onus et virgam asino*.[1] The peasants must have nothing but chaff. They do not hearken to the Word, and are foolish, so they must hearken to the rod and the gun, and that serves them right. We must pray for them that they obey. Where they do not there should not be much mercy. *Let the guns roar among them*, or else they will do it a thousand times worse.'

That was exactly what our late socialist and philanthropic bourgeoisie said when the proletariat claimed its share in the fruits of victory after the March events.

Luther had put a powerful weapon into the hands of the plebeian movement by translating the Bible. Through the Bible he contrasted the feudalized Christianity of his day with the moderate Christianity of the first century, and the decaying feudal society with a picture of a society that knew nothing of the ramified and artificial feudal hierarchy. The peasants had made extensive use of this instrument against the princes, the nobility, and the clergy. Now Luther turned it against them, extracting from the Bible such a veritable hymn to the God-ordained authorities as no bootlicker of absolute monarchy had ever been able to accomplish. Princedom by the grace of God, resigned obedience, even serfdom, were sanctioned with the aid of the Bible. Not the peasant revolt alone, but Luther's own mutiny against religious and lay authority was thereby disavowed; and not only the popular movement, but the burgher movement as well, were betrayed to the princes.

Need we name the bourgeois who recently also gave us examples of such a disavowal of their own past?

Let us now compare the plebeian revolutionary *Münzer*, with Luther, the burgher reformist.

Thomas Münzer was born in *Stolberg*, in the Harz, in 1498.[2] His father is said to have died on the scaffold, a victim of the obduracy of the Count of Stolberg. In his fifteenth year Münzer organized a secret union at the Halle school against the Archbishop of Magdeburg and the Roman Church in general. His

1. ['Food, pack, and lash to the ass.']   2. [Thomas Münzer was born about 1490.]

learning in the theology of his time brought him an early doctor's degree and the position of chaplain in a Halle nunnery. Here he treated the church dogmas and rites with the greatest contempt. At mass he omitted the words of the transubstantiation, and ate, as Luther said, the almighty gods unconsecrated. Medieval mystics, and particularly the chiliastic works of Joachim the Calabrese, were the main subject of his studies. The millennium and the Day of Judgement over the degenerated church and corrupted world propounded and described by that mystic, seemed to Münzer imminently close, what with the Reformation and the general unrest of his time. He preached in his neighbourhood with great success. In 1520 he went to Zwickau as the first evangelist preacher. There he found one of those fanatical chiliastic sects that continued their existence on the quiet in many localities, and whose momentary humility and detachment concealed the increasingly rampant opposition of the lowest strata of society to the prevailing conditions, and who were now coming into the light of day ever more boldly and persistently with the growing unrest. It was the sect of the Anabaptists headed by *Niklas Storch*. They preached the approach of the Day of Judgement and of the millennium; they had 'visions, transports and the spirit of prophecy'. They soon came into conflict with the Council of Zwickau. Münzer defended them, though he never joined them unconditionally, and would have rather brought them under his own influence. The Council took drastic measures against them; they had to leave the town, and Münzer with them. This was at the close of 1521.

He went to Prague and sought to gain a foothold by joining the remnants of the Hussite movement. But his proclamation only had the effect of compelling him to flee from Bohemia as well. In 1522 he became preacher at Allstedt in Thuringia. Here he started with reforming the cult. Even before Luther dared to go so far, he entirely abolished the Latin language and ordered the entire Bible, and not only the prescribed Sunday Gospels and epistles, to be read to the people. At the same time, he organized propaganda in his locality. People flocked to him from all directions, and Allstedt soon became the centre of the popular anti-priest movement of all Thuringia.

Münzer was as yet theologian before everything else. He still directed his attacks almost exclusively against the priests. He did not, however, preach quiet debate and peaceful progress, as Luther had begun at that time, but continued Luther's earlier violent sermons, calling upon the princes of Saxony and the people to rise in arms against the Roman priests. 'Does not Christ say, "I came not to send peace, but a sword"? What must you (the princes of Saxony) do with that sword? Only one thing if you wish to be the servants of God, and that is to drive out and destroy the evil ones who stand in the way of the Gospel. Christ ordered very earnestly (Luke, xix, 27) "bring hither mine enemies and slay them before me." Do not give us any empty phrases that the power of God will do it without the aid of your sword, since then it would rust in its sheath. . . . Those who stand in the way of God's revelation must be destroyed mercilessly, as Hezekiah, Cyrus, Josiah, Daniel and Elias destroyed the priests of Baal, else the Christian Church will never come back to its source. We must uproot the weeds in God's vineyard at harvest time. . . . God said in the Fifth Book of Moses, 7, "thou shalt not show mercy unto the idolators, but ye shall destroy their altars, and break down their images and burn them with fire that I shall not be wroth at you."'

But these appeals to the princes were of no avail, whereas revolutionary sentiments among the people grew day by day. Münzer, whose ideas became ever more sharply defined and bolder, now broke resolutely away from the burgher Reformation, and henceforth became an outright political agitator.

His philosophico-theological doctrine attacked all the main points not only of Catholicism, but of Christianity generally. Under the cloak of Christian forms he preached a kind of pantheism, which curiously resembles modern speculative contemplation[1] and at times even approaches atheism. He repudiated the Bible both as the only and the infallible revelation. The real and living revelation, he said, was reason, a revelation which existed, and still exists, among all peoples at all times. To hold up the Bible against reason, he maintained, was to kill the spirit

[1]. [Engels refers to the views of the German idealist philosophers Strauss and Feuerbach.]

by the letter, for the Holy Spirit of which the Bible speaks is not something that exists outside us; the Holy Spirit is our reason. Faith is nothing else but reason come alive in man, and pagans could therefore also have faith. Through this faith, through reason come to life, man became godlike and blessed. Heaven is, therefore, nothing of another world, and is to be sought in this life and it is the task of believers to establish this Heaven, the kingdom of God, here on earth. Just as there is no Heaven in the beyond, there is also no Hell, and no damnation. Similarly, there is no devil but man's evil lusts and greed. Christ was a man, as we are, a prophet and a teacher, and his supper is a plain meal of commemoration wherein bread and wine are consumed without any mystic garnish.

Münzer preached these doctrines mostly cloaked in the same Christian phraseology under which the new philosophy had to hide for some time. But the arch-heretical fundamental idea is easily discerned in all his writings, and he obviously took the biblical cloak much less in earnest than many a disciple of Hegel in modern times. And yet three hundred years separate Münzer from modern philosophy.

Münzer's political doctrine followed his revolutionary religious conceptions very closely, and just as his theology overstepped the current conceptions of his time, so his political doctrine went beyond the directly prevailing social and political conditions. Just as Münzer's religious philosophy approached atheism, so his political programme approached communism, and even on the eve of the February Revolution, more than one present-day communist sect lacked as comprehensive a theoretical arsenal as was Münzer's in the sixteenth century. This programme, less of a compilation of the demands of the plebeians of that day than a visionary anticipation of the conditions for the emancipation of the proletarian element that had scarcely begun to develop among the plebeians – this programme demanded the immediate establishment of the kingdom of God, of the prophesied millennium, by restoring the Church to its original status and abolishing all the institutions that conflicted with this allegedly early-Christian, but, in fact, very much novel church. By the kingdom of God Münzer understood a society without class differences, private property and a state authority independent of, and foreign to, the members of society. All the existing authorities, in so far as they refused to submit and join the revolution, were to be overthrown, all work and all property shared in common, and complete equality introduced. A union was to be established to realize all this, not only throughout Germany, but throughout all Christendom. Princes and lords were to be invited to join, and should they refuse, the union was to take up arms and overthrow or kill them at the first opportunity.

Münzer set to work at once to organize the union. His sermons became still more militant and revolutionary. He thundered forth against the princes, the nobility and the patricians with a passion that equalled the fervour of his attacks upon the clergy. He pictured the prevailing oppression in burning colours, and countered it with his dream-vision of the millennium of social republican equality. He published one revolutionary pamphlet after another, and sent emissaries in all directions, while personally organizing the union in Allstedt and its vicinity.

The first fruit of this propaganda was the destruction of St Mary's Chapel in Mellerbach near Allstedt, according to the command of the Bible (Deut. vii, 6): 'Ye shall destroy their altars, and dash in pieces their pillars, and burn their graven images with fire.' The princes of Saxony came in person to Allstedt to quell the unrest, and had Münzer come to the castle. There he delivered a sermon the like of which they had not heard from Luther, 'that easy-living flesh of Wittenberg', as Münzer called him. Münzer maintained that ungodly rulers, especially priests and monks, who treated the Gospel as heresy, should be killed, and referred to the New Testament for confirmation. The ungodly had no right to live save by the mercy of God's elect. If the princes would not exterminate the ungodly, God would take their sword from them, *because the entire community had the power of the sword*. The princes and lords are the prime movers of usury, thievery and robbery; they take all creatures into their private possession – the fish in the water, the birds in the air, and the plants in the soil – and still preach to the poor the commandment, 'Thou shalt not steal', while they themselves take everything they find, rob and oppress the peasant and the artisan; but when one of the latter commits the slightest transgression, he has to hang, and Dr Lügner[1] says to all this: Amen. 'The masters themselves are to blame that the poor man becomes their enemy. If they do not remove the causes of the upheaval, how can things go well in the long run? Oh, dear sirs, how the Lord will smite these old pots with an iron rod! But for saying so, I am regarded a rebel. So be it!'

Münzer had the sermon printed. His Allstedt printer was punished by Duke Johann of Saxony with banishment, while Münzer's writings were to be henceforth censored by the ducal government in Weimar. But he paid no heed to this order. He lost no time in publishing a highly inciting paper[2] in the imperial city of Mühlhausen, wherein he called on the people 'to widen the hole so that all the world may see and understand who our great personages are that have blasphemously turned our Lord into a painted mannikin', and which ended with the following words: 'All the world must suffer a big jolt. There will be such a game that the ungodly will be thrown off their seats, and the downtrodden will rise.' Thomas Münzer, 'the man with the hammer', wrote the following motto on the title page: 'Beware, I have put my words into thy mouth, I have put you over the people and over the Empire that thou mayest uproot, destroy, scatter and overthrow, and that thou mayest build and plant. A wall of iron against the kings, princes, priests, and against the people hath been erected. Let them fight, for victory will wondrously lead to the perdition of the strong and godless tyrants.'[3]

Münzer's breach with Luther and his party had taken place long before that. Luther had to accept some of the church reforms introduced by Münzer without consulting him. He watched Münzer's activities with a moderate reformer's nettled mistrust of a more energetic farther-aiming party. Already in the spring of 1524, in a letter to Melanchthon, that model of a hectic stay-at-home Philistine, Münzer wrote that he and Luther did

1. [Münzer refers to Luther; a play on the word 'Lügner' which is the German for 'liar'.]

2. [Münzer's pamphlet, *Open Denial of the False Belief of the Godless World on the Testimony of the Gospel of Luke, Presented to Miserable and Pitiful Christendom in Memory of its Error*, which appeared in Mühlhausen in 1524.]

3. [Münzer paraphrases words from the Book of the Prophet Jeremiah.]

not understand the movement at all. He said they sought to choke it by the letter of the Bible, and that their doctrine was worm-eaten. 'Dear brethren,' he wrote, 'cease your procrastinations and vacillations. It is time, summer is knocking at the door. Do not keep friendship with the ungodly who hinder the Word from working its full force. Do not flatter your princes, or you may perish with them. Ye tender bookish scholars, do not be wroth, for I can do nothing to change it.'

Luther had more than once challenged Münzer to an open debate. The latter, however, always ready to take up the battle before the people, had not the least desire to let himself in for a theological squabble before the partisan public of Wittenberg University. He did not wish 'to bring the testimony of the Spirit exclusively before the high school of learning'. If Luther were sincere he should use his influence to stop the chicaneries against his, Münzer's, printer, and lift the censorship so that their controversy might be freely fought out in the press.

But now, when Münzer's above-mentioned revolutionary brochure appeared, Luther openly denounced him. In his *Letter to the Princes of Saxony Against the Rebellious Spirit*, he declared Münzer to be an instrument of Satan, and demanded of the princes to intervene and drive the instigators of the upheaval out of the country, since they did not confine themselves to preaching their evil doctrine, but incited to insurrection, to violent action against the authorities.

On 1 August, Münzer was compelled to appear before the princes in the castle of Weimar on the charge of incitement to mutiny. Highly compromising facts were available against him; they were on the scent of his secret union; his hand was detected in the societies of the miners and the peasants. He was threatened with banishment. No sooner had he returned to Allstedt than he learned that Duke Georg of Saxony demanded his extradition. Union letters in his handwriting had been intercepted, wherein he called Georg's subjects to armed resistance against the enemies of the Gospel. The Council would have extradited him, had he not left the town.

In the meantime, the growing unrest among the peasants and plebeians had made Münzer's propaganda work incomparably easier. In the Anabaptists he found invaluable agents for that purpose. This sect, which had no definite dogmas, held together only by its common opposition to all ruling classes and by the common symbol of the second baptism, ascetic in their mode of living, untiring, fanatical and intrepid in carrying on propaganda, had grouped itself more and more closely around Münzer. Made homeless by persecutions, its members wandered all over Germany and carried word everywhere of the new teaching, in which Münzer had made their own demands and wishes clear to them. Countless Anabaptists were put on the rack, burned or otherwise executed, but the courage and endurance of these emissaries were unshakeable, and the success of their activities amidst the rapidly growing unrest of the people was enormous. Thus, on his flight from Thuringia, Münzer found the ground prepared wherever he turned.

Near Nürnberg, where Münzer first went, a peasant revolt had been nipped in the bud a month before.[1] Münzer conducted his propaganda on the quiet; people soon appeared who defended his most audacious theological propositions on the non-obligatory nature of the Bible and the meaninglessness of sacraments, who declared Christ a mere man, and the power of the lay authorities ungodly. 'There is Satan stalking, the Spirit of Allstedt!' Luther exclaimed. In Nuremberg Münzer printed his reply to Luther.[2] He accused him of flattering the princes and supporting the reactionary party through his insipid moderation. But the people would free themselves none the less, he wrote, and it would go with Dr Luther as with a captive fox. The Council ordered the paper confiscated, and Münzer had to leave Nürnberg.

Now he went across Swabia to Alsace, then to Switzerland, and then back to the Upper Black Forest, where an insurrection had broken out several months before, largely precipitated by his Anabaptist emissaries. This propaganda tour of Münzer's had unquestionably and substantially contributed to the estab-

1. [Münzer first went to the imperial town of Mühlhausen, from where he was banished in September 1524 for taking part in the disturbances among the city poor. From Mülhausen Münzer came to Nürnberg.]

2. [Münzer's reply to Luther was entitled: *A Well-Grounded Defence and Reply to the Godless, Easy-Living Flesh of Wittenberg, Which Has Pitifully Sullied Unhappy Christianity through Shameless Distortions of the Holy Scripture.*]

lishment of the people's party, to a clear formulation of its demands and to the final general outbreak of the insurrection in April 1525. It was through this trip that the dual effect of Münzer's activities appears particularly pronounced – on the one hand, on the people, whom he addressed in the only language they could then comprehend, that of religious prophecy; and, on the other hand, on the initiated, to whom he could disclose his ultimate aims. Even before his journey he had assembled in Thuringia a circle of resolute men from among the people and the lesser clergy, whom he had put at the head of his secret society. Now he became the soul of the entire revolutionary movement in South-western Germany, organized ties between Saxony and Thuringia through Franconia and Swabia up to Alsace and the Swiss border, and counted such South-German agitators as Hubmaier of Waldshut, Conrad Grebel of Zürich, Franz Rabmann of Griessen, Schappeler of Memmingen, Jakob Wehe of Leipheim, and Dr Mantel in Stuttgart, who were mostly revolutionary priests, among his disciples and the heads of the union. He himself stayed mostly in Griessen on the Schaffhausen border, journeying from there across the Hegau, Klettgau, etc. The bloody persecutions undertaken by the alarmed princes and lords everywhere against this new plebeian heresy, contributed not a little to fanning the spirit of rebellion and consolidating the ranks of the society. In this way Münzer conducted his agitation for about five months in Upper Germany, and returned to Thuringia when the outbreak of the conspiracy was near at hand, because he wished to lead the movement personally. There we shall find him later.

We shall see how truly the character and behaviour of the two party leaders reflected the attitude of their respective parties, how Luther's indecision and fear of the movement, that was assuming serious proportions, and his cowardly servility to the princes, fully corresponded to the hesitant and ambiguous policy of the burghers, and how Münzer's revolutionary energy and resolution was reproduced among the most advanced section of the plebeians and peasants. The only difference was that while Luther confined himself to expressing the conceptions and wishes of the majority of his class and thereby won an extremely cheap popularity among it, Münzer, on the contrary, went far beyond the immediate ideas and demands of the plebeians and peasants, and first organized a party of the élite of the then existing revolutionary elements, which, in as much as it shared his ideas and energy, always remained only a small minority of the in-insurgent masses.

3. The German Revolution of 1848 [1]

(i) The Vienna Insurrection

ON 24 February 1848, Louis Philippe was driven out of Paris, and the French Republic was proclaimed. On 13 March following, the people of Vienna broke the power of Prince Metternich, and made him flee shamefully out of the country. On 18 March, the people of Berlin rose in arms, and, after an obstinate struggle of eighteen hours, had the satisfaction of seeing the King surrender himself into their hands. Simultaneous outbreaks of a more or less violent nature, but all with the same success, occurred in the capitals of the smaller states of Germany. The German people, if they had not accomplished their first revolution, were at least fairly launched into the revolutionary career.

As to the incidents of these various insurrections, we cannot enter here into the details of them: what we have to explain is their character, and the position which the different classes of the population took up with regard to them.

The Revolution of Vienna may be said to have been made by an almost unanimous population. The bourgeoisie (with the exception of the bankers and stock-jobbers), the petty trading class, the working people, one and all arose at once against a Government detested by all, a Government so universally hated, that the small minority of nobles and money lords which had supported it made itself invisible on the very first attack. The middle classes had been kept in such a degree of political ignorance by Metternich that to them the news from Paris about

1 [Chapters from F. Engels, *Revolution and Counter Revolution in Germany in 1848* (1891). Appeared originally as articles in the *New York Daily Tribune* in 1851–2.]

the reign of Anarchy, Socialism, and terror, and about impending struggles between the class of capitalists and the class of labourers, proved quite unintelligible. They, in their political innocence, either could attach no meaning to these news, or they believed them to be fiendish inventions of Metternich, to frighten them into obedience. They, besides, had never seen working men acting as a class, or stand up for their own distinct class interests. They had, from their past experience, no idea of the possibility of any differences springing up between classes that now were so heartily united in upsetting a Government hated by all. They saw the working people agree with themselves upon all points: a constitution, trial by jury, liberty of the Press, etc. Thus they were, in March 1848, at least, heart and soul with the movement, and the movement, on the other hand, at once constituted them the (at least in theory) predominant class of the State.

But it is the fate of all revolutions that this union of different classes, which in some degree is always the necessary condition of any revolution, cannot subsist long. No sooner is the victory gained against the common enemy than the victors become divided among themselves into different camps, and turn their weapons against each other. It is this rapid and passionate development of class antagonism which, in old and complicated social organisms, makes a revolution such a powerful agent of social and political progress; it is this incessantly quick upshooting of new parties succeeding each other in power, which, during those violent commotions, makes a nation pass in five years over more ground than it would have done in a century under ordinary circumstances.

The Revolution in Vienna made the middle class the theoretically predominant class; that is to say, the concessions wrung from the Government were such as, once carried out practically and adhered to for a time, would inevitably have secured the supremacy of the middle class. But practically the supremacy of that class was far from being established. It is true that by the establishment of a national guard, which gave arms to the bourgeoisie and petty tradesmen, that class obtained both force and importance; it is true that by the installation of a 'Committee of Safety', a sort of revolutionary, irresponsible Government in which the bourgeoisie predominated, it was placed at the head of power. But, at the same time, the working classes were partially armed too; they and the students had borne the brunt of the fight, as far as fight there had been; and the students, about 4,000 strong, well-armed, and far better disciplined than the national guard, formed the nucleus, the real strength of the revolutionary force, and were no ways willing to act as a mere instrument in the hands of the Committee of Safety. Though they recognized it, and were even its most enthusiastic supporters, they yet formed a sort of independent and rather turbulent body, deliberating for themselves in the 'Aula', keeping an intermediate position between the bourgeoisie and the working classes, preventing by constant agitation things from settling down to the old everyday tranquillity, and very often forcing their resolutions upon the Committee of Safety. The working men, on the other hand, almost entirely thrown out of employment, had to be employed in public works at the expense of the state, and the money for this purpose had, of course, to be taken out of the purse of the taxpayers or out of the chest of the city of Vienna. All this could not but become very unpleasant to the tradesmen of Vienna. The manufacturers of the city, calculated for the consumption of the rich and aristocratic courts of a large country, were as a matter of course entirely stopped by the Revolution, by the flight of the aristocracy and Court; trade was at a standstill, and the continuous agitation and excitement kept up by the students and working people was certainly not the means to 'restore confidence', as the phrase went. Thus a certain coolness very soon sprung up between the middle classes on the one side and the turbulent students and working people on the other; and if for a long time this coolness was not ripened into open hostility, it was because the ministry, and particularly the Court, in their impatience to restore the old order of things, constantly justified the suspicions and the turbulent activity of the more revolutionary parties, and constantly made arise, even before the eyes of the middle classes, the spectre of old Metternichian despotism. Thus on 15 May, and again on 26, there were fresh risings of all classes in Vienna, on account of the Government having tried to attack, or to undermine some of the newly-conquered liberties, and on each occasion the alliance between the national guard or armed middle class, the students, and the working-men, was again cemented for a time.

As to the other classes of the population, the aristocracy and the money lords had disappeared, and the peasantry were busily engaged everywhere in removing feudalism down to its last vestiges. Thanks to the war in Italy, and the occupation which Vienna and Hungary gave to the Court, they were left at full liberty, and succeeded in their work of liberation, in Austria, better than in any other part of Germany. The Austrian Diet had very shortly after only to confirm the steps already practically taken by the peasantry, and whatever else the Government of Prince Schwartzenberg may be enabled to restore, it will never have the power of re-establishing the feudal servitude of the peasantry. And if Austria at the present moment is again comparatively tranquil, and even strong, it is principally because the great majority of the people, the peasants, have been real gainers by the Revolution, and because whatever else has been attacked by the restored Government, those palpable, substantial advantages, conquered by the peasantry, are as yet untouched.

(ii) The Berlin Insurrection

THE second centre of revolutionary action was Berlin, and from what has been stated in the foregoing papers, it may be guessed that there this action was far from having that unanimous support of almost all classes by which it was accompanied in Vienna. In Prussia, the bourgeoisie had been already involved in actual struggles with the Government; a rupture had been the result of the United Diet; a bourgeois revolution was impending, and that revolution might have been, in its first outbreak, quite as unanimous as that of Vienna, had it not been for the Paris Revolution of February. That event precipitated everything, while at the same time it was carried out under a banner totally different from that under which the Prussian bourgeoisie was preparing to defy its Government. The Revolution of February upset, in France, the very same sort of Government which the Prussian bourgeoisie were going to set up in their own country.

The Revolution of February announced itself as a revolution of the working classes against the middle classes; it proclaimed the downfall of middle-class government and the emancipation of the working man. Now the Prussian bourgeoisie had, of late, had quite enough of working-class agitation in their own country. After the first terror of the Silesian riots had passed away, they had even tried to give this agitation a turn in their own favour; but they always had retained a salutary horror of revolutionary Socialism and Communism; and, therefore, when they saw men at the head of the Government in Paris whom they considered as the most dangerous enemies of property, order, religion, family and of the other *Penates* of the modern bourgeois, they at once experienced a considerable cooling down of their own revolutionary ardour. They knew that the moment must be seized, and that, without the aid of the working masses, they would be defeated; and yet their courage failed them. Thus they sided with the Government in the first partial and provincial outbreaks, tried to keep the people quiet in Berlin, who, during five days, met in crowds before the royal palace to discuss the news and ask for changes in the Government; and when at last, after the news of the downfall of Metternich, the King made some slight concessions, the bourgeoisie considered the Revolution as completed, and went to thank His Majesty for having fulfilled all the wishes of his people. But then followed the attack of the military on the crowd, the barricades, the struggle, and the defeat of royalty. Then everything was changed; the very working classes, which it had been the tendency of the bourgeoisie to keep in the background, had been pushed forward, had fought and conquered, and all at once were conscious of their strength. Restrictions of suffrage, of the liberty of the Press, of the right to sit on juries, of the right of meeting – restrictions that would have been very agreeable to the bourgeoisie because they would have touched upon such classes only as were beneath them – now were no longer possible. The danger of a repetition of the Parisian scenes of 'anarchy' was imminent. Before this danger all former differences disappeared. Against the victorious working man, although he had not yet uttered any specific demands for himself, the friends and the foes of many years united, and the alliance between the bourgeoisie and the supporters of the over-turned system was concluded upon the very barricades of Berlin. The necessary concessions, but no more than was unavoidable, were to be made, a ministry of the opposition leaders of the United Diet was to be formed, and in return for its services in saving the Crown, it was to have the support of all the props of the old Government, the feudal aristocracy, the bureaucracy, the army. These were the conditions upon which Messrs Camphausen and Hansemann undertook the formation of a cabinet.

Such was the dread evinced by the new ministers of the aroused masses, that in their eyes every means was good if it only tended to strengthen the shaken foundations of authority. They, poor deluded wretches, thought every danger of a restoration of the old system had passed away; and thus they made use of the whole of the old state machinery for the purpose of restoring 'order'. Not a single bureaucrat or military officer was dismissed; not the slightest change was made in the old bureaucratic system of administration. These precious constitutional and responsible ministers even restored to their posts those functionaries whom the people, in the first heat of revolutionary ardour, had driven away on account of their former acts of bureaucratic overbearing. There was nothing altered in Prussia but the persons of the ministers; even the ministerial staffs in the different departments were not touched upon, and all the constitutional place hunters, who had formed the chorus of the newly-elevated rulers, and who had expected their share of power and office, were told to wait until restored stability allowed changes to be operated in the bureaucratic personnel which now were not without danger.

The King, chap-fallen in the highest degree after the insurrection of 18 March, very soon found out that he was quite as necessary to these 'Liberal' ministers as they were to him. The throne had been spared by the insurrection; the throne was the last existing obstacle to 'anarchy'; the Liberal middle class and its leaders, now in the ministry, had therefore every interest to keep on excellent terms with the Crown. The King, and the reactionary camerilla that surrounded him, were not slow in discovering this, and profited by the circumstance in order to fetter the march of the ministry even in those petty reforms that were from time to time intended.

The first care of the ministry was to give a sort of legal appearance to the recent violent changes. The United Diet was convoked in spite of all popular opposition, in order to vote as the legal and constitutional organ of the people a new electoral law for the election of an Assembly, which was to agree with the Crown upon a new constitution. The elections were to be indirect, the mass of voters electing a number of electors, who then were to choose the representative. In spite of all opposition this system of double elections passed. The United Diet was then asked for a loan of twenty-five millions of thalers, opposed by the popular party, but eventually agreed to.

These acts of the ministry gave a most rapid development to the popular, or as it now called itself, the Democratic party. This party, headed by the petty trading and shopkeeping class, and uniting under its banner, in the beginning of the Revolution, the large majority of the working people, demanded direct and universal suffrage, the same as established in France, a single Legislative Assembly, and full and open recognition of the Revolution of 18 March, as the base of the new governmental system. The more moderate faction would be satisfied with a thus 'democratized' monarchy, the more advanced demanded the ultimate establishment of the Republic. Both factions agreed in recognizing the German National Assembly at Frankfurt as the supreme authority of the country, while the Constitutionalists and Reactionists affected a great horror of the sovereignty of this body, which they professed to consider as utterly revolutionary.

The independent movement of the working classes had, by the Revolution, been broken up for a time. The immediate wants and circumstances of the movement were such as not to allow any of the specific demands of the Proletarian party to be put in the foreground. In fact, as long as the ground was not cleared for the independent action of the working men, as long as direct and universal suffrage was not yet established, as long as the thirty-six larger and smaller States continued to cut up Germany into numberless morsels, what else could the Proletarian party do but watch the – for them all-important – movement of Paris, and struggle in common with the petty shopkeepers for the attainment of those rights, which would allow them to fight afterwards their own battle?

There were only three points, then, by which the Proletarian party in its political action essentially distinguished itself from the petty trading class, or properly so-called Democratic party; firstly, in judging differently the French movement, with regard to which the democrats attacked, and the Proletarian Revolutionists defended, the extreme party in Paris; secondly, in proclaiming the necessity of establishing a German Republic, one and indivisible, while the very extremest ultras among the democrats only dared to sigh for a Federative Republic; and thirdly, in showing upon every occasion, that revolutionary boldness and readiness for action, in which any party headed by, and composed principally of petty tradesmen, will always be deficient.

The Proletarian, or really Revolutionary party, succeeded only very gradually in withdrawing the mass of the working people from the influence of the Democrats, whose tail they formed in the beginning of the Revolution. But in due time the indecision, weakness, and cowardice of the Democratic leaders did the rest, and it may now be said to be one of the principal results of the last years' convulsions, that wherever the working class is concentrated in anything like considerable masses, they are entirely freed from that Democratic influence which led them into an endless series of blunders and misfortunes during 1848 and 1849. But we had better not anticipate; the events of these two years will give us plenty of opportunities to show the Democratic gentlemen at work.

The peasantry in Prussia, the same as in Austria, but with less energy, feudalism pressing, upon the whole, not quite so hardly upon them here, had profited by the Revolution to free themselves at once from all feudal shackles. But here, from the reasons stated before, the middle classes at once turned against them, their oldest, their most indispensable allies; the democrats, equally frightened with the bourgeoisie, by what was called attacks upon private property, failed equally to support them; and thus, after three months' emancipation, after bloody struggles and military executions, particularly in Silesia, feudalism was restored by the hands of the, until yesterday, anti-feudal bourgeoisie. There is not a more damning fact to be brought against them than this. Similar treason against its best allies, against itself, never was committed by any party in history, and whatever humiliation and chastisement may be in store for this middle class party, it has deserved by this one act every morsel of it.

(iii) The Frankfurt National Assembly

IT will perhaps be in the recollection of our readers that in the preceding papers we followed up the revolutionary movement of Germany to the two great popular victories of 13 March in Vienna, and 18 March in Berlin. We saw, both in Austria and Prussia, the establishment of constitutional Governments and the proclamation, as leading rules for all future policy, of Liberal, or middle class principles; and the only difference observable between the two great centres of action was this, that in Prussia the Liberal bourgeoisie, in the persons of two wealthy merchants, Messrs Camphausen and Hansemann, directly seized upon the reins of power; while in Austria, where the bourgeoisie was, politically, far less educated, the Liberal bureaucracy walked into office, and professed to hold power in trust for them. We have further seen, how the parties and classes of society, that were heretofore all united in opposition to the old Government, got divided among themselves after the victory, or even during the struggle; and how that same Liberal bourgeoisie that alone profited from the victory turned round immediately upon its allies of yesterday, assumed a hostile attitude against every class or party of a more advanced character, and concluded an alliance with the conquered feudal and bureaucratic interests. It was, in fact, evident, even from the beginning of the revolutionary drama, that the Liberal bourgeoisie could not hold its ground against the vanquished, but not destroyed, feudal and bureaucratic parties except by relying upon the assistance of the popular and more advanced parties; and that it equally required, against the torrent of these more advanced masses, the assistance of the feudal nobility and of the bureaucracy. Thus, it was clear enough that the bourgeoisie in Austria and Prussia did not possess sufficient strength to maintain their power, and to adapt the institutions of the country to their own wants and ideas. The Liberal bourgeois ministry was only a halting-place from which, according to the turn circumstances might take, the country would either have to go on to the more advanced stage of Unitarian Republicanism, or to relapse into the old clerico-feudal and bureaucratic régime. At all events, the real, decisive struggle was yet to come; the events of March had only engaged the combat.

Austria and Prussia being the two ruling states of Germany, every decisive revolutionary victory in Vienna or Berlin would have been decisive for all Germany. And as far as they went, the events of March 1848, in these two cities, decided the turn of German affairs. It would, then, be superfluous to recur to the movements that occurred in the minor states; and we might, indeed, confine ourselves to the consideration of Austrian and Prussian affairs exclusively, if the existence of these minor states had not given rise to a body which was, by its very existence, a most striking proof of the abnormal situation of Germany and of the incompleteness of the late Revolution; a body so abnormal, so ludicrous by its very position, and yet so full of its own importance, that history will, most likely, never afford a pendant to it. This body was the so-called *German National Assembly* at Frankfurt am Main.

After the popular victories of Vienna and Berlin, it was a matter of course that there should be a Representative Assembly for all Germany. This body was consequently elected, and met at Frankfurt, by the side of the old Federative Diet. The German National Assembly was expected, by the people, to settle every matter in dispute, and to act as the highest legislative authority for the whole of the German Confederation. But, at the same time, the Diet which had convoked it had in no way fixed its attributions. No one knew whether its decrees were to have force of law, or whether they were to be subject to the sanction of the Diet, or of the individual Governments. In this perplexity, if the Assembly had been possessed of the least energy, it would have immediately dissolved and sent home the Diet – than which no corporate body was more unpopular in Germany – and replaced it by a Federal Government, chosen from among its own members. It would have declared itself the only legal expression of the sovereign will of the German people, and thus have attached legal validity to every one of its decrees. It would, above all, have secured to itself an organized and armed force in the country sufficient to put down any opposition on the parts of the Governments. And all this was easy, very easy, at that early period of the Revolution. But that would have been expecting a great deal too much from an Assembly composed in its majority of Liberal attorneys and *doctrinaire* professors, an Assembly which, while it pretended to embody the very essence of German intellect and science, was in reality nothing but a stage where old and worn-out political characters exhibited their involuntary ludicrousness and their impotence of thought, as well as action, before the eyes of all Germany. This Assembly of old women was, from the first day of its existence, more frightened of the least popular movement than of all the reactionary plots of all the German Governments put together. It deliberated under the eyes of the Diet, nay, it almost craved the Diet's sanction to its decrees, for its first resolutions had to be promulgated by that odious body. Instead of asserting its own sovereignty, it studiously avoided the discussion of any such dangerous question. Instead of surrounding itself by a popular force, it passed to the order of the day over all the violent encroachments of the Governments; Mainz, under its very eyes, was placed in a state of siege, and the people there disarmed, and the National Assembly did not stir. Later on it elected Archduke John of Austria Regent of Germany, and declared that all its resolutions were to have the force of law; but then Archduke John was only instituted in his new dignity after the consent of all the Governments had been obtained, and he was instituted not by the Assembly, but by the Diet; and as to the legal force of the decrees of the Assembly, that point was never recognized by the larger Governments, nor enforced by the Assembly itself; it therefore remained in suspense. Thus we had the strange spectacle of an Assembly pretending to be the only legal representative of a great and sovereign nation, and yet never possessing either the will or the force to make its claims recognized. The debates of this body, without any practical result, were not even of any theoretical value, reproducing, as they did, nothing but the most hackneyed commonplace themes of superannuated philosophical and juridical schools; every sentence that was said, or rather stammered forth, in that Assembly having been printed a thousand times over, and a thousand times better, long before.

Thus the pretended new central authority of Germany left everything as it had found it. So far from realizing the long-demanded unity of Germany, it did not dispossess the most insignificant of the princes who ruled her; it did not draw closer the bonds of union between her separated provinces; it never moved a single step to break down the custom-house barriers that separated Hanover from Prussia, and Prussia from Austria; it did not even make the slightest attempt to remove the obnoxious dues that everywhere obstruct river navigation in Prussia. But the less this Assembly did the more it blustered. It created a German Fleet – upon paper; it annexed Poland and Schleswig; it allowed German-Austria to carry on war against Italy, and yet prohibited the Italians from following up the Austrians into their safe retreat in Germany; it gave three cheers and one cheer more for the French Republic, and it received Hungarian embassies, which certainly went home with far more confused ideas about Germany than they had come with.

This Assembly had been, in the beginning of the Revolution, the bugbear of all German Governments. They had counted upon a very dictatorial and revolutionary action on its part – on account of the very want of definiteness in which it had been found necessary to leave its competency. These Governments, therefore, got up a most comprehensive system of intrigues in order to weaken the influence of this dreaded body; but they proved to have more luck than wits, for this Assembly did the work of the Governments better than they themselves could have done. The chief feature among these intrigues was the convocation of local Legislative Assemblies, and in consequence, not only the lesser states convoked their Legislatures, but Prussia and Austria also called Constituent Assemblies. In these, as in the Frankfurt House of Representatives, the Liberal middle class, or its allies, Liberal lawyers, and bureaucrats had the majority, and the turn affairs took in each of them was nearly the same. The only difference is this, that the German National Assembly was the Parliament of an imaginary country, as it had declined the task of forming what nevertheless was its own first condition of existence, viz. a United Germany; that it discussed the imaginary and never-to-be-carried-out measures of an imaginary Government of its own creation, and that it passed imaginary resolutions for which nobody cared; while in Austria and Prussia the constituent bodies were at least real parliaments, upsetting and creating real ministries, and forcing, for a time at least, their resolutions upon the princes with whom they had to contend. They, too, were cowardly, and lacked enlarged views of revolutionary resolutions; they, too, betrayed the people, and restored power to the hands of feudal, bureaucratic, and military despotism. But then they were at least obliged to discuss practical questions of immediate interest, and to live upon earth with other people, while the Frankfurt humbugs were never happier than when they could roam in 'the airy realms of dream', *im Luftreich des Traums*. Thus the proceedings of the Berlin and Vienna Constituents form an important part of German revolutionary history, while the lucubrations of the Frankfurt collective tomfoolery merely interest the collector of literary and antiquarian curiosities.

The people of Germany, deeply feeling the necessity of doing away with the obnoxious territorial division that scattered and annihilated the collective force of the nation, for some time expected to find, in the Frankfurt National Assembly at least, the beginning of a new era. But the childish conduct of that set of wiseacres soon disenchanted the national enthusiasm. The disgraceful proceedings occasioned by the armistice of Malmö (September 1848) made the popular indignation burst out against a body which, it had been hoped, would give the nation a fair field for action, and which, instead, carried away by unequalled cowardice, only restored to their former solidity the foundations upon which the present counter-revolutionary system is built.

(iv) The Prussian Assembly and the National Assembly

On 1 November Vienna fell, and on the 9th of the same month the dissolution of the Constituent Assembly in Berlin showed how much this event had at once raised the spirit and the strength of the counter-revolutionary party all over Germany.

The events of the summer of 1848 in Prussia are soon told. The Constituent Assembly, or rather 'the Assembly elected for the purpose of agreeing upon a Constitution with the Crown', and its majority of representatives of the middle class interest, had long since forfeited all public esteem by lending itself to all the intrigues of the Court, from fear of the more energetic elements of the population. They had confirmed, or rather restored, the obnoxious privileges of feudalism, and thus betrayed the Liberals and the interests of the peasantry. They had neither been able to draw up a Constitution, nor to amend in any way the general legislation. They had occupied themselves almost exclusively with nice theoretical distinctions, mere formalities, and questions of constitutional etiquette. The Assembly, in fact, was more a school of Parliamentary *savoir vivre* for its members, than a body in which the people could take any interest. The majorities were, besides, very nicely balanced, and almost always decided by the wavering centres whose oscillations from right to left, and vice versa, upset, first the ministry of Camphausen, then that of Auerswald and Hansemann. But while thus the Liberals, here as everywhere else, let the occasion slip out of their hands, the Court reorganized its elements of strength among the nobility, and the most uncultivated portion of the rural population, as well as in the army and the bureaucracy. After Hansemann's downfall, a ministry of bureaucrats and military officers, all staunch reactionists, was formed, which, however, seemingly gave way to the demands of the Parliament; and the Assembly acting upon the commodious principle of 'measures, not men', were actually duped into applauding this ministry, while they, of course, had no eyes for the concentration and organization of counter-revolutionary forces, which that same ministry carried on pretty openly. At last, the signal being given by the fall of Vienna, the King dismissed its ministers, and replaced them by 'men of action', under the leadership of the present premier, Manteuffel. Then the dreaming Assembly at once awoke to the danger; it passed a vote of no confidence in the Cabinet, which was at once replied to by a decree removing the Assembly from Berlin, where it might, in case of a conflict, count upon the support of the masses, to Brandenburg, a petty provincial town dependent entirely upon the Government. The Assembly, however, declared that it could not be adjourned, removed or dissolved, except with its own consent. In the meantime, General Wrangel entered Berlin at the head of some forty thousand troops. In a meeting of the municipal magistrates and the officers of the National Guard, it was resolved not to offer any resistance. And now, after the Assembly and its Constituents, the Liberal bourgeoisie, had allowed the combined reactionary party to occupy every important position, and to wrest from their hands almost every means of defence, began that grand comedy of 'passive and legal resistance' which they intended to be a glorious imitation of the example of Hampden, and of the first efforts of the Americans in the War of Independence. Berlin was declared in a state of siege, and Berlin remained tranquil; the National Guard was dissolved by the Government, and its arms were delivered up with the greatest punctuality. The Assembly was hunted down during a fortnight, from one place of meeting to another, and everywhere dispersed by the military, and the members of the Assembly begged of the citizens to remain tranquil. At last the Government having declared the Assembly dissolved, it passed a resolution to declare the levying of taxes illegal, and then its members dispersed themselves over the country to organize the refusal of taxes. But they found that they had been woefully mistaken in the choice of their means. After a few agitated weeks, followed by severe measures of the Government against the Opposition, everyone gave up the idea of refusing the taxes in order to please a defunct Assembly that had not even had the courage to defend itself.

Whether it was in the beginning of November 1848 already too late to try armed resistance, or whether a part of the army, on finding serious opposition, would have turned over to the side of the Assembly, and thus decided the matter in its favour, is a question which may never be solved. But in revolution as in war, it is always necessary to show a strong front, and he who attacks is in the advantage; and in revolution as in war, it is of the highest necessity to stake everything on the decisive moment, whatever the odds may be. There is not a single successful revolution in history that does not prove the truth of these axioms. Now, for the Prussian Revolution, the decisive moment had come in November 1848; the Assembly, at the head, officially, of the whole revolutionary interest, did neither show a strong front, for it receded at every advance of the enemy; much less did it attack, for it chose even not to defend itself; and when the decisive moment came, when Wrangel, at the head of forty thousand men, knocked at the gates of Berlin, instead of finding, as he and all his officers fully expected, every street studded with barricades, every window turned into a loop-hole, he found the gates open, and the streets obstructed only by peaceful Berliner burghers, enjoying the joke they had played upon him, by delivering themselves up, hands and feet tied, unto the astonished soldiers. It is true, the Assembly and the people, if they had resisted, might have been beaten; Berlin might have been bombarded, and many hundreds might have been killed, without preventing the ultimate victory of the Royalist party. But that was no reason why they should surrender their arms at once. A well-contested defeat is a fact of as much revolutionary importance as an easily-won victory. The defeats of Paris in June 1848, and of Vienna in October, certainly did far more in revolutionizing the minds of the people of these two cities than the victories of February and March. The Assembly and the people of Berlin would, probably, have shared the fate of the two towns above-named; but they would have fallen gloriously, and would have left behind themselves, in the minds of the survivors, a wish of revenge, which in revolutionary times is one of the highest incentives to energetic and passionate action. It is a matter of course that, in every struggle, he who takes up the gauntlet risks being beaten; but is that a reason why he should confess himself beaten, and submit to the yoke without drawing the sword?

In a revolution he who commands a decisive position and surrenders it, instead of forcing the enemy to try his hands at an assault, invariably deserves to be treated as a traitor.

The same decree of the King of Prussia which dissolved the Constituent Assembly also proclaimed a new constitution, founded upon the draft which had been made by a Committee of that Assembly, but enlarging in some points the powers of the Crown, and rendering doubtful in others those of the Parliament. This constitution established two Chambers, which were to meet soon for the purpose of confirming and revising it.

We need hardly ask where the German National Assembly was during the 'legal and peaceful' struggle of the Prussian Constitutionalists. It was, as usual, at Frankfurt, occupied with passing very tame resolutions against the proceedings of the Prussian Government, and admiring the 'imposing spectacle of the passive, legal, and unanimous resistance of a whole people against brutal force'. The Central Government sent commissioners to Berlin to intercede between the Ministry and the Assembly; but they met the same fate as their predecessors at Olmütz, and were politely shown out. The Left of the National Assembly, i.e. the so-called Radical party, sent also their commissioners; but after having duly convinced themselves of the utter helplessness of the Berlin Assembly, and confessed their own equal helplessness, they returned to Frankfurt to report progress, and to testify to the admirably peaceful conduct of the population of Berlin. Nay, more; when Herr Bassermann, one of the Central Government's commissioners, reported that the late stringent measures of the Prussian ministers were not without foundation, in as much as there had of late been seen loitering about the streets of Berlin sundry savage-looking characters, such as always appear previous to anarchical movements (and which ever since have been named 'Bassermannic characters'), these worthy deputies of the Left and energetic representatives of the revolutionary interest actually arose to make oath, and testify that such was not the case! Thus within two months the total impotency of the Frankfurt Assembly was signally proved. There could be no more glaring proofs that this body was totally inadequate to its task; nay, that it had not even the remotest idea of what its task really was. The fact that both in Vienna and in Berlin the fate of the Revolution was settled, that in both these capitals the most important and vital questions were disposed of, without the existence of the Frankfurt Assembly ever being taken the slightest notice of – this fact alone is sufficient to establish that the body in question was a mere debating club, composed of a set of dupes, who allowed the Governments to use them as a Parliamentary puppet, shown to amuse the shopkeepers and petty tradesmen of petty States and petty towns, as long as it was considered convenient to divert the attention of these parties. How long this was considered convenient we shall soon see. But it is a fact worthy of attention that among all the 'eminent' men of this Assembly there was not one who had the slightest apprehension of the part they were made to perform, and that even up to the present day ex-members of the Frankfurt Club have invariably organs of historical perception quite peculiar to themselves.

(v) The Close of the Insurrection

While the south and west of Germany was in open insurrection, and while it took the Governments from the first opening of hostilities at Dresden to the capitulation of Rastatt, rather more than ten weeks, to stifle this final blazing up of the first German Revolution, the National Assembly disappeared from the political theatre without any notice being taken of its exit.

We left this august body at Frankfurt, perplexed by the insolent attacks of the Governments upon its dignity, by the impotency and treacherous listlessness of the Central Power it had itself created, by the risings of the petty trading class for its defence, and of the working class for a more revolutionary ultimate end. Desolation and despair reigned supreme among its members; events had at once assumed such a definite and decisive shape that in a few days the illusions of these learned legislators as to their real power and influence were entirely broken down. The Conservatives, at the signal given by the Governments, had already retired from a body which, henceforth, could not exist any longer, except in defiance of the constituted authorities. The

Liberals gave the matter up in utter discomfiture; they, too, threw up their commissions as representatives. Honourable gentlemen decamped by hundreds. From eight or nine hundred members the number had dwindled down so rapidly that now one hundred and fifty, and a few days after one hundred, were declared a quorum. And even these were difficult to muster, although the whole of the Democratic party remained.

The course to be followed by the remnants of a parliament was plain enough. They had only to take their stand openly and decidedly with the insurrection, to give it, thereby, whatever strength legality could confer upon it, while they themselves at once acquired an army for their own defence. They had to summon the Central Power to stop all hostilities at once; and if, as could be foreseen, this power neither could nor would do so, to depose it at once and put another more energetic Government in its place. If insurgent troops could not be brought to Frankfurt (which, in the beginning, when the State Governments were little prepared and still hesitating, might have been easily done), then the Assembly could have adjourned at once to the very centre of the insurgent district. All this done at once, and resolutely, not later than the middle or end of May, might have opened chances both for the insurrection and for the National Assembly.

But such a determined course was not to be expected from the representatives of German shopocracy. These aspiring statesmen were not at all freed from their illusions. Those members who had lost their fatal belief in the strength and inviolability of the Parliament had already taken to their heels; the Democrats who remained were not so easily induced to give up dreams of power and greatness which they had cherished for a twelvemonth. True to the course they had hitherto pursued, they shrank back from decisive action until every chance of success, nay, every chance to succumb, with at least the honours of war, had passed away. In order, then, to develop a fictitious, busybody sort of activity, the sheer impotency of which coupled with its high pretension, could not but excite pity and ridicule, they continued insinuating resolutions, addresses, and requests to an Imperial Lieutenant, who did not even notice them; to ministers who were in open league with the enemy. And when at last William Wolff, member for Striegan, one of the editors of the new *Neue Rheinische Zeitung*, the only really revolutionary man in the whole Assembly, told them that if they meant what they said, they had better give over talking, and declare the Imperial Lieutenant, the chief traitor to the country, an outlaw at once; then the entire compressed virtuous indignation of these parliamentary gentlemen burst out with an energy which they never found when the Government heaped insult after insult upon them.

Of course, for Wolff's proposition was the first sensible word spoken within the walls of St Paul's Church; of course, for it was the very thing that was to be done, and such plain language going so direct to the purpose, could not but insult a set of sentimentalists, who were resolute in nothing but irresolution, and who, too cowardly to act, had once for all made up their minds that in doing nothing, they were doing exactly what was to be done. Every word which cleared up, like lightning, the infatuated, but intentional nebulosity of their minds, every hint that was adapted to aid them out of the labyrinth where they obstinated themselves to take up as lasting an abode as possible, every clear conception of matters as they actually stood, was, of course, a crime against the majesty of this Sovereign Assembly.

Shortly after the position of the honourable gentlemen in Frankfurt became untenable, in spite of resolutions, appeals, interpellations, and proclamations, they retreated, but not into the insurgent districts; that would have been too resolute a step. They went to Stuttgart, where the Württemberg Government kept up a sort of expectative neutrality. There, at last, they declared the Lieutenant of the Empire to have forfeited his power, and elected from their own body a Regency of five. This Regency at once proceeded to pass a Militia law, which was actually in all due force sent to all the Governments of Germany.

They, the very enemies of the Assembly, were ordered to levy forces in its defence! Then there was created – on paper, of course – an army for the defence of the National Assembly. Divisions, brigades, regiments, batteries, everything was regulated and ordained. Nothing was wanted but reality, for that army, of course, was never called into existence.

One last scheme offered itself to the General Assembly. The Democratic population from all parts of the country sent deputations to place itself at the disposal of the Parliament, and to urge it on to a decisive action. The people, knowing what the intentions of the Württemberg Government were, implored the National Assembly to force that Government into an open and active participation with their insurgent neighbours. But no. The National Assembly, in going to Stuttgart, had delivered itself up to the tender mercies of the Württemberg Government. The members knew it, and repressed the agitation among the people. They thus lost the last remnant of influence which they might yet have retained. They earned the contempt they deserved, and the Württemberg Government, pressed by Prussia and the Imperial Lieutenant, put a stop to the Democratic farce by shutting up, on 18 June 1849, the room where the Parliament met, and by ordering the members of the Regency to leave the country.

Next they went to Baden, into the camp of the insurrection; but there they were now useless. Nobody noticed them. The Regency, however, in the name of the Sovereign German people, continued to save the country by its exertions. It made an attempt to get recognized by foreign powers, by delivering passports to anybody who would accept of them. It issued proclamations, and sent commissioners to insurge those very districts of Württemberg whose active assistance it had refused when it was yet time; of course, without effect. We have now under our eye an original report, sent to the Regency by one of these commissioners, Herr Rössler (member for Oels), the contents of which are rather characteristic. It is dated, Stuttgart, 30 June 1849. After describing the adventures of half a dozen of these commissioners in a resultless search for cash, he gives a series of excuses for not having yet gone to his post, and then delivers himself of a most weighty argument respecting possible differences between Prussia, Austria, Bavaria and Württemberg, with their possible consequences. After having fully considered this, he comes, however, to the conclusion that there is no more chance. Next,

he proposes to establish relays of trustworthy men for the con-
veyance of intelligence, and a system of espionage as to the
intentions of the Württemberg Ministry and the movements of
the troops. This letter never reached its address, for when it was
written the 'Regency' had already passed entirely into the
'foreign department', viz., Switzerland; and while poor Herr
Rössler troubled his head about the intentions of the formidable
ministry of a sixth-rate kingdom, a hundred thousand Prussian,
Bavarian and Hessian soldiers had already settled the whole
affair in the last battle under the walls of Rastatt.

Thus vanished the German Parliament, and with it the first
and last creation of the Revolution. Its convocation had been the
first evidence that there actually *had been* a revolution in January;
and it existed as long as this, the first modern German Revolution, was not yet brought to a close. Chosen under the influence
of the capitalist class by a dismembered, scattered, rural population, for the most part only awaking from the dumbness of
feudalism, this Parliament served to bring in one body upon the
political arena all the great popular names of 1820–48, and then
to utterly ruin them. All the celebrities of middle class liberalism
were here collected. The bourgeoisie expected wonders; it earned
shame for itself and its representatives. The industrial and commercial capitalist class were more severely defeated in Germany
than in any other country; they were first worsted, broken, expelled from office in every individual state of Germany, and then
put to rout, disgraced and hooted in the Central German
Parliament. Political liberalism, the rule of the bourgeoisie, be it
under a monarchical or republican form of government, is forever impossible in Germany.

In the latter period of its existence, the German Parliament
served to disgrace forever that section which had, ever since
March 1848, headed the official opposition, the Democrats
representing the interests of the small trading, and partially of
the farming class. That class was, in May and June 1849, given
a chance to show its means of forming a stable Government in
Germany. We have seen how it failed; not so much by adverse
circumstances as by the actual and continued cowardice in all
trying moments that had occurred since the outbreak of the

revolution; by showing in politics the same short-sighted, pusill-animous, wavering spirit, which is characteristic of its commercial operations. In May 1849, it had, by this course, lost the confidence of the real fighting mass of all European insurrections, the working class. But yet, it had a fair chance. The German Parliament belonged to it, exclusively, after the Reactionists and Liberals had withdrawn. The rural population was in its favour. Two-thirds of the armies of the smaller states, one-third of the Prussian army, the majority of the Prussian Landwehr (reserve or militia), were ready to join it, if it only acted resolutely, and with that courage which is the result of a clear insight into the state of things. But the politicians who led on this class were not more clear-sighted than the host of petty tradesmen which followed them. They proved even to be more infatuated, more ardently attached to delusions voluntarily kept up, more credulous, more incapable of resolutely dealing with facts than the Liberals. Their political importance, too, is reduced below the freezing-point. But not having actually carried their commonplace principles into execution, they were, under *very* favourable circumstances, capable of a momentary resurrection, when this last hope was taken from them, just as it was taken from their colleagues of the 'pure Democracy' in France by the *coup d'état* of Louis Bonaparte.

The defeat of the south-west German insurrection, and the dispersal of the German Parliament, bring the history of the first German insurrection to a close. We have now to cast a parting glance upon the victorious members of the counter-revolutionary alliance; we shall do this in our next letter.

4. Introduction to *The Class Struggles in France*[1]

THIS newly republished work was Marx's first attempt, with the aid of his materialist conception, to explain a phase of contemporary history from the given economic situation. In *The*

---

1. [Preface to the new German edition of Karl Marx, *The Class Struggles in France*, 1895 (English translation in E. Burns, *A Handbook of Marxism* (1937), pp. 72–94).]

Communist Manifesto, the theory was applied in broad outline to the whole of modern history, while in the articles by Marx and myself in the *Neue Rheinische Zeitung*, it was constantly used to interpret political events of the day. Here, on the other hand, the question was to demonstrate the inner causal connexion in the course of a development which extended over some years, a development as critical, for the whole of Europe, as it was typical; that is, in accordance with the conception of the author, to trace political events back to the effects of what are, in the last resort, economic causes.

In judging the events and series of events of day-to-day history, it will never be possible for anyone to go right back to the final economic causes. Even today, when the specialized technical press provides such rich materials, in England itself it still remains impossible to follow day by day the movement of industry and trade in the world market and the changes which take place in the methods of production, in such a way as to be able to draw the general conclusion, at any point of time, from these very complicated and ever changing factors: of these factors, the most important, into the bargain, generally operate a long time in secret before they suddenly and violently make themselves felt on the surface. A clear survey of the economic history of a given period is never contemporaneous; it can only be gained subsequently, after collecting and sifting of the material has taken place. Statistics are a necessary help here, and they always lag behind. For this reason, it is only too often necessary, in the current history of the time, to treat the most decisive factor as constant, to treat the economic situation existing at the beginning of the period concerned as given and unalterable for the whole period, or else to take notice only of such changes in this situation as themselves arise out of events clearly before us, and as, therefore, can likewise be clearly seen. Hence, the materialist method has here often to limit itself to tracing political conflicts back to the struggles between the interests of the social classes and fractions of classes encountered as the result of economic development, and to show the particular political parties as the more or less adequate political expression of these same classes and fractions of classes.

It is self-evident that this unavoidable neglect of contemporaneous changes in the economic situation, of the very basis of all the proceedings subject to examination, must be a source of error. But all the conditions of a comprehensive presentation of the history of the day unavoidably imply sources of error – which, however, keeps nobody from writing contemporary history.

When Marx undertook this work, the sources of error mentioned were, to a still greater degree, impossible to avoid. It was quite impossible during the period of the Revolution of 1848–9 to follow the economic transformations which were being consummated at the same time, or even to keep a general view of them. It was just the same during the first months of exile in London, in the autumn and winter of 1849–50. But that was just the time when Marx began this work. And, in spite of these unfavourable circumstances, his exact knowledge both of the economic situation in France and of the political history of that country since the February Revolution made it possible for him to give a picture of events which laid bare their inner connexions in a way never attained since, and which later brilliantly withstood the double test instituted by Marx himself.

The first test resulted from the fact that after the spring of 1850 Marx once again found leisure for economic studies, and first of all took up the economic history of the last ten years. In this study, what he had earlier deduced, half *a priori*, from defective material, was made absolutely clear to him by the facts themselves, namely, that the world trade crisis of 1847 had been the true mother of the February and March Revolutions and that the industrial prosperity which had been returning gradually since the middle of 1848, and which attained full bloom in 1849 and 1850, was the revivifying force of the newly strengthened European reaction. That was decisive. Whereas in the three first articles (which appeared in the January, February and March numbers of the *Neue Rheinische Zeitung, politisch-ökonomische Revue*, Hamburg, 1850) there was still the expectation of an imminent upsurge of revolutionary energy, the historical review written by Marx and myself for the last number, which was published in the autumn of 1850 (a double number, May to October), breaks once and for all with these illusions: 'A new revolution is only possible as a result of a new crisis. It is just as certain, however, as this.' But that was the only essential change which had to be made. There was absolutely nothing to alter in the interpretation of events given in the earlier chapters, or in the causal connexions established therein, as the continuation of the narrative from 10 March, up to the autumn of 1850 in the review in question, proves. I have therefore included this continuation as the fourth article in the present new edition.

The second test was even more severe. Immediately after Louis Bonaparte's *coup d'état* of 2 December 1851, Marx worked out anew the history of France from February 1848, up to this event, which concluded the revolutionary period for the time being (*The Eighteenth Brumaire of Louis Bonaparte*, third edition, Meissner, Hamburg, 1885). In this brochure the period which we had depicted in our present publication is again dealt with, although more briefly. Compare this second production, written in the light of decisive events which happened over a year later, with our present publication, and it will be found that the author had very little to change.

The thing which still gives this work of ours a quite special significance is that, for the first time, it expresses the formula in which, by common agreement, the workers' parties of all countries in the world briefly summarize their demand for economic reconstruction: the appropriation by society of the means of production. In the second chapter, in connexion with the 'right to work', which is characterized as 'the first clumsy formula wherein the revolutionary aspirations of the proletariat are summarized', it is said: 'But behind the right to work stands the power over capital; behind the power over capital, the appropriation of the means of production, their subjection to the associated working class and, therefore, the abolition of wage labour as well as of capital and of their mutual relationships.' Thus, here, for the first time, the proposition is formulated by which modern working-class socialism is equally sharply differentiated both from all the different shades of feudal, bourgeois, petty-bourgeois, etc., socialism and also from the confused community of goods of Utopian and spontaneous worker-communism. If, later,

Marx extended the formula to appropriation of the means of exchange also, this extension, which, in any case, was self-evident after the *Communist Manifesto*, only expressed a corollary to the main proposition. A few wiseacres in England have of late added that the 'means of distribution' should also be handed over to society. It would be difficult for these gentlemen to say what these economic means of distribution are, as distinct from the means of production and exchange; unless political means of distribution are meant, taxes, poor relief, including the *Sachsenwald*[1] and other endowments. But, first, these are means of distribution now already in collective possession, either of the state or of the commune, and, secondly, it is precisely these we wish to abolish.

When the February Revolution broke out, we all of us, as far as our conception of the conditions and the course of revolutionary movements was concerned, were under the spell of previous historical experience, namely that of France. It was, indeed, the latter which had dominated the whole of European history since 1789, and from which now once again the signal had gone forth for general revolutionary change. It was therefore natural and unavoidable that our conceptions of the nature and the path of the 'social' revolution proclaimed in Paris in February 1848, of the revolution of the proletariat, were strongly coloured by memories of the models of 1789 and 1830. Moreover, when the Paris upheaval found its echo in the victorious insurrections in Vienna, Milan and Berlin; when the whole of Europe right up to the Russian frontier was swept into the movement; when in Paris the first great battle for power between the proletariat and the bourgeoisie was joined; when the very victory of their class so shook the bourgeoisie of all countries that they fled back into the arms of the monarchist-feudal reaction which had just been overthrown – for us, under the circumstances of the time, there could be no doubt that the great decisive struggle had broken out, that it would have to be fought out in a single, long and changeful period of revolution, but that it could only end with the final victory of the proletariat.

After the defeats of 1849 we in no way shared the illusions of

1. Bismarck's country estate near Hamburg.

the vulgar democracy grouped around the would-be provisional governments *in partibus*. This vulgar democracy reckoned on a speedy and finally decisive victory of the 'people' over the 'usurpers'; we looked to a long struggle, after the removal of the 'usurpers', between the antagonistic elements concealed within this 'people' itself. Vulgar democracy expected a renewed outbreak from day to day; we declared as early as autumn 1850 that at least the first chapter of the revolutionary period was closed and that nothing further was to be expected until the outbreak of a new world crisis. For this reason we were excommunicated, as traitors to the revolution, by the very people who later, almost without exception, have made their peace with Bismarck – so far as Bismarck found them worth the trouble.

But we, too, have been shown to have been wrong by history, which has revealed our point of view of that time to have been an illusion. It has done even more: it has not merely destroyed our error of that time; it has also completely transformed the conditions under which the proletariat has to fight. The mode of struggle of 1848 is today obsolete from every point of view, and this is a point which deserves closer examination on the present occasion.

All revolutions up to the present day have resulted in the displacement of one definite class rule by another; all ruling classes up till now have been only minorities as against the ruled mass of the people. A ruling minority was thus overthrown; another minority seized the helm of state and remodelled the state apparatus in accordance with its own interests. Thus was on every occasion the minority group able and called to rule by the degree of economic development, and just for that reason, and only for that reason, it happened that the ruled majority either participated in the revolution on the side of the former or else passively acquiesced in it. But if we disregard the concrete content of each occasion, the common form of all these revolutions was that they were minority revolutions. Even where the majority took part, it did so – whether wittingly or not – only in the service of a minority; but because of this, or simply because of the passive, unresisting attitude of the majority, this minority acquired the appearance of being the representative of the whole people.

As a rule, after the first great success, the victorious minority became divided; one half was pleased with what had been gained, the other wanted to go still further, and put forward new demands, which, to a certain extent at least, were also in the real or apparent interests of the great mass of the people. In individual cases these more radical demands were realized, but often only for the moment; the more moderate party again gained the upper hand, and what had eventually been won was wholly or partly lost again; the vanquished shrieked of treachery, or ascribed their defeat to accident. But in truth the position was mainly this: the achievements of the first victory were only safeguarded by the second victory of the more radical party; this having been attained, and, with it, what was necessary for the moment, the radicals and their achievements vanished once more from the stage.

All revolutions of modern times, beginning with the great English revolution of the seventeenth century, showed these features, which appeared inseparable from every revolutionary struggle. They appeared applicable, also, to the struggles of the proletariat for its emancipation; all the more applicable, since in 1848 there were few people who had any idea at all of the direction in which this emancipation was to be sought. The proletarian masses themselves, even in Paris, after the victory, were still absolutely in the dark as to the path to be taken. And yet the movement was there, instinctive, spontaneous, irrepressible. Was not this just the situation in which a revolution had to succeed, led certainly by a minority, but this time not in the interests of the minority, but in the real interests of the majority? If, in all the longer revolutionary periods, it was so easy to win the great masses of the people by the merely plausible and delusive views of the minorities thrusting themselves forward, how could they be less susceptible to ideas which were the truest reflex of their economic position, which were nothing but the clear, comprehensible expression of their needs, of needs not yet understood by themselves, but only vaguely felt? To be sure, this revolutionary mood of the masses had almost always, and usually very speedily, given way to lassitude or even to a revulsion to its opposite, so soon as illusion evaporated and disappointment set in. But here it was not a question of delusive views, but of giving effect to the very special interests of the great majority itself, interests which at that time were certainly by no means clear to this great majority, but which must soon enough become clear in the course of giving practical effect to them, by their convincing obviousness. And if now, as Marx showed in the third article, in the spring of 1850, the development of the bourgeois republic that had arisen out of the 'social' revolution of 1848 had concentrated the real power in the hands of the big bourgeoisie – monarchistically inclined as it was – and, on the other hand, had grouped all the other social classes, peasants as well as petty bourgeoisie, round the proletariat, so that, during and after the common victory, not they, but the proletariat grown wise by experience, must become the decisive factor – was there not every prospect here of turning the revolution of the minority into the revolution of the majority?

History has proved us, and all who thought like us, wrong. It has made it clear that the state of economic development on the Continent at that time was not, by a long way, ripe for the removal of capitalist production; it has proved this by the economic revolution which, since 1848, has seized the whole of the Continent, has really caused big industry for the first time to take root in France, Austria, Hungary, Poland and, recently, in Russia, while it has made Germany positively an industrial country of the first rank – all on a capitalist basis, which in the year 1848, therefore, still had great capacity for expansion. But it is just this industrial revolution which has everywhere for the first time produced clarity in the class relationships, which has removed a number of transition forms handed down from the manufacturing period and in Eastern Europe even from guild handicraft, and has created a genuine bourgeoisie and a genuine large-scale industrial proletariat and pushed them into the foreground of social development. But, owing to this, the struggle of these two great classes, which, apart from England, existed in 1848 only in Paris and, at the most, a few big industrial centres, has been spread over the whole of Europe and has reached an intensity such as was unthinkable in 1848. At that time the many obscure evangels of the sects, with their panaceas; today the one generally recognized, transparently clear theory of Marx, sharply formulating the final aims of the struggle. At that time the masses, sundered and differing according to locality and nationality, linked only by the feeling of common suffering, undeveloped, tossed to and fro in their perplexity from enthusiasm to despair; today a great international army of Socialists, marching irresistibly on and growing daily in number, organization, discipline, insight and assurance of victory. If even this mighty army of the proletariat has still not reached its goal, if, a long way from winning victory with one mighty stroke, it has slowly to press forward from position to position in a hard, tenacious struggle, this only proves, once and for all, how impossible it was in 1848 to win social reconstruction by a simple surprise attack.

A bourgeoisie split into two monarchist sections adhering to two dynasties, a bourgeoisie, however, which demanded, above all, peace and security for its financial operations, faced with a proletariat vanquished, indeed, but still a constant menace, a proletariat round which petty bourgeois and peasants grouped themselves more and more – the continual threat of a violent outbreak, which, nevertheless, offered no prospect of a final solution – such was the situation, as if created for the *coup d'état* of the third, the pseudo-democratic pretender, Louis Bonaparte. On 2 December 1851, by means of the army, he put an end to the tense situation and secured for Europe the assurance of domestic tranquillity, in order to give it the blessing of a new era of wars. The period of revolutions from below was concluded for the time being; there followed a period of revolutions from above.

The imperial reaction of 1851 gave a new proof of the unripeness of the proletarian aspirations of that time. But it was itself to create the conditions under which they were bound to ripen. Internal tranquillity ensured the full development of the new industrial boom; the necessity of keeping the army occupied and of diverting the revolutionary currents outwards produced wars, in which Bonaparte, under the pretext of asserting 'the principle of nationality', sought to sneak annexations for France. His imitator, Bismarck, adopted the same policy for Prussia; he made his *coup d'état*, his revolution from above, in 1868, against the German Confederation and Austria, and no less against the Prussian *Konfliktskammer*. But Europe was too small for two

Bonapartes and historical irony so willed it that Bismarck over-
threw Bonaparte, and King William of Prussia not only established the little German Empire, but also the French Republic. The
general result, however, was that in Europe the autonomy and
internal unity of the great nations, with the exception of Poland,
had become a fact. Within relatively modest limits, it is true, but,
for all that, on a scale large enough to allow the development of
the working class to proceed without finding national complications any longer a serious obstacle. The grave-diggers of the
Revolution of 1848 had become the executors of its will. And
alongside of them rose threateningly the heir of 1848, the proletariat, in the International.

After the war of 1870-1, Bonaparte vanishes from the stage and
Bismarck's mission is fulfilled, so that he can now sink back
again into the ordinary *Junker*. The period, however, is brought
to a close by the Paris Commune. An underhand attempt by
Thiers to steal the cannon of the Paris National Guard called
forth a victorious rising. It was shown once more that, in Paris,
none but a proletarian revolution is any longer possible. After
the victory power fell, wholly of its own accord, and quite undisputed, into the hands of the working class. And once again,
twenty years after the time described in this work of ours, it was
proved how impossible, even then, was this rule of the working
class. On the one hand, France left Paris in the lurch, looked on
while it bled from the bullets of MacMahon; on the other hand,
the Commune was consumed in unfruitful strife between the two
parties which divided it, the Blanquists (the majority) and the
Proudhonists (the minority), neither of which knew what was to
be done. The victory which came as a gift in 1871 remained just
as unfruitful as the surprise attack of 1848.

It was believed that the militant proletariat had been finally
buried with the Paris Commune. But, completely to the contrary,
it dates its most powerful advance from the Commune and the
Franco-German war. The recruitment of the whole of the population able to bear arms into armies that could be counted in
millions, and the introduction of firearms, projectiles and explosives of hitherto undreamt of efficacy created a complete
revolution in all warfare. This, on the one hand, put a sudden

end to the Bonapartist war period and insured peaceful industrial development, since any war other than a world war of unheard of cruelty and absolutely incalculable outcome had become an impossibility. On the other hand, it caused military expenditure to rise in geometrical progression, and thereby forced up taxes to exorbitant levels and so drove the poorer classes of people into the arms of Socialism. The annexation of Alsace-Lorraine, the most immediate cause of the mad competition in armaments, might set the French and German bourgeoisie chauvinistically at each other's throats; for the workers of the two countries it became a new bond of unity. And the anniversary of the Paris Commune became the first universal commemoration day of the whole proletariat.

The war of 1870–1 and the defeat of the Commune had transferred the centre of gravity of the European workers' movement for the time being from France to Germany, as Marx foretold. In France it naturally took years to recover from the bloodletting of May 1871. In Germany, on the other hand, where industry was, in addition, furthered (in positively hot-house fashion) by the blessing of the French milliards and developed more and more quickly, Social-Democracy experienced a much more rapid and enduring growth. Thanks to the understanding with which the German workers made use of the universal suffrage introduced in 1866, the astonishing growth of the Party is made plain to all the world by incontestable figures. 1871, 102,000; 1874, 352,000; 1877, 493,000 Social-Democratic votes. Then came recognition of this advance by high authority in the shape of the Anti-Socialist Law: the Party was temporarily disrupted; the number of votes sank to 312,000 in 1881. But that was quickly overcome, and then, though oppressed by the Exceptional Law, without press, without external organization and without the right of combination or meeting, the rapid expansion really began: 1884, 550,000; 1887, 763,000; 1890, 1,427,000 votes. Then the hand of the state was paralysed. The Anti-Socialist Law disappeared; socialist votes rose to 1,787,000, over a quarter of all the votes cast. The government and the ruling classes had exhausted all their expedients – uselessly, to no purpose, and without success. The tangible proofs of their impotence, which the authorities, from night watchman to the imperial chancellor, had had to accept – and that from the despised workers – these proofs were counted in millions. The state was at its wits' end, the workers only at the beginning of theirs.

But the German workers did a second great service to their cause in addition to the first, which they rendered by their mere existence as the strongest, best disciplined and most rapidly growing Socialist Party. They supplied their comrades of all countries with a new weapon, and one of the sharpest, when they showed them how to use universal suffrage.

There had long been universal suffrage in France, but it had fallen into disrepute through the misuse to which the Bonapartist government had put it. After the Commune there was no workers' party to make use of it. Also in Spain it had existed since the republic, but in Spain boycott of the elections was ever the rule of all serious opposition parties. The Swiss experiences of universal suffrage, also, were anything but encouraging for a workers' party. The revolutionary workers of the Latin countries had been wont to regard the suffrage as a snare, as an instrument of government trickery. It was otherwise in Germany. The *Communist Manifesto* had already proclaimed the winning of universal suffrage, of democracy, as one of the first and most important tasks of the militant proletariat, and Lassalle had again taken up this point. When Bismarck found himself compelled to introduce the franchise as the only means of interesting the mass of the people in his plans, our workers immediately took it in earnest and sent August Bebel to the first constituent Reichstag. And from that day on they have used the franchise in a way which has paid them a thousandfold and has served as a model to the workers of all countries. The franchise has been, in the words of the French Marxist programme, ' *transformé, de moyen de duperie qu'il a été jusqu'ici, en instrument d'émancipation*' – they have transformed it from a means of deception, which it was heretofore, into an instrument of emancipation. And if universal suffrage had offered no other advantage than that it allowed us to count our numbers every three years; that by the regularly established, unexpectedly rapid rise in the number of votes it increased in equal measure the workers' certainty of victory and the dismay of their opponents, and so became our best means of propaganda; that it accurately informed us concerning our own strength and that of all hostile parties, and thereby provided us with a measure of proportion for our actions second to none, safeguarding us from untimely timidity as much as from untimely foolhardiness – if this had been the only advantage we gained from the suffrage, then it would still have been more than enough. But it has done much more than this. In election agitation it provided us with a means, second to none, of getting in touch with the mass of the people, where they still stand aloof from us; of forcing all parties to defend their views and actions against our attacks before all the people; and, further, it opened to our representatives in the Reichstag a platform from which they could speak to their opponents in Parliament and to the masses without, with quite other authority and freedom than in the Press or at meetings. Of what avail to the government and the bourgeoisie was their Anti-Socialist Law when election agitation and socialist speeches in the Reichstag continually broke through it?

With this successful utilization of universal suffrage, an entirely new mode of proletarian struggle came into force, and this quickly developed further. It was found that the state institutions, in which the rule of the bourgeoisie is organized, offer still further opportunities for the working class to fight these very state institutions. They took part in elections to individual diets, to municipal councils and to industrial courts; they contested every post against the bourgeoisie in the occupation of which a sufficient part of the proletariat had its say. And so it happened that the bourgeoisie and the government came to be much more afraid of the legal than of the illegal action of the workers' party, of the results of elections than of those of rebellion.

For here, too, the conditions of the struggle had essentially changed. Rebellion in the old style, the street fight with barricades, which up to 1848 gave everywhere the final decision, was to a considerable extent obsolete.

Let us have no illusions about it: a real victory of an insurrection over the military in street fighting, a victory as between two armies, is one of the rarest exceptions. But the insurgents, also, counted on it just as rarely. For them it was solely a question of making the troops yield to moral influences, which, in a fight between the armies of two warring countries do not come into play at all, or do so to a much less degree. If they succeed in this, then the troops fail to act, or the commanding officers lose their heads, and the insurrection wins. If they do not succeed in this, then, even where the military are in the minority, the superiority of better equipment and training, of unified leadership, of the planned employment of the military forces and of discipline makes itself felt. The most that the insurrection can achieve in actual tactical practice is the correct construction and defence of a single barricade. Mutual support; the disposition and employment of reserves; in short, the cooperation and harmonious working of the individual detachments, indispensable even for the defence of one quarter of the town, not to speak of the whole of a large town, are at best defective, and mostly not attainable at all; concentration of the military forces at a decisive point is, of course, impossible. Hence the passive defence is the prevailing form of fight: the attack will rise here and there, but only by way of exception, to occasional advances and flank assaults; as a rule, however, it will be limited to occupation of the positions abandoned by the retreating troops. In addition, the military have, on their side, the disposal of artillery and fully equipped corps of skilled engineers, resources of war which, in nearly every case, the insurgents entirely lack. No wonder, then, that even the barricade struggles conducted with the greatest heroism – Paris, June 1848; Vienna, October 1848; Dresden, May 1849 – ended with the defeat of the insurrection, so soon as the leaders of the attack, unhampered by political considerations, acted from the purely military standpoint, and their soldiers remained reliable.

The numerous successes of the insurgents up to 1848 were due to a great variety of causes. In Paris in July 1830 and February 1848, as in most of the Spanish street fights, there stood between the insurgents and the military a civic militia, which either directly took the side of the insurrection, or else by its lukewarm, indecisive attitude caused the troops likewise to vacillate, and supplied the insurrection with arms into the bargain. Where this citizens guard opposed the insurrection from the outset, as in June 1848 in Paris, the insurrection was vanquished. In Berlin in 1848, the people were victorious partly through a considerable accession of new fighting forces during the night and the morning of the 19th, partly as a result of the exhaustion and bad victualling of the troops, and, finally, partly as a result of the paralysed command. But in all cases the fight was won because the troops failed to obey, because the officers lost their power of decision or because their hands were tied.

Even in the classic time of street fighting, therefore, the barricade produced more of a moral than a material effect. It was a means of shaking the steadfastness of the military. If it held out until this was attained, then victory was won; if not, there was defeat. This is the main point, which must be kept in view, likewise when the chances of contingent future street fights are examined.

The chances, however, were in 1849 already pretty poor. Everywhere the bourgeoisie had thrown in its lot with the governments, 'culture and property' had hailed and feasted the military moving against the insurrections. The spell of the barricade was broken; the soldier no longer saw behind it 'the people', but rebels, agitators, plunderers, levellers, the scum of society; the officer had in the course of time become versed in the tactical forms of street fighting, he no longer marched straight ahead and without cover against the improvised breastwork, but went round it through gardens, yards and houses. And this was now successful, with a little skill, in nine cases out of ten.

But since then there have been very many more changes, and all in favour of the military. If the big towns have become considerably bigger, the armies have become bigger still. Paris and Berlin have, since 1848, grown less than fourfold, but their garrisons have grown more than that. By means of the railways, the garrisons can, in twenty-four hours, be more than doubled, and in forty-eight hours they can be increased to huge armies. The arming of this enormously increased number of troops has become incomparably more effective. In 1848 the smooth-bore percussion muzzle-loader, today the small-calibre magazine breech-loading rifle, which shoots four times as far, ten times as accurately and ten times as fast as the former. At that time the relatively ineffective round-shot and grape-shot of the artillery;

today the percussion shells, of which one is sufficient to demolish the best barricade. At that time the pick-axe of the sapper for breaking through walls; today the dynamite cartridge.

On the other hand, all the conditions on the insurgents' side have grown worse. An insurrection with which all sections of the people sympathize will hardly recur; in the class struggle all the middle sections will never group themselves round the proletariat so exclusively that the reactionary parties gathered round the bourgeoisie well-nigh disappear. The 'people', therefore, will always appear divided, and with this a powerful lever, so extraordinarily effective in 1848, is lacking. Even if more soldiers who have seen service were to come over to the insurrectionists, the arming of them becomes so much the more difficult. The hunting and luxury guns of the gunshops – even if not previously made unusable by removal of part of the lock by the police – are far from being a match for the magazine rifle of the soldier, even in close fighting. Up to 1848 it was possible to make the necessary ammunition oneself out of powder and lead; today the cartridges differ for each rifle, and are everywhere alike only in one point, that they are a special product of big industry, and therefore not to be prepared *ex tempore*, with the result that most rifles are useless as long as one does not possess the ammunition specially suited to them. And, finally, since 1848 the newly-built quarters of the big towns have been laid out in long, straight, broad streets, as though made to give full effect to the new cannons and rifles. The revolutionary would have to be mad, who himself chose the working class districts in the North and East of Berlin for a barricade fight. Does that mean that in the future the street fight will play no further role? Certainly not. It only means that the conditions since 1848 have become far more unfavourable for civil fights, far more favourable for the military. A future street fight can therefore only be victorious when this unfavourable situation is compensated by other factors. Accordingly, it will occur more seldom in the beginning of a great revolution than in its further progress, and will have to be undertaken with greater forces. These, however, may then well prefer, as in the whole Great French Revolution on 4 September and 31 October 1870, in Paris, the open attack to the passive barricade tactics.

Does the reader now understand why the ruling classes decidedly want to bring us to where the guns shoot and the sabres slash? Why they accuse us today of cowardice, because we do not betake ourselves without more ado into the street, where we are certain of defeat in advance? Why they so earnestly implore us to play for once the part of cannon fodder?

The gentlemen pour out their prayers and their challenges for nothing, for nothing at all. We are not so stupid. They might just as well demand from their enemy in the next war that he should take up his position in the line formation of old Fritz, or in the columns of whole divisions *à la* Wagram and Waterloo, and with the flintlock in his hands at that. If the conditions have changed in the case of war between nations, this is no less true in the case of the class struggle. The time of surprise attacks, of revolutions carried through by small conscious minorities at the head of unconscious masses, is past. Where it is a question of a complete transformation of the social organization, the masses themselves must also be in it, must themselves already have grasped what is at stake, what they are going in for with body and soul. The history of the last fifty years has taught us that. But in order that the masses may understand what is to be done, long, persistent work is required, and it is just this work which we are now pursuing, and with a success which drives the enemy to despair.

In the Latin countries, also, it is being more and more recognized that the old tactics must be revised. Everywhere the unprepared onslaught has gone into the background, everywhere the German example of utilizing the suffrage, of winning all posts accessible to us, has been imitated. In France, where for more than a hundred years the ground has been undermined by revolution after revolution, where there is no single party which has not done its share in conspiracies, insurrections and all other revolutionary actions; in France, where, as a result, the government is by no means sure of the army and where, in general, the conditions for an insurrectionary *coup de main* are far more favourable than in Germany – even in France the Socialists are realizing more and more that no lasting victory is possible for them, unless they first win the great mass of the people, i.e., in this case, the peasants. Slow propaganda work and parliamentary activity are being recognized here, too, as the most immediate tasks of the Party. Successes were not lacking. Not only have a whole series of municipal councils been won; fifty Socialists have seats in the Chambers, and they have already overthrown three ministries and a President of the Republic. In Belgium last year the workers enforced the franchise, and have been victorious in a quarter of the constituencies. In Switzerland, in Italy, in Denmark, yes, even in Bulgaria and Rumania the Socialists are represented in the Parliaments. In Austria all parties agree that our admission to the Reichsrat can no longer be withheld. We will get in, that is certain; the only question still in dispute is: by which door? And even in Russia, when the famous *Zemsky Sobor* meets, that National Assembly to which young Nicholas offers such vain resistance, even there we can reckon with certainty on also being represented in it.

Of course, our foreign comrades do not renounce their right to revolution. The right to revolution is, after all, the only real 'historical right', the only right on which all modern states without exception rest, Mecklenburg included, whose aristocratic revolution was ended in 1755 by the 'hereditary settlement', the glorious charter of feudalism still valid today. The right to revolution is so incontestably recognized in the general consciousness that even General von Boguslawski derives the right to a *coup d'état*, which he vindicates for his Kaiser, solely from this popular right.

But whatever may happen in other countries, German Social-Democracy has a special situation and therewith, at least in the first instance, a special task. The two million voters, whom it sends to the ballot box, together with the young men and women who stand behind them as non-voters, form the most numerous, most compact mass, the decisive 'shock force' of the international proletarian army. This mass already supplies over a fourth of the recorded votes; and as the by-elections to the Reichstag, the diet elections in individual states, the municipal council and industrial court elections demonstrate, it increases uninterruptedly. Its growth proceeds as spontaneously, as steadily, as irresistibly, and at the same time as tranquilly as a natural process. All government interventions have proved powerless against it. We can count even today on two and a half million voters. If it continues in this fashion, by the end of the century we shall conquer the greater part of the middle section of society, petty bourgeois and small peasants, and grow into the decisive power in the land, before which all other powers will have to bow, whether they like it or not. To keep this growth going without interruption until of itself it gets beyond the control of the ruling governmental system, not to fritter away this daily increasing shock force in advance guard fighting, but to keep it intact until the day of the decision, that is our main task. And there is only one means by which the steady rise of the socialist fighting forces in Germany could be momentarily halted, and even thrown back for some time: a clash on a big scale with the military, a bloodbath like that of 1871 in Paris. In the long run that would also be overcome. To shoot out of the world a party which numbers millions – all the magazine rifles of Europe and America are not enough for this. But the normal development would be impeded, the shock force would, perhaps, not be available at the critical moment, the decisive struggle would be delayed, protracted and attended by heavy sacrifices.

The irony of world history turns everything upside down. We, the 'revolutionaries', the 'rebels' – we are thriving far better on legal methods than on illegal methods and revolt. The parties of order, as they call themselves, are perishing under the legal conditions created by themselves. They cry despairingly with Odilon Barrot: *la légalité nous tue*, legality is the death of us; whereas we, under this legality, get firm muscles and rosy cheeks and look like eternal life. And if we are not so crazy as to let ourselves be driven into street fighting in order to please them, then nothing else is finally left for them but themselves to break through this legality so fatal to them.

Meanwhile they make new laws against revolution. Again everything is turned upside down. These anti-revolt fanatics of today, are they not themselves the rebels of yesterday? Have we, perchance, evoked the civil war of 1866? Have we driven the King of Hanover, the Elector of Hesse, the Duke of Nassau from their hereditary, lawful domains, and annexed these hereditary domains? And do these rebels against the German Confederation and three crowns by the grace of God complain of overthrow? *Quis tulerit Gracchos de seditione querentes?* Who could allow the Bismarck worshippers to rail at revolt?

Let them, nevertheless, put through their anti-revolt bills, make them still worse, transform the whole penal law into india-rubber, they will achieve nothing but a new proof of their impotence. In order seriously to hit Social-Democracy, they will have to resort to quite other measures. They can only hold in check the Social Democratic revolt which is just now doing so well by keeping within the law, by revolt on the part of the parties of order, which cannot live without breaking the laws. Herr Rössler, the Prussian bureaucrat, and Herr von Boguslaw-ski, the Prussian general, have shown them the only way in which the workers, who refuse to let themselves be lured into street fighting, can still, perhaps, be held in check. Breach of the constitution, dictatorship, return to absolutism, *regis voluntas suprema lex!* Therefore, only courage, gentlemen; here is no backing out of it; here you are in for it!

But do not forget that the German Empire, just as all small states and generally all modern states, is a product of contract; of the contract, firstly, of the princes with one another and, secondly, of the princes with the people. If one side breaks the contract, the whole contract falls to the ground; the other side is then also no longer bound as Bismarck showed us so beautifully in 1866. If, therefore, you break the constitution of the Reich, then the Social Democracy is free, can do and refrain from doing what it will as against you. But what it will do then it will hardly give away to you today!

It is now, almost to the year, sixteen hundred years since a dangerous party of revolt made a great commotion in the Roman Empire. It undermined religion and all the foundations of the state; it flatly denied that Caesar's will was the supreme law; it was without a fatherland, international; it spread over all countries of the Empire from Gaul to Asia, and beyond the frontiers of the Empire. It had long carried on an underground agitation in secret; for a considerable time, however, it had felt itself strong enough to come out into the open. This party of revolt, who were known by the name of Christians, was also strongly represented in the army; whole legions were Christian. When they were ordered to attend the sacrificial ceremonies of the pagan established church, in order to do the honours there, the soldier rebels had the audacity to stick peculiar emblems – crosses – on their helmets in protest. Even the wonted barrack cruelties of their superior officers were fruitless. The Emperor Diocletian could no longer quietly look on while order, obedience and discipline in his army were being undermined. He intervened energetically, while there was still time. He passed an anti-Socialist, I should say, anti-Christian, law. The meetings of the rebels were forbidden, their meeting halls were closed or even pulled down, the Christian badges, crosses, etc., were, like the red handkerchiefs in Saxony, prohibited. Christians were declared incapable of holding offices in the state, they were not to be allowed even to become corporals. Since there were not available at that time judges so well trained in 'respect of persons' as Herr von Köller's anti-revolt bill assumes, the Christians were forbidden out of hand to seek justice before a court. This exceptional law was also without effect. The Christians tore it down from the walls with scorn; they are even supposed to have burnt the Emperor's palace in Nicomedia over his head. Then the latter revenged himself by the great persecution of Christians in the year 303, according to our chronology. It was the last of its kind. And it was so effective that seventeen years later the army consisted overwhelmingly of Christians, and the succeeding autocrat of the whole Roman Empire, Constantine, called the Great by the priests, proclaimed Christianity as the state religion.

5. Introduction to *The Civil War in France*[1]

... Thanks to the economic and political development of France since 1789, for fifty years the position in Paris has been such that no Revolution could break out there without assuming a proletarian character, that is to say, without the proletariat, which had bought victory with its blood, advancing its own demands after victory had been won. These demands were more or less unclear and even confused, corresponding to the state of evolution reached by the workers of Paris at the particular period, but the ultimate purpose of them all was the abolition of the class antagonism between capitalists and workers. It is true that no one could say how this was to be brought about. But the demand itself, however indefinite it still was in its formulation, contained a threat to the existing order of society; the workers who put it forward were still armed, and therefore the disarming of the workers was the first commandment for whatever bourgeois group was at the helm of the State. Hence, after every revolution won by the workers, a new struggle, ending with the defeat of the workers.

This happened for the first time in 1848. The liberal bourgeoisie of the Parliamentary opposition held banquets in support of the reform of the franchise, which was designed to secure supremacy for their Party. Forced more and more, in their struggle with the Government, to appeal to the people, they had to allow the radical and republican sections of the bourgeoisie and petty bourgeoisie gradually to take the lead. But behind these stood the revolutionary workers, and since 1830 these had acquired far more political independence than the bourgeoisie, and even the republicans, imagined. At the moment of the crisis between the Government and the opposition, the workers opened battle on the streets; Louis Philippe vanished, and with him the

1. [Written in 1891 on the 20th anniversary of the Paris Commune as a preface to a new German edition of Karl Marx, *The Civil War in France* (English translation from E. Burns, *A Handbook of Marxism* (1937), pp. 158–71).]

franchise reforms; and in their place arose the Republic, hailed by the victorious workers themselves as a 'social' Republic. No one, however, was clear as to what this social republic was to imply; not even the workers themselves. But they now had arms in their hands, and were a power in the State. Therefore, as soon as the bourgeois republicans in control felt the ground under their feet a little firmer, their first aim was to disarm the workers. This was carried into effect by driving them into the revolt of June 1848: by direct breach of faith, by open defiance and the attempt to banish the unemployed to a distant province. And then followed a blood-bath of defenceless prisoners the like of which has not been seen since the days of the civil wars which led to the overthrow of the Roman Republic. It was the first time that the bourgeoisie showed to what insane cruelties of revenge they will resort, the moment that the proletariat ventures to take its stand against them as a class apart, with its own interests and demands. And yet 1848 was only child's play compared with their frenzy in 1871.

Punishment followed hard at heel. If the proletariat was not yet able to rule France, the bourgeoisie could no longer do so. At least not at that period, when it had not yet a majority in favour of the monarchy, and was divided into three dynastic parties and a fourth republican party. Their internal dissensions allowed the adventurer Louis Bonaparte to take possession of all the strategic points – army, police and the administrative machinery and, on 2 December 1851, to torpedo that last stronghold of the bourgeoisie, the National Assembly. The Second Empire opened – the exploitation of France by a band of political and financial adventurers, but at the same time also an industrial development such as had never been possible under the narrowminded and timorous system of Louis Philippe, with its exclusive domination by only a small section of the big bourgeoisie.

Louis Bonaparte took the political power from the capitalists under the pretext of protecting them, the bourgeoisie, from the workers, and on the other hand the workers from them; but in compensation for this his rule encouraged speculation and industrial activity – in a word the rise and enrichment of the whole bourgeoisie to an extent which was hitherto unknown. To an even greater extent, it is true, corruption and mass robbery developed, clustering round the imperial Court, and drawing their heavy percentages from this enrichment.

But the Second Empire was the appeal to French Chauvinism, the demand for the restoration of the frontiers of the First Empire, which had been lost in 1814, or at least those of the First Republic. A French Empire within the frontiers of the old monarchy and, in fact, within the even more amputated frontiers of 1815 – such a thing was impossible for any long duration of time. Hence the necessity for brief wars and the extension of frontiers. But no extension of frontiers was so dazzling to the imagination of the French Chauvinists as the extension which would take in the German left bank of the Rhine. One square mile on the Rhine was more to them than ten in the Alps or anywhere else. Given the Second Empire, the demand for the restoration to France of the left bank of the Rhine, either all at once or by degrees, was merely a question of time. The time came with the Prusso-Austrian war of 1866; swindled by Bismarck and by his own over-cunning, vacillating policy in regard to the expected 'territorial compensation', there was now nothing left for Napoleon but war, which broke out in 1870 and drove him first to Sedan, and thence to Wilhelmshöhe.

The inevitable result was the Paris Revolution of 4 September 1870. The Empire collapsed like a house of cards, and the Republic was again proclaimed. But the enemy was standing at the gates; the armies of the Empire were either hopelessly beleaguered in Metz or held captive in Germany. In this dire situation the people allowed the Paris deputies to the former legislative body to constitute themselves into a 'Government of National Defence'. They were the more ready to allow this because, for the purposes of defence, all Parisians capable of bearing arms had enrolled in the National Guard and were armed, so that now the workers constituted a great majority. But almost at once the antagonism between the almost completely bourgeois government and the armed proletariat broke into open conflict. On 31 October workers' battalions stormed the town hall and captured some members of the Government. Treachery, the Government's breach of its undertakings, and the intervention of some petty bourgeois battalions set them free again, and in order not to occasion the outbreak of civil war inside a city which was already beleaguered by foreign armies, they left the former Government in office.

At last, on 8 January 1871, Paris, almost starving, capitulated; but with honours unprecedented in the history of war. The forts were surrendered, the outer wall disarmed, the weapons of the regiments of the line and of the mobile guard were handed over, and the troops considered prisoners of war. But the National Guard kept their weapons and guns, and only entered into an armistice with the victors, who themselves did not dare enter Paris in triumph. They only dared to occupy a tiny corner of Paris, which, into the bargain, consisted partly of public parks, and even this they only occupied for a few days! And during this time they, who had maintained their encirclement of Paris for 131 days, were themselves encircled by the armed workers of Paris, who kept a sharp watch that no 'Prussian' should overstep the narrow bounds of the corner yielded up to the foreign conquerors. Such was the respect which the Paris workers inspired in the army before which all the armies of the Empire had laid down their arms; and the Prussian Junkers, who had come to take revenge at the very centre of the revolution, were compelled to stand by respectfully, and salute just precisely this armed revolution!

During the war the Paris workers had confined themselves to demanding the vigorous prosecution of the fight. But now, when peace had come with the capitulation of Paris, at this moment Thiers, the new head of the government, was compelled to realize that the supremacy of the propertied classes – large landowners and capitalists – was in constant danger so long as the workers of Paris had arms in their hands. His first action was to attempt to disarm them. On 18 March he sent troops of the line with orders to deprive the National Guard of the artillery belonging to them, which had been constructed during the siege of Paris and had been paid for by subscription. The attempt did not come off; Paris rallied as one man in defence of the guns, and war between Paris and the French Government sitting at Versailles was declared. The Central Committee of the National

Guard, which up to then had carried on the government, handed in its resignation to the National Guard, after it had first decreed the abolition of the scandalous Paris 'Morality Police'. On the 30th the Commune abolished conscription and the standing army, and declared that the National Guard, in which all citizens capable of bearing arms were to be enrolled, was to be the sole armed force. They released the citizens from all payments of rent for dwelling houses from October 1870 to April, taking also into account amounts already paid in advance, and stopped all sales of articles pledged in the hands of the municipal pawnshops. On the same day the foreigners elected to the Commune were confirmed in office, because 'the flag of the Commune is the flag of the World Republic'.

On 1 April it was decided that the highest salary received by any employee of the Commune, and therefore also by its members themselves, might not exceed 6,000 francs. On the following day the Commune decreed the separation of the Church from the State, and the abolition of all State payments for religious purposes as well as the transformation of all Church property into national property; on 8 April this was followed up by a decree excluding from the schools all religious symbols, pictures, dogmas, prayers – in a word, 'all that belongs to the sphere of the individual's conscience' – and this decree was gradually applied. On the 5th, in reply to the shooting, day after day, of soldiers of the Commune captured by the Versailles troops, a decree was issued ordering the imprisonment of hostages, but it was never carried into effect. On the 6th the guillotine was brought out by the 137th battalion of the National Guard, and publicly burnt, amid great popular rejoicing. On the 12th the Commune decided that the Column of Victory on the Place Vendôme, which had been cast from captured guns by Napoleon after the war of 1809, should be demolished, as the symbol of chauvinism and incitement to national hatreds. This decree was carried out on 16 May. On 16 April the Commune ordered a statistical registration of factories which had been closed down by the manufacturers, and the working out of plans for the carrying on of these factories by workers formerly employed in them, who were to be organized in cooperative societies; and also plans for the organization of these cooperatives in one great Union. On the 20th the Commune abolished night work for bakers, and also the workers' registration cards, which since the Second Empire had been run as a monopoly by nominees of the police – exploiters of the first rank; the issuing of these registration cards was transferred to the mayors of the twenty districts of Paris. On 30 April the Commune ordered the closing of the pawn-shops, on the ground that they were a form of individual exploitation of the worker, and stood in contradiction with the right of the workers to their instruments of labour and to credit. On 5 May it ordered the demolition of the Chapel of Atonement, which had been built in expiation of the execution of Louis XVI.

Thus, from 18 March onwards the class character of the Paris movement, which had previously been pushed into the background by the fight against the foreign invaders, emerged sharply and clearly. As almost without exception workers, or recognized representatives of the workers, sat in the Commune, its decisions bore a decidedly proletarian character. Either they decreed reforms which the republican bourgeoisie had failed to pass only out of cowardice, but which provided a necessary basis for the free activity of the working class – such as the adoption of the principle that *in relation to the State*, religion is a purely private affair – or they promulgated decrees which were in the direct interests of the working class and to some extent cut at the foundations of the old order of society. In a beleaguered city, however, it was possible to do no more than make a start in the realization of all these measures. And from the beginning of May on all their energies were required for the fight against the ever-growing armies assembled by the Versailles Government.

On 7 April the Versailles troops had captured the Seine crossing at Neuilly, on the west front of Paris; on the other hand they were driven back with heavy losses by General Eudes in an attack on the south front. Paris was continuously bombarded and, moreover, by the very people who had stigmatized as a sacrilege the bombardment of the same city by the Prussians. These same people now besought the Prussian government to hasten the return of the French soldiers who had been taken prisoner at Sedan and Metz, in order that they might recapture

Paris for them. From the beginning of May the gradual arrival of these troops gave the Versailles forces a decided ascendancy. This already became evident when, on 23 April, Thiers broke off the negotiations for the exchange, proposed by the Commune, of the Archbishop of Paris and a whole number of other priests held as hostages in Paris, for only one man, Blanqui, who had twice been elected to the Commune but was a prisoner in Clairvaux. And even more in the changed attitude of Thiers; previously procrastinating and double-faced, he now suddenly became insolent, threatening, brutal. The Versailles forces took the redoubt of Moulin Saquet on the south front, on 3 May; on the 9th Fort Issy, which had been completely reduced to ruins by gunfire; and on the 14th Fort Vanves. On the west front they advanced gradually, their weight of numbers capturing the villages and buildings which extended up to the city wall, and at last reached the wall itself; on the 11th, thanks to treachery and the carelessness of the National Guards stationed there, they succeeded in forcing their way into the city. The Prussians who held the northern and eastern forts allowed the Versailles troops to advance across the land north of the city, which was forbidden ground to them under the armistice, and thus to march forward and attack on a long front, which the Parisians naturally thought covered by the armistice, and therefore held only with weak forces. As a result of this, only a weak resistance was put up in the western half of Paris, the luxury quarter proper; it grew stronger and more tenacious the nearer the attacking troops approached the eastern half, the real working-class quarter. It was only after eight days' fighting that the last defenders of the Commune were overwhelmed on the heights of Belleville and Ménilmontant; and then the massacre of defenceless men, women and children, which had been raging all through the week on an increasing scale, reached its zenith. The breech-loaders could no longer kill fast enough; the vanquished workers were shot down in hundreds by mitrailleuse fire. The 'Wall of the Federals' at the Père Lachaise cemetery, where the final mass murder was consummated, is still standing today, a mute but eloquent testimonial to the savagery of which the ruling class is capable, as soon as the working class dares to demand its rights.

Then came mass arrests; when the slaughter of them all proved to be impossible, the shooting of victims arbitrarily selected from the prisoners' ranks, and the removal of the rest to great camps, where they had to await trial by courts-martial. The Prussian troops surrounding the northern half of Paris had orders not to allow any fugitives to pass; but the officers often shut their eyes when the soldiers paid more obedience to the dictates of humanity than to their general's orders; particular honour is due to the Saxon army corps for its humane conduct in letting through many workers who had obviously been fighting for the Commune.

Today, when after twenty years we look back at the work and historical significance of the Paris Commune of 1871, we find that it is necessary to supplement the account given in *The Civil War in France* with a few additional points.

The members of the Commune were divided into a majority, the Blanquists, who had also been predominant in the Central Committee of the National Guard; and a minority: members of the International Working Men's Association, chiefly consisting of adherents of the Proudhon school of Socialism. The great majority of the Blanquists at that time were Socialists only by revolutionary and proletarian instinct; only a few had attained greater clarity on the essential principles, through Vaillant, who was familiar with German scientific Socialism. It is therefore comprehensible that in the economic sphere much was neglected which, as we see today, the Commune should have done. The hardest thing to understand is the holy awe with which they remained standing outside the gates of the Bank of France. This was also a serious political mistake. The bank in the hands of the Commune – this would have been worth more than ten thousand hostages. It would have meant that the whole of the French bourgeoisie would have brought pressure to bear on the Versailles government in favour of peace with the Commune. But what is more astonishing is the correctness of so much that was actually done by the Commune, composed as it was of Blanquists and Proudhonists. Naturally the Proudhonists were chiefly responsible for the economic decrees of the Commune, for their praiseworthy and their less praiseworthy aspects; as the Blanquists were for its political achievements and failings. And in both cases the irony of history willed – as often happens when doctrinaires come into power – that both did the opposite of what the doctrines of their school prescribed.

Proudhon, the Socialist of small farmers and master-craftsmen, regarded the principle of association with positive hatred. He said of it that there was more bad than good in it; that it was by nature sterile, even harmful, because it was a fetter on the freedom of the workers; that it was a pure dogma, unproductive and burdensome, in conflict as much with the freedom of the workers as with economy of labour; that its disadvantages multiplied more swiftly than its advantages; that, as compared with it, competition, division of labour and private property were sources of economic strength. Only for the exceptional cases – as Proudhon called them – of large-scale industry and large industrial units, such as railways, was there any place for the association of workers.

And by 1871, even in Paris, the great centre of handicrafts, large-scale industry had already to such a degree ceased to be an exceptional case, that by far the most important decree of the Commune instituted an organization of large-scale industry and even of manufacture which was not based only on the association of workers in each factory, but also aimed at combining all these associations in one great Union; in short an organization which as Marx quite rightly says in *The Civil War* must necessarily have led in the end to Communism, that is to say, the direct antithesis of the Proudhon doctrine. And, therefore, the Commune was also the grave of the Proudhon school of Socialism. Today this school is no longer to be found in French working-class circles; among the Possibilists no less than among the 'Marxists', the Marxian theory now rules there unchallenged. Only among the 'radical' bourgeoisie can Proudhonists still be found.

The Blanquists fared no better. Brought up in the school of conspiracy, and held together by the severe discipline which went with it, they worked on the theory that a proportionately small number of resolute, well-organized men would be able, at a given favourable moment, not only to seize the helm of the

State, but also by energetic and relentless action, to keep power until they succeeded in drawing the mass of the people into the revolution and ranging them round the small band of leaders. This conception involved, above all, the strictest dictatorship and centralization of all power in the hands of the new revolutionary government. And what did the Commune, with its majority of these same Blanquists, actually do? In all its proclamations to the French in the provinces the Commune proposed to them a free federation of all French Communes with Paris, a national organization, which for the first time was really to be created by the nation itself. It was precisely the oppressing power of the former centralized Government – the army, political police and bureaucracy which Napoleon had created in 1789 and since then had been taken over by every new government and used against its opponents – it was precisely this power which should have fallen everywhere, just as it had already fallen in Paris.

The Commune was compelled to recognize from the outset that the working class, once come to power, could not carry on business with the old State machine; that in order not to lose again its but newly-won supremacy, this working class must, on the one hand, do away with all the old repressive machinery previously used against it, and on the other, safeguard itself against its own deputies and officials, by declaring them all, without exception, subject to recall at any moment. What had been the special characteristics of the former State? Society had created its own organs to look after its common interests, first through the simple division of labour. But these organs, at whose head was the State power, had in the course of time, in pursuance of their own special interests, transformed themselves from the servants of society into the masters of society; as can be seen for example, not only in the hereditary monarchy, but equally also in the democratic republic. There is no country in which 'politicians' form a more powerful and distinct section of the nation than in North America. There each of the two great parties which alternately succeed each other in power is itself in turn controlled by people who make a business of politics, who speculate on seats in the legislative assemblies of the Union as well as of the separate States, or who make a living by carrying on agitation for their party and on its victory are rewarded with positions. It is common knowledge that the Americans have been striving for thirty years to shake off this yoke, which has become intolerable, and that in spite of all they can do they continue to sink ever deeper in this quicksand of corruption. It is precisely in America that we have the best example of the growing independence of the State power in opposition to society, whose mere instrument it was originally intended to be. Here there was no dynasty, no nobility, no standing army, beyond the few men keeping watch on the Indians; no bureaucracy with permanent posts or the right to pensions. And nevertheless we find here two great groups of political speculators, who alternately take possession of the State machine, and exploit it by the most corrupt means and for the most corrupt ends – and the nation is powerless against these two great cartels of politicians, who are ostensibly its servants but in reality exploit and plunder it.

Against this transformation of the State and the organs of the State from the servants of society into masters of society – a process which had been inevitable in all previous States – the Commune made use of two infallible expedients. In the first place, it filled all posts – administrative, judicial and educational – by election on the basis of universal suffrage of all concerned, with the right of these electors to recall their delegate at any time. And in the second place, all officials, high or low, were paid only the wages received by other workers. The highest salary paid by the Commune to anyone was 6,000 francs. In this way an effective barrier to place-hunting and careerism was set up, even apart from the imperative mandates to delegates to representative bodies which were also added in profusion.

This shattering of the former State power and its replacement by a new and really democratic State is described in detail in the third section of *The Civil War*. But it was necessary to dwell briefly here once more on some of its features because in Germany particularly the superstitious faith in the State has been carried over from philosophy into the general consciousness of the bourgeoisie and even of many workers. According to the philosophical conception the State is the 'realization of the idea' or, translated into philosophical language, the Kingdom of God on earth; the sphere in which eternal truth and justice is or should be realized. And from this follows a superstitious reverence for the State and everything connected with it, which takes root the more readily as people from their childhood are accustomed to imagine that the affairs and interests common to the whole of society could not be managed and safeguarded in any other way than as in the past, that is through the State and its well-paid officials. And people think they are taking quite an extraordinarily bold step forward when they rid themselves of faith in a hereditary monarchy and become partisans of a democratic republic. In reality, however, the State is nothing more than a machine for the oppression of one class by another, and indeed in the democratic republic no less than in the monarchy; and at best an evil inherited by the proletariat after its victorious struggle for class supremacy whose worst sides the proletariat, just like the Commune, will have at the earliest possible moment to lop off, until such time as a new generation, reared under new and free social conditions, will be able to throw on the scrap-heap all the useless lumber of the State.

Of late the Social Democratic philistine has once more been filled with wholesome terror at the words: Dictatorship of the Proletariat. Well and good, gentlemen, do you want to know what this dictatorship looks like? Look at the Paris Commune. That was the Dictatorship of the Proletariat.

V. THE PHILOSOPHER

Introduction

WHEN Engels was performing his military service in Berlin he made contact – as Marx had done before him – with a radical group of Young Hegelians known as 'The Free'. The most important members of this group were Arnold Ruge, Bruno Bauer, Max Stirner[1] and Ludwig Feuerbach. They employed the tools provided by Hegel's system of philosophy to reach conclusions very different from those of Hegel himself. They boldly criticized the dominant conceptions and institutions of their day. Feuerbach's *The Essence of Christianity*, for example, had a considerable influence both inside and outside Germany. But the Young Hegelians were, for the most part, content to criticize only on paper and they played little active part in the political struggle against the reactionary German governments of that time.

Marx and Engels believed that the logical outcome of the Young Hegelian movement was communism and they tried to put their plans into action through revolutionary agitation. In 1844 in the *Deutsch-Französische Jahrbücher*[2] both Marx and Engels contributed articles affirming their faith in communism. In *The Holy Family* (1845) and in *The German Ideology*[3] they criticized the theories of Feuerbach, Bruno Bauer, Max Stirner and the so-called 'true Socialists'.[4] Some years later Marx wrote that in *The German Ideology* he and Engels had tried 'to work out in common the opposition of our view to the ideological view of German philosophy – in fact to settle accounts with our erstwhile philosophical conscience. The resolve was carried out in the form of a criticism of post-Hegelian philosophy.' Many ideas originally put forward in *The German Ideology* were

1. [Pseudonym of Johann Kaspar Schmidt.]
2. [*Franco-German Yearbooks*.]
3. [Only the last section of *The German Ideology* was published in the lifetime of Marx and Engels. The book was first published in full in 1932 in *Gesamtausgabe*.]
4. [i.e. Grün, Lüning, Püttman, Kuhlmann and Hess who were followers of Fourier.]

subsequently elaborated in *The Communist Manifesto*, in *Das Kapital* and in *Anti-Dühring*.

After a brief period of collaboration with Marx on these philosophical works Engels turned his attention to economics, politics and military affairs. In his old age, however, he returned to his first love and in his *Ludwig Feuerbach and the End of Classical German Philosophy* (1888), which appeared first in 1886 in articles in the periodical *Die Neue Zeit*, he wrote a short account of the views of Marx and himself on the Hegelian philosophy. In the introduction Engels observed that 'a full acknowledgement of the influence which Feuerbach, more than any other post-Hegelian philosopher, had upon us during our period of storm and stress, appeared to me to be an undischarged debt of honour'.

1. Marxist Philosophy[1]

IN so far as they did not abandon the study of philosophy Strauss, Bauer, Stirner and Feuerbach carried on the traditions of the Hegelian system. After Strauss had produced his *Life of Jesus* and his *Dogmatics*, he wrote only literary studies (like those of Renan) on philosophy and on the history of religion. Bauer's only book of any significance was his history of the origins of Christianity. Stirner remained something of a curiosity even after Bakunin blended his ideas with those of Proudhon and labelled the mixture 'Anarchism'.

Feuerbach alone is worthy of attention as a philosopher. He regarded philosophy as an inviolable and holy branch of knowledge. He believed that beyond its limits no further progress was possible. He thought that philosophy was superior to all specialist branches of knowledge. It was 'the science of sciences' which linked all sciences. Feuerbach's philosophical system was a half-way house between materialism and idealism. Feuerbach was unable to dispose of Hegel by critical arguments. So he simply threw Hegel overboard as useless. Compared with the encyclopedic knowledge of Hegel's system that of Feuerbach had nothing positive to offer beyond a turgid religion of love and an impotent morality.

When Hegel's school of philosophy declined there developed another system of philosophy which is indissolubly linked with Karl Marx. This was the only new system of philosophy which bore real fruit. Both Marx and Feuerbach broke from Hegel's system and returned to materialism. Marx got rid of all the preconceived views of the Hegelian idealists. He was determined to understand the real world as revealed by science and by history. He ruthlessly sacrificed idealist principles which did not fit the actual facts. He ignored the traditional fantastic links between

---

1. [Part 4 of F. Engels, *Ludwig Feuerbac hand the End of Classical German Philosophy*. The first edition appeared in German in 1888 (this version is based upon the translation issued by the Foreign Languages Publishing House, Moscow, 1950).]

the 'real' and the 'ideal' world. This approach is the essence of Marx's materialism. Marx was the first thinker to take materialism seriously and he consistently applied the basic principles of materialism in his studies of all the varied branches of knowledge.

Hegel was not simply ignored. On the contrary Marx started out by using the dialectical method, which was the revolutionary side of Hegel's system. In its original Hegelian form this method could not be used satisfactorily. According to Hegel dialectics is 'the self-development of the idea'. He argued that the 'absolute concept' is eternal – though no one knows where it exists – and that it also represented the actual living soul of the whole world. In his *Logic* Hegel discusses at length the development of the absolute concept through all its preliminary stages. Then it 'alienates' itself by changing into Nature. In that form it unconsciously goes through a new development and finally comes again to self-consciousness in Man. This new self-consciousness then elaborates itself once more in History from its original crude form until the final absolute concept again comes completely into its own in the Hegelian system of philosophy. Thus according to Hegel a dialectical development can be traced both in Nature and in History. This is a progressive movement from a lower to a higher form of life – a movement which continually asserts itself through all fluctuations and all temporary setbacks. And this movement is only a poor reflection of the absolute concept which exists throughout eternity quite independently of any human brain.

It was necessary to do away with this ideological perversion of the truth. Marx and I tried to understand the ideas in our minds from a materialist point of view. We considered that ideas were images of real things. We did not consider real things to be reflections of some stage of Hegel's 'absolute concept'. For Marx dialectics became the science of the general laws of motion both of the external world and of human thought. These two sets of laws are identical in substance but they express themselves in different ways. These laws can be consciously understood by the human mind but they only assert themselves unconsciously in Nature – and largely also in History. The laws assert themselves unconsciously in the form of external pressure and this occurs in the midst of an endless succession of apparent accidents.

Regarded from this point of view Hegel's dialectic concepts became merely the conscious reflection of dialectical changes in the real world. So Marx stood Hegel's dialectic on its head – or rather he turned it upside down and placed it on its feet! And Marx's materialist dialectic has been our best practical tool for years. It is remarkable that the discovery of the materialist dialectic was made not only by Marx and myself but – independently of us and independently of Hegel – also by a German worker named Joseph Dietzgen.[1]

The revolutionary side of Hegel's philosophy came into its own again without its idealist trimmings which had prevented its application in a logical manner. Hegel's fundamental principle is that the world cannot be understood if it is simply regarded as being a complex system of ready-made *things*. It can be understood only as a complex system of *processes*. Looked at in this way we realize that both *things* (which appear to be stable) and the *images of things in our minds* (i.e. the concepts) pass through an uninterrupted cycle from birth to decay. This cycle is a progressive development which eventually always asserts itself despite all apparent accidents and temporary setbacks. Since Hegel's day this fundamental idea has so completely permeated people's minds that hardly anyone questions it. But the validity of the fundamental principle may well be accepted without applying the principle in detail to every branch of knowledge. If we pursue knowledge with this principle as our guide we cease to look for 'final solutions' or for 'eternal truths'. We are conscious of the inevitable limitations of all knowledge because we realize that knowledge is conditioned by the circumstances in which it is acquired. On the other hand we are no longer inhibited by the idea of 'antithesis' – which was an integral part of the old metaphysics. We are no longer interested in the traditional 'antithesis' between truth and error, between good and evil, between identity and contrast, between inevitable and chance. We know that these 'antitheses' are valid only in a relative fashion. We

1. See *Das Wesen der menschlichen Kopfarbeit*, dargestellt von einem Handarbeiter (Hamburg).

realize that something which is now regarded as 'true' has also its latent 'false' side which will eventually manifest itself. We appreciate that what is now regarded as 'false' has its 'true' aspect by virtue of which it could previously be regarded as 'true'. And we know that what is regarded as 'inevitable' is composed of sheer accidents, and that so-called 'accidents' disguise events that follow in logical sequence.

Hegel called the old method of investigation and thought 'metaphysical'. Philosophers investigated *things* in the belief that 'things' were fixed and stable and this traditional line of inquiry still has a strong hold upon people's minds. In its day there was a good deal of historical justification for this method. It was necessary to examine 'things' before it was possible to examine 'processes'. It was necessary to know what a particular thing *was* before we could observe how it was changing. This certainly applied to natural science. The old metaphysics which accepted 'things' as complete objects was derived from natural science which investigated dead and living things as complete objects. But a time came when this investigation had reached a stage when it could take a decisive step forward and examine systematically the *changes* which these things undergo in nature itself. When that happened the last hour of the old metaphysics had struck – not only as far as natural science was concerned but also in the realm of philosophy itself. Before 1800 scientists were concerned mainly with *collecting* and identifying objects. Natural Science was the knowledge of static substances. In our century scientists are concerned with *classification* and the study of *processes*. They examine the origin and the development of things as well as the links which bind all natural processes into one great unity. Physiology, which investigates the processes occurring in plant and animal organisms; embryology, which deals with the growth of individual organisms from germ to maturity; geology, which examines the gradual formation of the earth's surface – these new sciences all belong to our century.

Above all, there are three great discoveries which have enabled our knowledge of the links between various natural processes to advance by leaps and bounds. The first has been the discovery of the cell as the unit from which plants and animals develop by the multiplication and differentiation of the cells. We have recognized that a single general law governs the development and growth of all higher organisms. And we realize that since a cell has the capacity to change it is possible for organisms to alter their species and to undergo a change of a more radical character than the development of an individual organism. Secondly, we now know that all the so-called forces which, in the first instance, act upon inorganic nature are different forms of the manifestation of universal motion. These forces include mechanical force (and its complement potential energy), heat, radiation, electricity, magnetism and chemical energy. And the different kinds of universal motion change from one form to another in definite proportions so that when a certain quantity of the one disappears a certain quantity of another makes its appearance. In this way the whole process of motion in nature is reduced to this single incessant process of transformation from one form into another. Thirdly, Darwin has proved that the stock of nature's organic products (including mankind) is in fact the result of a long process of evolution from a few germs which were originally single cells. And these cells have developed from protoplasm (or albumen) which came into existence by chemical means.

These great discoveries and the other immense advances in natural science, have shown us the connexion between various natural processes. We can see the links between the various sciences and those between particular branches of science and the whole body of scientific knowledge. By examining the facts provided empirically by natural science we can secure a reasonably comprehensive view of the various interconnexions in nature. Formerly a study of 'natural philosophy' gave us this comprehensive view. But it did this by inventing 'ideal' fictitious links instead of the real links which were not yet known. The old philosophers filled in missing facts and bridged gaps by figments of the imagination. They had many brilliant ideas and they pointed the way to many later discoveries. But they also wrote a great deal of nonsense. We only have to understand the results of scientific investigation 'dialectically' – i.e. in the sense of their own interconnexions – to arrive at a 'system of nature' sufficient for our own time. The scientists themselves – however much they may resist it because of their own metaphysical training – are coming to accept the dialectical character of this inter-communication. Today we have no further use for the old 'natural philosophy' and any attempt to revive it would be a reactionary step.

Nature is now recognized as a historical process of evolution. This applies also to the development of the history of society in all its branches. It applies equally to all aspects of knowledge dealing with things human and divine. In the philosophy of history, the philosophy of law, and the philosophy of religion the old metaphysical approach consisted in substituting links invented by the philosopher himself for the true links which we can discover by studying history. The metaphysical approach attempted to understand history – both as a whole and in its separate parts – as the gradual realization of 'ideas' and these 'ideas' were of course always the pet notions of the philosopher himself. The metaphysical philosophers thought that history worked inevitably, though unconsciously, towards a certain predetermined ideal goal. For Hegel this was the realization of his 'absolute idea'. And the unalterable trend towards this absolute idea formed the essential link between historical events. A mysterious providence – unconscious or gradually coming into consciousness – replaced the real, though as yet unknown, links between historical events. As in the natural sciences so in history these invented and artificial links had to be abolished by discovering the real links. Before this could be done it was necessary to identify the principal laws of change in the evolution of human society.

But there is an important difference between the development of society and the changes that occur in nature. In nature – leaving out of account the intervention of man – there are only blind unconscious agencies which act upon one another. General natural laws emerge from the interplay of these unconscious agencies. Nothing that happens in nature occurs as the result of an aim that has been consciously desired. This applies both to the innumerable apparent accidents observable upon the surface and to the ultimate results which confirm the regularity which is inherent in these accidents. On the other hand, all the actors in the drama of human history are men with minds and their actions are influenced by thoughts or by emotions. They are men who are working with definite objectives in mind. In history nothing happens without a conscious purpose or an intended aim.

This distinction is important in the study of history – especially in the investigation of particular periods and events. But the distinction that has been made does not alter the fact that the course of history is governed by fundamental general laws. In spite of the consciously desired aims of all individuals it appears, at first sight, as if accidental circumstances have a powerful influence upon what happens in history. It is rare that the final results coincide with the aims of those who play a part in the drama of history. Various people have different aims and these aims may well clash. On the other hand, people's aims may, from the outset, be incapable of realization or the means of attaining the aims may be inadequate. The clash of innumerable individual aims and actions produces a state of affairs which is similar to that prevailing in the unconscious world of science. In history the aims of actions are consciously intended but the results which *actually* follow from these actions are not intended. When the results *appear* to correspond to the original aims they *ultimately* have consequences quite different from those which were expected. Both historical events and changes in nature, seem to be governed by chance. Although on the surface the influence of accidental factors appears to be all important, history is actually always governed by basic hidden laws – and it is only a matter of finding out what these laws are.

Men make their own history, whatever its outcome may be, because everybody endeavours to realize the aims which he consciously desires. History is the result of all these minds being directed towards different aims and having a great variety of effects upon the world. The aims of many individuals must therefore be examined. Both conscious deliberation and emotion play a part in determining men's aims. But there are many different factors which determine thought or emotion. These factors may be external objects, or ideal motives, or ambition, or 'enthusiasm for truth and justice', or personal hatred, or purely individual whims of all kinds. We have seen that the many individual wills which are active in history generally produce quite different – often the very opposite – results from those originally intended. We have observed that people's motives are of only secondary importance in relation to the result finally achieved. There are further questions to be asked: What driving forces determine human motives? What historical causes transform themselves into motives in the minds of those who influence events?

The old materialism never asked these questions. Its conception of history – in so far as it has one at all – is essentially pragmatic since it judges everything according to the motives behind actions. It divides historical figures into good and bad characters and then finds that normally the good people are defrauded and that the bad people are victorious. For the old materialists the study of history was far from edifying. The old materialism had a mistaken view of history since it regarded 'ideal' factors as ultimate causes and failed to investigate the driving forces *behind* the ideal factors. The inconsistency of the old materialism lies not in its emphasis on 'ideal' driving forces but in its failure to carry the investigation a step further back to find out what lies behind the driving forces. Hegel's philosophy of history does not recognize that neither the ostensible nor the real motives of men are the ultimate causes of historical events. Hegel saw that unknown primary motives lie behind secondary motives. Hegel did not look for fundamental motives in history itself. He looked for them outside history in philosophical ideology. Instead of explaining the development of the ancient Greeks in terms of the links between the events in Greek history, Hegel maintained that Greek history was simply the working out of 'forms of beautiful individuality' and the creation of a 'work of art' as such. Much that Hegel writes about the ancient Greeks is fine and profound but that does not mean that we are any longer prepared to be fobbed off with such an 'explanation' of Greek history.

When investigating the factors which – often unconsciously – determine the motives of men we are examining the real ultimate driving forces in history. There is no need to examine the motives of particular individuals, however eminent they may be. What is necessary is the investigation of the motives lying behind the actions of peoples and of social classes. Motives which influence people for only a short time may be ignored. We are not interested in the transient flaring up of a fire which quickly dies down. We are concerned with motives that lead to lasting actions and ultimately to great historical changes. Our aim must be to discover the driving forces which act upon the minds of great masses of people and of their leaders – the so-called 'great men'. These driving forces are revealed as conscious motives in many varied forms. Only investigation of this kind can put us on the track of fundamental laws which influence all historical development as well as events in particular periods or in particular lands. Everything which causes men to act must go through their minds. But the form that it will take in their minds will depend very much upon particular circumstances. The workers have by no means become reconciled to capitalist machine industry even though they no longer break machinery to pieces as they still did in the Rhineland in 1848.

At one time the investigation of all the driving forces in history was almost impossible because the links between historical events were complicated and hidden from view. Today these links have been simplified and the riddle can be solved. Since the establishment of large-scale industry – i.e. since 1815 – it has been quite obvious that in England the political struggle has turned upon the rival claims of two classes – the landed aristocracy and the middle classes. In France, the same thing happened when the Bourbons were restored – French historians (Thierry, Guizot, Mignet, Thiers) writing about that period agreed that class rivalry was the key to the understanding of French history ever since the Middle Ages. In both Britain and France the working classes have, since 1830, been recognized as a third competitor for power. By that time conditions had become so simplified that everybody – who did not deliberately close his eyes to the facts – was bound to see that in the two most advanced countries in the world the conflict between the interests of these three great classes was the driving force in history.

How did these classes come into existence? The origin of the old feudal landed aristocracy could, at least in the first instance, be ascribed to political causes. The feudal lords seized land by force. Such an explanation, however, would not be satisfactory as far as the middle classes and the working classes were concerned. The origin and the development of those two great classes were obviously to be found in purely economic – and not in political – causes. It is equally clear that *economic* interests were the mainspring in the struggles between the landed aristocracy and the middle classes, and in the struggle between the middle classes and the working classes. In these struggles political power merely served economic ends. Both the middle classes and the working classes arose as the result of changes in economic conditions. They arose because of changes in methods of producing goods. The development of the two social classes has been brought about first by the change from craft industry to manufacturing industry and then from small-scale manufacturing industry to large-scale production by means of steam power and modern machinery. The middle classes set new productive forces in motion. These changes included the introduction of the division of labour and the bringing together in a single factory of a number of different kinds of (skilled and unskilled) workers. The *new* methods of making goods and the *new* method of buying and selling could not exist side by side with *old* methods of producing goods – methods sanctified by law and by custom. Numerous privileges existed under the old system – privileges of private persons, of particular places and of guilds. These privileges were part and parcel of feudal society and they were opposed by those who had no privileges. The productive forces represented by the middle classes rebelled against the methods of industrial production which belonged to the age of feudal landlords and privileged guilds.

We know what happened. In England feudal restrictions gradually disappeared while in France they were destroyed by a single blow. In Germany the process is not yet finished. Just as – at a particular stage of its development – manufacturing industry came into conflict with feudal methods of industrial production so now modern large-scale industry has already come into conflict with the type of production which the middle classes put in the place of feudal production. Industry is cramped by the methods of production invented by the middle classes. Capitalist production – because of its self-imposed limitations – has two fundamental drawbacks. First, the great mass of the people became poorer under this system and secondly an ever-increasing mass of unsaleable goods appeared upon the market. The absurd contradiction of modern capitalism is the simultaneous appearance of over-production and mass misery. This situation obviously calls for the liberation of productive forces through a change in the means of production.

There can therefore be no doubt that, at any rate in modern times, all political struggles have been class struggles. Moreover it is clear that all class struggles for emancipation – although they are necessarily political in form – turn ultimately on the question of *economic* emancipation. So in this case the State (the political order) is subordinate to civil society (the realm of economic relations). The traditional view – and this was the view taken by Hegel – regarded the State as the determining element in human affairs while civil society was determined by the State. At first sight this view might appear to be correct. In an individual the driving forces which lead to action must first pass through his brain and transform themselves into motives of his will. Similarly all the needs of civil society – whichever class happens to rule – must pass through the will of the State before they can secure general validity in the form of laws. That is the formal aspect of the matter and it is the aspect which is self-evident. But what is the real content of this formal will and where does it come from? Why is one thing willed rather than another? These questions arise both for the individual and the State. And, if we examine this problem, we discover that in modern times the will of the State is normally determined by the changing needs of civil society. It is determined by the supremacy of one class or another. And in the last resort it is determined by the productive forces and by the exchange mechanism of the economy.

Even in modern times, when the means of production and communication have greatly increased, the State is not something independent which develops by its own volition. The existence of the State and its development must, in the last resort, be explained in terms of prevailing economic conditions. If this is true of the situation today it must be still more correct for all previous history. It must apply to earlier times when the production of food and goods was a much more difficult matter than it is today. At one time the production of material things must have exercised a greater mastery over men than it does today. At the present time – in an era of great industries and railways – the State simply mirrors (in concentrated form) the economic needs of the class which controls production. This situation must have existed in the past in an exaggerated form because in earlier ages men had to spend more of their time in satisfying purely material needs. An examination of the history of earlier periods, as soon as it is seriously undertaken from this angle, must confirm this.

It is not only the State and public law which are determined by economic influences. Private law, of course, is in essence simply a sanction for the normal existing relations between individuals. The form in which this occurs can vary considerably. In England, for example, it was found possible (within the framework of the historical development of the country) to retain the forms of feudal laws though they were adapted to the needs of the middle classes. On the other hand, Roman law became the basis of new economic relationships in the western states on the Continent. Roman law was the first world law of a society producing commodities and it elaborated, with unsurpassed skill, all the essential relations of owners of commodities, of buyers and sellers, of debtors and creditors. Roman law can be adapted to the simple needs of semi-feudal and petty bourgeois society by judicial practice (common law). Alternatively – with the aid of moralizing lawyers who are supposed to be 'enlightened' – the principles of Roman law can be worked into a special code of law to meet the needs of a relatively underdeveloped society. In these circumstances such a code – the Prussian *Landrecht* for example – will be a bad code from a legal standpoint. It is also possible for such a classic code of laws (suitable for a middle class society) to be worked out on the basis of Roman law after a great bourgeois revolution. The French civil code is an example of this. Middle class legal rules merely express in legal form the economic conditions of society. The quality of these legal rules will vary according to circumstances.

The State is the first ideological authority over mankind. Society creates the State to safeguard its common interests against internal and external attacks. Hardly has it come into being than the State makes itself *independent* of society. As the State becomes the organ of a particular class it enforces the supremacy of that class. The struggle of an oppressed class against a ruling class must be a political struggle. It is above all a struggle against the political dominance of its rival. Those engaged in such a conflict may cease to be fully aware of the limits between the political struggle on the surface and the economic struggle which goes on underneath. The participants in the conflict may not completely forget the economic basis of the struggle but historians nearly always do forget it. Appian, for example, is the only ancient historian who tells us clearly that landed property was the real issue in the struggles within the Roman Republic.

Once the State has become an independent power in its own right it produces a new ideology. And in this ideology (as interpreted by professional politicians, theorists of public law and jurists of private law) the connexion between politics and economics is lost for good. In each particular case economic facts must assume the form of legal motives in order to receive legal sanction. The lawyer has to apply the particular case within the framework of a legal system which already exists. In these circumstances the outward legal form becomes all-important while the basic economic factors are ignored. Public law and private law are treated as if they were independent. Each is supposed to have had its own historical development and each has to be presented in such a way as to eliminate any inner contradictions.

Philosophy and religion may be regarded as ideologies of a still higher order since they are still further removed (than politics or law) from the material basis of life. Here the links between ideas and facts become even more complex and are even more obscured by intermediate links. Nevertheless the links between ideas and material facts do exist. The whole period of the Renaissance (from the middle of the fifteenth century onwards) was dominated by the cities and therefore by the urban middle class. And we find that the new philosophy of that period was also dominated by the urban middle classes. The essence of this philosophy was really only an ideological expression of the thoughts of the urban middle classes who were then in a stage of transition from the small and middle bourgeoisie to the big bourgeoisie. The same is true of certain English and French thinkers of the eighteenth century, many of whom were as much economists as they were philosophers. And in previous discussion we have shown that this is also true of Hegel.

We will deal only briefly with religion which is farthest removed from material life and seems to be most alien to it. Religion arose in very primitive times and was based upon the mistaken and primitive ideas which men had concerning both their own nature and the world in which they lived. Once an ideology has established itself it develops its basic conceptions. The ability to do this is a function of an ideology which may be defined as the examination of thoughts as independent entities. These entities expand and are subject only to their own laws. In primitive times religious ideas were common to a group of kindred peoples. When the original group splits each of the smaller units develop its own particular religious ideas which are influenced by its economic environment. A study of comparative mythology has made this process clear in respect of several groups of peoples, particularly the Aryans. The popular gods fashioned in this way were national deities whose domain extended no farther than the national territory which they protected. Beyond the national frontiers other gods held undisputed sway. These dieties could continue to exist only so long as the nation existed. When the nation fell they disappeared. Such a downfall of old nationalities occurred when the Roman Empire was established. (There is no need to examine here the economic conditions which contributed to the rise of this empire.) When old nationalities collapsed so did the old national gods. Even the Roman gods decayed because they were suitable only within the narrow limits of the city of Rome. It was necessary to find a world religion for a world empire and so attempts were made to provide in Rome itself altars for all those foreign gods which could be regarded as in any degree respectable. But no imperial decree can create a new world religion. Christianity had already come into being. It was a mixture of Eastern (particularly Jewish) theology and vulgarized Greek (particularly Stoic) philosophy. The original Christian beliefs had to be laboriously reconstructed since the official Christianity that has been handed down to us is merely the Christianity which was adopted by the Council of Nicaea as the State religion of the Empire. The fact that after only 250 years Christianity became the State religion shows that its beliefs corresponded with the conditions of that time. In the same way when feudalism arose in the Middle Ages Christianity developed – with its own hierarchy – as the religious counterpart to the new political and social order.

When the urban middle classes began to thrive, the Protestant heresy developed in opposition to feudal Catholicism. The first Protestant heresy appeared in the south of France among the Albigense when the cities in that part of the country reached their maximum expansion. In medieval times the various ideologies – philosophy, politics, jurisprudence and so forth – had been regarded as subdivisions of theology. Consequently all social and political movements tended to adopt a theological form. The masses were fed with religious ideas to the exclusion of everything else. If the masses wished to further their own interests they had to put their views in a religious form so as to gain support for them. Just as the urban middle classes brought into being the precursors of the later proletariat (day labourers, servants and other workers who owned no property), so religious heresy came to be divided into a moderate heresy supported by the urban middle classes and a revolutionary heresy supported by the poor workers. The middle-class heretics of course abominated the rival heresy of the proletariat.

Just as no one could halt the advance of the urban middle classes so no one could stamp out the Protestant heresy. When the new urban middle classes became strong enough their struggle against the old feudal nobility began to assume national – instead of purely local – dimensions. The first great clash occurred in Germany. This was the so-called Reformation. The urban middle classes had not yet reached a stage in their development which would give them the power to secure the allegiance of other discontented elements in society, such as the workers in the towns, the peasants on the land, and the lower nobility. At first the nobles were defeated. The peasants rose in revolt and this was the climax of the revolutionary rising. But the cities left the peasants in the lurch and the revolution was defeated by the armies of the secular princes. And it was only the princes who gained any advantage from the revolt. For three centuries after the Peasant Revolt Germany ceased to be a country which was able to play an active part in world affairs.

Beside the German Luther there appeared the Frenchman Calvin. With true French acuteness he put the bourgeois character of the Reformation in the forefront of his movement. He founded a democratic republican church. While the Lutheran Reformation in Germany degenerated and reduced the country to ruin the Calvinist Reformation inspired the republicans in Geneva, Holland and Scotland. Calvinism freed Holland from Spain and from the Holy Roman Empire. And Calvinism provided the ideological framework for the second phase of the revolution of the middle classes which was taking place in England. It was in England that Calvinism showed it was the religion best suited to the interests of the middle classes at that time. This was why Calvinism was not fully recognized when the revolution ended in 1689 as a compromise between one part of the aristocracy and the bourgeoisie. The Church of England was not re-established in its earlier form of a Catholic Church which had the king for its pope. Instead it was re-established in a strongly Calvinized form. The old Church of England had celebrated the merry Catholic Sunday and had fought against the dull Calvinist Sabbath. But the new Church of England, now strongly influenced by middle-class ideas, introduced the Calvinist Sabbath which survives to the present time.

In France the Calvinist minority was suppressed in 1685. The Huguenots either left the country or turned Catholic. But what good did that do? Pierre Bayle, the free-thinker, was already at the height of his activity at that time while Voltaire was born in

1694. Louis XIV's forcible measures against the Huguenots merely made it easier for the French middle classes to carry out their revolution in a fully-political – and not a religious – form. And this suited a fully-developed bourgeoisie. Free thinkers sat in the National Assemblies instead of Protestants. And so Christianity entered into its final phase. No longer could a progressive social class use Christianity as a cloak for its political aspirations. Only the ruling classes now had a vested interest in Christianity. And the ruling classes simply regarded Christianity as a means of governing. They used religion as a method of checking the advance of the lower classes. Each class had its own appropriate religion. The landed aristocracy are Catholics or orthodox Protestants. The liberal and radical middle classes are rationalists. And whether these gentlemen actually believe in their respective religions is a matter of little importance.

We have seen that tradition is a powerful conservative force in all ideologies and that once a religion has been established it always has its traditional aspect. The transformations which take place in the traditional aspects of any religion spring from the relations between different classes in society. They are due ultimately to the economic interests of classes.

It has been possible to give only a general sketch of the Marxist conception of history, illustrated by a few examples. The proof of our arguments must be derived from history itself. And this has been done in other books and articles. The Marxist view of history excludes philosophy from the realm of history just as the Marxist view of nature makes all natural philosophy both unnecessary and impossible. We no longer have to invent links (between historical or scientific facts); we have to discover the links by studying the facts themselves. Philosophy has been expelled from nature and history and must now concern itself solely with logic and dialectics in the realm of pure thought.

After the Revolution of 1848 'educated' Germany gave up theory for practice. Manufacturing on a small scale with manual labour was replaced by industry on a large scale. Germany again appeared on the markets of the world. The new Reich of 1871 abolished the most scandalous of the abuses which had formerly checked industrial expansion. It got rid of petty states, feudal relics and bureaucratic management. Germans ceased to speculate in the philosopher's study in order to speculate on the stock exchange. And so educated Germans lost their great aptitude for theory which had been Germany's glory in the days of her deepest political humiliation. At one time the Germans had shown an exceptional aptitude for purely scientific investigations which they pursued without considering whether the results that they obtained had any practical application or were likely to offend the police. It is true that the high reputation of German investigations in the natural sciences has retained its reputation, especially in the field of specialized research. But even the American journal *Science* rightly observes that the decisive advances in the sphere of the correlation of particular facts – and their generalization into scientific laws – are now being made in England rather than in Germany. In the sphere of philosophy and the historical sciences the disappearance in Germany of the old classical philosophy has been accompanied by the disappearance of the former fearless zeal for original theoretical speculation. The Germans now borrow doctrines from every school of thought. They are concerned with mundane affairs such as making a career for themselves, getting better jobs and accumulating money. The official representatives of philosophy and history have completely identified themselves with the middle classes and with the existing state. Now the bourgeoisie and the State are openly opposed to the working classes. The German aptitude for theoretical speculation survives only among the workers for they are not concerned with careers or profits or gracious patronage from above. As science makes greater progress – by determined and disinterested research – it finds itself more and more in harmony with the interests and the aspirations of the workers. Marxist scientific thought recognizes that the whole evolution of society lies in the history of the development of labour. Marxist scientists from the first preferred to address themselves to the working classes. It was amongst the workers that Marxist science found the responses which it neither sought nor expected from officially recognized science. The German working-class movement is the inheritor of German classical philosophy.

2. Engels to Bloch[1]

London, 21-22 September 1890

... According to the materialist conception of history, the *ultimately* determining element in history is the production and reproduction of real life. More than this neither Marx nor I have ever asserted. Hence if somebody twists this into saying that the economic element is the *only* determining one, he transforms that proposition into a meaningless, abstract, senseless phrase. The economic situation is the basis, but the various elements of the superstructure – political forms of the class struggle and its results, to wit: constitutions established by the victorious class after a successful battle, etc., juridical forms, and even the reflexes of all these actual struggles in the brains of the participants, political, juristic, philosophical theories, religious views and their further development into systems of dogmas – also exercise their influence upon the course of the historical struggles and in many cases preponderate in determining their *form*. There is an interaction of all these elements in which, amid all the endless host of accidents (that is, of things and events whose inner interconnexion is so remote or so impossible of proof that we can regard it as non-existent, as negligible) the economic movement finally asserts itself as necessary. Otherwise the application of the theory to any period of history would be easier than the solution of a simple equation of the first degree.

We make our history ourselves, but, in the first place, under very definite assumptions and conditions. Among these the economic ones are ultimately decisive. But the political ones, etc., and indeed even the traditions which haunt human minds, also play a part, although not the decisive one. The Prussian state also arose and developed from historical, ultimately economic, causes. But it could scarcely be maintained without pedantry that among the many small states of North Germany, Brandenburg was specifically determined by economic necessity to become the

1. [From Marx and Engels, *Selected Correspondence* (Foreign Language Publishing House, Moscow) pp. 498-500.]

great power embodying the economic, linguistic and, after the Reformation, also the religious difference between North and South, and not by other elements as well (above all by its entanglement with Poland, owing to the possession of Prussia, and hence with international political relations – which were indeed also decisive in the formation of the Austrian dynastic power). Without making oneself ridiculous it would be a difficult thing to explain in terms of economics the existence of every small state in Germany, past and present, or the origin of the High German consonant permutations, which widened the geographic partition wall formed by the mountains from the Sudeten range to the Taunus to form a regular fissure across all Germany.

In the second place, however, history is made in such a way that the final result always arises from conflicts between many individual wills, of which each in turn has been made what it is by a host of particular conditions of life. Thus there are innumerable intersecting forces, an infinite series of parallelograms of forces which give rise to one resultant – the historical event. This may again itself be viewed as the product of a power which works as a whole *unconsciously* and without volition. For what each individual wills is obstructed by everyone else, and what emerges is something that no one willed. Thus history has proceeded hitherto in the manner of a natural process and is essentially subject to the same laws of motion. But from the fact that the wills of individuals – each of whom desires what he is impelled to by his physical constitution and external, in the last resort economic, circumstances (either his own personal circumstances or those of society in general) – do not attain what they want, but are merged into an aggregate mean, a common resultant, it must not be concluded that they are equal to zero. On the contrary, each contributes to the resultant and is to this extent included in it.

I would furthermore ask you to study this theory from its original sources and not at second-hand; it is really much easier. Marx hardly wrote anything in which it did not play a part. But especially *The Eighteenth Brumaire of Louis Bonaparte* is a most excellent example of its application. There are also many allusions to it in *Capital*. Then may I also direct you to my writings:

Herr Eugen Dühring's Revolution in Science and *Ludwig Feuerbach and the End of Classical German Philosophy*, in which I have given the most detailed account of historical materialism which, as far as I know, exists.

Marx and I are ourselves partly to blame for the fact that the younger people sometimes lay more stress on the economic side than is due to it. We had to emphasize the main principle vis-á-vis our adversaries, who denied it, and we had not always the time, the place or the opportunity to give their due to the other elements involved in the interaction. But when it came to presenting a section of history, that is, to making a practical application, it was a different matter and there no error was permissible. Unfortunately, however, it happens only too often that people think they have fully understood a new theory and can apply it without more ado from the moment they have assimilated its main principles, and even those not always correctly. And I cannot exempt many of the more recent 'Marxists' from this reproach, for the most amazing rubbish has been produced in this quarter, too. . . .

VI. THE MILITARY CRITIC

Introduction[1]

ENGELS established a considerable reputation for himself as a military critic and his friends called him 'the General'. His actual experience of army life was quite limited. As a young man he performed his military service in Berlin in the Guards Artillery (1841–2) and in 1849 he took part – as August Willich's adjutant – in a minor insurrection in Baden. In four weeks the Prussian troops drove the insurgents out of Baden into Switzerland and the campaign was over. In the following year Engels described the campaign in articles which appeared in the *Neue Rheinische Zeitung*. When Engels settled down to office work in Manchester in 1851 he soon began to devote his scanty leisure to a systematic study of military history. His original idea was to write a history of the campaigns of 1848–9 in order to explain to the workers the reasons for the failure of the revolutionary movements from a military point of view. He believed that 'if the working class was to overcome the bourgeoisie it would first have to master the art and strategy of war'.[2]

Engels never wrote a military study of the campaigns of 1848. He did however use some of the material in a series of articles on the revolutions in Germany. They appeared under Marx's name in the *New York Daily Tribune*. Marx and Engels wrote regularly for this newspaper in the 1850s and Engels's contributions were often on military topics. Engels also wrote articles on military affairs for the *New American Cyclopaedia*. His pamphlet on *Po und Rhein* (1859) discussed the political and military implications for Germany of the war between Austria and France in Italy. Marx declared that this pamphlet had established Engels's position as a military critic in Germany.

In the 1860s Engels contributed articles on the volunteer movement for the *Volunteer Journal for Lancashire and Cheshire*

1. [See W.H. Chaloner and W.O. Henderson (eds.), *Engels as Military Critic* (1959).]
2. [Introduction to Karl Marx and Frederick Engels, *The Civil War in the United States* (edn of 1961), p. xiii.]

and on the Seven Weeks War for the *Manchester Guardian*. In Engels's correspondence with Marx the campaigns of the American civil war were frequently discussed. Marx often incorporated parts of these letters in articles on the war which he contributed to *Die Presse* in Vienna. During the Franco-Prussian war Engels wrote sixty articles for the *Pall Mall Gazette* on the campaigns of 1870–1.

Engels was not able to offer his readers the kind of information that was available to war correspondents who followed campaigns on the spot. He depended entirely on the daily papers for news of the campaigns which he discussed. But he had a profound knowledge of the history of warfare and he was able to compare the problems that had faced commanders in the past with those with which contemporary generals had to deal. He was prepared to make confident predictions which sometimes proved to be wrong. But he erred in the company of other experts on military affairs.

1. The Invasion of Britain[1]

ENGELS TO WEYDEMEYER *23 January 1852*

Here are some additional points by way of comment on the possibility of invading Britain, to clear up the matter for you:

1. Any landing west of Portsmouth runs the risk of being driven into the angle of Cornwall – hence impracticable.

2. Any landing further to the north of, or too close to, Dover runs the risk of suffering the same fate between the Thames and the sea.

3. The initial objectives of the operation would be London and Woolwich. Detachments would have to be assigned to take Portsmouth and Sheerness (Chatham). A strong garrison would have to be kept in London, with strong detachments between London and the coast. With a landing force of 150,000 men, this would require at least 60,000 (and even that would be insufficient). Hence, 90,000 men would be available for the advance.

4. The second objective of the operation would be Birmingham (the arms factories are located there). The area south of Bristol Channel and the Wash would have to be secured, i.e. the line from Gloucester to King's Lynn, together with a powerful attack on Birmingham. No matter how weak and overwhelmed the enemy's army might be, I think that to deal with it with a force of 90,000 men would be impossible. But even if this should succeed, it would not gain a tenable defensive position, especially if British sea power came into play. The line is too long and too weak. That is why the advance would have to be maintained.

5. The third objective of the operation would be Manchester. The whole area south of the Mersey (or the Ribble) and the Aire (the Humber) must be secured, and this line held. It is shorter

1. [From Karl Marx and F. Engels, *Letters to Americans, 1845-95* (International Publishers, New York, 1953 and New World Paperbacks edition 1963), pp. 34-5. When Louis Napoleon seized power in France there was a war scare in England.]

and easier to defend; but here too the invading forces would be greatly weakened by the detaching of troops. Since the defence would still have enough territory and adequate facilities to re-organize its forces, the invaders would have to either advance or soon retreat.

6. The first line that could be held in the extremely narrow north of England is either the Tees or, even better, the Tyne, from Carlisle to Newcastle (the line of the Roman Wall, erected against the Picts). But then the defenders would still have the agricultural, industrial and commercial resources of the Scottish Lowlands.

7. The conquest of *England proper* may be considered complete, *even though only temporarily,* only when Glasgow and Edinburgh are taken, the defenders are forced back into the Highlands, and the invaders occupy the excellent, short, strong line between the Clyde and the Firth of Forth, which is adequately provided with rail lines to the rear.

But the real difficulties – the difficulties of maintaining the position – begin after the conquest, since communications with France will certainly be cut off.

How many men would be required, under these conditions, to conquer the whole country from Dover to the Clyde and to set up a decent front on the Clyde?

I think 400,000 would not be too high a figure.

These considerations are too detailed for the newspaper, and I am setting them down for you solely as a professional man. Take a look at the map of England and tell me what you think of this. This is one side of the question that the British lose sight of completely.

2. The Volunteer Movement in England

(i) A Review of the English Volunteer Riflemen[1]

The Allgemeine Militärzeitung, *published at Darmstadt, and considered the first military paper in Germany, in its number of 8*

1. [*Volunteer Journal for Lancashire and Cheshire,* Vol. 1, No. 2, pp. 26–28, 14 September, 1860.]

September, gives an account by a correspondent of the Newton Review and of the rifle movement in general. The following is a translation of this article (prepared specially for the Volunteer Journal) *which no doubt will prove interesting to the volunteers of Lancashire and Cheshire and especially to those who were present at the review. As may be expected, this account is not made up of that unqualified praise which the British press generally gives as its contribution to the movement; still the character of the contemporary in question ought to be a sufficient guarantee that it is not written by an incompetent hand, and the sympathetic tone of the whole article proves that the writer had no inclination for wanton fault-finding. As to the suggestions contained in the article, we shall leave our readers to form their own opinion upon them.*[1]

England, as well as Germany, is arming to repel the attack with which Bonapartism threatens her; the British Volunteer Riflemen arose for the same cause which made Prussia double the number of her battalions of the line. It will, therefore, be of interest to the German military public to receive some detailed information on the present state and the fitness for actual service of the British Volunteer Army; for this army, from its very origin, and in virtue of its fundamental idea, is an enemy of Bonapartism, an ally of Germany. A very few battalions excepted, this army of volunteers dates from the latter half of last year; the great body has not been put in uniform and drilled more than a twelvemonth. At present, its strength, on paper, is 120,000 men; but if we may draw conclusions from what is the fact in some districts, there will not be more than 80,000 men really effective and drilled; the remainder take no interest in the matter, and had better be erased from the lists.

The organization is very simple. Wherever 60 to 100 volunteers (in the artillery 50 to 80) are brought together, in any locality, they form themselves into a company, subject to the consent of the Lord Lieutenant of the county. They elect candidates for officers (a captain, a lieutenant, and an ensign), whom the Lord Lieutenant, in most cases, appoints to their respective companies; but there have also been instances of rejection.

1. [This introductory paragraph was written by the editor of the *Volunteer Journal*.]

Several companies may form themselves into a battalion, in which case the Lord Lieutenant appoints the major and lieutenant-colonel, mostly according to the wishes of the officers, or according to the seniority among the captains. Thus there are corps varying from one to eight companies and more, numbered in the order of their formation in their respective counties; but only full battalions of eight companies receive a lieutenant-colonel. The officers may, all of them, be appointed from among the volunteers, and they are not subjected to any examination. The adjutant, however, must be an officer from the line of militia, and he alone receives regular pay. The volunteers find their own clothing, etc., but if desired, the Government furnishes them with rifle and bayonet by way of loan. The colour and cut of the uniform is fixed by the various corps, subject to the approval of the Lord Lieutenant. The corps have also, upon the whole, to find their own drill and practice grounds, ammunition, instructors and music.

The uniforms of the various infantry or rifle corps are mostly dark green, dark or light grey, or brown drab. The shape is something intermediate between the French and English pattern; for a headdress they mostly wear the French *képi*, or the French or English officer's cap. The artillery is dressed in dark blue, and has adopted, for appearance's sake, the rather unserviceable and lumbering fur-cap or busby of the horse artillery. There are also a few mounted rifles whose uniform imitates that of the English cavalry, but they are a mere article of luxury.

At the time when the formation of these rifle corps was first agitated, the whole matter savoured very strongly of our own national and civic guards; there was a great deal of playing at soldiers; the way in which officers were manufactured, and the appearance and helplessness of some of these officers, when on duty, were rather amusing. It may well be imagined, the men did not always elect the most capable, or even those who had the movement most at heart. During the first six months, almost all battalions and companies made the same effect upon the beholder as our own defunct civic guard of 1848.

This, then, was the material handed over to the drill-sergeants, in order to shape it into a body of serviceable field-troops.

The manual and platoon was gone through mostly at nights, between seven and nine o'clock, in covered rooms and by gas-light, twice or three times a week. On Saturday afternoons, if possible, the whole body made a short march and went through company movements. To drill on Sunday was forbidden by both law and custom. The instructors were sergeants and corporals of the line, the militia, or pensioners; and they, too, had to form the officers into shape. But the English non-commissioned officer is an excellent man in his way. There is, on duty, less swearing and coarse language in the English army than in any other; on the other hand, punishment is so much the more certain to be applied. The non-commissioned imitates the commissioned officer, and thus (has) adopted manners far superior to those of our German sergeants. Then he does not serve because of the prospect of some pettifogging office in the civil service being held out to him, as is the case with us; he has engaged himself voluntarily for twelve years, and promotion, up to the rank of sergeant-major even, offers him considerable fresh advantages at every step; in every battalion one or two commissions (adjutant and paymaster) are mostly reserved to old non-commissioned officers; and, on active service, every sergeant may attach the golden star to his collar by distinguishing himself before the enemy. The drill-sergeants belonging to this class of men have, indeed, upon the whole, made the volunteers what it was possible to make them in so short a time; they have not only made them steady in company movements, but also licked the officers into shape.

In the meantime, the single companies, at least in the large towns, formed themselves into battalions and received adjutants from the regular troops. Similar to the Austrian, the English subaltern is far less theoretically educated than the North German; but same as the Austrian, if he likes his profession, he knows his duty exceedingly well. Among the adjutants who have passed over from the line to the volunteers, there are men who, as instructors, could not be better; and the results which they obtained in a very short time in their battalions are surprising indeed. Up to the present time, however, only a minority of the volunteers have been formed into permanent battalions, and as a matter of course, these are considerably superior to the mass of companies not so formed.

The volunteers of Lancashire and Cheshire had organized a Review at Newton, half way between Manchester and Liverpool, for the 11th of August, the commanding General of the district, Sir George Wetherall, taking the command. The volunteers who met here were the contingents of the manufacturing districts around Manchester; there were not very many present either from Liverpool or from the neighbouring agricultural districts of Cheshire. To judge from our own German recruiting experience, these corps must have been physically below the average; but it is not to be forgotten that by far the minority of the volunteers belong to the working classes.

The soil of Newton race-course, of itself spongy enough, had been considerably softened by the continuous rains; it was very uneven and very sticky. On one side of it there is a small brook, with here and there some thick gorse on its banks. The ground was just right for a parade of young volunteers; they most of them stood ankle deep in water and mud, and the officers' horses often sank into the clay until above the fetlock-joint.

The 57 corps which had sent in their adhesion were divided into four brigades – the first of four, the remainder of three battalions each; every battalion of eight companies. Lieutenant-Colonels of the line commanded the brigades; officers of volunteers were appointed to the battalions. The first brigade had three battalions deployed, the fourth in column behind the centre. The three remaining brigades stood in second line, nine battalions in continuous columns of companies at quarter distance, right in front.

After saluting the general, a change of front to the left was to be effected, under shelter of the battalion which stood in column behind the first line. To effect this, the two centre companies of the battalion deployed in front of it, wheeled outwards, upon which the column passed through the opening thus formed, and then extended along the water-course – four companies skirmishing, and four forming the supports. The ground and the gorse were both so wet that the men could not be expected to take a correct advantage of the ground; besides, most battalions of volunteers are still occupied with the A B C only of skirmishing and outpost duty, so that it would not be fair to measure them by too high a standard in this respect. In the meantime, the deployed line effected its change of front around its own centre as a pivot; the two centre companies of the middle battalions wheeled a quarter of a circle – the one forwards, the other backwards – after which the remaining companies took up the new alignment. The two battalions on the wings of the first line formed columns at quarter distance, marched into the alignment, and deployed again. It may be imagined what a time was occupied by this complicated and rather clumsy manoeuvre. At the same time, the right battalion of the line of columns advanced straight on until halted behind the new right wing of the first line; the remaining battalions faced to the right and followed in double files (fours right), each battalion turning to the front, and following the right battalion as soon as it arrived on the spot originally occupied by this right battalion. When the last column had thus arrived upon the new alignment, each column independently wheeled to the left, and thus restored the front of the line of columns.

The third brigade now advanced from the centre of this line of columns; arrived about two hundred paces behind the first or deployed line, the three battalions opened out to deploying distance and deployed in their turn. The chain of skirmishers, in the meantime, having gained considerable ground, both deployed lines advanced a couple of hundred paces, upon which the first line was relieved by the second. This is effected by the first line forming fours right, and the head of each company disengaging and wheeling to the right; files in the second line give way, thus affording room for the first line to pass through; after which, companies form front and wheel into line. This is one of those drill-ground movements which are superfluous wherever they are practicable, and which are not practicable where they would be necessary. After this, the four brigades were drawn together again into a mass of columns, and the troops marched past the general in open column of companies (25 to 35 files front).

We shall not attempt to criticize this system of evolutions

which, no doubt, will appear rather old-fashioned to our readers. It is evident that, whatever may be its value in an army of the line with twelve years' service, it is certainly less adapted than any other for volunteers who can afford a few spare hours per week only for their drill. What interests us most on this occasion, is the manner in which these movements were performed by the volunteers; and here we must say that, although there was a slight hitch here and there, upon the whole, these evolutions were gone through steadily and without confusion. The most defective parts were, the wheeling in column and the deployments, which latter were done very slowly; in both evolutions, it was visible that the officers were not sufficiently formed and not yet at home in their duty. But on the other hand, the advance in line, this chief and cardinal movement of British tactics, was good beyond all expectation; the English appear, indeed, to have quite an exceptional talent for this movement, and to learn it uncommonly quick. The marching-past also came off, upon the whole, very well – and what was most amusing, it came off under a drenching shower of rain. There were a few mistakes against British military etiquette, and besides, by the fault of the officers, distances were very badly kept.

Besides a sham fight organized in London, by some over-sanguine commanders of Volunteers, and gone through rather wildly, this was the first time that a larger body of volunteers performed evolutions, which had something more in view than eventual marching-past. If we consider that the great mass of the troops present at Newton consisted of corps which, counting one, two, or at the outside three companies, are not formed into permanent battalions, have no officers from the regulars, have been drilled by drill-sergeants alone, and have only now and then been brigaded together in a battalion, we shall have to allow that the volunteers have done everything that was possible, and that they are no longer on the same level with our civic guards. As a matter of course, the corps which formed permanent battalions, and are directed by adjutants from the line (for the adjutants, so far, are the virtual commanders of battalions), were also those which went most steadily through their evolutions at the review.

The men upon the whole looked well. There were, indeed, some companies as puny as Frenchmen, but others surpassed in stature the average of the present British line. Mostly, however, they were very unequal in size and breadth of chest. The pallor peculiar to the inhabitants of towns gave to most of them a rather unpleasantly unwarlike look, but eight days' encampment would soon get the better of that. The uniforms, some of them a little over-ornamental, made a very good effect in the mass.

The first year's drill has taught the volunteers so much of the elementary movements, that they may now enter upon skirmishing and rifle practice. They will be far more handy at both these kinds of work than the English line, so that by summer 1861 they would form a very useful army, if only their officers knew more about their business.

This is the weak point of the whole formation. Officers cannot be manufactured in the same time and with the same means as privates. Up to now it has been proved that the willingness and the zeal of the mass may be relied upon, as far as is required, for making every man a soldier as far as necessary. But this is not sufficient for the officers. As we have seen, even for simple battalion movements, wheeling in column, deployments, keeping distances (so important in the English system of evolutions, where open columns are very often employed), the officers are not by far sufficiently formed. What is to become of them on outpost and skirmishing duty, where judgement of ground is everything, and where so many other difficult matters are to be taken into consideration? How can such men be entrusted with the duty of taking care of the safety of an army on the march? Government has made it binding upon every officer of volunteers to go to Hythe for three weeks, at least. So far, so good; but that will neither teach him to conduct a patrol, nor to command a picket. And yet, the volunteers are chiefly to be used for light-infantry service – for that very kind of duty which requires the cleverest and most reliable of officers.

If the whole movement is to lead to something, this is the point where Government will have to step in. All companies which are still existing – singly, or by twos and threes – ought to be compelled to combine together in permanent battalions, (and) to engage adjutants from the regulars. These adjutants should be bound to give to all the officers of their respective battalions a regular course of instruction in elementary tactics, light-infantry service in all its branches, and the regulations affecting the internal routine of service in a battalion. The officers should be bound, besides attending Hythe, to do duty, for at least three weeks, with a regiment of the line or militia in some encampment; and, finally, they should, after a certain time, be all made to pass an examination, proving that they have learnt at least the most indispensable part of their business. Such a course of instruction and examination of the officers; further, a medical examination of the men, in order to weed out those who are physically unfit for field-service (and there are not a few); and an annual revision of the company-lists, for the removal of those men who do not attend drill, who only play at soldiers and will not learn their duty – if this was done, the 120,000 men now existing on paper would be considerably reduced, but you would have an army worth three times the one which now counts 120,000 men on paper.

Instead of that, it is reported that the military authorities are busy discussing the important question, whether it would not be desirable to clothe, at the first opportunity, all rifle volunteers in the so very desirable brick colour of the line.

(ii) Volunteer Officers[1]

'Lieutenant A.B., dishonourably discharged; Second Lieutenant C.D., struck off the list; Captain E.F., dismissed the United States service' – such are a few specimens of the latest items of military news we receive by wholesale from America.

The United States have had a very large volunteer army in the field for the last eight months; they have spared neither trouble nor expense to make this army efficient; and, moreover, it has had the advantage of being posted, almost all that time, in sight of the outposts of an enemy who never dared to attack it in a mass or pursue it after a defeat. These favourable circumstances ought to make up, to a very large extent, for the dis-

1. [*Volunteer Journal*, Vol. III, No. 64, p. 315, 22 November 1861.]

advantages under which the United States volunteers were organized; for the poor support they got from a very small army of the line, forming their nucleus; and for the want of experienced adjutants and drill instructors. For we must not forget that in America there were many men both fit and ready to assist in the organization of the volunteers – partly German officers and soldiers who had undergone regular training and seen service in the campaigns of 1848–9, partly English soldiers emigrated during the last ten years.

Now, if under these circumstances a regular weeding of the officers becomes necessary, there must be some weakness inherent, not to the volunteer system in itself, but to the system of officering volunteers by men chosen indiscriminately by themselves from among themselves. It is only after an eight months' campaign in the face of the enemy that the United States Government ventures to call upon volunteer officers to qualify themselves, in some degree, for the duties they undertook to perform when they accepted their commissions; and see what an amount of voluntary or forced resignations, what a heap of dismissals, more or less dishonourable, is the consequence....

These facts may well serve as a lesson to the volunteers of England. Some of our readers may recollect that, from the very starting of the *Volunteer Journal*, we maintained that the officers were the weak point of the volunteer system, and insisted upon an examination, after a certain time, calling upon the officers to prove that they were at least in a fair way of becoming fit for performing the duties they had undertaken. Most of the gentlemen who had taken upon themselves to command and to instruct men in a line of business of which they were as perfectly ignorant at the time as the men themselves – most of these gentlemen scorned the idea. That was the time when all Government assistance and Government interference were equally scorned. But since then the call upon the pockets of these same gentlemen has been heavy enough to make them apply for pecuniary assistance from the Government; and, as Governments run, this means, at the same time, a call for Government interference. Moreover, a two years' experience has brought out pretty plainly the defects of the present system of officering volunteer corps;

and we are now informed by a metropolitan commanding officer, and apparently upon authority, that before long the volunteer officers will be called upon to prove their fitness for command, before a board of examination.

We heartily wish this to be the case. The fact is, the English volunteer officers, too, do require weeding to a certain extent. Look at a line regiment at drill and compare it to a volunteer battalion. What it takes the volunteers an hour and a half to go through, the line men go through in less than half an hour. We have seen a deal of square-forming by some of the best volunteer regiments in the country, and we cannot help saying they must be wretched cavalry that would not have cut them up each time before they had their flanks ready for firing. That was not the fault of the men. They appeared to know their duty as well as could be expected, and to do it sometimes even as mechanically as you see in a line regiment. But the men had to wait for the company officers, who appeared to hesitate about the word of command to be given, and about the moment when they ought to give it. Thus, hesitation and sometimes confusion was thrown into a formation which, above all others, requires a promptness, both of command and execution, imparted by long practice only. Now, if this be the case after two years' practice, is this not a proof that there are plenty of volunteer officers holding responsible situations which they are not fit to hold?

Again, the commanders of battalions have lately received some very high praise from the hands of highly competent authority. It was said that they appeared to be up to their work, while the company officers were not always so. We are not at all inclined, as will have been seen above, to dispute the latter statement; but we must say that if the high authority alluded to had seen the lieutenant-colonels and majors, not at a great review, but at plain battalion drill, the opinion given would probably have been slightly different. At a great review, no field officer in command of a battalion, if not perfectly up to his work, would attempt to act on his own responsibility. He has his adjutant – who knows what he is about – for a prompter; and he is prompted by him accordingly, and goes through his work creditably, while the poor captain has to bungle through his performance without any prompter at all. But look at the same field officer at battalion drill. There he has no vigilant general's eye watching him; there he reigns supreme; and there the adjutant, often enough, has to take the post assigned to him by the Queen's regulations, and must keep his advice to himself until asked for it, or until the mess is complete. This is the place where you see the volunteer field officer in his true light. He is there to instruct his men in battalion drill; but not being himself perfect in that science, he profits of their being there to instruct himself in it. As the old saying goes, *docendo discimus*. But if the teacher is not well on his legs in the art he has to teach, blunders and confusion are apt to occur, and, unfortunately, do occur often enough. It will not contribute either to the proficiency in drill of a volunteer battalion, or to its confidence in its commander, if the men find out that battalion drill, for them, means nothing but giving their field officer in command an opportunity of learning his drill himself, while they are tossed about here and there, without any purpose even, and expected to rectify, by their superior knowledge, the blunders of their superior officer.

We do not mean to say that commanding officers of volunteers have not put themselves to some trouble to learn their duty; but we do mean to say that if company officers cannot be manufactured out of civilians as easily as private soldiers, field officers are far more difficult to manufacture. We must come to the conclusion, on the mere ground of battalion drill experience, that none but professional soldiers are fit to command battalions. And if we consider that drill is but one part of a field officer's duty, that the commander of a battalion, being liable to be detached for independent duty, where he has to act on his own responsibility, requires a knowledge of higher tactics, we must say that we should be very sorry to see the lives of 600 or 1,000 men entrusted to the guidance of such civilians as now form the great majority of commanders of battalions.

Depend upon it, if the English volunteers ever will have to face an enemy, it will not be under the favourable circumstances which now permit the American Government to clear the ranks of their volunteer officers the most incapable subjects. If the English volunteers are called out, it will be to fight, not a volunteer army like themselves, but the most highly disciplined and most active army in Europe. The very first engagements will be decisive; and, depend upon it, if any hesitation or confusion arises, either by the wrong commands of the colonels, or by the uncertainty of the captains, that will be taken advantage of at once. There will be no time for weeding when once before the enemy, and therefore we hope it will be done while there is time.

3. The American Civil War[1]

(i)

WHEN, a few weeks back, we drew attention to the process of weeding which had become necessary in the American volunteer army, we were far from exhausting the valuable lessons this war is continually giving to the volunteers on this side of the Atlantic. We therefore beg leave again to revert to the subject.

The kind of warfare which is now carried on in America is really without precedent. From the Missouri to Chesapeake Bay, a million of men, nearly equally divided into two hostile camps, have now been facing each other for some six months without coming to a single general action. In Missouri, the two armies advance, retire, give battle, advance, and retire again in turns, without any visible result; even now, after seven months of marching and counter-marching, which must have laid the country waste to a fearful degree, things appear as far from any decision as ever. In Kentucky, after a lengthened period of apparent neutrality, but real preparation, a similar state of things appears to be impending; in Western Virginia, constant minor actions occur without any apparent result; and on the Potomac, where the greatest masses on both sides are concentrated, almost within sight of each other, neither party cares to attack, proving that, as matters stand, even a victory would be of no use at all. And unless circumstances foreign to this state of things cause a

1. [*Volunteer Journal*, Vol. III, No. 66, pp. 334–5, 6 December 1861 and Vol. IV. No. 80, pp. 9–10, 14 March 1862.]

great change, this barren system of warfare may be continued for months to come.

How are we to account for this?

The Americans have, on either side, almost nothing but volunteers. The little nucleus of the former United States regular army has either dissolved, or it is too weak to leaven the enormous mass of raw recruits which have accumulated at the seat of war. To shape all these men into soldiers, there are not even drill-sergeants enough. Teaching, consequently, must go on very slowly, and there is really no telling how long it may take until the fine material of men collected on both shores of the Potomac will be fit to be moved about in large masses, and to give or accept battle with its combined forces.

But even if the men could be taught their drill in some reasonable time, there are not officers enough to lead them. Not to speak of the company officers – who necessarily cannot be taken from among civilians – there are not officers enough for commanders of battalions, even if every lieutenant and ensign of the regulars were appointed to such a post. A considerable number of civilian colonels are therefore unavoidable; and nobody who knows our own volunteers will think either McClellan or Beauregard over-timid if they decline entering upon aggressive action or complicated strategical manoeuvres with civilian colonels of six months' standing to execute their orders.

We will suppose, however, that this difficulty was, upon the whole, overcome; that the civilian colonels, with their uniforms, had also acquired the knowledge, experience and tact required in the performance of their duties – at least, as far as the infantry is concerned. But how will it be for the cavalry? To train a regiment of cavalry, requires more time, and more experience in the training officers, than to get a regiment of infantry into shape. Suppose the men join their corps, all of them, with a sufficient knowledge of horsemanship – that is to say, they can stick on their horses, have command over them, and know how to groom and feed them – this will scarcely shorten the time required for training. Military riding, that control over your horse by which you make him go through all the movements necessary in cavalry evolutions, is a very different thing from the riding commonly practised by civilians. Napoleon's cavalry, which Sir William Napier (*History of the Peninsular War*)[1] considered almost better than the English cavalry of the time, notoriously consisted of the very worst riders that ever graced a saddle; and many of our best cross-country riders found, on entering mounted volunteer corps, that they had a deal to learn yet. We need not be astonished, then, to find that the Americans are very deficient in cavalry, and that what little they have consists of a kind of Cossacks or Indian irregulars (rangers) unfit for a charge in a body.

For artillery, they must be worse off still; and equally so for engineers. Both these are highly scientific arms, and require a long and careful training in both officers and non-commissioned officers, and certainly more training in the men too, than infantry does. Artillery, moreover, is a more complicated arm than even cavalry; you require guns, horses broken in for this kind of driving, and two classes of trained men – gunners and drivers; you require, besides, numerous ammunition-waggons, and large laboratories for the ammunition, forges, workshops, etc.; the whole provided with complicated machinery. The Federals are stated to have, altogether, 600 guns in the field; but how these may be served, we can easily imagine, knowing that it is utterly impossible to turn out 100 complete, well-appointed and well-served batteries out of nothing in six months.

But suppose, again, that all these difficulties had been overcome, and that the fighting portion of the two hostile sections of Americans was in fair condition for their work, could they move even then? Certainly not. An army must be fed; and a large army in a comparatively thinly-populated country such as Virginia, Kentucky and Missouri, must be chiefly fed from magazines. Its supply of ammunition has to be replenished; it must be followed by gunsmiths, saddlers, joiners and other artisans, to keep its fighting tackle in good order. All these requisites shone by their absence in America; they had to be organized out of almost nothing; and we have no evidence whatever to show that even now the commissariat and transport of either army has emerged from babyhood.

1. [The correct title is *History of the War in the Peninsula* (1828-40).]

America, both North and South, Federal and Confederate, had no military organization, so to speak. The army of the line was totally inadequate, by its numbers, for service against any respectable enemy; the militia was almost non-existent. The former wars of the Union never put the military strength of the country on its mettle; England, between 1812 and 1814, had not many men to spare, and Mexico defended herself chiefly by the merest rabble. The fact is, from her geographical position, America had no enemies who could anywhere attack her with more than 30,000 or 40,000 regulars at the very worst; and to such numbers the immense extent of the country would soon prove a more formidable obstacle than any troops America could bring against them; while her army was sufficient to form a nucleus for some 100,000 volunteers, and to train them in reasonable time. But when a civil war called forth more than a million of fighting men, the whole system broke down, and everything had to be begun at the beginning. The results are before us. Two immense, unwieldy bodies of men, each afraid of the other, and almost as afraid of victory as of defeat, are facing each other, trying at an immense cost to settle down into something like a regular organization. The waste of money, frightful as it is, is quite unavoidable, from the total absence of that organized ground-work upon which the structure could have been built. With ignorance and inexperience ruling supreme in every department, how could it be otherwise? On the other hand, the return for the outlay, in efficiency and organization, is extremely poor; and could that be otherwise?

The British volunteers may thank their stars that they found, on starting, a numerous, well-disciplined, and experienced army to take them under its wings. Allowing for the prejudices inherent to all trades, that army has received and treated them well. It is to be hoped that neither the volunteers nor the public will ever think that the new service can ever supersede, in any degree, the old one. If there are any such, a glance at the state of the two American volunteer armies ought to prove to them their own ignorance and folly. No army newly formed out of civilians can ever subsist in an efficient state unless it is trained and supported by the immense intellectual and material resources which are deposited in the hands of a proportionately strong regular army, and principally by that organization which forms the chief strength of the regulars. Suppose an invasion to threaten England, and compare what would be then done with what is unavoidably done in America. In England, the War Office, with the assistance of a few more clerks, easily to be found among trained military men, would be up to the transaction of all the additional labour an army of 300,000 volunteers would entail; there are half-pay officers enough to take, say, three or four battalions of volunteers each under their special inspection, and, with some effort, every battalion might be provided with a line-officer as adjutant and one as colonel. Cavalry, of course, could not be improvised; but a resolute reorganization of the artillery volunteers – with officers and drivers from the Royal Artillery – would help to man many a field-battery. The civil engineers in the country only wait for an opportunity to receive that training in the military side of their profession which would at once turn them into first-rate engineer officers. The commissariat and transport services are organized, and may soon be made to supply the wants of 400,000 men quite as easily as those of 100,000. Nothing would be disorganized, nothing upset; everywhere there would be aid and assistance for the volunteers, who would nowhere have to grope in the dark; and – barring some of those blunders which England cannot do without when first she plunges into a war – we can see no reason why in six weeks everything should not work pretty smoothly.

Now, look to America, and then say what a regular army is worth to a rising army of volunteers.

(ii)

The real opening of the campaign in this war dates from the advance of the Union forces in Kentucky. Not before Missouri and Western Virginia had been finally reconquered did this advance commence. The Secessionist troops held three strong positions – entrenched camps – in the State of Kentucky; Columbus, on the Mississippi, on their left; Bowling Green, in the centre; Mill Spring, on the Cumberland River, on their right. Their line thus extended fully 250 miles as the crow flies. By road, the distance certainly was 300 miles east and west. Such an extended line precluded all possibility of these corps supporting each other, and gave the Federal forces a chance of attacking each of them separately with superior forces. There was no great risk in such a course, as none of the three Secessionist corps were strong enough to advance, even if unopposed, beyond the Ohio River. The great mistake in the Secessionist position was the attempt to occupy everything, and the consequent dissemination of the troops. One strong central entrenched camp, destined to be the prepared battlefield for a decisive action, and held by the main body, would have defended Kentucky far more efficiently; for it must either have attracted the main body of the Federals, or placed them in a disadvantageous position if they attempted to march past it without noticing this strong concentration of troops. As it was, the Federals attempted to attack these three camps one after another, and to manoeuvre their enemy out of them, so as to compel him to fight in the open. This plan was completely in accordance with the rules of military art, and it was executed with a vigour and rapidity which deserves much commendation, as well as the perfect success obtained. Towards the middle of February, a body of 15,000 Federals moved upon Mill Spring, which was held by about 10,000 Confederates. The Federals manoeuvred so as to make their adversaries believe that but a weak force was in the neighbourhood, and the Confederate general, Zollicoffer, at once took the bait thrown out to him. He marched out of his works, attacked the first Federal body he met, but very soon found that he had to do with a force superior to his own in numbers, and at least its equal in spirit and discipline. He fell, and his troops were as completely routed as the Federals had been at Bull Run. But this time the victory was followed up far differently. The beaten army were pursued very closely until they arrived, broken, demoralized, and deprived of their field artillery and baggage, at their camp of Mill Spring. The camp was constructed on the northern shore of the Cumberland River, so that the troops, in case of another defeat, had no retreat but by a few steamers and boats across the river. We shall find that almost all these Secessionist camps were thus placed on the enemy's side of a river. Such an encampment is perfectly correct, and of the greatest utility – when there is a bridge. The camp, in that case, serves as a bridge-head, and gives to its occupants the chance of throwing their forces at will on either bank of the river, by which alone they obtain a perfect command over it. But to do the same thing when there is no bridge, is to place your troops in a position where they have no retreat after an unlucky engagement, and when, therefore, they will either have to surrender or be massacred and drowned, same as the Federals were whom General Stone's treachery had sent across the Potomac at Ball's Bluff. Accordingly, when the defeated Secessionists reached their camp at Mill Spring, the fact at once became patent to them that unless they could beat off an attack on their entrenchments, they would have to surrender very speedily. After the experience of the morning, they had no longer any confidence in their powers of resistance; and when the Federals, next morning, advanced to attack the entrenched camp, they found that the enemy had taken advantage of the night to cross the river, abandoning camp, baggage, artillery and stores. Thus the extreme right of the Confederate line was driven back into Tennessee; and Eastern Kentucky, where the population are chiefly Union men, was reconquered for the Union.

About the same time – the second half of January – the preparations for dislodging the Secessionists from Columbus and Bowling Green were commenced. A strong fleet of mortar-boats and iron-clad gunboats had been got ready, and the news was spread everywhere that they were to accompany the march of a strong army down the Mississippi, from Cairo to Memphis and New Orleans. A ridiculously conspicuous reconnaissance was made toward Columbus. The retreat of this strong body of troops, which did not effect anything, even looked like a serious check to the Union troops. But it seems that all these demonstrations on the Mississippi were mere blinds. When everything was ready, the gunboats were quietly removed into the Ohio, and thence into the Tennessee River, which they steamed up to Fort Henry. This place, together with Fort Donelson, on the Cumberland River, formed a second line of defence of the Secessionists in Tennessee. The position was well chosen; for if they had retreated behind the Cumberland River, this would have covered their front, and the Tennessee River their left flank, while the narrow strip of land between the two would have been sufficiently covered by the two camps just named. But the rapid action of the Federals broke through the second line before even the left and centre of the first was attacked.

In the first week of February, the Federal gunboats appeared before Fort Henry, and shelled it with such effect that it at once surrendered. The garrison escaped to Fort Donelson, the land force of the expedition not being strong enough to invest the place. Then the gunboats steamed down the Tennessee again, up the Ohio, and up the Cumberland, towards Fort Donelson; only one gunboat boldly steamed up the Tennessee, right through the heart of the State of Tennessee, skirting the State of Mississippi, and penetrating as far as Florence, in Northern Alabama, where a series of flats and swamps (the so-called mussle (sic) shoals) stop further navigation. The single fact of one gunboat performing this long journey (at least 150 miles) and returning without ever being attacked, proves in itself that there must be, along this river at least, a strongly prevailing Union sentiment, which no doubt will tell very powerfully if the Federals should penetrate so far.

The naval expedition up the Cumberland now concerted its movements with those of the land forces under Generals Halleck and Grant. The Secessionists at Bowling Green were deceived as to the Federal movements, and remained quiet and confident in their camp, while a week after the fall of Fort Henry, Fort Donelson was invested on the land side by 40,000 Federals and menaced on the river by a powerful fleet of gunboats. Same as Mill Spring and Fort Henry, the entrenched camp of Fort Donelson was constructed with its rear to the river and no bridge for a retreat. It was the strongest place the Federals had as yet attacked. The works were not only constructed with much greater care, but, besides, it was large enough to shelter the 20,000 men which held it. On the first day of the attack, the gunboats silenced the fire of the batteries facing the river and shelled the interior of the works, while the land forces drove in the enemy's outposts and compelled the main body to take shelter close under the guns of their works. On the second day, the gunboats, having suffered severely the day before, appear to have done little work, but the land forces had to fight a long and sometimes severe battle with the columns of the garrison, which tried to break through their right in order to keep open the line of retreat towards Nashville. But a vigorous attack of the Federal right upon the Secessionist left, and strong reinforcements sent to the Federal left, decided the victory in favour of the assailants. Several outworks had been stormed; the garrison, hemmed in within their inner lines of defence, without any chances of retreat and evidently not in a condition to resist an assault next morning, surrendered on the third day unconditionally. General Floyd escaped on the evening of the second day, it is said, with 5,000 men. It is not quite clear how that was possible; the number is too large to have been stowed away on steamers during the night; but still they may have successively crossed the river, and escaped along its right bank. The whole of the artillery, baggage and stores, together with 13,300 prisoners, fell into the hands of the Unionists; 1,000 more prisoners were made next day, and on the appearance of the Federal advanced guard, Clarksville, a town higher up the river, surrendered with great quantities of stores, collected there for the Secessionist troops.

Whether Nashville has also fallen, appears very uncertain, and we can scarcely believe it. As it is, these successes of the Federals, in the short space of three weeks, are quite enough for them to be satisfied with. Columbus, the only place the Secessionists now hold in Kentucky, they can continue to hold at very great risks only. If they lose a decisive battle in Tennessee, the garrison of Columbus cannot escape being compelled to surrender, unless the Federals commit very great blunders. And that the Confederates are now compelled to fight a decisive battle in Tennessee, is one of the great results of the Federal victories. They have concentrated, we are told, 65,000 men at and about Nashville; it may be that they have succeeded in collecting even a larger force. But the combined troops of Halleck, Grant, Buell and Thomas, together with the reserve now hurrying up from the camps of instruction in Kentucky, Ohio, Indiana and Illinois, will enable the Federals to outnumber them; and with their *morale* necessarily much raised above that of their adversaries by the late successes, and with a strong Union party among the population to keep them well informed of the movements of the enemy, we do not see that they have any reason to be afraid of the issue.

4. The Seven Weeks War

Notes on the War, No. 1[1]

THE following notes are intended to comment impartially, and from a strictly military point of view, upon the current events of the war, and, as far as possible, to point out their probable influence upon impending operations.

The locality where the first decisive blows must be struck is the frontier of Saxony and Bohemia. The war in Italy can scarcely lead to any decisive results so long as the Quadrilateral remains untaken, and to take that will be rather a lengthy operation. There may be a good deal of warlike action in Western Germany, but from the strength of the forces engaged, it will be altogether subordinate in its results to the events on the Bohemian frontier. To this neighbourhood, therefore, we shall, for the present, exclusively direct our attention.

In order to judge of the strength of the contending armies it will suffice, for all practical purposes, if we take into account the infantry only, keeping in mind, however, that the strength of the Austrian cavalry will be to the Prussian as three to two. The artillery will be, in both armies, in about the same proportion as the infantry, say three guns per 1,000 men.

The Prussian infantry consists of 253 battalions of the line, 83½ depot battalions, and 116 battalions of the Landwehr (first levy, containing the men from 27 to 32 years of age). Of these, the depot battalions and Landwehr form the garrisons of the fortresses, and are intended, besides, to act against the smaller German states, while the line is massed in and around Saxony to oppose the Austrian army of the north. Deducting about 15

1. [Unsigned article in the *Manchester Guardian*, 20 June 1866.]

battalions occupying Schleswig-Holstein, and another 15 battalions – the late garrisons of Rastatt, Mainz and Frankfurt, now concentrated at Wetzlar – there remain about 220 battalions for the main army. With cavalry and artillery, and such Landwehr as may be drawn from the neighbouring fortresses, this army will contain about 300,000 men, in nine army corps.

The Austrian army of the north counts seven army corps, each of which is considerably stronger than a Prussian one. We know very little at present of their composition and organization, but there is every reason to believe that they form an army of from 320,000 to 350,000 men. Numerical superiority, therefore, seems assured to the Austrians.

The Prussian army will be under the command-in-chief of the King – that is to say, of a parade soldier of at best very mediocre capacities, and of weak, but often obstinate, character. He will be surrounded, firstly, by the general staff of the army, under General Moltke, an excellent officer; secondly, by his 'private military cabinet', composed of personal favourites; and thirdly, by such other unattached general officers as he may call to his suite. It is impossible to invent a more efficient system for ensuring defeat at the very headquarters of an army. Here is, at the very beginning, the natural jealousy between the staff of the army and the Cabinet of the King, each of which sections will struggle for supreme influence and will concoct and advocate its own pet plan of operations. This alone would render almost impossible all singleness of purpose, all consistent action. But then come the interminable councils of war, which, in nine cases out of ten, end in the adoption of some half measure – the very worst course in war. The orders of today, in such cases, generally contradict those of yesterday, and when matters become complicated or threaten to go wrong, no orders at all are given out, and things take their own course. 'Ordre, contre-ordre, désordre,' as Napoleon used to say. Nobody is responsible, because the irresponsible King takes all responsibility upon himself, and, therefore, nobody does anything until distinctly ordered to do so. The campaign of 1806 was commanded in a similar way by the father of the present King; the defeats of Jena and Auerstädt, and the destruction of the whole Prussian army within three weeks, was the consequence. There is no reason to suppose that the present King is superior in mettle to his father; and if he has found in Count Bismarck a man whose political direction he can implicitly follow, there is no man of sufficient standing in the army to take exclusive charge, in a similar way, of military matters.

The Austrian army is under the unconditional command of General Benedek, who is an experienced officer and who, at least, knows his mind. The superiority of supreme command is decidedly on the side of the Austrians.

The Prussian troops are subdivided into two 'armies'; the first, under Prince Frederick Charles, composed of the 1st, 2nd, 3rd, 4th, 7th and 8th corps; the second, under the Crown Prince, of the 5th and 6th corps. The Guards, forming the general reserve, will probably join the first army. Now this subdivision not only breaks the unity of command, but it also induces, very often, the two armies to move on two different lines of operation, to make combined movements, to lay their mutual point of junction within the reach of the enemy; and in other words, it tends to keep them separated whereas they ought, as much as possible, to keep them together. The Prussians in 1806, and the Austrians in 1859, under very similar circumstances, followed the same course, and were beaten. As to the two commanders, the Crown Prince is an unknown magnitude as a soldier; and Prince Frederick Charles certainly did not show himself to be a great commander in the Danish war.

The Austrian army has no such subdivision; the commanders of the army corps are placed directly under General Benedek. They are, therefore, again superior to their opponents as far as the organization of the army goes.

The Prussian soldiers, especially the men of the reserve and such Landwehr men as had to be taken to fill up vacancies in the line (and there are many) go to war, against their will; the Austrians, on the contrary, have long wished for a war with Prussia, and await with impatience the order to move. They have, therefore, also the advantage in the *morale* of the troops.

Prussia has had no great war for fifty years; her army is, on the whole, a peace army, with the pedantry and martinetism inherent to all peace armies. No doubt a great deal has been done latterly, especially since 1859, to get rid of this; but the habits of forty years are not so easily eradicated, and a great number of incapable and pedantic men must still be found, particularly in the most important places – those of the field officers. Now the Austrians have been fundamentally cured of this complaint by the war of 1859, and have turned their dearly-bought experience to the very best use. No doubt, in organization of detail, in adaptation for, and experience in, warfare, the Austrians again are superior to the Prussians.

With the exception of the Russians the Prussians are the only troops whose normal formation for fighting is the deep close column. Imagine the eight companies of an English battalion in a quarter-distance column, but two companies instead of one forming the front, so that four rows of two companies each form the column, and you have the 'Prussian column of attack'. A better target for rifled fire-firms than this could not be imagined, and, since rifled cannon can throw a shell into it at 2,000 yards range, such a formation must render it almost impossible to reach the enemy at all. Let one single shell explode in the midst of this mass, and see whether that battalion is fit for anything afterwards on that day.

The Austrians have adopted the loose open column of the French, which is scarcely to be called a column; it is more like two or three lines following each other at 20 or 30 yards distance, and is scarcely, if anything, more exposed to losses by artillery than a deployed line. The advantage of tactical formation is, again, on the side of the Austrians.

Against all these advantages the Prussians have but two points to set off. Their commissariat is decidedly better, and the troops will therefore be better fed. The Austrian commissariat, like all Austrian administration, is one den of bribery and peculation scarcely better than in Russia. Even now we hear of the troops being badly and irregularly fed in the field and in the fortresses it will be worse still, and the Austrian Administration may happen to be a more dangerous enemy to the fortresses in the Quadrilateral than the Italian artillery.

The second set-off the Prussians have is their superior armament. Although their rifled artillery is decidedly better than that of the Austrians, this will make very little difference in the open field. The range, trajectory, and accuracy of the Prussian and Austrian rifles will be about on a par; but the Prussians have breech-loaders, and can deliver a steady well-aimed fire in the ranks at least four times a minute. The immense superiority of this arm has been proved in the Danish war, and there is no doubt the Austrians will experience it in a far higher degree. If they, as it is said Benedek has instructed them to do, will not lose much time with firing, but go at the enemy at once with the bayonet, they will have enormous losses. In the Danish war, the loss of the Prussians was never more than one fourth, sometimes only one tenth, of that of the Danes; and, as a military correspondent of *The Times* a short time ago very correctly pointed out, the Danes were almost everywhere beaten by a minority of troops actually engaged.

Still, in spite of the needle gun, the odds are against the Prussians; and if they refuse to be beaten in the first great battle by the superior leadership, organization, tactical formation and *morale* of the Austrians, and last, not least, by their own commanders, then they must certainly be of a different mettle from that of which a peace army of 50 years' standing may be expected to be.

Notes on the War, No. 2[1]

People begin to grow impatient at the apparent inactivity of the two great armies on the Bohemian frontier. But there are plenty of reasons for this delay. Both the Austrians and the Prussians are perfectly aware of the importance of the impending collision, which may decide the result of the whole campaign. Both are hurrying up to the front whatever men they can lay their hands on; the Austrians from their new formations (the fourth and fifth battalions of the Infantry regiments), the Prussians from the Landwehr, which at first was intended for garrison duty only.

At the same time, there appears to be on either side an attempt to out-manoeuvre the opposing army, and to enter upon the

1. [Unsigned article in the *Manchester Guardian*, 25 June 1866.]

campaign under the most favourable strategical conditions. To understand this, we shall have to look at the map and examine the country in which these armies are placed.

Taking it for granted that Berlin and Vienna are the normal points of retreat of the two armies, and that therefore the Austrians will aim at the conquest of Berlin and the Prussians at that of Vienna, there are three routes by which they might operate. A large army requires a certain extent of country from the resources of which it has to live on the march, and is compelled, in order to move quick, to march in several columns on as many parallel roads; its front will, therefore, be extended on a line which may vary between, say, sixty and sixteen miles, according to the proximity of the enemy and the distance of the roads from each other. This will have to be kept in mind.

The first route would be on the left bank of the Elbe and Moldau, by Leipzig and Prague. It is evident that on this route each of the belligerents would have to cross the river twice, the second time in the face of the enemy. Supposing either army to attempt to turn, by this route, the flank of its opponent, the latter, having the shorter, because straighter, road, could still anticipate the turning force on the line of the river, and if successful in repelling it, could march straight upon the enemy's capital. This route, equally disadvantageous to both parties, may therefore be dismissed from consideration.

The second route is on the right bank of the Elbe, between it and the Sudeten mountain chain which divides Silesia from Bohemia and Moravia. This is almost on the straight line from Berlin to Vienna; the portion now lying between the two armies is marked out by the railway from Lobau to Pardubitz. This railway passes through that portion of Bohemia which is bounded by the Elbe to the south and west, and the mountains to the north-east. It has plenty of good roads, and if the two armies were to march straight at each other, here would be the point of collision.

The third route is that by Breslau, and thence across the Sudeten chain. This chain, of no considerable elevation, on the Moravian frontier, where it is crossed by several good roads, rises to greater elevation and abruptness in the Riesengebirge, which forms the boundary of Bohemia. Here there are but few roads across; in fact, between Trautenau and Reichenberg, a distance of forty miles, the whole north-eastern portion of the range is not traversed by a single military road. The only road in existence there, that from Hirschberg to the valley of the Iser, stops short at the Austrian frontier. It follows, then, that this whole barrier of forty miles in length, is impassable, at least for a large army, with its innumerable impediments, and that an advance upon or by Breslau must pass the mountains to the south-west of the Riesengebirge.

Now, what are the relative positions of the two armies, with regard to their communications, if engaged on this route?

The Prussians, by advancing due south from Breslau, lay open their communications with Berlin. The Austrians might, if strong enough to command the almost absolute certainty of victory, leave them to advance as far as the entrenched camp of Olmütz, which would stop them, while they themselves could march upon Berlin, trusting to re-open any temporarily-interrupted communications by a decisive victory; or they might meet the Prussian columns singly as they debouch from the mountains, and, if successful, drive them back upon Glogau and Posen, whereby Berlin and the greater portion of the Prussian states would be at their mercy. Thus an advance by Breslau would be advisable for the Prussians in case of a great numerical superiority only.

The Austrians are in a far different position. They have the advantage that the bulk of the monarchy lies south-east of Breslau; that is, in the *direct prolongation* of a line drawn from Berlin to Breslau. Having fortified the northern bank of the Danube near Vienna, so as to shelter the capital from a surprise, they may, temporarily and even for a length of time, sacrifice their direct communication with Vienna, and draw their supplies of men and stores from Hungary. They can, therefore, with equal safety operate by way of Lobau and by way of Breslau, to the north or to the south of the hills; they have far greater freedom in manoeuvring than their opponents.

The Prussians, moreover, have further reasons to be cautious. From the northern frontier of Bohemia, the distance to Berlin is not much more than half of that to Vienna; Berlin is so much more exposed. Vienna is sheltered by the Danube, behind which a beaten army can find protection; by the fortifications erected to the north of that river; and by the entrenched camp of Olmütz, which the Prussians could not pass unnoticed with impunity, if the mass of the Austrian army, after a defeat, were to take up a position there. Berlin has no protection of any kind, except the army in the field. Under these circumstances, and those detailed in our first number, the part destined for the Prussians appears to be clearly marked out as a defensive one.

The same series of circumstances, and strong political necessity besides, almost compels Austria to act on the offensive. A single victory may ensure to her great results, while her defeat would not break her power of resistance.

The strategical plan of campaign in its fundamental features is necessarily very simple. Whichever of the two attacks first, he has only this alternative: either a false attack *north-west* of the Riesengebirge, and the true attack south-east of it, or *vice versa*. The forty-mile barrier is the decisive feature of the seat of war, and round it the armies must gravitate. We shall hear of fighting at both its extremities, and a very few days afterwards will clear up the direction of the true attack, and probably the fate of the first campaign. Yet, with two such unwieldy armies opposed to each other, we feel inclined to think that the most direct route is the safest, and that the difficulty and danger of moving such bodies of troops in separate columns on different roads through a difficult mountain country, will almost naturally draw both opposing armies on the route Lobau-Pardubitz.

The actual movements which have taken place are as follow: The Prussians, in the first week of June, massed their army of Saxony along the Saxon frontier, from Seitz to Görlitz and their Silesian army from Hirschberg to Neisse. By the 10th of June they drew nearer together, having their right wing on the Elbe near Torgau, and their extreme left near Waldenburg. From the 12th to the 16th, the army of Silesia, now consisting of the 1st, 5th, and 6th corps and the Guards, were again extended to the east, this time as far as Ratibor, that is to say, into the extreme south-eastern corner of Silesia. This looks like a feint, especially the parading of the Guards, which are supposed to be always with the main army. If it be more than a feint, or if measures have not been taken to move these four corps back towards Görlitz at the shortest notice and in the shortest time, then this massing of more than 120,000 men in a remote corner is a palpable mistake; they may be cut off from all possibility of retreat and certainly from all connexion with the remainder of the army.

Of the Austrians we know little more than that they were concentrated around Olmütz. *The Times* correspondent in their camp states that their sixth corps, 40,000 strong, arrived on the 19th from Weisskirchen at Olmütz indicating a movement to the westward. He adds that on the 21st headquarters were to be shifted to Trübau, on the frontier between Moravia and Bohemia. This move would point in the same direction, if it did not look exceedingly like a *canard* sent on to London with the intention of being thence telegraphed to the Prussian headquarters in order to mislead them. A general who acts with such secrecy as Benedek, and who has such objections to newspaper correspondents, is not likely to inform them on the 19th where his headquarters will be on the 21st, unless he has his reasons for it.

Before concluding, we may be allowed to cast a glance at the operations in North-western Germany. The Prussians had more troops here than was at first known. They had 15 battalions disposable in Holstein, 12 in Minden, and 18 in Wetzlar. By rapid concentric moves, during which the troops showed a quite unexpected capability of supporting forced marches, they took possession in two days of all the country north of a line from Coblenz to Eisenach, and of every line of communication between the eastern and western provinces of the kingdom. The Hessian troops, about 7,000 strong, managed to escape, but the Hanoverians, 10,000 or 12,000, had their direct line of retreat towards Frankfurt cut off, and already on the 17th the rest of the 7th Prussian army corps, 12 battalions, together with the two Coburg battalions arrived in Eisenach from the Elbe. Thus the Hanoverians appear to be hemmed in on all sides, and could escape only by a miracle of stupidity on the part of the Prussians. As soon as their fate will be settled, a force of 50 Prussian battalions

will be available against the Federal army which Prince
Alexander of [Hesse]-Darmstadt is forming at Frankfurt, and
which will consist of about 23,000 Württembergers, 10,000
Darmstaders, 6,000 Nassauers, 13,000 Badeners (only mobilizing
now), 7,000 Hessians and 12,000 Austrians, now on the road
from Salzburg; in all about 65,000 men, who may be possibly
reinforced by from 10,000 to 20,000 Bavarians. About 60,000
men of these are now reported as already concentrated at Frankfurt, and Prince Alexander has ventured upon a forward move
by re-occupying Giessen on the 22nd. This, however, is of no
consequence. The Prussians will not advance against him until
they are well concentrated, and then, with 70,000 men of all arms,
and their superior armament, they ought to make short work of
this motley army.

Notes on the War, No. 3[1]

The first great battle has been fought, not in Bohemia, but in
Italy, and the Quadrilateral has again given the Italians a lesson
in strategy. The strength of this famous position, as indeed of
all fortified positions of any value, consists, not so much in the
high defensive capabilities of its four fortresses, but in their being
so grouped in a country with strongly-marked military features
that the attacking force is almost always induced, and often
compelled, to divide itself and attack on two different points,
while the defending force can send its whole combined strength
against one of these attacks, crush it by superior numbers, and
then turn against the other. The Italian army has been induced
to commit this fault. The King stood with eleven divisions on
the Mincio, while Cialdini with five divisions faced the Lower
Po, near Ponte Lagoscuro and Polesalla. An Italian division
counts 17 battalions of 700 men each; consequently, Victor
Emmanuel would have, with cavalry and artillery, at least 120,000
or 125,000 men, and Cialdini about half that number. While the
King crossed the Mincio on the 23rd, Cialdini was to cross the
Lower Po and act upon the rear of the Austrians; but up to the
moment we write, no certain news has arrived of this latter

1. [Unsigned article in the *Manchester Guardian*, 28 June 1866.]

movement having been effected. At all events, the 60,000 men whose presence might, and probably would, have turned the scale on Sunday last at Custozza, cannot so far have obtained any advantage at all commensurate to the loss of a great battle.

The Lake of Garda lies encased between two spurs of the Alps, forming, to the south of it, two clusters of hills, between which the Mincio forces its way towards the lagoons of Mantua. Both of these groups form strong military positions; their slopes towards the south overlook the Lombard plain, and command it within gun-range. They are well known in military history. The western group, between Peschiera and Lonato, was the scene of the battles of Castiglione and Lonato in 1797, and of Solferino in 1859; the eastern group, between Peschiera and Verona, was contested during three days in 1848, and again in the battle of last Sunday.

This eastern group of hills slopes down on one side towards the Mincio, where it ends in the plain at Valleggio; on the other side, in a long arc, facing south-east, towards the Adige, which it reaches at Bussolengo. It is divided, from north to south, in two about equal portions by a deep ravine, through which flows the rivulet Tione; so that a force advancing from the Mincio will have first to force the passage of the river, and immediately afterwards find itself again arrested by this ravine. On the edge of the slope, facing the plain, and east of the ravine, are the following villages: Custozza, on the southern extremity; further north, in succession, Somma Campagna, Sona and Santa Giustina. The railway from Peschiera to Verona crosses the hills at Somma Campagna, the high road at Sona.

In 1848, after the Piedmontese had taken Peschiera, they blockaded Mantua and extended their army from beyond that place to Rivoli, on the Lake of Garda, their centre occupying the hills in question. On 23 July Radetzky advanced with seven brigades from Verona, broke through the centre of this over-extended line, and occupied the hills himself. On the 24th and 25th the Piedmontese tried to re-take the position, but were decisively beaten on the 25th, and retreated at once through Milan beyond the Ticino. This first battle of Custozza decided the campaign of 1848.

The telegrams from the Italian headquarters about last Sunday's battle are rather contradictory; but, with the assistance of those from the other side, we get a pretty clear insight into the circumstances under which it was fought. Victor Emmanuel intended his 1st corps (General Durando, four divisions or 68 battalions), to take up a position between Peschiera and Verona, so as to be able to cover a siege of the former place. This position must, of course, be Sona and Somma Campagna. The 2nd corps (General Cucchiari, three divisions or 51 battalions) and 3rd corps (General Della Rocca, of the same strength as the second) were to cross the Mincio at the same time, to cover the operations of the 1st. The 1st corps must have crossed near or south of Saliongo, and taken the road of the hills at once, the 2nd seems to have crossed at Valleggio, and the 3rd at Goito, and advanced in the plain. This took place on Saturday the 23rd. The Austrian brigade Pulz, which held the outposts on the Mincio, fell slowly back on Verona; and on Sunday, the anniversary of Solferino, the whole of the Austrian army debouched from Verona to meet the enemy. They appear to have arrived in time to occupy the heights of Sona and Somma Campagna, and the eastern edge of the ravine of the Tione before the Italians. The struggle then would principally be fought for the passage of the ravine. At the southern extremity the two corps in the plain could cooperate with the 1st Italian corps in the hills, and thus Custozza fell into their hands. Gradually the Italians in the plain would advance more and more in the direction of Verona, in order to act upon the Austrian flank and rear, and the Austrians would send troops to meet them. Thus the front lines of the two armies which were originally facing east and west respectively, would wheel round a quarter circle, the Austrians facing south and the Italians north. But, as the hills retreat from Custozza to the north-east, this flank movement of the Italian 2nd and 3rd corps could not immediately affect the position of their 1st corps in the hills because it could not be extended far enough without danger to the flanking troops themselves. Thus the Austrians appear merely to have occupied the 2nd and 3rd corps by troops sufficient to break their first impetus, while they launched every available man upon the 1st corps, and crushed it by superior numbers.

They were perfectly successful; the first corps was repulsed, after a gallant struggle, and at last Custozza was stormed by the Austrians. By this, the Italian right wing, advanced east and north-east beyond Custozza, appears to have been seriously endangered; consequently a new struggle for the village took place, during which the lost connexion must have been restored, and the Austrian advance from Custozza checked, but the place remained in their hands, and the Italians had to re-cross the Mincio the same night.

We give this sketch of the battle, not as a historical account – for which every detail is yet wanting – but merely as an attempt, map in hand, to reconcile the various telegrams relating to it amongst each other, and with military common sense; and if the telegrams were anything like correct and complete, we feel confident that the general outline of the battle would appear to be not very different from what we have stated.

The Austrians lost from 600 prisoners, the Italians 2,000, and a few guns. This shows the battle to have been a defeat, but no disaster. The forces must have been pretty equally matched, although it is very probable that the Austrians had less troops under fire than their opponents. The Italians have every reason to congratulate themselves that they were not driven back into the Mincio; the position of the 1st corps between that river and the ravine, on a strip of land between two and four miles wide, and a superior enemy in front, must have been one of considerable danger. It was undoubtedly a mistake to send the main body of the troops into the plain, while the commanding heights, the decisive points, were neglected; but the greatest mistake was, as we pointed out before, to divide the army, to leave Cialdini with 60,000 men on the Lower Po, and to attack with the remainder alone. Cialdini could have contributed to a victory before Verona, and then, marching back to the Lower Po, have effected his passage much more easily, if this combined manoeuvre was to be insisted upon at all hazards. As it is, he seems no further advanced than on the first day, and may now have to meet stronger forces than hitherto. The Italians ought, by this time, to know that they have a very tough opponent to deal with. At Solferino, Benedek, with 26,000 Austrians, held the whole

Piedmontese army of fully double that number at bay for the whole day, until he was ordered to retreat in consequence of the defeat of the other corps by the French. That Piedmontese army was much superior to the present Italian army; it was better schooled, more homogeneous, and better officered. The present army is but of very recent formation and must suffer from all the disadvantages inherent to such; while the Austrian army of today is much superior to that of 1859. National enthusiasm is a capital thing to work upon, but until disciplined and organized, nobody can win battles with it. Even Garibaldi's 'Thousand' were not a crowd of mere enthusiasts, they were drilled men who had learnt to obey orders and to face powder and shot in 1859. It is to be hoped that the staff of the Italian army, for their own good, will refrain from taking liberties with an army which – if numerically inferior – is instrinsically superior to theirs, and, moreover, holds one of the strongest positions in Europe.

Notes on the War, No. 4[1]

Suppose a young Prussian ensign or cornet, under examination for a lieutenancy, to be asked what would be the safest plan for a Prussian army to invade Bohemia? Suppose our young officer were to answer, – 'Your best way will be to divide your troops into two about equal bodies, to send one round by the east of the Riesengebirge, the other to the west, and effect their junction in Gitschin.' What would the examining officer say to this? He would inform the young gentleman that this plan sinned against the two very first laws of strategy: Firstly, never to divide your troops so that they cannot support each other, but to keep them well together; and, secondly, in case of an advance on different roads, to effect the junction of the different columns at a point which is not within reach of the enemy; that, therefore, the plan proposed was the very worst of all; that it could only be taken into consideration at all in case Bohemia was quite unoccupied by hostile troops, and that, consequently, an officer proposing such a plan of campaign was not fit to hold even a lieutenant's commission.

1. [Unsigned article in the *Manchester Guardian*, 3 July 1866.]

Yet, this is the very plan which the wise and learned staff of the Prussian army have adopted. It is almost incredible; but it is so. The mistake for which the Italians had to suffer at Custozza, has been again committed by the Prussians, and under circumstances which made it ten-fold worse. The Italians knew at least that, with ten divisions, they would be numerically superior to the enemy. The Prussians must have known that if they kept their nine corps together they would be at best barely on a par, as far as numbers went, with Benedek's eight corps; and that by dividing their troops they exposed the two armies to the almost certain fate of being crushed in succession by superior numbers. It would be completely inexplicable how such a plan could ever be discussed, much less adopted, by a body of such unquestionably capable officers as form the Prussian staff – if it was not for the fact of King William being in chief command. But nobody could possibly expect that the fatal consequences of kings and princes taking high command would come out so soon and so strong. The Prussians are now fighting, in Bohemia, a life-and-death struggle. If the junction of the two armies at or about Gitschin is prevented, if each of the two, being beaten, has to retire out of Bohemia, and, by retiring, to get further away again from the other, then the campaign may be said to be virtually over. Then Benedek may leave the army of the Crown Prince unnoticed while it retires towards Breslau, and follow up, with all his forces, the army of Prince Frederick Charles, which can hardly escape utter destruction.

The question is, Will this junction have been prevented? Up to the moment we write we have no news of events later than Friday evening, the 29th. The Prussians, beaten out of Gitschin (the name of the place, in Bohemian, is spelt Jicin) on the 28th by General Edelsheim, claim to have stormed the town again on the 29th, and this is the last information we possess. The junction was not then effected; at least four Austrian and parts of the Saxon army corps had then been engaged against about five or six Prussian corps.

The various columns of the army of the Crown Prince, as they descended into the valley on the Bohemian side of the hills, were met by the Austrians at favourable points where the valley, widening out, allowed them to offer a larger front to the Prussian columns, and to attempt to prevent them from deploying; while the Prussians would send troops, wherever practicable, through the lateral valleys, to take their opponents in flank and rear. This is always the case in mountain warfare, and accounts for the great number of prisoners that are always made under such circumstances. On the other side, the armies of Prince Frederick Charles and Herwarth von Bittenfeld appear to have got through the passes almost unopposed; the first engagements took place on the line of the Iser river, that is almost midway between the starting points of the two armies. It would be idle to try to disentangle and bring into harmony the fearfully contradictory, and often totally unauthenticated, telegrams which have come to hand these last three or four days.

The fighting has been necessarily very much chequered in its results; as new forces came up, victory favoured first one and then the other side. Up to Friday, however, the general result appears to have been, so far, in favour of the Prussians. If they maintained themselves in Gitschin, no doubt the junction was effected on Saturday or Sunday, and then their greatest danger would be passed. The final fight for the junction would probably be fought with concentrated masses on both sides, and decide the campaign for some time, at least. If the Prussians were victorious, they would be at once out of all their self-begotten difficulties, but they might have obtained the same, and even greater, advantages without exposing themselves to such unnecessary dangers.

The fighting appears to have been very severe. The very first Austrian brigade which met the Prussians in battle, was the 'black and yellow' brigade, which, in Schleswig, stormed the Königsberg, near Oberselk, the day before the evacuation of the Dannevirke. It is called black and yellow after the facings of the two regiments composing it, and was always considered one of the best brigades in the service. They were, however, beaten by the needle-gun, and above 500 men of one of its regiments (Martini) were taken prisoners after they had charged the Prussian lines five times in vain. In a later engagement, the colours of the 3rd battalion of the Deutschmeister regiment were taken. This regiment, recruited in Vienna exclusively, is considered the best in the whole army. Thus the very best troops have been already in action. The Prussians must have behaved splendidly for an old peace army. When war was actually declared, a totally different spirit came over the army, brought on, chiefly, by the clearing-out of the small fry of potentates in the north-west. It gave the troops – rightly or wrongly, we merely register the fact – the idea that they were asked to fight, this time, for the unification of Germany, and the hitherto sullen and sulky men of the reserve and Landwehr then crossed the frontier of Austria with loud cheers. It is owing to this chiefly that they fought so well; but at the same time we must ascribe the greater portion of whatever success they have had to their breech-loaders; and if they ever get out of the difficulties into which their generals so wantonly placed them, they will have to thank the needle-gun for it. The reports as to its immense superiority over the muzzle-loaders are again unanimous. A sergeant from the Martini regiment, taken prisoner, said to the correspondent of the *Cologne Gazette*: 'We have surely done whatever may be expected from brave soldiers, but no man can stand against that rapid fire.' If the Austrains are beaten, it will be not so much General Benedek or General Ramming as General Ramrod who is to blame for the result.

In the north-west, the Hanoverians, brought to a sense of their position by a sharp attack from General Manteuffel's advanced guard, under General Flies, have surrendered, and thereby 59 Prussian battalions will be at liberty to act against the Federal troops. It was high time, too, that this should be done before Bavaria had completed all her armaments, for otherwise much stronger forces would be required to subdue South-western Germany. Bavaria is notoriously always slow and behindhand with her military arrangements, but when they are complete, she can bring into the field from 60,000 to 80,000 good troops. We may now soon hear of a rapid concentration of Prussians on the Main and of active operations against Prince Alexander of Hesse-Darmstadt and his army.

Notes on the War, No. 5[1]

The campaign which the Prussians opened with a signal strategic blunder has been since carried on by them with such a terrible tactical energy that it was brought to a victorious close in exactly eight days.

We said in our last note that the only case in which the Prussian plan of invading Bohemia by two armies separated by the Riesengebirge could be justified was that in which Bohemia was unoccupied by hostile troops. The mysterious plan of General Benedek appears to have mainly consisted in creating a situation of that sort. There appear to have been but two Austrian army corps – the 1st (Clam Gallas) and the 6th (Ramming) – in the north-western corner of Bohemia, where, from the beginning, we expected the decisive actions would be fought. If this was intended to draw the Prussians into a trap, Benedek has succeeded so well that he got caught in it himself. At all events, the Prussian advance on two lines, with from forty to fifty miles of impassable ground between them, towards a point of junction two full marches from the starting points, and within the enemy's lines, – this advance remains a highly dangerous manoeuvre under all circumstances, and one which would have been followed by signal defeat but for Benedek's strange slowness, for the unexpected dash of the Prussian troops, and for their breech-loading rifles.

The advance of Prince Frederick Charles took place with three corps (the 3rd, 4th and 2nd, the latter in reserve), by Reichenberg, north of a difficult range of hills, on the southern side of which General Herwarth advanced with a corps and a half (the 8th and one division of the 7th). At the same time, the Crown Prince stood, with the 1st, 5th, and 6th corps, and the Guards, in the mountains about Glatz. Thus the army was divided into three columns – one on the right, of 45,000, one in the centre, of 90,000, and one on the left, of 120,000 men – none of which could support either of the others for at least several days. Here, if ever, there was a chance for a general commanding at least an equal number of men to crush his opponents in detail. But no-

1. [Unsigned article in the *Manchester Guardian*, 6 July 1866.]

thing appears to have been done. On the 26th Prince Frederick Charles had the first serious engagement, at Turnau, with a brigade of the 1st corps, by which he established his communication with Herwarth; on the 27th, the latter took Münchengratz, while, of the army of the Crown Prince, a first column, the 5th corps, advanced beyond Nachod, and beat the 6th Austrian corps (Ramming) severely; on the 28th, the only slightly unlucky day for the Prussians, Prince Frederick Charles's advance guard took Gitschin, but was again dislodged by General Edelsheim's cavalry, while the 1st corps of the army of the Crown Prince was checked with some loss at Trautenau by the 10th Austrian corps of Gablenz, and only disengaged by the advance of the Guards towards Eipel, on an intermediate road between the 1st and 5th Prussian corps. On the 29th, Prince Frederick Charles stormed Gitschin, and the army of the Crown Prince totally defeated the 6th, 8th and 10th Austrian corps. On the 30th, a fresh attempt of Benedek's to re-take Gitschin by the 1st corps and the Saxon army was signally foiled, and the two Prussian armies effected a junction. The Austrian loss represents men to the number of at least a corps and half, while that of the Prussians is less than one fourth that number.

Thus we find that on the 27th there were only two Austrian army corps, of about 33,000 men each, at hand; on the 28th, three; on the 29th, four, and if one Prussian telegram be correct, part of a fifth (the 4th corps); while on the 30th the Saxon army corps only had been able to come up in support. There were, then, two, if not three, corps absent from the contested ground during all that time, while the Prussians brought every man down into Bohemia. In fact, up to the evening of the 29th, the whole of the Austrian troops on the spot were barely superior in numbers to either of the two Prussian armies, and being brought into line successively, the supports arriving only after the defeat of the troops first engaged, the result was disastrous.

The 3rd army corps (Archduke Ernest), which fought at Custozza, is reported to have been sent to the north by rail immediately after that battle, and is, in some accounts, set down among Benedek's available forces. This corps, which would make the whole force, including the Saxons, nine corps, could not have been up in time for the battles in the latter days of June.

The Prussians, whatever the faults of their plan of operations were, made up for them by their rapidity and energy of action. No fault can be found with the operations of either of their two armies. Short, sharp and decisive were all their blows, and completely successful. Nor did this energy forsake them after the two armies were joined; on they marched, and already on the 3rd they met Benedek's combined forces with the whole of theirs, and gave them a last crushing blow.

It is hardly possible to suppose that Benedek accepted this battle of his own free will. No doubt the rapid pursuit of the Prussians compelled him to take a strong position with all his army, in order to re-form his troops, and to give a day's start to his retiring army train, expecting not to be attacked in force during the day, and to be able to draw off during the night. A man in his position, with four of his corps completely shattered, and after such tremendous losses, cannot have desired, there and then, to deliver a decisive battle, if he could draw off in safety. But the Prussians appear to have compelled him to fight, and the result was the complete rout of the Austrians, who, if the armistice be not granted, will now be trying to make towards Olmütz or Vienna, under the most disadvantageous circumstances, for the slightest out-flanking movement of the Prussians on their right must cut off numerous detachments from the direct road, and drive them into the hills of Glatz, to be made prisoners. The 'army of the north', as splendid a host as there was in Europe ten days ago, has ceased to exist.

No doubt the needle-gun, with its rapid fire, has done a great part of this. It may be doubted whether without it the junction of the two Prussian armies could have been effected; and it is quite certain that this immense and rapid success could not have been obtained without such superior fire, for the Austrian army is habitually less subject to panic than most European armies. But there were other circumstances cooperating. We have already mentioned the excellent dispositions and unhesitating action of the two Prussian armies, from the moment they entered Bohemia. We may add that they also deviated, in this campaign, from the column system, and brought their masses forward principally in deployed lines, so as to bring every rifle into activity, and to save their men from the fire of artillery. We must acknowledge that the movements both on the march and before the enemy were carried out with an order and punctuality which no man could have expected from an army and administration covered with the rust of fifty years' peace. And, finally, all the world must have been surprised at the dash displayed by these young troops in each and every engagement without exception. It is all very well to say the breech-loaders did it, but they are not self-acting, they want stout hearts and strong arms to carry them. The Prussians fought very often against superior numbers, and were almost everywhere the attacking party; the Austrians, therefore, had the choice of ground. And in attacking strong positions and barricaded towns, the advantages of the breech-loader almost disappear; the bayonet has to do the work, and there has been a good deal of it. The cavalry, moreover, acted with the same dash, and with them cold steel and speed of horses are the only weapons in a charge. The French *canards* of Prussian cavalry lines first peppering their opponents with carbine fire (breech-loading or otherwise) and then rushing at them sword in hand, could only originate among a people whose cavalry has very often been guilty of that trick, and always been punished for it by being borne down by the superior impetus of the charging enemy. There is no mistaking it, the Prussian army has, within a single week, conquered a position as high as ever it held, and may well feel confident now to be able to cope with any opponent. There is no campaign on record where an equally signal success, in an equally short time, and without any noteworthy check, has been obtained, except that campaign of Jena which annihilated the Prussians of that day, and, if we except the defeat of Ligny, the campaign of Waterloo.

VII. THE LETTER WRITER

Introduction

ENGELS was a prolific correspondent. The letters he exchanged with Marx, particularly between 1850 and 1870 when Marx was living in London and Engels in Manchester, have long been accepted as one of the Communist classics. Lenin observed that in their letters Marx and Engels were continually applying materialist dialectics 'to the reshaping of all political economy, from its foundations up – to history, natural science, philosophy and to the policy and tactics of the working class'. The Marx–Engels correspondence throws light on the famous partnership of the founders of Marxism. Engels, of course, had many other correspondents. He was in close touch with the old revolutionaries of 1848 some of whom were in exile in England and America, though others continued to live in Germany. In the 1870s and 1880s, particularly after the collapse of the First International, Engels maintained a correspondence with Socialist leaders in many countries – in Germany, France, Spain, Italy, Russia and the United States. Engels had great gifts as a linguist and he often wrote to his foreign correspondents in their own languages. The letters from Engels reproduced in this section range from personal matters – such as his unsatisfactory relationship with his father – to his views on the natural sciences.

1. Engels and his Father

ENGELS TO MARX[1]   *Barmen, 20 January 1845*
.... In view of the glum faces of my parents I took the advice of my brother-in-law and had another shot at a business career by working for a few weeks in the office. Circumstances connected with my love affair have also influenced my decision. But I disliked the prospect from the start. Petty trade is too horrible, Barmen is too horrible, and the waste of time is too horrible. Above all it is too horrible to belong to the middle classes and actually to be associated with factory owners. It is too horrible to play the part of a member of the bourgeoisie and to be actively engaged in opposing the interests of the workers. A few days in my old man's factory were enough to remind me forcibly of the horrors that I have been in danger of forgetting ...

ENGELS TO MARX[2]   *Barmen, 17 March 1845*
.... I am indeed living a dog's life here. All the religious fanaticism of my old man has been aroused by the Communist meetings and by the 'dissolute character' of several of our local Communists with whom I am of course in close contact. And the old man's wrath has been increased by my firm refusal to go into petty trading. Finally my appearance in public as an avowed Communist has aroused in him a truly middle-class fury. Now try to put yourself in my place. Since I want to leave in a fortnight or so I cannot afford to have a row. So I simply ignore all the criticisms of the family. They are not used to that and so get even angrier. If a letter comes for me everyone has a sniff at it even before it comes into my hands. They know that all my correspondence is from Communists so that every time the post arrives there is a howl of holy terror that is enough to drive me off my head. If I go out – the same gloomy faces. If I sit in my room and write – and they know that I am writing about Communism – it is just the same. ... Moreover my old man is so

1. [Translated from *Gesamtausgabe*, Part III, Vol. 1, pp. 12–13.]
2. [Translated from *Gesamtausgabe*, Part III, Vol. 1, pp. 19–21.]

stupid that he lumps Communism and Liberalism together as 'revolutionary' movements and – in spite of all that I can say to him – he actually tries to make me responsible for the infamies perpetrated by the middle classes in the English Parliament.

To cap it all it is the season of piety at home just now. Two of my sisters were confirmed last week and today all our relations have turned up for Holy Communion. The consecrated bread has done its work all right and this morning's faces are gloomier than ever. It was just my luck to have spent yesterday evening with Hess in Elberfeld. We argued about Communism until two in the morning. So today there are naturally long faces because of the late hours that I keep and dark hints that I was probably in the lock up. At last someone summons up enough courage to ask straight out where I was. 'I was with Hess,' I reply. 'With Hess! Good God!' A pause. Rising Christian consternation on every face. 'What company you choose to keep!' And then more sighs. It is enough to drive me mad. You can have no notion of the sheer malice that lies behind this wild Christian hunt after my 'soul' . . . I have a great affection for my mother who has a fine and noble character. It is only in relation to my father that she has no spirit of independence at all. Were it not for my mother I would not hesitate for one moment to refuse to make even the most trifling concession to my fanatical and despotic old man. . . .

ENGELS TO MARX[1]   *Manchester, 6 July 1851*
I have been trotting round with my old man for a week and now that I have packed him off safe and sound I can at last send you a postal order for £5. On the whole I am satisfied with the meeting. My old man needs me here for at least three years. He did not ask for any promises and I made none. I did not agree to stay here for good or even for three years. Nor was I asked to give any undertaking about my literary work or about staying here if a revolution breaks out . . .

But if my old man had stayed here for a few days more we should have quarrelled. The fellow cannot stand good fortune.

1. [Translated from *Gesamtausgabe*, Part III, Vol. 1, pp. 212–3.]

When things go well for him he gets above himself and becomes provoking by acting like a schoolmaster. He is stupid and tactless into the bargain. On his last day here, for example, he took advantage of the fact that one of the Ermens was present to try to get the better of me by bursting into a song of praise about the excellence of Prussia's institutions. He thought that I would have to behave myself and keep my trap shut. Of course a few words and a furious look were enough to silence him. But they were also enough to put our relations back onto a colder footing just when he was leaving. I am sure that he will try to have his revenge. We shall see. The contretemps cannot prejudice my future here – i.e. my financial position – and I would naturally prefer a cool business relationship to any protestations of friendship that would be mere humbug. . . .

ENGELS TO MARX[1]   *Manchester, 8 September 1851*
On Friday evening I suddenly received a letter from my old man in which he says that I am spending too much money and must manage on £150 a year. Of course I will not accept this ridiculous suggestion, particularly since it was accompanied by the threat that the Ermens will, if necessary, be instructed to limit my allowance to that figure. I will naturally reply at once that if he tries this mean trick on me I will not set foot in the office but will leave for London immediately. The fellow is really quite mad. The whole affair is all the more ridiculous and unsavoury since we have settled all this by word of mouth and I have given him absolutely no cause to change his mind. I think that with my brother's help I shall be able to settle the matter. All the same I shall have to economize a bit. I have already spent £230 and I do not want this sum to grow very much before November when I shall have been here for a year. This new trick is most disagreeable and I am furious at the mean way in which my old man has behaved. It is true that he will not earn anything like as much here this year as compared with last year but that is due entirely to the bad management of his partners and I have no control over that.

1. [Translated from *Gesamtausgabe*, Part III, Vol. 1, p. 258.]

ENGELS TO MARX[1] *Manchester, 4 March 1853*

.... A reform of my personal expenses has become imperative. In a week or a fortnight I shall move to less expensive lodgings and shall change over to lighter drinks so as to be prepared for the great moment when the balance is struck. Thank God that in the past year I have managed to gobble up half my old man's profits in this business. When my old man comes here I will move into good lodgings again and order some fine wine and cigars so as to impress him. *Voilà la vie* ...

2. Engels's Quarrel with Marx, 1863

ENGELS TO MARX[2] *13 January 1863*

You will appreciate that your callous attitude to my misfortune has made it absolutely impossible for me to reply sooner. The affair really affected me very intimately and all my friends – including philistine middle-class acquaintances – showed more friendship and understanding than I expected. You considered this to be an opportune moment to show how heartless you could be.[3] So be it. You know the state of my finances. You know too that I will do all that I can to ease your financial situation. But you must know that I cannot at this moment raise the larger sum that you mention ...

ENGELS TO MARX[4] *26 January 1863*

Thank you for being so straightforward. You have recognized the impression that your last letter but one made upon me. It is

1. [Translated from *Gesamtausgabe*, Part III, Vol. 1, p. 451.]

2. [Translated from *Gesamtausgabe*, Part III, Vol. 3, p. 118. Mary Burns, with whom Engels had lived for many years, died in January 1863. Engels considered that Marx had failed to show any sympathy for his friend's loss.]

3. [In the first draft of this letter Engels wrote at this point: 'Enjoy your triumph. No one will begrudge you it.']

4. [Translated from *Gesamtausgabe*, Part III, Vol. 3, p. 121. In his reply to Engels's letter of 13 January 1863, Marx wrote: 'It was very wrong of me to write to you as I did and I was sorry that I had sent the letter as soon as it was posted.' Marx explained that his attitude was not due to 'heartlessness' but to his own grave financial worries.]

impossible to live with a girl for years without being deeply affected by her death. With her I felt that I was burying the last bit of my youth. When your letter came she was not yet in her grave. I can tell you that I thought about your letter for a week. I could not forget it. Never mind – your last letter puts things right again and I am glad that when I lost Mary I did not at the same time lose my oldest and best friend.

3. Engels in Manchester, 1850–70

ENGELS TO MARX[1]   *Manchester, 17 December 1850*
... Please thank your wife for her kind letter. I doubt if I will ever become a 'cotton lord'. My old man does not seem to want me here any longer than is absolutely necessary. Well, we shall see. Peter Ermen[2] runs round like a fox who has lost his brush in a trap and intrigues to get rid of me. The poor devil really thinks that *he* can annoy me ....

ENGELS TO WEYDEMEYER[3]   *Manchester, 23 January 1852*
.... For the present I am here in Manchester to stay, luckily in a very independent job with many advantages: Marx and other friends come to visit me now and again from London, and so long as Weerth is in Bradford, we have established a regular switchback service between the two cities, since the rail trip takes only two and a half hours. But he will probably be leaving soon: he cannot stand that filthy hole Bradford and he does not possess the composure to stay in one place for a whole year ...

ENGELS TO MARX[4]   *Manchester, 1 July 1869*
Hurrah! I have finished with sweet commerce today and I am a free man. I settled all the main points yesterday with the worthy

1. [Translated from *Gesamtausgabe*, Part III, Vol. 1, pp. 122–3.]
2. [Partner of Engels's father.]
3. [Karl Marx and Frederick Engels, *Letters to Americans 1848–1895* (International Publishers, New York: New World Paperbacks edition, 1963), p. 33.]
4. [Translated from *Gesamtausgabe*, Part III, Vol. 4, p. 198.]

Gottfried[1] and he had to give way completely. Tussy[2] and I celebrated my first free day by taking a long walk in the fields . . .

ENGELS TO MARX[3]   *Manchester, 15 May 1870*

. . . . During the last few days I have again spent a good deal of time sitting at the four-sided desk in the alcove[4] where we sat together twenty-four years ago. I am very fond of the place. The stained glass window ensures that the weather is always fine there. Old Jones, the librarian, is still alive but he is very old and no longer active.[5] I have not seen him on this occasion . . .

4. The Natural Sciences

ENGELS TO MARX[6]   *30 May 1873*

This morning when I was in bed I had some dialectical ideas about the natural sciences.

Science is concerned with matter – or bodies – in motion. Matter and motion must be considered together. It is only in relation to motion that the nature and type of matter can be recognized. Nothing can be said about bodies except when they are in motion and have a relationship to other bodies. Only when it is in motion does a body reveal what it is. So science recognizes bodies by examining them in motion and in relation to one another. To identify the different kinds of motion is to identify the bodies themselves. The examination of these different kinds of motion is the chief task of scientific research.[7]

1. [Gottfried Ermen, partner of Engels.]
2. [Eleanor Marx (Mrs. Aveling): Marx's youngest daughter.]
3. [Translated from *Gesamtausgabe*, Part III, Vol. 4, p. 328.]
4. [In Chetham's Library.]
5. [Thomas Jones was Chetham's Librarian between 1845 and 1875.]
6. [Translated from *Gesamtausgabe*, Part III, Vol. 4, pp. 396–8.]
7. [Marginal note by Carl Schorlemmer: 'Very good. I agree.' Carl Schorlemmer (1834–92) was born in Darmstadt. He studied chemistry at Universities of Giessen and Heidelberg and came to Owens College, Manchester, in 1859 as assistant to Professor Roscoe. Schorlemmer was one of the founders of the study of organic chemistry in England and collaborated with Roscoe in writing a standard textbook on the subject. He met Engels in Manchester and shared his political views. Marx and

1. *Mechanical* motion. This is the simplest kind of motion. It is a change from one place to another place (in time – to oblige old Hegel).

(a) Normally an isolated body is incapable of motion, though – relatively speaking – *falling* could be regarded as motion of this kind. Next we must consider the situation in which several bodies move towards the same central point. If an isolated body moves in a direction other than towards the centre it is still subject to the laws of falling though these laws are modified.[1]

(b) They are modified into the laws of trajectories and lead directly to the reciprocal motion of several bodies. This brings us to a consideration of the motion of planets and stars and of the phenomenon of temporary or apparent equilibrium of bodies in motion. The *real* result of this kind of motion is always the *contact* between the moving bodies – i.e. they fall into one another.

(c) The laws of the mechanics of contact when moving bodies collide. This involves a consideration of levers, inclined planes, etc. But the study of the consequences of the contact of bodies should go further. There are two aspects of bodies that have come into contact with one another – friction and impact. A characteristic of both forms of contact is this. Under certain conditions if the contact is sufficiently violent the contact of bodies has *new* results which are not merely mechanical results. The contact of bodies may lead to the creation of heat or light or electricity or mechanism.

2. *Physics* proper is the science which is concerned with these forms of motion. After examining each form of motion the physicist can show that, in certain circumstances, they all merge into one another. He finally discovers that all the forms of motion – at a certain degree of intensity which varies according to the different sorts of bodies set in motion – produce results which transcend physics. They are *chemical* changes in the inner structure of the bodies themselves.

3. *Chemistry*. When investigating the forms of motion already

---

Engels frequently consulted Schorlemmer when they were studying scientific problems. Schorlemmer joined the International Working Men's Association.]

1. [Marginal note by Carl Schorlemmer: 'Quite right'.]

discussed it is more or less immaterial whether the bodies in motion are animate or inanimate. The phenomena which we have been considering can actually be seen most clearly in the movement of inanimate bodies. But the chemist can distinguish the chemical nature of the most important bodies only in living substances. In future chemistry will more and more be concerned with the problem of producing living substances artificially. Chemistry is the connecting link between the inorganic and the organic sciences. The dialectical transition will come only when chemistry has either made the real transition to an organic science or is on the point of doing so.[1]

4. Organism. For the time being I refrain from embarking upon any dialectics on this aspect of the subject.[2]

If you think that I have got hold of something here please keep it to yourself. I do not want some lousy Englishman to steal the idea. And it will take a long time to get it into shape.

5. Death of Marx, 1883

ENGELS TO SORGE[3]   *15 March 1883*

.... Schorlemmer and I planned to visit Marx on New Year's Day[4] when news came that it was necessary for Tussy[5] to join him at once. Then Jenny's death[6] followed and he came back with another attack of bronchitis. After all that had gone before, and at his age, this was dangerous. A number of complications set in, particularly an abscess of the lung and a terribly rapid loss of strength. Despite this the general course of the illness progressed favourably and last Friday the chief physician in attendance on him, one of the foremost young doctors in London and specially recommended to him by Ray Lankester, gave us the most brilliant hope for his recovery. Yet anyone who has ever

1. [Marginal note by Carl Schorlemmer: 'That's the point.']
2. [Marginal note by Carl Schorlemmer: 'I too.']
3. [From Karl Marx and Frederick Engels, *Letters to Americans 1848–95* (International Publishers, New York: New World Paperbacks edition, 1963), pp. 134–6.]
4. [Marx had been on a visit to the Isle of Wight.]
5. [Eleanor Marx (Mrs Aveling): Marx's daughter.]
6. [Jenny Marx (Mme Longuet): Marx's daughter.]

examined lung tissue under the microscope knows how great is the danger of a blood vessel being broken through a suppurating lung. And that is why I had a deathly fear, every morning for the past six weeks, of finding the shades down when I turned the corner of the street. Yesterday afternoon at 2.30, the best time for visiting him, I arrived to find the house in tears. It seemed that the end was near. I asked what had happened, tried to get to the bottom of the matter, to offer comfort. There had been a slight haemorrhage, but suddenly he had begun to sink rapidly. Our good Lenchen[1] who had looked after him better than any mother cares for her child went upstairs and came down again. He was half asleep, she said and I might come in. When we entered the room he lay there asleep, but never to wake again. His pulse and breathing had stopped. In those two minutes he had passed away, peacefully and without pain . . . .

Mankind is shorter by a head, and the greatest head of our time. The movement of the proletariat goes on, but gone is the central point to which Frenchmen, Russians, Americans and Germans spontaneously turned at decisive moments to receive always that clear incontestable counsel which only genius and a perfect knowledge of the situation could give. Local lights and small talents, if not the humbugs, obtain a free hand. The final victory is certain, but the detours, the temporary and local errors – even now so unavoidable – will grow more than ever. Well, we must see it through. What else are we here for? And we are far from losing courage because of it.

6. The Danger of World War, 1888

ENGELS TO SORGE[2]   *7 January 1888*

. . . . A war . . . would throw us back for years. Chauvinism would swamp everything, for it would be a struggle for existence. Germany would put about five million armed men into the field,

---

1. [Helene Demuth, Marx's housekeeper.]
2. [From Karl Marx and Frederick Engels, *Letters to Americans, 1848–95* (1963) pp. 194–5.]

or ten per cent of the population, the others about four or five per cent, Russia relatively less. But there would be ten to fifteen million combatants. I should like to see how they would be fed. There would be devastation like that in the Thirty Years' War. And nothing could be settled quickly despite the colossal fighting forces. For France is protected on the north-east and the south-east by very extensive fortifications along the frontier, and the new works round Paris are exemplary. So it will last a long time. And Russia is not to be taken by storm either. If, therefore, everything goes as Bismarck wishes, more will be demanded of the nation than ever before, and it is quite possible that post-ponement of the decisive victory and partial defeats will produce an internal upheaval. But if the Germans were defeated from the outset and forced into a permanent defensive, things would certainly start. If the war were fought out to the end without internal disturbance, a state of exhaustion would ensue such as Europe has not experienced for two hundred years. American industry would then win out all along the line and would place all of us before the alternative – either a relapse to pure agricul-ture for *self-consumption* (American grain prohibits anything else) or social transformation. I imagine therefore, that the plan is not to push matters to the extreme, to more than a sham war. But once the first shot is fired, control ceases, the horse may bolt. ...

7. Engels's Visit to Germany in 1893

ENGELS TO LAURA LAFARGUE[1]   *Zürich, 21 August 1893*

.... I found Germany completely metamorphosed. Steam chim-neys all over the country, but where I passed, not numerous enough over a small district, to create a nuisance by their smoke. Cologne and Mainz are transformed. The old town is still there where it was, but around or aside of it has arisen a larger and

1. [From *Frederick Engels – Paul and Laura Lafargue Correspondence*, Vol. III (Foreign Languages Publishing House, Moscow), p. 283. This letter was written in English.]

newer town with splendid buildings disposed according to a well-arranged plan, with large industrial establishments occupying distinct quarters so as not to interfere with the aspect or the comfort of the rest. Cologne has made most progress, having nearly trebled its inhabitants – the Ring is a splendid street, there is nothing equal to it in all England. Mainz is growing but at a slower rate. In Strasbourg you see too distinctly the separation between the old town and the new district formed by university and government buildings, an external addition, not a natural growth ...

ENGELS TO SORGE[1]   *London, 7 October 1892*

.... I found Germany completely revolutionized after 17 years' absence – industry enormously developed, agriculture, big and small, *very much* improved, and as a result our movement progressing excellently. Our people themselves have had to win the bit of freedom they have – especially win it from the police and the *Landräte*[2] *after* the respective laws have already been proclaimed on paper. And so you find a confident, firm demeanour, such as has never been found among the German bourgeois. Of course, there is much to be criticized in minor details – the party press, for instance, is not up to the level of the party, especially in Berlin – but the masses are excellent and usually better than the leaders or at least than many who have assumed the role of leaders. One can do everything with these people: they feel really happy only in the struggle, they live only for the struggle and are bored when their opponents don't give them any work to do. It is positively a fact that most of them would greet a new Socialist Law with scornful laughter, if not with actual rejoicing – for they would have something new to do every day ...

1. [From Karl Marx and Frederick Engels, *Letters to Americans, 1848–95* (International Publishers, New World Paperbacks edition, 1963), p. 255.]
2. [District Commissioners.]

Principal Writings of Friedrich Engels[1]

Books and Articles   To 1845

Articles on English economic and social affairs in the *Rheinische Zeitung* (9 December 1842), the *Schweizerischer Republikaner* (2 June 1853) (in *Gesamtausgabe*, I(2), pp. 351–75), *The New Moral World* (4 November 1843 – 3 February 1844) (in *Gesamtausgabe*, I(2), pp, 435–55), *Vorwärts* (Paris) (31 August – 11 September 1844 and 18 September – 19 October 1844) (in *Gesamtausgabe*, I(4), pp. 291–334).

Review of Thomas Carlyle, *Past and Present*, in the *Deutsch-Französische Jahrbücher* (Paris 1844) (in *Gesamtausgabe*, I(2), pp. 405–31).

'Umrisse zu einer Kritik der Nationalökonomie' (*Deutsch-Französische Jahrbücher*, 1844) (in *Gesamtausgabe*, I(2), pp. 379–404); English translation in appendix to Karl Marx, *Economic and Philosophic Manuscripts of 1844* (Foreign Languages Publishing House, Moscow 1961).

Articles and speeches on Communism in the *Deutsches Bürgerbuch* (Darmstadt 1845) (in *Gesamtausgabe*, I(4), pp. 351–66) and in the *Rheinische Jahrbücher* (Darmstadt 1845) (in *Gesamtausgabe* I(4), pp. 369–90).

Die Lage der arbeitenden Klasse in England (1845) (in *Gesamtausgabe* I(4), pp. 5–282, ed. by V. Adoratskij). First English translation – *The Condition of the Working-Class in England in 1844* – by Florence Kelley Wischnewetzky (published in the U.S.A. in 1887 and in the United Kingdom in 1892). A new English translation by W. O. Henderson and W. H. Chaloner – *The Condition of the Working Class in England* – was published by Basil Blackwell in 1958. A French translation by Brache was issued in 1933.

Article on builders' strike in Manchester in *Das Westfälische Dampfboot* (January and February 1846) (in *Gesamtausgabe*, I(4), pp. 393–405), English translation in Henderson and Chaloner's edition of *The Condition of the Working Class in England*, pp. 337–52.

Karl Marx and Friedrich Engels, *The German Ideology* (Lawrence & Wishart, London 1965).

1. Based upon the appendix on Engels's works in Maximilien Rubel, *Bibliographie des oeuvres de Karl Marx* (1956), pp. 242–58.

1846–9

Das Manifest der kommunistischen Partei (*The Communist Manifesto*)
by Marx and Engels (1848). Three editions were printed in 1848 – two
by J. E. Burghard of 46 Liverpool Street, Bishopsgate, London, and
one by R. Hirschfeld of 48 Clifton Street, Finsbury Square, London
(*Gesamtausgabe* I(6), pp. 682–6). English translation by Helen
Macfarlane in *The Red Republican* (23 and 30 November 1850).
Centenary translation – Harold Laski (ed.), *The Communist Manifesto:
Socialist Landmark* (1948); new introductions by Marx and Engels to
reprints of 1872 and 1882 and by Engels to reprints of 1883, 1888 and
1890.

Numerous articles on current affairs were contributed by Engels to
the *Neue Rheinische Zeitung* between 1 June 1848 and 29 April 1849, in
Gesamtausgabe I(7) and K. Marx and F. Engels, *Die Revolution von
1848: Auswahl aus der Neuen Rheinischen Zeitung* (1955); see 'Marx
und die *Neue Rheinische Zeitung*' in the *Sozialdemokrat* (13 March
1884).

1850

Article on 'The Ten Hours Question' in the *Democratic Review*
(March 1850).

Articles in the *Neue Rheinische Zeitung* (London, Hamburg: New
York 1850; reprinted in 1955):

'Die deutsche Reichsverfassungs-Campagne' (January and February 1850).

'Für die Republik zu sterben' (March 1850).

'Die englische Zehnstundenbill' (April 1850).

Review of Thomas Carlyle, *Latter Day Pamphlets* (April 1850).

'Der deutsche Bauernkrieg' (May–October 1850), republished by
Engels as a book in 1870. English translation: *The Peasant War in
Germany* (with appendices on 'The Mark' and 'The History of the
Prussian Peasantry') issued by the Foreign Languages Publishing
House, Moscow 1956.

1851–2

Twenty articles on the revolution of 1848 in Germany in the *New
York Daily Tribune* (25 October 1851 to 22 December 1852) signed by
Karl Marx but written by Engels. Appeared as a book – *Revolution
and Counter Revolution in Germany* – in 1896: edited by Eleanor
Marx-Aveling who attributed the articles to her father. An American
edition (*Germany: Revolution and Counter Revolution*) appeared in 1933.

1853–5

Articles on the Eastern Question and the Crimean War in the *New York Times* (1853–4). Some were reprinted in 1897 by Eleanor Marx-Aveling and E. Aveling – who attributed them to Marx – as *The Eastern Question*. 'Deutschland und der Panslawismus' in the *Neue Oder Zeitung* (Breslau) (21 and 24 April 1855).

Three articles on European armies in *Putnam's Monthly Magazine* (New York, August–December 1855).

1857–8

Articles on military subjects in the *New America Cyclopaedia*. Engels's articles included those on 'Army', 'Cannon', 'Fortification', 'Infantry', 'Navy', 'Blücher', 'Armada' and 'Aboukir'.

1859

Po und Rhein (1859): anonymous pamphlet. The name of the author was soon revealed by Marx in *Das Volk* (London).

Two articles in *Das Volk* (London, 6 and 20 August 1859) on Karl Marx, *Zur Kritik der politischen Ökonomie*.

1860–2

Savoyen, Nizza und der Rhein (1860): sequel to *Po und Rhein*. The two pamphlets (ed. by E. Bernstein) were reprinted by Dietz at Stuttgart in 1915.

Article on the English volunteers in the *Allgemeine Militär-Zeitung* (Darmstadt, 8 September 1860); reprinted in English in the *Volunteer Journal for Lancashire and Cheshire* (14 September 1860). Twenty-eight further articles by Engels appeared in this journal between September 1860 and March 1862; reprinted in *Engels as Military Critic* (ed. by W. H. Chaloner and W. O. Henderson, 1959). Articles on military subjects in the *New York Daily Tribune* (February to September 1860) and in the *Allgemeine Militär-Zeitung* (1 and 8 November 1862).

Two articles on the American Civil War in the *Volunteer Journal* (6 December 1861 and 14 March 1862); reprinted in *Engels as a Military Critic* (ed. by W. H. Chaloner and W. O. Henderson, 1959).

1864

Letter on the Schleswig-Holstein war in the *Manchester Guardian* (16 February 1864); reprinted in *Engels as Military Critic* (ed. by W. O. Henderson and W. H. Chaloner, 1959).

1865

Die Preussische Militärfrage und die deutsche Arbeiterpartei (1865): pamphlet criticizing the followers of Lassalle.

1866

Three articles on Poland in *The Commonwealth* (24 and 31 March and 5 May 1866).

1869

Article on Marx in *Die Zukunft*.

Five articles in the *Manchester Guardian* on the Seven Weeks' War; reprinted in *Engels as Military Critic* (ed. by W. O. Henderson and W. H. Chaloner, 1959).

1870–1

Sixty articles in the *Pall Mall Gazette* on the Franco-Prussian war. Reprinted as a book in Vienna under the title *Notes on the War. Sixty Articles reprinted from the 'Pall Mall Gazette'* (ed by F. Adler, 1923). German translation 1957.

1872

Six articles on the housing question in the *Volksstaat* (1872). Revised and reprinted as a pamphlet in Zürich in 1887. English translation: *The Housing Question* (1935).

1873

L'Alliance de la democratie socialiste et l'Association internationale des travailleurs (1873). Sharp attack on Bakunin.

1878

Herrn Eugen Dührings Umwälzung der Wissenschaft (1878). Appeared originally as articles in *Vorwärts*. English translation entitled *Anti-Dühring* (published by the Foreign Languages Publishing House, Moscow 1959).

1882

Die Entwicklung des Sozialismus von der Utopie zur Wissenschaft (3 chapters from *Anti-Dühring* with an appendix on 'The Mark'). An English translation by E. Aveling entitled *Socialism, Utopian and Scientific* appeared in 1892.

1884

Der Ursprung der Familie, des Privateigentums und des Staates (Hottingen-Zürich 1884). English translation: *The Origin of the Family, Private Property and the State* (Foreign Languages Publishing House, Moscow).

1886

Essay on the history of the Prussian peasants which was printed as the second part of an introduction to W. Wolff, *Die Schlesische Milliarde* (Zürich 1886). English translation appeared as appendix to *The Peasant War in Germany*.

1888

Ludwig Feuerbach und der Ausgang der klassischen deutschen Philosophie (Stuttgart 1888), an expansion of a review of C. N. Starke, *Ludwig Feuerbach* which appeared in *Die Neue Zeit* in 1886. English translation: *Ludwig Feuerbach and the End of Classical German Philosophy* (Foreign Languages Publishing House, Moscow 1950).

1890

Article on Russian foreign policy in *Die Neue Zeit* (1890); in English in *The Times* (June 1890).

1891

In Sachen Brentano contra Marx wegen angeblicher Zitatsfälschung (Hamburg 1891).
Preface to new edition of K. Marx, *Der Bürgerkrieg in Frankreich*.

1892

Articles on Marx in *Handwörterbuch der Staatswissenschaften*, Vol. IV (1892), and on Schorlemmer in *Vorwärts*, (3 July 1892).
'Der Sozialismus in Deutschland' (in *Die Neue Zeit*, 1892).

1893

'Kann Europa abrüsten?' (in *Die Neue Zeit*, 1893).

1895

Preface to new edition of Karl Marx, *Die Klassenkämpfe in Frankreich*. Complete text in D. Riazanov (ed.), *Unter dem Banner des Marxismus*, Vol. I (1925).

1896

'Gewalt und Ökonomie bei der Herstellung des neuen Deutschen Reiches' (incomplete manuscript printed by Eduard Bernstein in *Die Neue Zeit*, 1896: reprinted in *Über die Gewaltstheorie*, 1946).

Correspondence

K. Marx and F. Engels, *Briefwechsel*, 4 vols, (*Marx-Engels Gesamtausgabe*, 1929–31: new edition 1936 and 1950). Replaces the unsatisfactory edition of 1913 edited by August Bebel and Eduard Bernstein.

K. Marx and F. Engels, *Ausgewählte Briefe* (Berlin, 1953). English translation: *Selected Letters* (London 1936).

E. Eichorn (ed.), *Vergessene Briefe* (Briefe Friedrich Engels an Johann Philipp Becker (Berlin 1920).

E. Bernstein (ed.), *Die Briefe von Friedrich Engels an Eduard Bernstein* (Berlin 1925).

G. Mayer (ed.), 'Briefe von Friedrich Engels an Mutter und Geschwister' (in the *Deutsche Revue*, 1920–1).

'Aus der Flüchtlingszeit von Marx und Engels' (letters from Marx and Engels to J. Weydemeyer and others) (in *Die Neue Zeit*, Vol. XXV, 1906–7).

Victor Adlers Aufsätze, Reden und Briefe (Vienna 1922).

K. Mandelbaum (ed.), *Die Briefe von Karl Marx und Friedrich Engels an Danielson* (introduction by G. Mayer) (Leipzig 1929).

'Engels' Briefe an Conrad Schmidt' (in *Sozialistische Monatshefte*, 1920).

B. Kautsky (ed.), *Friedrich Engels' Briefwechsel mit K. Kautsky* (new edition, 1955).

G. Eckert (ed.), *Wilhelm Liebknecht. Briefwechsel mit Karl Marx und Friedrich Engels* (The Hague 1963).

F. Engels' Briefe an Bebel (1959).

Correspondence of Friedrich Engels with Paul and Laura Lafargue, 3 vols. (1959).

K. Marx and F. Engels, *Letters to Americans, 1845–95* (New York 1953).

Index

Items which appear frequently in the book, such as Marx, Engels, England, Germany, France, Socialism, London, Manchester, have been omitted from the index.